Kālacakra and the Tibetan Calendar

TREASURY OF THE BUDDHIST SCIENCES series

Editor-in-Chief: Robert A.F. Thurman
Jey Tsong Khapa Professor of Indo-Tibetan Buddhist Studies,
Columbia University
President, American Institute of Buddhist Studies

Executive Editor: Thomas F. Yarnall
Department of Religion
Columbia University

Editorial Board:
Ryuichi Abe, Jay Garfield, David Gray, Laura Harrington, Thubten Jinpa, Joseph Loizzo, Gary Tubb, Christian Wedemeyer, Chun-fang Yu

The American Institute of Buddhist Studies (AIBS), in affiliation with the Columbia University Center for Buddhist Studies (CBS) and Tibet House US (THUS), has established the *Treasury of the Buddhist Sciences* series to provide authoritative English translations, studies, and editions of the texts of the Tibetan Tengyur (*bstan 'gyur*) and its associated literature. The Tibetan Tengyur is a vast collection of over 3,600 classical Indian Buddhist scientific treatises (*śāstra*) written in Sanskrit by over 700 authors from the first millennium CE, now preserved mainly in systematic 7th–12th century Tibetan translation. Its topics span all of India's "outer" arts and sciences, including linguistics, medicine, astronomy, socio-political theory, ethics, art, and so on, as well as all of her "inner" arts and sciences such as philosophy, psychology ("mind science"), meditation, and yoga.

Kālacakra and the Tibetan Calendar

by
Edward Henning

Treasury of the Buddhist Sciences series

Published by
The American Institute of Buddhist Studies
at Columbia University in New York

Co-published with
Columbia University's Center for Buddhist Studies
and Tibet House US

New York
2007

Treasury of the Buddhist Sciences series
A refereed series published by:

American Institute of Buddhist Studies
Columbia University
80 Claremont Avenue, room 303
New York, NY 10027

http://www.aibs.columbia.edu

Co-published with Columbia University's Center for Buddhist Studies and Tibet House US.

Distributed by Columbia University Press.

Printed in Canada on acid-free paper.

ISBN 978-0-9753734-9-1 (cloth)

Library of Congress Cataloging-in-Publication Data

Henning, Edward, 1949–
Kālacakra and the Tibetan calendar / by Edward Henning.
p. cm. — (Treasury of the Buddhist sciences series)
"Co-published with Columbia University's Center for Buddhist Studies and Tibet House US."
Includes bibliographical references and index.
ISBN 978-0-9753734-9-1 (alk. paper)
1. Calendar, Tibetan. I. Title.

CE38.5.H46 2007
529'.309515--dc22

2007060675

Dedicated to the memory of
Khenpo Tseundru

Contents

Series Editor's Preface ix

Author's Preface and Acknowledgements xiii

Introduction 1

Chapter I: Five Components of the Calendar 7

Chapter II: The Five Planets 55

Chapter III: Rāhu and Eclipses 95

Chapter IV: The Tibetan Almanac 141

Chapter V: The Kālacakra Tantra and Vimalaprabhā 211

Chapter VI: Different Calculation Systems 295

Appendix I: The Sixty-Year Cycles 351

Appendix II: Chronology of the Sambhala Kings 365

Glossary 375

Bibliography 381

Index 387

Series Editor's Preface

We are extremely pleased to present this fascinating book by Edward Henning, our first monograph associated with the Tibetan Tengyur Translation Initiative underlying this *Treasury of the Buddhist Sciences* series. It is a labor of love and deep erudition on the part of an exceptional independent Buddhist scholar, physicist, mathematician, and linguist. Herein, with the help of the most insightful Tibetan teachers and a wide range of the central texts of the tradition, he elucidates the principles of Tibetan astronomy. He shows how a Tibetan scientist calculates the yearly calendar, the times of eclipses of sun and moon (extremely precise although calculated within a cosmological model quite different from the modern one), and the positions of the planets. Based on that thorough and clear elucidation, he translates the textual *locus classicus* of the Tibetan Buddhist method, verses 13 to 52 of the First Chapter of the *Kālacakra Tantra*, and its commentary the *Stainless Light* (*Vimalaprabhā)*, showing how the instructions therein function as the foundation of the later works.

The Kālacakra Tantra, or "Wheel of Time Technology," as it can be impressionistically translated, is a scientific way of understanding and engaging the universe—including the inner realm of the mind as well as the outer realm of the environment—that enables the scientific explorer to consciously maximize her or his evolutionary progress toward happiness and fulfillment through also assisting others. One of its central insights is that we are completely interwoven with our environment in time and space, and that therefore the more we know about the events around us, the better we are positioned to help ourselves and others avoid suffering and achieve happiness. We need to know what we are as evolutionary beings, where we are in the cosmos, and what time it is in regard to the dangers and opportunities we face. Therefore, the understanding of astronomical events is foundationally important to the quality of our lives, and an accurate and thorough calendar is something like a weather report, necessary for us to be prepared for the realities ahead of us.

I personally do not pretend to understand the details of this subject well, though in my youth I learned the rudimentary principles of one Tibetan system as I worked with fellow students on the Tibetan calendar for the year 1964 under Tsipay Gen Amdo Lotreu, the State Astronomer of the Tibetan Government in Exile in Dharamsala, India. From whatever of that remains dimly in memory, I know just enough to be able to recognize and admire the excellence of Henning's accomplishment. Not only has he mastered the intricacies of the system and the ability to use it in practice, while understanding in detail the differences between the different systems, but also he has found a key problem with the current practice, based on a modern critical understanding as well as on his teacher's and his own rediscovery in the root sources of the principle needed to resolve this problem—a principle totally in consonance with modern science.

Indeed, it is absolutely marvelous that the Kālacakra system, after giving detailed instructions on the calculation of the calendar, recommends one indispensable practice to keep its practice effective—the actual observation of nature. Such attention to precise and careful examination befits the Buddhist scientific emphasis on the importance of experience, and its critical observation. That is, in the present context, no matter how sophisticated any mathematical system may be, based on no matter what theory or worldview, you have to get out at the winter and summer solstices, at least one of them, and observe the exact moment when the sun's shadow at noon changes its motion relative to previous days, signaling the yearly shift from the southern to the northern passage of the sun, or vice versa. Only by fixing this time and adjusting calculations to fit it can subtle corrections be made to the yearly calculations, avoiding the gradual compounding of error over decades and centuries that would otherwise ruin the accuracy of the calendar.

One of the first books in our Tengyur series was the English translation of the Second Chapter of the *Kālacakra Tantra* together with its *Stainless Light* commentary, beautifully accomplished by Dr. Vesna Wallace. We have the three other later chapters in the pipeline in various stages of completion, and we hope to publish eventually the First Chapter in its entirety. The present book by Edward Henning will serve as a precious key to unlock the all-important astronomical perspective of this the First Chapter, leading the way and continuing to provide the great benefit of showing the actual use of this remarkable system.

My congratulations go to Edward Henning for his careful perseverance and outstanding accomplishment. It is our honor to publish his work.

Robert A. F. Thurman
American Institute for Buddhist Studies
Columbia University Center for Buddhist Studies
Tibet House US

February 18, 2007
New Year's Day, Fire Pig Year

Author's Preface and Acknowledgements

The catalyst that started me on the task of learning Tibetan was an artefact closely related to the Tibetan calendar; this was also an important factor that eventually led to the writing of this book. My background had been in mathematics and physics, with a strong interest in astronomy—all good grounding for working on any calendar, but an oriental language was a major departure.

I was given a fascinating present in 1973, that turned out to be a Tibetan *srid pa ho*—a copper plaque depicting the great golden turtle of Chinese mythology, together with various other astrological signs. These are intended to ward off negative influences of the planets, lunar mansions, and so forth.

Around this time I had developed an interest in northern, particularly Tibetan, Buddhism and was somewhat frustrated by having read everything I could find in the English language on the subject. The thought had crossed my mind that if I wanted to study and practise it properly, I would have to turn to original sources—which would not be in English. My curiosity regarding this plaque quickly had me learning Tibetan.

Over the next few months I started collecting from various sources Tibetan texts and photocopies of others. I was lucky to have the collection in the British Library close at hand, and soon came across some important astrological and astronomical material, but found it mostly indecipherable.

Two years later, whilst on a long visit to India, I spent a very brief amount of time with a Tibetan teacher, the late Khenpo Tseundru. He was renowned as one of the greatest experts in Tibetan astrology, and very easily pointed me in the right direction with my studies, particularly with regard to the accuracy of the calendar.

On my return to England, partly thanks to his guidance, I found I was increasingly able to make sense of the basic texts I had acquired, but still I did nothing about writing any of this up. I knew that microcomputers were about to become available and I waited impatiently for this to become a reality.

As soon as I was able to buy a PC (in 1984), I set about computerizing a version of the Tibetan lunar calendar. Very often I translated directly from Tibetan into the C programming language, and then, once I had ascertained that a certain algorithm worked correctly, translated into English.

I completed this program and first printed out my computerized version of the lunar calendar during the afternoon of what I discovered later that evening to be the day of the centenary of the adoption of the Greenwich meridian. A good omen indeed for an Englishman, but I still made no plans to write about the calendar.

Eventually I realized that in order to examine the calendar properly, it would not be enough simply to look at the calendar as used by Tibetans today, but it would be necessary to go back to the original sources and create a translation and analysis of the basic calculations in the original Indian Kālacakra system, the source of the calculations used by the Tibetans.

As time has passed I have come to consider the translation and analysis of the original Indian material the most important and interesting aspect of this project. One could also make a fascinating study of the early Tibetan origins of some aspects of the calendar as well as its Chinese and Mongolian background, but the Kālacakra influence is certainly the most important, and has been my main focus.

As will be clear by the end of this work, the Tibetans in part either did not understand or did not accept the intentions of the Kālacakra system for the calendar. This is a great pity, as the Kālacakra system itself seems to me to have a positive reforming spirit to it. The Tibetan calendar, particular in its most common form, from the Phugpa tradition, is now in a sorry state, itself very much in need of just the kind of reform encouraged in the Kālacakra literature.

I know that most Tibetans do not accept this point of view, but I also know that some do, and it was, after all, a most distinguished Tibetan Kālacakra expert, Khenpo Tseundru, who directed my studies in such a way that led to this conclusion.

As he passed on just a couple of years after our meeting, I have no way of thanking him for his help or of checking if this present work satisfies his intentions, but I am reasonably confident that it does. He confirmed what I had been told about him, that he held a secret key (presumably a method of some kind) that enabled proper accuracy of the calendar, and told me that if I applied a western (scientific) analysis in the particular areas that he suggested, I would not need this key. In this he has certainly been proved correct.

Apart from Khenpo Tseundru, I would like to single out a couple of other individuals for particular thanks, the first of whom I happened to meet in the same year as the Khenpo, 1976. At that time Gene Smith was running the U.S. Library of Congress' Tibetan Text Publication Project (PL480) out of New Delhi. During this work he accumulated a most impressive personal library of Tibetan materials, now housed in a continuous state of chaotic expansion in the Tibetan Buddhist Resource Center, New York. Some of the Tibetan texts mentioned in the bibliography at the back of this book were made available to me by Gene, and the present work would be much poorer were it not for his help and support.

The other is Günther Grönbold, of the Bayerische Staatbibliothek, Munich. Günther was a student of the famous Kālacakra scholar Helmut Hoffmann, and shares my interest in Kālacakra. This interest usefully influenced acquisitions at the library, and on the many occasions that I visited during the last 20 years, there was nearly always a pile of recommended reading awaiting me, as well as the materials I had requested before travelling.

My hope is that this book will help in some small way towards a better understanding of both the Tibetan calendar and the Kālacakra system. To that end I am also particularly grateful to Dr. Robert Thurman, Dr. Thomas Yarnall, and the AIBS for accepting this book into their series. I could not ask for a more suitable home for this work, and they have even been willing to accommodate my request to preserve native British spellings throughout the book! In particular, Dr. Yarnall has paid meticulous attention to the editing, design, and layout of this book, which is somewhat complex due to the number of calculations, tables, and graphics that it contains. Any errors that may remain are of course entirely my own.

Edward Henning
February 2007

Introduction

In the west, we take the existence of an almanac, or ephemeris, with its precise planetary positions, as a given. For the Tibetans, and their predecessors in India, the situation was very different. The calendar itself had to be calculated by hand from fundamental formulae, and I have been told that it could take an individual seven months to perform the calculations for a calendar for one year.

Tibetan astronomy and astrology have three main sources: Indian Buddhist and Hindu systems, and Chinese. The Indian systems include what we could call 'positional' astrology. Much of this is familiar to westerners, and includes such concepts as the 12 signs of the zodiac, the 12 houses, and takes into consideration the positions of the planets within these. One interesting addition is the use of the 27 lunar mansions as an additional division of the ecliptic. These are known in the west, but are used very infrequently.

The Indian and Chinese systems both use a method that I term 'cyclic' astrology. Here, most of the cycles depend upon the actual positions of the Sun and Moon. The cycles are the years, lunar months, lunar days, and so forth. The definition of these, particularly of the months, is different in Chinese and Indian systems, but sufficiently compatible that the Tibetans have been able to combine them.

The work of calculating the Tibetan lunar calendar consists in determining these basic cycles, and onto this structure then dropping the symbolic elements from the Indian and Chinese traditions. The calculations derive the position of the Sun and Moon, and then go on to determine the positions of Rāhu (the ascending node of the Moon's orbit) and the five visible planets.

No aspect of the calculations has been derived from Chinese sources (although there is certainly some Chinese influence in later almanacs), and the single source for the calculations is the Kālacakra Buddhist system. The main source text for this tradition is the Kālacakra Tantra, which, together with its main commentary, has been one of the main sources for this current work.

The commentary is called the Vimalaprabhā, and this appears to have been written around the beginning of the 11th century. The text describes two epochs for calculation. The basic one for which planetary positions are given is 806 CE, and the one that calculations are described as starting from is 1027.

Fortunately, both the Kālacakra Tantra itself and the Vimalaprabhā are available in both Sanskrit and Tibetan, and this enables the comparison of technical terms in both languages. This is useful, as much has been written in English about Indian systems of astronomy and astrology, based on Sanskrit sources.

The other main commentary that I have used on the Kālacakra Tantra itself has been the "Illumination of the Vajra Sun" (MiKal), an excellent work by Mipham (*mi pham rgya mtsho*). He died early last century (1912), and is one of the most recent authoritative writers on the Kālacakra. His style is clear and lucid, and is particularly suitable in my opinion for translation into western languages.

Also useful in helping understand parts of the original Tantra and the Vimalaprabhā has been a work by Pawo Tsuklag (*dpa' bo gtsug lag*) called the "Treasury of Jewels" (Tlkuntu). This is a commentary to an earlier work by the third Karmapa, Rangjung Dorje (*rang byung rdo rje*), called the "Compendium of Astronomy" (*rtsis kun btus pa*), which was the first native Tibetan text on the subject. The date for the epoch given in Pawo Tsuklag's text is 1536, and that in Rangjung Dorje's text, unfortunately not now available, 1326.

The other main texts that I have used have been specific works on astronomy and astrology rather than commentaries on the original Kālacakra system. There are now two main calendrical traditions in Tibet, the Phugpa (or Phugluk) and Tsurphu (or Tsurluk), and most of these texts come from one of these traditions. There were others, and perhaps pockets of their practice survive still in Tibet, but these two seem to be the only ones that remain in extensive use.

The most important of these that I have used has been one written less than a hundred years ago in the Phugpa tradition. This is the "Essence of the Kalkī" (Rigthig, 1927) by Chenrab Norbu (*mkhyen rab nor bu*). For many Tibetans creating calendars today, this will be the definitive source book. It is this text that I have mainly used as the basis for my discussion of the main calculations in the calendar. Older texts tend to give shorter versions of the calculations, sometimes missing details that were either preserved in an oral tradition, or perhaps devised later.

Chenrab Norbu's work is itself based on another text from the Phugpa tradition, written over 200 years earlier, and arguably the most famous Tibetan book on the subject: the "White Beryl" (Baidkar, 1687), attributed to Desi Sangje Gyatso (*sde srid sang rgyas rgya mtsho*). Regarding this particularly important work, Gene Smith (Smith, p. 243) points out that the actual author was almost certainly Dumbu Dondrup Wangyal (*ldum bu don grub dbang rgyal*).

Another text from the same tradition of which I have made extensive use is the "Illumination of the Day-maker" (Nangrtsa, 1681) and its commentary, the "Golden Chariot" (Nangser), by Minling Lochen Dharmaśrī (*smin glin lo chen dharma śrī*). This is a particularly lucid work, and I have used it mainly for the calculation of eclipse predictions.

I have also made use of the original work in the Phugpa tradition, the "The Oral Instructions of Puṇḍarīka" (Padzhal, 1447) by Lhundrup Gyatso (*lhun grub rgya mtsho*), Norzang Gyatso (*nor bzang rgya mtsho*) and others. This does not contain specific data for the creation of a calendar as do later texts in the Phugpa tradition, but contains considerable discussion of the theory underlying the creation of the Phugpa calendar.

The other main tradition, Tsurphu, follows on from the work of Pawo Tsuklag, and I have referred to two other texts in this tradition. The first is the "Excellent Flask of Essentials" (Bumzang, 1732) of Karma Ngelek Tendzin (*karma nges legs bstan 'dzin*). This text revived the Tsurphu calendrical tradition. I have not had access to the original work (1429) in this tradition by Jamyang Dondrup Wozer (*'jam dbyangs don grub 'od zer*).

The other main work of the Tsurphu tradition of which I have made use is the "Compendium of Practical Astronomy" (Kongleg, 1852) of Jamgon Kongtrul (*'jam mgon kong sprul*).

One particularly interesting writer to whose works I have also referred is Banda Gelek (*'ba' mda' dge legs*). He is one of the most important writers in the Jonang tradition of Buddhism. The Jonang mainly followed the Phugpa system of calculation, but he is the only author of astronomical texts that I have come across who has displayed an eclectic attitude towards the calendrical systems, and written in detail about both the Phugpa and Tsurphu systems.

The only text from other specific calendrical traditions that I have used is the work by the famous historian Geu Lotsawa Zhonnu Pal (*'gos lo tsā ba gzhon nu dpal*). He is well known in the west as the author of the historical work "The Blue Annals," translated into English by George Roerich. His work on the calendar, the title of which translates as "The

Correction of Errors in Astronomy" (Khrulsel, 1443) takes a significantly different approach to that in the Phugpa and Tsurphu traditions, but as we shall see, in my opinion, apart from one major problem his method came closer to embodying the intentions of the original Kālacakra Tantra and Vimalaprabhā, as well as avoiding the errors in those other systems when combining the Chinese and Indian calendrical systems.

There are several other more minor and some modern texts that I have also used. These are listed in the bibliography.

This present work is therefore a compendium based on many sources. The first chapters are not a straight translation as this would not be much help in describing the calculations. The original works are very tersely written, and the first chapters of this book follow the methods of Chenrab Norbu and others, but expand considerably on their texts.

In chapter five I give a translation of the original material from both the Kālacakra Tantra and the Vimalaprabhā, and have added my explanations to these texts.

One point about language: I only give Sanskrit equivalents to words when they are either very well known, or I have managed to trace a Tibetan-Sanskrit pair in the original Kālacakra texts. Some terms used in the Tibetan literature seem to have evolved after the translation period, and have no original Sanskrit equivalents—although it may be that I have simply not come across them. However, except for a few safe cases, I have refrained from taking Sanskrit equivalents from dictionaries, or reverse engineering them, as this strikes me as artificial and potentially misleading.

As far as Tibetan is concerned, there is always a problem when representing Tibetan words in a western text. People who understand the language prefer to see the correct spelling of Tibetan words, using a transcription system such as that devised by Wylie. But this produces problems for westerners who are not familiar with the language because of the unpronounced consonants. It is better for them to have an approximate representation of the pronunciation.

For Tibetan words such as names of persons that need to be included in the main body of the text, rather than simply be referenced, I have followed this latter course. However for the first occurrence of each such Tibetan word I give the Wylie transcription in brackets, together with the Sanskrit or Chinese equivalents where relevant. For Chinese transcription I have followed the pinyin system.

There is also a glossary of technical terms at the back of this book, together with lists of the more common groupings of terms—such as the names of the lunar mansions, the solar terms, and so forth.

CHAPTER I

Five Components of the Calendar

There are several aspects of the Tibetan calendar that have often surprised or confused westerners. The years start at different times relative to the western calendar and they are not always of equal length. Months (identified by a number and name) can be repeated, and days—at least the numbers associated with them, what we might call Tibetan dates—can be both duplicated and omitted.

The calendar is a luni-solar one, and these variations are due to the fact that the length of the lunar month varies, and is a little less than one-twelfth of a solar year. Most years have twelve months, but in order to keep in step with the seasons, some years have thirteen. All the details of the calendar—the months and the dates of the days they contain—are calculated on the basis of the lunar cycle and subdivisions of it.

Some have suggested that the doubled months and added and omitted days are due to superstition—that an inauspicious day is removed, for example. There may well be plenty of scope for superstition in any calendrical system that is also used for astrology, but this is not the reason for these variations. Calculation of the relative and absolute positions of the Sun and Moon yields all the details of the calendar.

Any calendar needs a uniform measure of time, and the Tibetan system uses a method that at first sight might seem back to front. In modern western methods of astronomical calculation we usually take a measure of time from some epoch, and calculate astronomical phenomena at that time. Ignoring the most modern and accurate methods that use integration techniques, this would involve a count of days and then a fraction of a day for the time concerned.

The Tibetan system instead uses one of the astronomical phenomena as the basic time scale: the mean synodic month (the period between successive new Moons), subdivided into 30 equal parts called lunar days. The time of day at which new Moon occurs is itself treated as a phenomenon that varies and is the subject of calculation. (Similar methods are sometimes used in the west. See, for example, Meeus, p. 349 ff., for new Moon calculations. The details and style are very different and much more complex, but the principle is exactly the same as that used in the Tibetan calculations.)

It is worth bearing in mind that measuring time in this way is a very reliable method to use. (See Neugebauer, p. 128, for why the Babylonians originally devised a similar system which was almost certainly the original source of the Tibetan one.) This is because the mean relative position of the Sun and Moon—irrespective of their actual longitudes—is the easiest and most reliably accurate quantity to measure and predict. The reason for this is that not only is the monthly cycle clear and easy to measure, but both lunar and solar eclipses help make the determination of the lengths of months very accurate indeed.

The first steps in calculating the Tibetan calendar are to derive mean values for the time when new Moon for a particular month occurs and the longitude of the Sun at that time. Once the mean values for the time of certain relative positions of the Sun and Moon are known, then adjustments are made to derive the correct, or true, time.

Once that is known, the next logical step to take would be to determine the actual longitudes for the Sun and Moon, and then move on to consider the planets. As the lunar longitude varies in a much more complicated fashion throughout the year than that of the Sun, the solar longitude should be the easiest to calculate.

Just as with any western calculation, an epoch is needed from which to measure time. Basically, the calculations contain a snapshot of the mean planetary positions (*rtsis 'phro*) at the moment of the epoch. Measuring forwards from then in time one calculates the mean positions at some future date, and then makes corrections for actual positions.

The epoch often coincides with the time that a particular text describing the calculations was written, or at least a suitably convenient time. For the purposes of this book, I shall take the 1927 epoch, as defined in the "Essence of the Kalkī" (*rigs ldan snying thig*, Rigthig) by Chenrab Norbu (*mkhyen rab nor bu*, born 1883). 1927 is the year Prabhava in the Indian calendars on which the Tibetan system is based. These use a sixty-year cycle of years, of which the first is Prabhava. Many texts on Tibetan calendars use the start of one of these sixty-year cycles as their epoch. This particular text belongs to a tradition of Tibetan astronomical calculation called the Phugluk (*phug lugs*), or Phugpa, started in 1447 by Phugpa Lhundrub Gyatso (*phug pa lhun grub rgya mtsho*) and Khedrub Norzang Gyatso (*mkhas grub nor bẕang rgya mtsho*). The other main tradition in use today is the Tsurluk (*mtshur lugs*), associated with Tsurphu (*mtshur phu*) monastery, and started around the same time by Jamyang Dondrub Wozer (*'jam dbyangs don grub 'od zer*).

There are several other calculation systems that survive, but these two are by far the most prominent, and the Phugpa is the most commonly used. If somebody today buys one of the common almanacs available in such places as Lhasa, Dharamsala or Kathmandu, it will almost certainly be from the Phugpa system.

I shall later give the necessary constants from earlier works of both the Phugpa and Tsurphu traditions, and show how the values in one text lead directly to the values given in another. In other words, in any particular tradition, you could take any source with its own epoch, and come up with the same answers for a current lunar calendar. It just makes the calculations much easier to handle if you take a base epoch in relatively recent times rather than several centuries ago. I shall also later describe a couple of the more important of the other traditions; however, apart from the Phugpa and Tsurphu traditions, most have fallen into disuse, apart from their calculations being preserved in textbooks.

Both of these two main traditions describe two sets of calculations, one of which is actually used to derive a calendar, and the other which is really only given for historical reasons—the calculations are "kept going," but not actually used apart from a couple of results. These are, respectively, called siddhānta and karaṇa calculations (*grub rtsis & byed rtsis*). Interestingly, this exact distinction is not held in the original Sanskrit works from which these calculations are derived.

In their original sense, siddhānta is often translated as textbook (Newman, 1987, p. 531), and karaṇa as handbook. The intention here is a contrast that is very similar to the use of the terms 'theory' and 'practice' in English.

The siddhānta provides the basic, perhaps quite complex, theory of the motions of the Sun, Moon, and planets, and the karaṇa is the simplified set of algorithms for producing a calendar from a particular epoch. In the original intentions of the Kālacakra Tantra, from which the Tibetan system is derived, the karaṇa calculations would be used for the actual calendar, and the siddhānta provides a set of values and methods for use in setting up and, most importantly, correcting a particular karaṇa.

For reasons that I shall investigate later, the Tibetans adapted the siddhānta data and used this for the basic calculations of their calendars. The original Indian data was not presented in this way and so was open to multiple interpretation, and this is one of the reasons that there is more than one calendrical system in Tibet. There are even sets of calculations that try to blend together by a sort of averaging method the calculations of both siddhānta and karaṇa methods, an idea that would presumably seem bizarre to the original Indian developers of these systems.

The main Tibetan systems that are used to produce calendars are of the siddhānta calculation type, and from amongst these, the rest of this chapter follows the description of calculations as given by Chenrab Norbu. It matters little which system I describe, as the principles are the same for all, and once one is understood, the differences with the others simply lie in the values used in the calculations. With some minor variations, they all use the same calculation methods. As the Phugpa tradition is the main one in use today, it makes sense to use the most recent textbook of that tradition as the basis for explaining the calculations of the Tibetan calendar.

This chapter is a loose translation if it can be considered a translation at all, because I have added much in the way of explanation, including comments from other texts where they are perhaps more clear or informative than Chenrab Norbu.

The epoch that is going to be used here is the start of the third month in the Tibetan calendar (*nag pa'i zla ba, caitramāsa*) in the Fire-Rabbit year, 1927. The date in western terms is Friday 1st April 1927. This western date is not explicitly given in the original material, but as modern almanacs have for many years included western dates it is easily calculated.

The first step is to calculate the number of (lunar) months that have elapsed from the epoch. As an example, I shall take the Tibetan new year in 1995, which fell on 1st March of that year. (Strictly speaking, the new Moon at the very end of the previous year fell on this date.)

Most of the calculations involve the use of a main unit of some quantity, with subdivisions of various fractions. As one would expect in a text on astronomy and calendars, the main quantities that will be used are time and angular measure. The easiest to describe first is time.

The basic unit of time is the solar day (*nyin zhag, dina*), which starts from what is best described as mean daybreak (*nam langs, pratyūṣa*). The most common definition one finds of this start of the day states that it is the moment when one is able to see the lines on the palms of the hands.

I have not been able to find any more mathematical definition than this, but calculations based on texts that measure time from that point make it clear that mean daybreak occurs at what we would call in the west, 5 AM L.M.S.T. (Local Mean Solar Time)—seven hours before the mean Sun crosses the meridian at noon. It should be considered to be the mean because the Tibetan calculations take no account of the variations through the year of the time of sunrise or daybreak.

Each solar day is therefore equal in length, and each is assigned a number, from 0 to 6. This value refers to the weekday (*res gza', vāra*), which corresponds to the planet associated with the day of the week: the Moon for our Monday, Mars for Tuesday, and so on. The Tibetan word *gza'* means planet, and the term *res gza'* could be translated as "successive planet," indicating the cycle of planets associated with successive solar days.

In some contexts the terms 'weekday' and 'solar day' are interchangeable, but strictly speaking the solar day is the general period from one daybreak to the next, and each solar day has a weekday assigned to it. So, unlike a western civil day in which, say, a Wednesday would last from one midnight to the next, in the Tibetan calendar the day lasts from 5 AM to the following 5 AM.

The weekdays are associated with the planets and assigned numerical values, in the following way:

0 Saturday	Saturn
1 Sunday	Sun
2 Monday	Moon
3 Tuesday	Mars
4 Wednesday	Mercury
5 Thursday	Jupiter
6 Friday	Venus

Each day is subdivided into smaller units. There does not seem to be any satisfactory equivalent to these in English and so I have chosen the most suitable Sanskrit equivalents for two of these. These are not necessarily the most commonly used in Sanskrit texts, but they occur in the Kālacakra literature, and are short and easy to remember and pronounce for anybody not familiar with Sanskrit.

Each solar day is divided into 60 nāḍī (*chu tshod*), also called ghaṭikā, or daṇḍa (*dbyug gu*), and each of these is further divided into 60 pāṇīpala (*chu srang*) or pala. These stand in a similar relationship to each other as do western hours and minutes, or minutes and seconds, and presumably for this reason Newman (Newman, 1987, p. 519ff.) translates nāḍī as half-hour. I was tempted to do something similar, but half-minute would seem awkward, and comparisons with western timing could become confusing.

The Tibetan term for a nāḍī translated literally into English would be something like "water-measure." This derives from an ancient method of measuring time using water clocks. The other term for the same measure of time, daṇḍa, literally means stick, and this refers to an ancient Indian custom of beating a drum or gong with a stick to mark each nāḍī.

The nāḍī is a little less than half an hour in length at 24 minutes, and the pala is 24 seconds. Each pala is further divided into 6 breaths (*dbugs, śvāsa*), each of four seconds duration. The term 'breath' is used as it is considered to be the length of time for a cycle of inhalation and exhalation in a mature person, free from illness, and breathing naturally.

Each of these breaths is divided into further sub-units, but these are variable in number depending on the context. The most common subdivision is of each breath into 707 sub-units or fractional parts (*cha shas, bhāga*), but these are not given particular names. There are therefore 15,271,200 of these final units or 21,600 breaths in each whole solar day. (There are two other different types of day defined, but I'll leave the discussion of these until later for the sake of clarity.)

So, how should one express values like these in a western book? It would be misleading to convert everything to decimals, and accuracy would also be lost that way.

The way I have chosen to represent values such as these is a method similar to that used by modern writers (see Neugebauer, p. 13) to represent ancient Babylonian sexagesimal values, from which, of course, the Indian and Tibetan systems are descended. The integer part of the value is separated from the fractional parts by a semicolon, and the fractional parts are themselves separated by commas.

Where the values of the fractional units, or denominators, are not clear (for example, the final unit mentioned above was said to depend on context), they will follow in brackets. So, a value of: 3;10,49,2,347 (60,60,6,707) will represent a Tuesday, at 10 nāḍī, 49 pala, etc., after mean daybreak. Usually it is only the last fractional unit that should be uncertain, and so that value will normally be written: 3;10,49,2,347 (707).

My use of semicolons and commas is simply for clarity in representing these quantities in a western book. There is no equivalent to these in a Tibetan text—although modern Tibetan texts printed in China have started to use commas—and the normal way of representing these values is to write the units one on top of the other, with the most significant unit at the top.

Of course, this use of commas could produce some ambiguity when representing normal numbers greater than three figures, where we place commas between powers of a thousand. I expect that the context should make it clear which notation is being used, and of course sexagesimal style values will nearly always include a semi-colon (sometimes fractions alone need to be represented) whereas normal numbers will not.

Very often it is necessary to multiply values such as these by some number, and add two values together. For example, we will later use a calculation where a weekday value has to be multiplied by an integer, and the result added to another weekday. This will be represented by:

840 × 1;31,50,0,480 + 6;57,53,2,20 (707)

This means that the second weekday value is added to the result of multiplying the first weekday value by 840. Each time we encounter a new type of calculation like this, I shall give a worked example. Needless to say, calculations such as these are best performed on a computer, and routines are easily written to represent them.

One word of warning though for anybody thinking of computerizing these calculations. Very large integer values often result, and so in the computer programs that I have written for creating and analysing Tibetan calendars, it was necessary to use binary coded decimal integers—just using long integers was not enough.

The second main quantity we will be using is angular measure. Both Indian and Tibetan systems of astronomy use the division of the ecliptic (the path the Sun appears to take through the stars during a year) into the familiar 12 signs (*khyim, rāśi*) of the zodiac: Aries, Taurus, etc.

However, much more important is a similar division of the ecliptic into 27 lunar mansions. The first lunar mansion (*tha skar, Aśvinī*) starts at the first point of Aries in the zodiac, and these mansions are used as a measure of longitude from that point. It is therefore easy to convert between longitudes using mansions and zodiac signs as they both have the same starting point.

The measure of longitude in terms of the zodiac of 12 signs (*khyim gyi 'khor lo, rāśicakra*) is not as commonly used as that of the 27 lunar mansions. When it is used, each zodiac sign is subdivided into 30 zodiacal days (*khyim zhag*), equivalent to degrees.

The clearest definition I have found of a zodiacal day is by Banda Gelek (Bgbumrin, p. 42) and he gives it unambiguously as a measure of time: the time taken for the mean Sun to move through a thirtieth of one sign of the zodiac. However, the term is also often used effectively as a measure of angle.

A value of longitude then, is normally expressed by the number of lunar mansion (starting with the first numbered zero), followed by several fractional parts. Just as with the solar days, each lunar mansion is divided into 60 nāḍī, each of these into 60 pala, and again each of these into six breaths. There are usually one or more other fractional units in a longitude value, but again, the denominators are not fixed, and vary according to the quantity being described, and some other factors.

It will be clear that with 27 lunar mansions of 60 nāḍī each, the entire circle of the ecliptic contains 1,620 nāḍī. Therefore each of the twelve zodiacal signs contains 135 nāḍī. These are the figures that are used when converting between the two measurement systems. The normal western subdivision of the zodiac signs into 30° each is used, but very rarely.

It may seem a little odd that the same subdivisions are used for both the main units of time and angular measure. But this is very similar to the western system (which also has Babylonian origins) in which both hours of time and degrees of angle are each subdivided into minutes and seconds. We also use hours, minutes, and seconds as angular measures of right ascension in the sky.

These units demonstrate the importance of the Moon in the Tibetan system. In the western definition the whole ecliptic measures 360°, and each degree therefore represents the approximate distance in the sky travelled by the Sun in one day. However, in the Tibetan system, the ecliptic measures 27 lunar mansions, and each mansion represents the approximate distance in the ecliptic travelled by the Moon in one day.

Also, as there are both 60 angular nāḍī in a lunar mansion and also 60 nāḍī of time in a solar day, the time taken for the Moon to move through approximately one nāḍī of angular measure in the sky is also approximately one nāḍī of time. This simple relationship is actually used as an approximation in the calendrical calculations.

Regarding the ecliptic, there is a question I shall answer later about whether these lunar mansions start at the first point of Aries in a tropical zodiac, or in a sidereal zodiac (as most people seem to assume), but this is not relevant to the present discussion.

First calculation—the true month

As one would expect, it would be normal to calculate a calendar for a whole year at a time, but of course the calculations for the months, lunar days, and so forth can be performed for any month one chooses. Whatever month is chosen, the first value that has to be calculated in deriving a Tibetan lunar calendar is the true lunar month (*zla ba rnam par dag pa*, or, *tshes zla rnam par dag pa*, *māsa viśuddha*). The point is to establish the exact number of lunar months that have elapsed from the epoch up to the new Moon for which calculations are being performed—the target date.

There are more lunar months in each year than the normal 12 of the western calendar months. The actual value of a lunar month (the number associated with it: the second month, third month, etc.) is defined in terms of the solar longitude during that month, and so the first month in each year must fall at roughly the same time (in the western calendar) each year.

This means that there has to be an extra (intercalary) month every so often—once every 32 1/2 lunar months, on average—and the exact determination of this I shall leave until later.

There are two steps in calculating the true month. In the first an intermediate figure is derived which does not include the intercalary months, and in the second that figure is corrected for the intercalations in order to derive the true month count. This simple structure applies to many of the more complex calculations that we shall encounter later.

For the first step, take the number of years that have elapsed from the epoch, multiply this by 12, and then add the number of months that have elapsed since the month of Caitra—this is counted as the third Tibetan lunar month in most Tibetan calendars, but not in all.

So, for the current example (1995), as the first month of the year is before the third month, instead of using negative values, it is easier if it is considered to be the 13th month of the previous year.

Between 1927 and 1994 there are 67 years, and there are ten months between the 3rd and 13th months. So the first step of the calculation is:

$$67 \times 12 + 10 = 814$$

In one year the Sun passes through 12 zodiac signs, and approximately one each month. Therefore this value is almost exactly equal to the total number of zodiac signs the Sun has passed through since the epoch, and for this reason it is sometimes called the number of zodiacal months (*khyim zla*).

Next, the correction has to be applied which adjusts for the intercalary months. This requires a fractional unit with 65 parts. The calculation is, where M is the intermediate value for the true month:

$$M \times 1;2 + 0;55 \ (65)$$

Tibetans and their predecessors in India did not write the calculations in this way, and instead wrote the different steps of the calculation one above the other. To write this calculation in their way on paper, write the intermediate value for the month down twice, one above the other. Multiply the lower of these by 2, add 55 to the result, and then divide by 65, noting both the whole value that results as the quotient, and the remainder:

814
$814 \times 2 + 55 = 1683 \div 65 = 25$ rem. 58 (rem. indicates a remainder)

The quotient of 25 then has to be added to the upper intermediate value, and this, together with the fractional part—the remainder from the division, which I term the intercalation index, for reasons that will become clear later—yields the true month. Note that there is no value to be multiplied by the first intermediate result for the month, neither is there a constant to be added to it. In order that the calculation looks more like those we shall encounter later, if these facts are written into the calculation, representing them as a 1 and a 0 respectively, it will look like this:

814 × 1 + 0 + 25 = 839
814 × 2 + 55 ÷ 65 = 25 rem. 58

Remember that the 25 on the top line is the quotient from the lower division carried over to the next step in the calculation. Using the notation I described earlier, this value for the true month would be written as: 839;58 (65). These are fractional calculations, and in western arithmetic terms this whole calculation could be written as:

$$814 \times 1\frac{2}{65} + \frac{55}{65} = 839\frac{58}{65}$$

The reason for using a different notation is that most of the calculations that come later in the derivation of a Tibetan calendar are much more complicated than this, and would be less understandable if they were represented in western fractional form. Without writing the calculation out in full, it could also be represented by:

814 × 1;2 + 0;55 = 839;58 (65)

As it happens, due to the rules for calculating for intercalary months, which will be explained later, the value that has been calculated here has to be considered to be that for the previous month, the last month of the previous year, and what is actually needed is the value for the next month for the start of the year. In effect this means that the calculation has to be done for the second month of the year, and the resulting value applies for the first month. This is easily done by adding the necessary factors. The true month becomes:

839;58 + 1;2 = 840;60.

The mean weekday

The next step is to calculate the monthly mean weekday (*gza' yi dhru ba*). This is a mean value for the weekday at which the new Moon occurs. I use the term 'mean' here in the same sense as is used in western astronomical texts. To get the exact weekday further corrections have to be applied to the mean value to give a final result either greater or less than the mean. As mentioned earlier, first determine the mean time at which an event occurs, and then find the true time. The time is described in terms of a certain number of nāḍīs, etc., during a particular weekday.

The mean is simply derived by multiplying the period of time elapsed since the epoch (measured in whole lunar months) by a constant, and then adding a value equivalent to the value of the mean weekday at the epoch.

The calculation is to take only the whole part (840) of the true month, multiply this by a weekday value, and then add another weekday value to the result:

840 × 1;31,50,0,480 + 6;57,53,2,20 (7,60,60,6,707)

The traditional way of performing this calculation is to write the true month value down five times, with the least significant term at the bottom, and multiply by each of the first fractional units in turn, also adding the values from the constant. Starting at the bottom, multiply the true month (840) by 480, and then add to this 20. This gives a result of 403,220. This needs to be divided by 707, keeping both the quotient (570) and the remainder (230):

840
840
840
840
840 × 480 + 20 = 403220 ÷ 707 = 570 rem. 230

The quotient needs to be added (carried) to the result on the line above, before performing the division on that line. On that line the multiplication is by 0, so the calculation is simply to add 2 to the previous quotient and then divide by 6, still preserving both the new quotient and remainder:

840
840
840
840 × 0 + 2 + 570 = 572 ÷ 6 = 95 rem. 2
840 × 480 + 20 = 403220 ÷ 707 = 570 rem. 230

Then continue, carrying the quotient up each time to the next line, leaving the remainder as the respective derived value. One final point is that the top line result is not left as a whole value but is divided by 7 and the remainder only preserved. What is needed is a weekday, and as there is a total of seven of those, the arithmetic on that line has to be performed modulo 7.

840 × 1 + 6 + 446 = 1292 ÷ 7 = 184 rem. 4
840 × 31 + 57 + 702 = 26799 ÷ 60 = 446 rem. 39
840 × 50 + 53 + 95 = 42148 ÷ 60 = 702 rem. 28
840 × 0 + 2 + 570 = 572 ÷ 6 = 95 rem. 2
840 × 480 + 20 = 403220 ÷ 707 = 570 rem. 230

This gives the final value for the mean weekday as 4;39,28,2,230 (60,60,6,707). This indicates a Wednesday (4), at 39 nāḍī, 28 pala, etc. We could otherwise write this calculation as:

840 × 1;31,50,0,480 + 6;57,53,2,20 = 4;39,28,2,230 (707)

These first two steps in the calculations are expressing two of the fundamental relationships that underlie the calendar—between the length of the month and the solar year, and between solar days and synodic months, and we should compare these to modern figures. (In this chapter I shall make other such comparisons, but all of these are only of the rates of various motions, such as the length of the synodic month, speed of the Sun, etc. These figures apply to most of the calendrical systems in use in Tibet. Where they differ is with regard to the absolute values at any time—the mean positions or values at their epochs—and comparisons of these data with modern values are in chapter six.)

First, the calculation for the true month involved a simple fraction of 65. The number of years was multiplied by 12, this result was multiplied by 1;2 and then the epoch value was added. Clearly, if one considers starting from an epoch value of 0;0, after a total of 65 years, there occurs once again an epoch value of 0 for the same lunar month within the year.

In arithmetical terms, this means that:

$$65 \times 12 \times 1;2 = 804;0 \qquad (804 = 67 \times 12)$$

This relationship tells us that 65 years, or solar cycles, is exactly equal to 804 lunar months. The cycle of different intercalary months repeats itself, and every 65 years there are 780 normal months and 24 intercalary, giving a total of 804.

The other relationship is that between solar days and synodic months. Here, we have the change in weekday from one new Moon to the next as 1;31,50,0,480 (707). The length of a synodic month is actually about 29 1/2 days, and clearly the weekday figure is represented modulo 7. The actual figure for the mean length of the synodic month then, is: 29;31,50,0,480 (707).

Converting this to decimals works out to 29.5305870 solar days. It must be borne in mind that the exact value of the synodic month is changing very slowly with time, as is the length of the solar day against which we would measure it, but this is in very close agreement with the modern western value.

Between 1000 CE and the present day the length of the synodic month has varied between 29.5305867 and 29.5305889 days. The figure used in the derivation of Tibetan calendars is therefore very accurate indeed. To give an idea of the accuracy of this value, based on the present value of the length of the synodic month, the time that would need to elapse for the timing of the mean relative position of the Sun and Moon to be out by about an hour would be nearly two thousand years. (Of course, I am ignoring initial positions here, and just considering the mean length of the month. If the first full Moon in this calendrical system was out by a day, so would all those that follow it. This is an issue I shall investigate later.)

Although there are many other greater errors in the calculation of Tibetan calendars, it is this figure that ensures that the calendars do indeed keep close step with the lunar cycles, and that, say, new and full Moons do usually fall on the days indicated. For example, a check on a few Tibetan calendars in recent years revealed a 15 per cent error rate in the indicated solar day for new Moons. This is reasonable for calculations that have not been adjusted or corrected in over 500 years.

It is worth at this point looking at the length of the synodic month in order to reveal the relationship between solar and lunar days. One mean synodic month, or 30 lunar days, is equivalent to 29;31,50,0,480 solar days. If we multiply this figure out to its smallest fractional part, we find that one lunar day is equal to 15032250/15271200 solar days. Dividing these numbers by common factors, we find that one lunar day equals 11135/11312 solar days, or, 11,312 lunar days equals 11,135 solar days.

The anomaly

The next step in the calculation is to derive the anomaly (*ril po, piṇḍa*) and its fractional part (*ril po'i cha shas, piṇḍāvayava*). The reason for my use of this term 'anomaly' will be explained later, but for now it is sufficient to state that this is a value that will be used to derive the exact weekday. The calculation is simple. Take the true month, and perform the following calculation:

840 × 2;1 + 13;103 (28,126)

The extra divisor is given because the value of the anomaly is calculated modulo 28. Writing this calculation out as before, with the lower line being calculated first, yields:

840 × 2 + 13 + 7 = 1700 ÷ 28 = 60 rem. 20
840 × 1 + 103 = 943 ÷ 126 = 7 rem. 61

This gives the anomaly as 20;61 (28,126).

The mean solar longitude

The next step is to calculate the monthly mean solar longitude (*nyi ma'i dhru ba*). Again, take the true month, multiply it by a constant which will represent the mean motion of the Sun in a month, and then add a value equivalent to the mean longitude of the Sun at the epoch.

The calculation required is this:

840 × 2;10,58,1,17 + 25;9,10,4,32 (27,60,60,6,67)

This gives as a result 22;44,6,1,41. If this calculation is written out in full, starting from the bottom as usual and showing the values carried on each line, it would be:

840 × 2 + 25 + 153 = 1858 ÷ 27 = 68 rem. 22
840 × 10 + 9 + 815 = 9224 ÷ 60 = 153 rem. 44
840 × 58 + 10 + 176 = 48906 ÷ 60 = 815 rem. 6
840 × 1 + 4 + 213 = 1057 ÷ 6 = 176 rem. 1
840 × 17 + 32 = 14312 ÷ 67 = 213 rem. 41

It is worth looking at a couple of these numbers more carefully. For a start, one thing needs to be explained. The final value is calculated modulo 27. This reflects the method described earlier of measuring longitude by dividing the ecliptic into 27 lunar mansions.

With 27 of them all of equal length, this gives the number of degrees in each one as 13 1/3. So, the first lunar mansion starts at 0° Aries, the second at 13° 20' Aries, etc.

The value derives as the mean solar longitude is 22;44,6,1,41. What does this translate to in western terms? The easiest way of doing this calculation is to consider the lunar mansion itself, and then the fractional part. The lunar mansion is number 22, and so it starts at 22 × 13 1/3 degrees from the first point of Aries. This gives 293° 20'. This is equivalent to 23° 20' of Capricorn.

The fractional part is more complicated. Subtracting the lunar mansion we are left with 44,6,1,41 (60,60,6,67), where the fractions are parts of a lunar mansion of 13 1/3 degrees. If this is multiplied out to the smallest unit, we find that there are a total of 60 × 60 × 6 × 67 = 1,447,200 of these divisions in a single lunar mansion. The fraction is then: 41 + 67 × (1 + 6 × (6 + 60 × 44)) = 1063800.

So we can represent the longitude as 22 1063800/1447200 lunar mansions. The extra fraction is 9° 48', which when added to the start of the lunar mansion (23° 20' of Capricorn) yields 3° 8' of Aquarius.

There is another step that has to be taken here if the calculation is being performed for a date other than the new Moon itself. The new Moon is taken as the 30th lunar day of the month. If the first, second or any other such lunar day is needed, one has to perform another calculation to derive the mean weekday and the mean solar longitude for the lunar day in question. Simply multiply the day required by the constant 0;59,3,4,16 (707) and add this to the weekday for the new Moon.

Similarly, multiply the lunar day value by the constant 0;4,21,5,43 (67) and then add to the value for the mean solar longitude at new Moon. If values are required for the third lunar day, for example, multiply by 3, and then add to the original mean values:

Weekday:	4;39,28,2,230 + 3 × 0;59,3,4,16
Sun:	22;44,6,1,41 + 3 × 0;4,21,5,43

The lunar day (*tshes zhag, tithi*) is a period of time dependent on the phase of the Moon. There are thirty of these in a lunar month, and the first starts when the Moon is new—when the Sun and Moon are in conjunction, each having the same longitude. It finishes when, about a day after new Moon, the Sun and Moon are 12° apart. The second lunar day finishes when the Sun and Moon are 24° apart, and so on.

The original calculations determined the mean weekday and solar longitude at the precise point of new Moon, i.e., at the end of the 30th lunar day, and the beginning of the first of the next month. If the multiplication by 3, described above, is performed, this would add values for three whole lunar days, and so this would yield the mean weekday and solar longitude for the end of the third lunar day—the beginning of the fourth—when the Sun and Moon are 36° apart.

When this calculation is performed, the results are simply called the mean weekday (*gza' bar pa*) and mean solar longitude (*nyi ma bar pa*). In this current worked example, I'll continue with the values for the new Moon itself (the very start of the first lunar day), and so the mean weekday and solar longitude are equal to the monthly mean values that were first obtained.

True weekday and solar longitude—first steps

The next step in the calculation is to apply corrections in order to derive the true weekday and solar longitude. For the true weekday, a calculation first has to be performed using the anomaly. The value derived earlier for the anomaly was 20;61 (28,126). In Tibetan notation the 20 would be written above the 61.

If the calculation is being done for a lunar day other than the exact new Moon, that lunar date first has to be added to the top value for the anomaly. The total is then divided by 14, preserving both the quotient and the remainder. In the current example there is nothing to add, and dividing by 14 gives a quotient of 1 and remainder of 6.

The corrections that are going to be derived here are calculated from a step function, and the second part of the calculation interpolates between two step values to give greater accuracy. This step function, and others like it that will be encountered later, is equivalent to the third term in simplified Western calculations for planetary motion.

The first term is a value for the longitude of the Sun or a planet at a particular epoch, the second term will usually then give the mean longitude, and be formed simply by multiplying a value by the time elapsed since the epoch. The third term will usually be a sine or cosine function that corrects for the ellipticity of the orbit. The step function that we are going to use now, represented by a table of values given in Table 1-1, is an approximation to the range of values that would be yielded by such a sine or cosine function.

Index	Coefficient	Total
1	5	5
2	5	10
3	5	15
4	4	19
5	3	22
6	2	24
7	1	25
8	1	24
9	2	22
10	3	19
11	4	15
12	5	10
13	5	5
0	5	0

Table 1-1

In using this table of values, the quotient from the division by 14 determines the way the resulting correction is later going to be applied. If the quotient is even (0, 2 or 4) it will be used additively, and if it is odd (the only possible odd values are 1 and 3) it will be used subtractively.

The Tibetan terms that are used here are respectively 'progressive' (*rim pa, krama*) and 'regressive' (*rim min, utkrama*), indicating that the value of the true weekday is ahead of the mean value (in which case the correction is added) or behind the mean value (in which case it is subtracted).

The remainder was 6 and this is used as an index (*rkang 'dzin*) into the table.

The value in the total column (*rkang sdom*) is taken as a number of nāḍī—in this case this is 24. This is the first step in the adjustment calculation, and next will be found another value, intermediate between two steps, which will be subtracted from, or added to, this number of nāḍī.

First, take the fractional part of the anomaly (61), multiply it by 30, and then add the number of the lunar day required in the particular month. There is nothing to add as the calculation is for new Moon, so the result is 1,830.

This is then multiplied by the coefficient in the next column to the index, but taking the next value down—this represents the difference between the two steps, and so the next value down is required, given the way the table is organized. The next total value is 25, 1 greater than the current step. It is that difference that is in the middle column.

In this example, as the value is 1, the calculation is simple, resulting in 1,830. This is placed in the position of a nāḍī, and divided by 3,780. The quotient is placed in the nāḍī position, and is called the interpolation correction. The remainder is carried on to the next line down, the pala position. The calculation so far would look like this:

1830 ÷ 3780 = 0 rem. 1830
1830

The carried remainder (1,830) is then multiplied by 60, and again divided by 3,780. Once more the quotient is left in the pala position, and the remainder carried down to the next position:

1830 ÷ 3780 = 0
1830 × 60 = 109800 ÷ 3780 = 29 rem. 180
180

The calculation continues, multiplying by 6 and then 707, each time dividing by 3,780. In the last line there is a whole number result, with no remainder:

$1830 \div 3780 = 0$
$1830 \times 60 = 109800 \div 3780 = 29$
$180 \times 6 = 1080 \div 3780 = 0$
$1080 \times 707 = 763560 \div 3780 = 202$

This value of 0,29,0,202 is then added to the nāḍī value that was written down earlier (24), to give 24,29,0,202. The original quotient when dividing the anomaly was odd, and so now the correction is subtracted from the mean weekday:

4;39,28,2,230 - 0;24,29,0,202 = 4;14,59,2,28

This value is called the semi-true weekday (*gza' phyed dag pa*). Before going any further, there are a couple of points to be made about this calculation.

From index value 7 onwards, the total is decreasing, and so the values calculated from the table are subtracted from the total value that had been written down in the nāḍī position. The result of this is then either subtracted from or added to the mean weekday, depending on whether the anomaly quotient was odd or even.

Also, the method I have described is a little more complex, and theoretically more accurate, than is often used by modern calendar makers. The adjustment of multiplying by 30 and adding the lunar day value is not used, and instead the fractional part of the anomaly is simply multiplied by the coefficient, and the result then divided by 126.

Interpolation techniques

The calculation that has just been described using the table is of a type that we shall encounter again, and so it is worth some further explanation. A correction was calculated and this was based on a main index and a fractional part of that index. The index was 6, and the fractional part of the anomaly was 61.

The value 6 referred to a total value for the correction of 24 nāḍī, but, the fractional part indicated that we were part of the way between the exact value of 6, with its total of 24, and the next value of 7, with its total of 25. The difference between these two is one nāḍī and so interpolation was used based on the fractional part. The denominator of the fraction is 126, and so it was needed to add to the total of 24 nāḍī, 61/126 of the difference with the next total.

So, the calculation that was performed was:

$$24 + \frac{61}{126} \times 1$$

The full calculation is a little more complicated than that because if individual lunar days are considered, the fractional part increases by 1 every 30 lunar days, and therefore by 1/30 every lunar day. For this reason, both the numerator and the denominator in the fraction are multiplied by 30, and an increment added to the numerator equal to the number of lunar day concerned. This lunar day value would be added before the first division by 3,780. In the example case of new Moon there is no such addition, and the calculation simply became:

$$24 + \frac{1830}{3780} \times 1$$

In other examples, the numerator of the fraction will be a number of nāḍī, pala, etc. The way to perform the calculation then is to multiply that value by the coefficient, and then divide by the denominator. Usually, the final division of such a calculation results in no remainder, and that should always be the case with calculations involving the weekday and solar longitude.

Regarding the use here of the term 'anomaly,' I should point out that I am using the term in the sense in which it is used in older Indian literature. In normal western use the word means the distance (in longitude) of the Moon from its perigee, the point of closest approach to the Earth in its orbit. In the case of these Tibetan calculations, they are fractions of a whole cycle, and are equivalent to the mean distance, not from the perigee, but from the apogee, the point when the Moon is furthest away from the Earth.

This is easily understood if one considers small values of the quantity I am calling the anomaly. In such a case, the division by 14 would result in a quotient of zero, and the resulting correction would be added to the weekday value. In other words, the Moon is travelling slower than its mean motion, and is taking longer to reach the required position for new Moon or other exact lunar day position. Its slowest speed, is of course, when it is furthest from the Earth, at apogee.

If these calculations actually used the western anomaly, the only difference this would make to the algorithm is that one would add for odd quotients and subtract for even ones. Bearing that in mind, it seems justified to use the term 'anomaly' here, as long as it is remembered that the actual figure is a half-circle different from the usual western meaning of the term.

The principle is exactly the same, although it is of course not described this way in Tibetan texts. Such texts describe the mathematics without giving any physical description of what underlies that mathematics. In texts translating Indian systems of astronomy into English, an equivalent word of the measure of longitude from the apogee, kendra, is often also translated as anomaly. See for example *Pañcasiddhāntikā* (Pañca), p. 31.

In the next section a similar adjustment will be made for the variable speed of the Sun, but first, I should compare the values that result from this current step function with modern western figures.

Regarding the length of this cycle, the mean time between two consecutive passages of the Moon through its perigee, the anomalistic month, it can be seen that the main value of the Tibetan anomaly advances by two each synodic month, and the fractional part by one.

But notice that in the step calculation where these values are used, the lunar day value is added to the anomaly. Also, the fractional part of the anomaly is multiplied by 30, and then added to the lunar day value. So, the anomaly increases each day by a value of one, and its fractional part increases by one thirtieth.

In a full month of thirty lunar days, the anomaly will increase by 30, and its fractional part by one. The anomaly is calculated modulo 28, and so in the monthly calculation it increases by two.

The increase each lunar day in the fractional part by one thirtieth means that this increase has to happen 30 × 126 times for it to be carried over to the anomaly itself. 30 multiplied by 126 is 3,780, and this number was used in the calculation for the weekday correction.

After 3,780 lunar days then, the fractional part will carry over to the anomaly itself. How many cycles of 28 is this? Well, 3,780 divided by 28 is 135.

The full cycle for the anomaly then is clearly just less than 28 lunar days. To calculate it fully, note that after 3,780 lunar days, 135 cycles are complete, plus the fractional part has carried, so we have 135 1/28 cycles. A quick calculation shows that one full cycle takes:

$$\frac{28 \times 3780}{3781} \text{ lunar days.}$$

Another way of expressing these figures would be to say that 3,781 anomalistic months are equal to 28 × 3,780 lunar days, or, 3,528 lunar, or synodic, months. Using the relationship that 11,312 lunar days equals 11,135 solar days, we can find that the length of the anomalistic month is:

$$\frac{28 \times 3780 \times 11135}{3781 \times 11312} = 27.55459 \text{ solar days.}$$

The modern figure for the length of the anomalistic month is 27.55455 days, showing quite a small error in the Tibetan figure. The position of the apogee, from which the anomaly is measured, is slowly moving in time, and I shall investigate the Tibetan handling of this factor after I have first considered the longitude of the Sun.

Regarding the steps of the correction, in "Astronomical Algorithms," Jean Meeus (Meeus, p. 349 ff.) gives a set of formulae for determining the time of the main phases (new, first quarter, full, and last quarter) of the Moon. The method is much more complex than the Tibetan system, but if his method is simplified it can be seen that the principles are exactly the same.

First, the time for the mean phases of the Moon are calculated by multiplying the number of months from the epoch by the length of the synodic month, and then adding an epoch value of the mean time of new Moon at the epoch. The next step corrects for many factors, the largest of which is the eccentricity of the Moon's orbit, represented by the mean anomaly of the Moon.

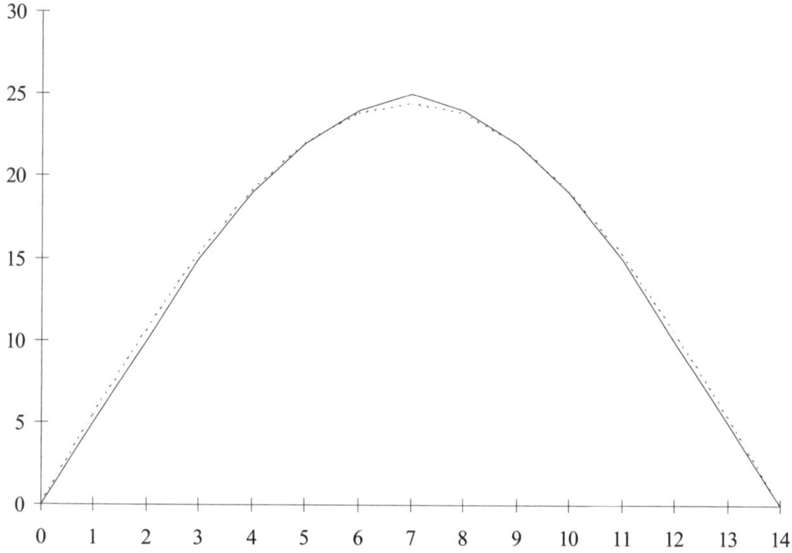

Figure 1a

Averaging the figures Meeus gives for new and full Moons, the value of the correction is the sine of the mean anomaly multiplied by 0.40690. This is in terms of days, and the correction will therefore vary between extremes of -0.40690 and +0.40690 days, just as one would expect.

The Tibetan corrections vary between extremes of plus and minus 25 nāḍī, and for comparison we need to convert Meeus' figure to nāḍī. This is easily done by multiplying by 60, with the result of 24.414 nāḍī.

For further comparison, Figure 1a shows the Tibetan step function for this correction and the same steps calculated from Meeus' formula (dotted line), both drawn to the same scale. The next largest factor in the calculation given by Meeus corrects for the eccentricity of the orbit of the Sun. There is also an equivalent to this in the Tibetan calculations, and it is derived in the next part of the calculation.

True weekday and solar longitude

Before the next step, an adjustment is needed to be made to the smallest fractional part of the semi-true weekday. The value that was derived is:

4;14,59,2,28 (707)

The purpose of this adjustment is to make this value for the semi-true weekday compatible with the value for the solar longitude, and in order to do this, the smallest fractional part (28 in our example) is multiplied by 67. This gives a result of 1,876. This is then divided by 707, and the quotient (2) remains as the fifth fractional part, and the remainder (462) becomes an extra sixth part. (This can usually later be ignored.) The sixth part still has the divisor of 707, and the fifth now has the divisor of 67. This is needed for the next step in the calculation, and the value of the semi-true weekday has now become:

4;14,59,2,2,462 (7,60,60,6,67,707)

The next steps will derive a final adjustment which will be applied to both the semi-true weekday and the mean solar longitude, finally to yield the true values of both. The first step is to subtract a value of 6 mansions and 45 nāḍī from the mean solar longitude:

22;44,6,1,41 - 6;45,0,0,0 = 15;59,6,1,41 (27,60,60,6,67)

This position in the zodiac represented by 6;45 is known as the birth-sign (*skyes khyim, janmarāśi*) of the Sun, and is equivalent to the Sun's apogee when it is at its furthest from the Earth. It is equivalent in zodiacal signs to the very beginning of Cancer.

The principle here is very similar to the earlier correction using the Moon's anomaly—the distance of the Moon from its apogee. Here, the calculation is finding the distance of the Sun from its apogee, and this is used to calculate the correction. As before, in western methods the Sun's anomaly is measured from the perigee, not the apogee.

If the subtraction of 6;45 will not work without creating a negative value—i.e., the mean solar longitude is less than 6;45,0,0,0—then first add a whole circle of 27 lunar mansions (360°) to the longitude.

A check is now made to determine whether the value just derived is greater or less than a half-circle of 13;30,0,0,0 (180°). In our case it is greater, and so a half a circle is subtracted from it:

15;59,6,1,41 - 13;30,0,0,0 = 2;29,6,1,41 (27,60,60,6,67)

Whether or not this subtraction of half a circle has been needed should be noted down, as this will determine whether the correction that will now be derived is added or subtracted. There was a similar need in the previous calculation for the weekday, which depended on whether the quotient from the original division by 14 was even or odd.

The lunar mansion value just derived (in the example, 2) is multiplied by 60 and then added to the nāḍī value (29). In the example, this gives 149. Divide this total by 135, and the quotient (1) is noted down to be used later as an index into a table (Table 1-2).

Before continuing with the calculation, some explanation is useful here as the physics underlying this calculation is easy to describe. 60 is the number of nāḍī in a lunar mansion, and 135 is the number of nāḍī in a zodiac sign, and so this last step has converted from a measure of longitude in terms of lunar mansions and nāḍī into a measure of zodiac signs and nāḍī. The nāḍī are the same size in each case.

There are now two possibilities: a measure of zodiac signs from the birth-sign of the Sun if no half-circle was subtracted, and from the opposite point in the zodiac if the half-circle did have to be subtracted.

In the first case these are the signs Cancer, Leo, Virgo, Libra, Scorpio, and Sagittarius. This half of the Sun's course is called progressive because at the beginning of Cancer, according to the Tibetan system, the Sun is at its apogee, when it is furthest from the Earth and travelling at its slowest speed. At the apogee, its true position is equal to its mean position. During the following six months, as the Sun starts by travelling at its slowest it falls behind its mean position, but as it is continually gathering speed this half of its course is called progressive. In this case the correction that is going to be calculated will have to be subtracted from the Sun's mean position.

In the second case, if the half-circle had been subtracted, then the calculation is dealing with the signs Capricorn, Aquarius, Pisces, Aries, Taurus, and Gemini. At the very beginning of Capricorn the Sun's true position is again the same as its mean, it is at is perigee, when it is closest to the Earth and travelling at its fastest speed. After it has passed this point, the true position quickly overtakes the mean position, and so the correction that is about to be derived will need to be added to the Sun's mean position. As it is gradually slowing down through these six signs this half of its course is called regressive.

I should point out that this usage of the terms 'progressive' and 'regressive' appears to be contrary to the way they are employed with the weekday calculation. In that calculation when the result of the division by 14 is even, this is the progressive half of the cycle and the step correction is added; with the solar calculation the correction is subtracted in the progressive half.

This contradiction is explained by the fact that in both calculations, the progressive half of the cycle immediately follows the anomaly of the body in question starting from zero and travelling through half a circle. The progressive half therefore starts at that body's apogee, when it is travelling at its slowest, after which, in the case of the Sun, the longitude correction has to be subtracted. In both cases, the body in question is accelerating throughout the progressive half of the cycle.

Index	Coefficient	Total
1	6	6
2	4	10
3	1	11
4	1	10
5	4	6
0	6	0

Table 1-2

With the weekday, when the anomaly is zero, the Moon is travelling at its slowest, but the weekday is therefore increasing at its fastest relative to the lunar days, and the correction to the weekday has to be added in the two quadrants that follow. The words progressive and regressive are with respect to the speed of the Moon, not the correction to the weekday. In the progressive half of the cycle the Moon is accelerating, and in the regressive half it is decelerating, just as with the Sun.

Getting back to the calculation, the remainder after the division by 135 is a number of nāḍī. This is taken together with the pala and other fractional parts remaining from the result just obtained. In the example the remainder was 14, and so this results in 0;14,6,1,41. The point here is that multiples of 135 (whole zodiac signs) in the nāḍī unit are removed and used as an index. The rest of the value that remains (position within the next zodiac sign) is then going to be used as a fractional multiplier, properly called an interpolation variable. (The fractions are 135th parts of the difference between successive 'total' values.)

To this end, multiply all the units down to the lowest fractional part:

$$((14 \times 60 + 6) \times 6 + 1) \times 67 + 41 = 340200$$

Reference is now made to the table, using the earlier quotient as an index. The quotient was 1, and this refers to the first row. As a coefficient, take the next row, in this case the second one, and find the coefficient of 4. This is now multiplied by the number just obtained:

$$340200 \times 4 = 1360800$$

Now divide up (starting at the bottom) by the respective fractional parts, until the nāḍī unit is reached:

56
$3385 \div 60 = 56$ rem. 25
$20310 \div 6 = 3385$ rem. 0
$1360800 \div 67 = 20310$ rem. 30

This gives a result of 56,25,0,30. Work downwards, starting with the nāḍī figure, each time dividing by 135 and carrying the remainder down to the next line, multiplying by the respective fractional parts:

$56 \div 135 = 0$ rem. 56
$25 + 56 \times 60 = 3385 \div 135 = 25$ rem. 10
$0 + 10 \times 6 = 60 \div 135 = 0$ rem. 60
$30 + 60 \times 67 = 4050 \div 135 = 30$

This gives an intermediate correction of 0;0,25,0,30.

As before, the total value (6 in the example) from the index row is used as a number of nāḍī, and the intermediate correction is now added to or subtracted from this.

Just as with the earlier weekday calculation, if the index was 0, 1 or 2 this value of 0;0,25,0,30 is added to the nāḍī value taken from the total column. If the index was 3, 4 or 5, it is subtracted. In this case, the index was 1, and so it is added. The total it is added to is 6, and so the final value of the correction is 0;6,25,0,30.

This correction is to be applied to both the semi-true weekday and the mean solar longitude. First, reference has to be made to the note about whether half a circle was subtracted when starting this correction calculation. If the subtraction was performed, the correction is added to both the semi-true weekday and the mean solar longitude. If the subtraction was not needed, then we subtract the correction.

In the example, the subtraction was needed, and so the correction is added. The true weekday therefore becomes:

4;14,59,2,2 + 0;6,25,0,30 = 4;21,24,2,32 (7,60,60,6,67)

In that calculation, the final fractional part (of 707) derived earlier is ignored. The true solar longitude becomes:

22;44,6,1,41 + 0;6,25,0,30 = 22;50,31,2,4 (27,60,60,6,67)

The point here is that in the half-circle after the Sun has passed its apogee, the correction has to be subtracted from the mean longitude, and in the half-circle after the perigee it has to be added. There is a very similar calculation that will be used later for the motions of the planets.

One question that needs to be answered here is: why is the same correction applied to both the weekday and the solar longitude? One is a measure of time, and the other of angular position around the ecliptic.

This is best described in western terms. Both the tables that we have used make adjustments for the fact that the Moon and Sun do not move in perfectly circular, but elliptical orbits. The first table, used to derive the semi-true weekday, adjusts for the ellipticity of the Moon's orbit only, and as the weekday needs to be calculated according to the relative position of both the Sun and Moon, an additional correction needs to be made for the position of the Sun.

The second table adjusts for the ellipticity of the Sun's (apparent) orbit, and for the sake of illustrating the point, let's say that we are calculating for new Moon, and the correction applied means that the true Sun is actually one nāḍī ahead of the mean position. This one nāḍī is actually one sixtieth part of a lunar mansion, and is 13 1/3 minutes of arc. This one nāḍī will be the correction, which will have to be added to the mean value in order to calculate the true solar longitude.

If the Sun is ahead of the mean position, there is no longer a new Moon, because the Moon is behind the Sun by one nāḍī—still taken as a measure of angular position. The Moon has to catch up with the Sun, and so how long does it take to reach it? As was described earlier, the Moon travels through approximately one lunar mansion each day, and as it has to move through one sixtieth of a lunar mansion, it will therefore take one sixtieth of a day to do this. One sixtieth of a day is one nāḍī as a measure of time, and so this correction of one nāḍī also needs to be added to the value of the weekday.

This makes it clear why the same correction is applied to both the weekday and the solar longitude, and also why the previous calculation for the weekday is called "semi-true"—that calculation adjusts for the lunar cycle only, and not the variations from the mean of the solar longitude.

We should now consider the accuracy of this calculation of the solar longitude and the correction that is applied to it.

The first point to consider is the length of the solar year—the time for the mean Sun to complete a full circle of the zodiac. The mean motion of the Sun in a single lunar day was given as 0;4,21,5,43 (67). Reducing this value to its lowest fractional part yields: 105,300. The total number of those lowest fractional parts in an entire circle of the zodiac is:

$$27 \times 60 \times 60 \times 6 \times 67 = 39074400$$

The mean motion of the Sun in one lunar day can therefore be represented as a fraction of the whole circle of the zodiac:

$$\frac{105300}{39074400} = \frac{13}{4824}$$

The length of the solar year in terms of solar days can then be found by converting this to solar days using the relationship that 11,135 solar days is equal to 11,312 lunar days, and then dividing into a full circle:

$$\frac{4824}{13} \times \frac{11135}{11312} = 365.270645 \text{ solar days.}$$

There is another way that this same figure can be derived. In the calculation of the true month I showed that 65 years, or solar cycles, is exactly equal to 804 lunar months. 804 lunar months is 24,120 lunar days, and so, converting again to solar days:

24120 × 11135 = 65 × 11312 solar cycles, which when simplified gives:

6714405 solar days = 18382 solar cycles.

Both of these numbers will be used in a later part of the calendar calculations. Dividing them again yields the value of the length of the

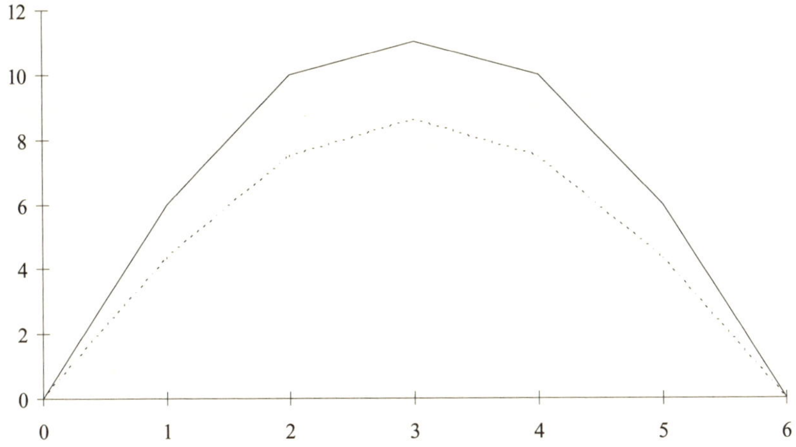

Figure 1b

year as 365.270645 days.

For comparison with modern figures for the length of the mean tropical solar year, in 1000 CE this was 365.24225087 days and in 2000 CE, 365.24218967 days. There is quite an error in the Tibetan length of the year here, and the Tibetan figure is much closer to the length of the sidereal solar year—relative to the fixed stars. However, as we shall see later, the definition of the solar longitude is dependent on seasonal points, and this can only imply a tropical year.

With regard to the accuracy of the correction that is applied to the mean solar longitude, in a similar fashion to the calculation for the timing of the phases of the Moon, a simplified modern calculation of the longitude of the Sun would take an epoch value of the mean longitude, add to this a second term where the mean motion is multiplied by time, and then add a third trigonometric term involving the anomaly of the Sun.

The trigonometric term is a sine function that will vary between extremes of plus and minus 1°.9146 (Meeus, p. 164). The Tibetan corrections vary between extremes of plus and minus 11 nāḍī. Again Meeus' figure can be converted to nāḍī, by dividing by 360, and then multiplying by 1,620 (27×60). This gives a result of 8.62 nāḍī, and so the Tibetan figures are not particularly accurate. As before, Figure 1b compares at the same scale the Tibetan step function for this correction and the same steps calculated from Meeus' data (dotted line).

I stated before that the position of the Moon's apogee, from which the Tibetan anomaly is measured, is moving in time, and that this would be investigated after having described the determination of the solar longitude.

The position of the Moon's apogee moves forward through the zodiac by just less than 41° per year. The Tibetan figure must be close to this due to the accuracy in the Tibetan anomalistic month. The easiest way to compare properly is to find two new Moons when the anomaly was precisely zero.

This has happened twice since the Phugpa calculations were established, at the new Moons at the start of the first month of the year starting in 1603 (Monday 10th February 1603) and of the 4th month of the year starting in 1888 (Thursday 10th May 1888).

At those times, as the anomaly is zero, and as it is new Moon, both the longitudes of the mean Moon and its apogee must equal that of the mean Sun. Using data from an early epoch of the Phugpa tradition, the relevant values are easily calculated, converted into degrees of longitude, and then compared with modern figures:

		Tibetan Apogee	**Modern Value**	**Difference**
1603	22;9,51,0,18 =	295°.522	314°.058	-18°.536
1888	1;12,32,1,29 =	16°.119	40°.662	-24°.543

Although I have not made any attempt to define the Tibetan zodiac and its relation with the western one yet, what matters here are the differences between the figures. Clearly the Tibetan value for the position of the Moon's perigee is slowly falling further behind the real perigee.

This might seem surprising at first because the length of the Tibetan anomalistic month was slightly longer than the modern figure. If the Moon is taking slightly longer each month to reach its perigee, then its longitude will be increasing slightly each month relative to the modern figures.

The reason that this is not the case is that the error in the length of the anomalistic month is proportionately very much smaller than that in the length of the solar year. For this reason the Tibetan values for the longitude of the Sun, and therefore also for the Moon and its perigee, are decreasing relative to modern figures as time progresses. This effect is much greater than that due to the small error in the anomalistic month.

Later I shall be describing other calculation systems, and it would be useful to summarise here the basic calculations of the calendar that have been described so far, as based on the "Essence of the Kalkī" (Rigthig) of Chenrab Norbu:

Epoch: Friday 1st April 1927. Julian day: 2424972.

True month:	m × 1;2	+ 0;55 (1,65)
Mean weekday:	M × 1;31,50,0,480	+ 6;57,53,2,20 (707)
Anomaly:	M × 2;1	+ 13;103 (28,126)
Mean Sun:	M × 2;10,58,1,17	+ 25;9,10,4,32 (67)

In the above, "m" is the result of the first calculation of the month count, from multiplying the year count by 12 and adding months elapsed since Caitra. There is no need to represent this calculation here as it the same for every system. "M" is the true month count, after adjustment for intercalation. The Julian day number is a count of days used in western astronomy. It serves as a useful common reference point when comparing different calendars and their epochs.

More modern texts that have been published in the last few years (e.g., Kunnor 1, p. 58) have started to use a more recent epoch, the start of the latest sexagenary cycle in 1987—exactly 60 years after the epoch of the "Essence of the Kalkī." This epoch is 743 lunar months after that of the "Essence of the Kalkī," and its epoch values are easily calculated as:

Epoch: Tuesday 28th April 1987. Julian day: 2446914.

True month:	m × 1;2	+ 0;0 (1,65)
Mean weekday:	M × 1;31,50,0,480	+ 3;11,27,2,332 (707)
Anomaly:	M × 2;1	+ 21;90 (28,126)
Mean Sun:	M × 2;10,58,1,17	+ 0;0,0,0,0 (67)

Five components of the calendar

The above calculation provides the basic elements needed with which to derive the lunar calendar. That calendar consists of five specific components (*lnga bsdus*, or, *yan lag lnga*, *pañcāṅga*). These are the weekdays, lunar days, lunar mansions, yogas (*sbyor ba*) and karaṇas (*byed pa*).

The weekdays are the normal days from mean daybreak to daybreak, and have the names of the seven planets: Sunday for the Sun, Monday for the Moon, etc. As mentioned earlier, the start of each weekday is best described as 5 AM Local Mean Solar Time. The lunar days were also described earlier, and are the periods of time between exact separations of the Sun and Moon by multiples of 12°, starting at new Moon.

The third component of the calendar, the lunar mansion, refers to the position of the Moon in the ecliptic, and this, together with the yogas and karaṇas, will be explained later.

The basis of the calendar is the solar day, to each of which is assigned a weekday, and at the start of each solar day one of the other components of the calendar will also be in force.

For example, if a new Moon occurs late afternoon on a Wednesday, then the end of the first lunar day of the new month—when the Sun and Moon are exactly 12° apart—will be sometime in the late afternoon of the next day, the Thursday. Therefore at daybreak on the Thursday the first lunar day will be in progress, and so the whole of the Thursday—from daybreak until the following daybreak at the beginning of the Friday—will be given the lunar day number, what we might call a lunar date, of 1. The Thursday is therefore the first day of the new month.

The previous day, the Wednesday, is the new Moon day of the previous month, and at its daybreak the lunar day in progress will be the last in the cycle, the 30th. The Wednesday will therefore be given the lunar date 30. This number applies to the whole of the Wednesday, just as the number 1, the first of the next month, will apply to the whole of the Thursday. The calculation for the weekday that we have used gives the time during the particular weekday when the lunar day changes—the time that the Sun and Moon are an exact multiple of 12° apart.

When a calendar is being drawn up, these lunar dates are assigned to the solar days by simply inspecting the results of the weekday calculation. However, sometimes the calculations for successive lunar days result in a weekday value being skipped, or one occurring twice.

For example, if calculations are performed for the month previous to the one used in the above example calculations, the true weekdays for the 9th and 10th lunar days are:

9th lunar day - 4;59,8,0,5
10th lunar day - 6;3,23,2,29

The first of these is a Wednesday (8th February) and the second is a Friday (10th February). The first value indicates that the 9th lunar day finished, and the 10th started, right at the very end of the Wednesday. The 10th lunar day did not end until very early on the Friday, and so at daybreak on both the Thursday and the Friday, the lunar day in progress was number 10. This means that there is an extra or duplicated (*lhag pa, adhika*) lunar date, and the number 10 is associated with both the Thursday and the Friday.

Looking later in the same month, exactly the opposite happens. The calculations for the true weekday for the 21st, 22nd, and 23rd lunar days yield:

21st lunar day - 3;5,23,3,66
22nd lunar day - 3;59,38,5,26
23rd lunar day - 4;53,54,0,52

The first two of these are both for a Tuesday (21st February) and the third is for a Wednesday (22nd February). This means that the 22nd lunar day started very early on the Tuesday, just after daybreak, and finished very late on the same day. So, at daybreak on the Tuesday the lunar day in progress was 21, and at daybreak on the Wednesday the lunar day was 23. These numbers are associated with these two consecutive weekdays, and the 22nd lunar date is omitted (*chad pa, ūna*).

As I mentioned at the beginning of this chapter, it is often said that the Tibetans add or omit certain dates because of superstition regarding some being lucky and others unlucky. From this it can be seen that this is not the case at all, and a rigorous mathematical formula produces these variations.

One further point regarding the weekday calculation that is worth mentioning here is that the calendar is, or certainly should be, sensitive to geographic longitude. If at a certain point on the Earth's surface a lunar day ends just before daybreak, a little further east, that same lunar day will end just after daybreak, resulting in a different assignment of lunar to solar days. (The lunar day ends at the same time for both locations, but daybreak occurs earlier in the more eastern location.)

In a later chapter I shall look more closely at this issue, and consider the longitude for which the original Tibetan calendars were calculated.

Similarly to the lunar days, the other components of the calendar are generally considered to apply to the whole weekday, depending on which was in effect at daybreak. The next step in calculating the calendar then, is to derive the lunar mansion, the third of the three components. The example I have been using for the calculations is too simple, being new Moon itself, and so I shall take another day to illustrate the calculation.

This is the 10th day of the same month that was used in the previous calculations. For this day, the true weekday calculates as: 0;50,13,4,57 and the true solar longitude as: 23;35,28,2,10.

As the solar longitude refers to exactly the end of a lunar day, when the Sun and Moon are a multiple of 12° apart, to find the longitude of the Moon at the same time one simply has to calculate the separation between the Sun and Moon, and add this to the solar longitude. 12° is 54 nāḍī of longitude, and so the number of the lunar day is multiplied by 54. This gives a total of 540 for the example. This is a number of nāḍī, and dividing by 60 gives the separation in terms of lunar mansions and nāḍī. The quotient becomes the number of lunar mansions, and the remainder, the number of nāḍī.

The result of this is 9;0. This is the angular separation between the Sun and the Moon—the Moon is moving ahead of the Sun, so this is the Moon's longitude minus that of the Sun. Therefore this is added to the true solar longitude to find the longitude of the Moon itself:

23;35,28,2,10 + 9;0,0,0,0 = 5;35,28,2,10

In this example, the result of adding the lunar mansions is 32, but as there are a total of 27 lunar mansions, 27 was subtracted to leave 5. This is a value for the longitude of the Moon, but not at daybreak.

This value applies at the very end of the tenth lunar day. Now, as the Moon moves through approximately one nāḍī of longitude in each nāḍī of time, a simple calculation can be performed to determine the position of the Moon at daybreak.

The true weekday is 0;50,13,4,57, meaning that the weekday, at the point of the exact end of the tenth lunar day, is 50 nāḍī, 13 pala, etc., old. This is the time of the end of the tenth lunar day, measured from daybreak. It is therefore necessary to subtract this time, 50,13,4,57, from the lunar longitude just derived:

5;35,28,2,10 - 0;50,13,4,57 = 4;45,14,3,20

This method does not give the Moon's position at the beginning of the first of two days when there is an extra day. I have not found a description in Tibetan texts of how to do this. The obvious assumption to make is that one would take the lunar day end that would have occurred shortly before the beginning of the current solar day, and add the time remaining of that particular weekday to the Moon's longitude.

It is also worth pointing out that normal practice does not entail making a similar correction to the longitude of the Sun. The value derived is also for the moment of the exact end of the lunar day, and so to derive the longitude at daybreak would require a certain amount to be subtracted.

For a full listing of the Tibetan and Sanskrit names of the lunar mansions, see Appendix 1.

The next component of the calendar is easy to calculate. The yoga is simply the sum of the solar and lunar longitudes, with 27 subtracted if the total is greater than 26. In the example, the longitudes of the Sun and Moon are:

Sun: 23;35,28,2,10 Moon: 4;45,14,3,20

The longitude of the Moon being used here is that calculated for daybreak, and as no correction is made to the longitude of the Sun for daybreak, there is an odd situation in that the longitude of the Sun at the time of the end of the lunar day is to be added to that of the Moon at daybreak—the beginning of the weekday. There is an obvious inconsistency here that could be corrected, but generally is not.

Banda Gelek (Bgbumrin, p. 45) states that the longitude of the Moon is taken at daybreak because the yoga is needed at that moment in time as it will apply to the solar day, but unfortunately, in common with other writers, he does not explain why no correction is applied to the Sun.

The calculation for the yoga is, then:

23;35,28,2,10 + 4;45,14,3,20 = 1;20,42,5,30

The yogas are numbered similarly to the lunar mansions, from 0 to 26, and the one calculated here is therefore number 1, Prīti (*mdza' ba*). For a full list of these, see Appendix 1.

The last step is to calculate the karaṇa. There are eleven of these in total, four of which occur only once in each lunar month, and seven that repeat in a cycle through the month. The karaṇas are simply halves of a lunar day—there are two to each lunar day, and they therefore represent the time between successive separations between the Sun and Moon in multiples of 6°.

Tibetan texts rarely give a calculation for the karaṇa, presumably as it is considered trivial, but Banda Gelek (Bgbumrin, p. 35) does.

Banda Gelek states that one should multiply the lunar date by two, and write the result in two places. Subtract 2 from the upper of these, and subtract 1 from the lower. Divide both by 7 and the remainder in the upper place gives the karaṇa in the first half of the lunar day and the remainder in the lower place that in the second half of the lunar day.

A result of 1 indicates Vava, a result of zero, Viṣṭi, and so forth. These results are for the seven changing karaṇas and he expects the position of the four unchanging karaṇas to be determined by inspection. See Appendix 1 for a list of the two types of karaṇa.

It is still needed to determine the timing of the karaṇas, and the determination of which half of the lunar day is in effect at daybreak is best done by examining the time of the exact lunar day either side of daybreak. The timing of the half lunar day would be determined by simply halving the time between the beginning and end of the lunar day in question, but this information is not normally given in almanacs.

In the example, on the day in question the true weekday is 0;50,13,4,57, meaning that the exact end of the tenth lunar day occurred 50 nāḍī, 13 pala, etc., after daybreak.

The true weekday on the previous day is 6;46,2,1,53. Ignoring the weekday value, and subtracting from a whole day, we get:

1;0,0,0,0 - 0;46,2,1,53 = 0;13,57,4,14

This means that after the exact moment of the lunar day (the beginning of the tenth lunar day), there are 13 nāḍī, 57 pala, etc., until the start of the next weekday. It is clear that at the relevant daybreak, we are much nearer to the beginning of the tenth lunar day than the end of it—therefore the karaṇa that occupies the first half of the tenth lunar day is in progress—this is Taitila (*til rdung*).

The karaṇas are not applied to the solar days as is the case with the weekdays and lunar dates, but are considered to be in effect from whatever times their relevant lunar days and half lunar days start.

Correlation with western dates

I stated at the start of these calculations for the five components of the calendar that the correlation of the epoch of 1927 with western dates was easily calculated. I simply gave the epoch as Friday 1st April 1927, and I shall now describe how this is determined. Using a similar method one can correlate Tibetan and western dates back through history, if required.

To do this, a calculation is needed that will be used in the next chapter for calculating the positions of the five planets. This determines the whole number of solar days that have elapsed since the epoch, and once this is determined, the lunar calendar can easily be matched to the familiar western one.

Take the value for the true lunar month, multiply by 30, and then add the number of the lunar day under consideration. Keeping with the previous example of new Moon day at the start of the new year in 1995, this simply means:

$$840 \times 30 = 25200$$

This result is clearly the number of lunar days that have elapsed since the epoch. Write this number down three times, add 2 to the middle one, and 178 to the lower one:

25200
25200 + 2 = 25202
25200 + 178 = 25378

The lower result is divided by 707, and the quotient added to the figure above. This is then divided by 64, and the quotient is subtracted from the upper figure:

25200 - 394 = 24806
25200 + 2 = 25202 + 35 = 25237 ÷ 64 = 394 rem. 21
25200 + 178 = 25378 ÷ 707 = 35 rem. 633

The resulting value of 24,806 is known as the general day (*spyi zhag*).

These two values of 2 and 178 are particular to the epoch, and it is a simple job to demonstrate their meaning. The above calculation is multiplying the number of lunar days by a certain ratio in order to derive solar days. That ratio is best represented by the following:

$$1 \text{ lunar day} = 1 - \left(\frac{1}{64} + \frac{1}{64 \times 707}\right) \text{ solar days.}$$

This is exactly equivalent to the ratio we calculated earlier, that one lunar day equals 11135/11312 solar days.

In this calculation a fraction of a solar day is subtracted. The fact that it is being subtracted may not be obvious at first as the first figures are actually added. However, they add to values that eventually result in a quotient that is subtracted on the top line. This fraction that is subtracted can be represented by:

$$\frac{2}{64} + \frac{178}{64 \times 707} \text{ solar days.}$$

This fraction can be converted to a measure of solar days in terms of nāḍī, pala, etc.

$$\text{This equals } \frac{(2 \times 707) + 178}{64 \times 707} = \frac{1592}{64 \times 707} = \frac{199}{8 \times 707} \text{ solar days}$$

$$= \frac{199 \times 15 \times 30 \times 6}{60 \times 60 \times 6 \times 707} = \frac{537300}{60 \times 60 \times 6 \times 707} \text{ solar days.}$$

Subtract this from a whole day:

$$\frac{60 \times 60 \times 6 \times 707 - 537300}{60 \times 60 \times 6 \times 707} = \frac{14733900}{60 \times 60 \times 6 \times 707}$$

Now, simply divide this through, from the bottom upwards.

$3473 \div 60 = 57$ rem. 53.
$20840 \div 6 = 3473$ rem. 2
$14733900 \div 707 = 20840$ rem. 20

This result of 57,53,2,20 matches exactly the value for the fractional part of the mean weekday at the epoch, which was 6;57,53,2,20. So, the fraction of a solar day that was subtracted in the general day calculation, represented at the epoch by the numbers 2 and 178, is equal to the fraction of the solar day remaining at the time of mean lunar day (new Moon in the example). The epoch values of 2 and 178 effectively take the start of the calculation to the end of the solar day of the epoch, and the general day is determined from there.

The calculation results in two remainders, 21 and 633. These are effectively negative (the quotient was subtracted on the top line), and so the result of the calculation could be represented as:

$$24806-\left(\frac{21}{64}+\frac{633}{64\times707}\right)$$

If this fractional part is subtracted, another way the final result could be represented is:

$$24805+\frac{42}{64}+\frac{74}{64\times707}\text{ solar days.}$$

This fractional part, the numerators 42 and 74, represents the time of the exact current mean lunar day. If this is converted into nāḍī, etc., the result is 39,28,2,230. The value that was originally calculated for the mean weekday was 4;39,28,2,230, and so the remainder figures for the general day calculation (21 and 633) represent the time between mean new Moon and the end of the solar day during which it occurred.

Since the end of the solar day of the epoch, 24,805 whole solar days have elapsed up to the start of the new Moon solar day in question, leaving this fraction of a solar day left up to the time of the current mean lunar day (in this current example, mean new Moon). Therefore 24,806 solar days elapsed between the end of the solar day of the epoch, and the end of the solar day in question.

There is one more step in this calculation. As the true weekday can either be equal to the mean weekday, or one greater or one less than it, all that now has to be done is for the general day result to be checked and a possible correction applied. The weekday value at the epoch was 6, and so 6 is added to 24,806, and then the result is divided by 7:

$$24806 + 6 = 24812 \div 7 = 3544 \text{ rem. } 4$$

This remainder now has to be compared with the true weekday that was determined earlier. This was 4;21,24,2,32—a Wednesday. The remainder was 4, also a Wednesday. This means that the value for the general day is correct. If the remainder had been different from the true weekday, and it should only differ by plus or minus 1, then it should be adjusted to bring it in line with the true weekday.

Now, the epoch was given earlier as Friday 1st April 1927. There is a slight difficulty here as the Tibetan calculations seem to use the day before the new Moon itself. In the calculation above, a 6 was added in order to correct the general day. This is the value for a Friday, and in fact the value for the mean weekday at the epoch is 6;57,53,2,20. However, the true weekday at the epoch is a Saturday: 0;8,58,4,40. So, it is clear that the calculations are actually using the mean value for the weekday, which is the value 6 that is added to perform the correction.

The best way of using this data to correlate with a western calendar is to use Julian day numbers. Although there are some (see for example Meeus, p. 59) who disapprove of this, I find it useful to follow the convention of the Explanatory Supplement to the Astronomical Almanac (ESAA, p. 600) in distinguishing between Julian day numbers (or simply Julian days) and Julian dates.

This system of counting starts with 1st January 4713 BCE. (This date is according to the Julian calendar applied retrospectively before the actual reform of the calendar by Julius Caesar in 45 BCE.) That day is Julian day number 0, and for each successive day the count increases by 1. The Julian date includes decimal fractions of a day and is therefore a uniform measure of time. This measure starts from noon Greenwich on 1st January 4713 BCE. This means, for example, that 6 PM on the next day, 2nd January, would have a Julian date of 1.25. The Julian day number of that day was 1.

Regarding the day of the current example, Wednesday 1st March 1995, at midnight at the beginning of that day the Julian date was 2,449,777.5, and at midnight at the end of that day it was 2,449,778.5. However, the Julian day number for that day was 2,449,778, and for most purposes in dealing with calendars it is easiest to deal with Julian day numbers. However, it is important to bear in mind these two different uses of Julian day counts.

To find the date of the epoch, all that is needed is to subtract the general day count from the Julian day:

2449778 - 24806 = 2424972

This is the Julian day number for Friday 1st April 1927, the day I gave originally as the epoch of the "Essence of the Kalkī."

Correction for intercalary months

Another point from early in the calculations that needs further clarification concerns the numbering of the months.

The calculation for the first month of the year starting in 1995 resulted in a month count of 839, but this was increased to 840. The reason for this lies in the intercalation of months—some months, as defined by their number, name, and so on, such as the third Tibetan month Caitra, are duplicated.

This correction depends on the solar longitude at successive new Moons, and the Tibetans do not use the true solar longitude, but the mean instead. The figures that are used here are different between the various calendrical traditions, and in keeping with the other calculations in this chapter the following description concerns the Phugpa tradition. Unfortunately, the Phugpa uses the most complex system of intercalation, although the principle underlying it is very simple.

The months are defined by the passage of the mean Sun past one of 12 definition points around the zodiac. These are called *sgang* in Tibetan, short for *dbugs sgang*. The word *sgang* is problematic. It may mean height or elevation in this context.

However, these terms are derived from Chinese astronomy, not Indian, and it could also be a Tibetan phonetic representation of the first syllable of the equivalent Chinese term, zhōng qì (中氣). This literally translates as something like "central-chi," where "chi" (sometimes "chhi") is the well-known Chinese term for wind, breath, etc. In the Chinese system these points in the zodiac are the beginnings of each of the tropical signs of the zodiac, and just as in the original Kālacakra system, the months are defined by the change of sign of the Sun, when it passes one of these points.

There are in addition twelve points in the middle of each of these signs, at the 15 degree points, called in Chinese jié qì (节氣), which Needham (Needham 3, p. 404) translates as "chhi-nodes." The equivalent Tibetan term for these points is *dbugs thob*, which literally translates as "obtaining-breath," indicating the beginning of some cycle or phase. Collectively these 24 points are called seasonal indicators or definitions (*dus gzer*).

The word zhōng (中), in zhōng qì (中氣), means centre or central, indicating that the cycle has reached its peak, height or centre. The Tibetan *dbugs sgang* would then translate as "central-breath" or "maximum-breath."

More modern translations from the Chinese often refer to these as solar terms, jié qì being the minor solar terms and zhōng qì the major solar terms, coinciding with the beginning of the tropical signs. See Appendix 1 for a list of these 24 solar terms.

I have decided to use the term 'definition point' because the actual positions of the points that are used in most Tibetan systems do not match those in use in Chinese astronomy or the original Kālacakra system. The reason for this is discussed in chapter six.

The Phugpa definition of the first month of a year is that between two new Moons, the mean Sun passes a definition point of longitude 23;6. This equates to 8° Aquarius. The second month is defined by the Sun passing 8° Pisces (25;21), the third by 8° Aries (0;36), etc. The difference between successive values here is the length of a zodiac sign in terms of mansions and nāḍī, 2;15.

The reason for this value of 8° in each zodiac sign is something that will also be described in chapter six when comparing the main Tibetan calendrical traditions. I should also point out that Chenrab Norbu, and other writers, states that the index values of 48 and 49 indicate an intercalary month, and that values of 50 and 51 indicate the absence of one of the definition points during a month, but this is not quite how the calendar actually works.

It is worth remembering that months can only be added—one is never omitted in a similar fashion to the lunar days. However, if the calendar had ever been evolved to use the true Sun to define the months, as happened in China, then occasionally a month could occur containing two of these defining points, suggesting that it should be omitted.

The intercalation of months and the decision regarding any adjustment to the calculated true month depends on the fractional part of the true month calculation. There is no specific name for this value in Tibetan texts, and so I have found it useful to call this the intercalation index.

It is stated in Phugpa calculations that when the value of the intercalation index is either 48 or 49, an intercalary month is needed. An adjustment is needed for the following months, up until the fractional part becomes equal to or larger than 65 and then carries over to the true month figure, when the index starts again at either 0 or 1.

In the example calculation for the first month of the year starting in 1995, just such an adjustment was needed as the intercalation index was greater than 49; it was 58. This meant that the month count had to be adjusted and was therefore increased from 839 to 840. As the fractional part was greater than 49, an intercalary month had been inserted, and so the months had 'moved along' by one.

There are two definitions here of the requirements for an intercalary month, one depending directly on mean solar longitude, and the other on the fractional part of the true month. The first of these certainly seems to be the main intention in the theory of the calendar, but it is the fractional part of the month that is normally used.

In the example calculation, if the adjustment had not been made, the main data that would have been derived if the extra month had not been added would have been:

True month: 839;58
True weekday: 2;48,0,5,34 (Monday 30th January 1995)
Mean solar longitude: 20;33,8,0,24

The fractional part of the true month is greater than 49, and the solar longitude is just less than the definition for the 12th month: 20;51. Clearly the mean Sun passes the point 20;51 during that month, and so it is not the first month, but the twelfth of the previous year. This is in line with the adjustment rule based on the intercalation index.

Looking at the next two successive new Moons, the main data is:

True month: 840;60
True weekday: 4;21,24,2,32 (Wednesday 1st March 1995)
Mean solar longitude: 22;44,6,1,41

True month: 841;62
True weekday: 5;58,22,0,10 (Thursday 30th March 1995)
Mean solar longitude: 24;55,4,2,58

Clearly the mean Sun passes the point 23;6 between these two new Moons, and so the first month of the new year is the one starting with the new Moon of 1st March, and the first day of the new year is 2nd March 1995.

This fits the theory fine, but the Tibetans actually use the indicator of 48 or 49 in the fractional part of the true month to determine the intercalary month, the following month having the same number.

The intercalary month relevant here actually occurs a few months earlier in 1994. The data for the start of the 8th, 9th, and 10th months in that year (as calculated according to the true month definition) is:

True month: 834;48
True weekday: 2;44,27,1,40 (5th September 1994)
Mean solar longitude: 9;38,17,0,6

True month: 835;50
True weekday: 4;7,15,5,39 (5th October 1994)
Mean solar longitude: 11;49,15,1,23

True month: 836;52
True weekday: 5;29,5,3,61 (3rd November 1994)
Mean solar longitude: 14;0,13,2,40

For the month starting the 5th September, the fractional part of the true month is 48, and this suggests an intercalary month. The solar longitude definitions for the 7th, 8th, and 9th months are: 9;36, 11;51, and 14;6, and the month between 5th September and 5th October contains none of these.

9;36 occurs just before the new Moon of 5th September, and 11;51 occurs just after the next new Moon, during the month between 5th October and 3rd November. 14;6 occurs during the following month.

As the mean Sun does not pass any of the points defining a month during the month starting 5th September, that month is called an intercalary, or extra, month (*zla ba bshol, zla ba lhag pa, adhikamāsa*), and takes the number of the month following it. It would usually be called the "earlier eighth."

The next month, between the new Moons on 5th October and 3rd November, is styled the "later eighth," and is numbered the 8th because during the period of time between its new Moons the mean Sun passes the point defining the 8th month, 11;51.

Whichever definition is used, the result is the same, as the two methods of defining the intercalary month are compatible. Given an intercalary month indicated by the fractional parts 48 or 49, the mean Sun never passes any defining point between the two relevant new Moons. The whole cycle of intercalary months repeats itself every 65 years, with exactly the same mean solar longitudes and the same values for the intercalation index.

The theory on which the timing of intercalary months rests is described by the mean Sun passing these points in the zodiac that define the months. However, as the fractional indicators of 48 and 49 correctly show when the Sun will not pass such a point, this is the easiest system to use when drawing up a calendar.

It should now be clear why a month was added in the original calculation for the first month of 1995. An intercalary month had been added a few months earlier, and so the calculation was out of step. The only other problem of this kind occurs when it gets back into step, when the fractional part of the true month passes 65. When this happens, the true month value increases by 2, and the fractional part results in either 0 or 1.

From this point there is no adjustment needed until the index again reaches a value of 48 or 49.

It is easiest to illustrate this with data from later in 1995. Calculating for the three months starting with the 4th month of the year yields:

Calculating for:	True month:	Adjusted month:
4th Month	842;64	3rd
5th Month	844;1	5th
6th Month	845;3	6th

The true month value of 843 has not occurred because of the fractional part carrying over to the true month value. That value of 843 is used however, and it is taken as the month count for the 4th month. From then on no further adjustments to the month count are needed.

This has now covered all the calculations relevant to the main structure of the lunar calendar according to the Siddhānta methods of the Phugpa tradition. In chapter four I shall describe the symbolic elements that are associated with this structure, and in chapter six describe the calculations of other calendrical traditions. The next two chapters continue with the Phugpa calculations, first for the five planets, and then for eclipses.

CHAPTER II

The Five Planets

So far I have described the main structure of the calendar: the cycles of the years, months, and days. It is this overall structure that is normally referred to by the use of the word "calendar," and in a society like Tibet or ancient India, it is this aspect of the calendar that was most useful for the general organization of society, individual lives, and for agriculture.

Components of the calendar, particularly details such as the lunar mansions, and so forth, are also used for astrology. But for that purpose other information is also needed, in particular the positions of the five planets. Calculations for these are included in the original calendar as described in the Kālacakra Tantra, and in most subsequent Tibetan books on the production of calendars.

Calculating the positions of the planets (*gza', graha*) is more complicated than dealing with the Sun and the Moon, simply because there are two cycles to be taken into consideration for each planet. Looked at from the point of view of the Earth, all the planets rotate around the Sun, which in turn appears to rotate around the Earth .

But, Mercury and Venus, often referred to in Tibetan texts as the two peaceful planets, are within the orbit of the Earth, and so they need to be treated differently from the others. When we calculate a mean rotation for Mercury and Venus around the Earth, this is the same as the mean rotation of the Sun, because they appear from the Earth only to swing either side of the Sun. The proper mean motion of these two planets around the Sun is a different quantity.

With the outer planets—Mars, Jupiter, and Saturn, also called the wrathful planets—the mean motion around the Sun is equal to the mean motion from the point of view of the Earth. This is because the outer planets rotate around the Sun with the Earth inside their orbits. However, the apparent motion from the point of view of the Earth is complicated by the Sun's apparent rotation around the Earth, which changes the relative position of these planets from the mean. Putting it very loosely, with the outer planets it is the Sun that swings either side of the Earth, changing the apparent position of the planets.

So, for each planet there are two cycles to be considered. One of these represents the mean motion of the planet from the point of view of the Earth, and this is adjusted for the eccentricity of the orbit, in just the same way as was done for the motion of the Sun in chapter one. Perhaps surprisingly, no such adjustment is normally made for the other cycle. (Some writers in the Tsurphu tradition advocate the use of the true Sun in planetary calculations, and this would in effect make just this adjustment.)

There are three different sets of calculations given in some Tibetan texts. These are for the three different days: solar days, lunar days, and zodiacal days. The first of these is by far the most important, and like some Tibetan texts I shall not cover the last two as the principles are very similar—the mean motion per day is the main difference. The results of calculating for solar days will yield the planetary positions at the very end of the solar day during which the mean lunar day ends that is taken as the base for calculation.

I shall first deal with the three outer planets, and take Mars as the example, calculating still for the new Moon of the new year in 1995 (1st March), and still following the method of Chenrab Norbu, as given in the "Essence of the Kalkī."

Heliocentric longitude of the outer planets

The calculation starts with the mean longitude of the outer planets, with a calculation that is effectively determining the longitude of a planet from the point of view of the Sun. It is not described that way in the Tibetan or Sanskrit texts, but the use of terms such as 'heliocentric' and 'geocentric' longitude is very useful here in order to help illustrate the meaning behind the calculation.

For the outer planets, and care is needed here as these terms are used somewhat differently for the inner planets, the actual term used in the Tibetan texts for the heliocentric longitude is 'slow (or steady) longitude' (*dal ba, manda*) and that used for geocentric longitude is 'fast (or complex) longitude' (*myur ba, śīghra*).

These terms are very similar to those used in early Indian astronomy to describe the two components of a planet's motion in epicyclic theory. The epicycles for each planet that moved in circles around the earth were called manda-vṛttas. These described, mathematically at least, the elliptical motion of the planet around the Sun. Then each planet moved in another epicycle which effectively described the addition of the motion of the earth around the Sun—translating from a heliocentric position to a geocentric one. These were called śīghra-vṛttas.

I have not come across any description in Tibetan texts that describe the mechanics of planetary motion in any way similar to epicycle theory, but it seems clear that the mathematics, and the terminology employed, relies on Indian epicyclic planetary (see Pañca, p. 206) theory, which itself, of course, was based on Ptolemaic theory.

When determining the western date for the main calendar a calculation was used that is now needed again. This determines the whole number of solar days that have elapsed since the epoch, and is called the general day. In chapter one the general day number for the example day of Wednesday 1st March 1995 was found to be 24,806.

It is now necessary to find the particular day (*sgos zhag*) for each planet. This is equivalent to the number of whole days the planet has been orbiting since it last crossed the first point of Aries (it might be more pertinent to use lunar mansions, and call this instead the first point of Aśvinī). For each planet a value is added to the general day, and then the remainder from dividing the total by another value is the particular day.

The values used are:

	Add:	Divide by:
Mars	157	687
Jupiter	3964	4332
Saturn	6286	10766

Clearly, the numbers used to divide are the periods of the planets in days, and the numbers added represent the mean position of the planet at the epoch in 1927.

For Mars, this gives:

$24806 + 157 = 24963 \div 687 = 36$ rem. 231

So, the particular day for Mars is 231.

The mean position is now easy to calculate. As the planet has moved for 231 days of a full orbit cycle of 687 days, its longitude is 231/687 of a full circle. Therefore take the full circle of 27 lunar mansions, multiply by the particular day, and then divide by the period (of 687).

The lowest fractional parts for the planets vary. They are: Mars, 229, Jupiter, 361, and Saturn, 5,383. (These numbers are the largest prime factors of each of the planetary periods, and will yield a remainder of zero in the final fractional part calculation.)

For Mars, the calculation is:

27 × 231 = 6237

As this is a division, the calculation proceeds downwards:

6237 ÷ 687 = 9 rem. 54
54 × 60 = 3240 ÷ 687 = 4 rem. 492
492 × 60 = 29520 ÷ 687 = 42 rem. 666
666 × 6 = 3996 ÷ 687 = 5 rem. 561
561 × 229 = 128469 ÷ 687 = 187 rem. 0

This calculation, which should always have a last remainder of zero, gives the mean longitude of Mars as 9;4,42,5,187 (229). This is usually called the mean slow longitude (*dal bar*, or, *dal ba bar pa*).

An adjustment now has to be applied to this to derive the true heliocentric longitude of the planet. This calculation is just the same as the one in chapter one for the true longitude of the Sun, and as with that calculation, the first step is to subtract a value for the position of each planet's birth-sign. This is equivalent to the longitude of the planet's aphelion—the point in its orbit where the planet is at its greatest distance from the Sun, and travelling at its slowest.

The values (in mansions and nāḍī) for the birth-signs for the outer planets are:

Mars:	9;30
Jupiter:	12;0
Saturn:	18;0

For Mars, the calculation is therefore:

9;4,42,5,187 - 9;30 = 26;34,42,5,187 (229)

Mars		
Index	Coefficient	Total
1	25	25
2	18	43
3	7	50
4	7	43
5	18	25
0	25	0
Jupiter		
Index	Coefficient	Total
1	11	11
2	9	20
3	3	23
4	3	20
5	9	11
0	11	0
Saturn		
Index	Coefficient	Total
1	22	22
2	15	37
3	6	43
4	6	37
5	15	22
0	22	0

Table 2-1

If this value is greater than half a full circle of 13;30, that much needs to be subtracted from it. As before, a note is made of whether this subtraction was done, and in this case the subtraction is needed:

26;34,42,5,187 - 13;30 = 13;4,42,5,187

Next, the mansion value of this result is multiplied by 60 and is added to the nāḍī value to give a total number of nāḍī. In this example the result is 784. This is then divided by 135, the number of nāḍī in a zodiacal sign. Just as with the calculation for the Sun, this coverts the value of 13;4,42,5,187 from a number of lunar mansions plus nāḍī, pala, etc., into an equivalent number of zodiacal signs, nāḍī, etc.

The division by 135 yields a quotient of 5 and remainder of 109. As with the similar calculation for the correction to solar longitude, the quotient is to be used as an index into a table, and the remainder will be used as a fractional part for interpolation. As there has just been a conversion into units of zodiacal signs, of which there are a total of 12, each half of the table has six places. The tables of figures for the three outer planets are given in Table 2-1.

There are two steps in the process of using these tables. As the example index into the table for Mars is 5, the total value is 25, and it is then necessary to interpolate between this total value and the next one of zero, using the coefficient in the next row.

The last three units of the earlier subtraction are added to the remainder (109) from the division by 135, taken as a number of nāḍī. This gives 109,42,5,187. This is then multiplied by the coefficient from the table. The index is 5, and so the coefficient, taken from the next row, is 25. The multiplication yields:

$$25 \times 0;109,42,5,187 = 0;2742,54,1,95$$

As the next step is going to divide this quantity, there is no need to round up to the mansion position, and the number of nāḍī can just be left as it is.

The division is by 135 to determine the intermediate correction:

$$0;2742,54,1,95 \div 135 = 0;20,19,0,94$$

This then needs to be added to or subtracted from the total figure, taken as a number of nāḍī.

Just the same as with the solar longitude correction, if the index values are 3, 4 or 5, as the total value is decreasing, the intermediate correction needs to be subtracted, otherwise it is added. In this example, it is subtracted:

$$0;25,0,0,0 - 0;20,19,0,94 = 0;4,40,5,137$$

This correction then has to be added to, or subtracted from the mean heliocentric longitude for the planet, depending on whether the earlier subtraction of half a circle was needed. If the half-circle was subtracted, the correction is added, otherwise it is subtracted. For this example of Mars, the half-circle was subtracted, and so the correction is added:

$$9;4,42,5,187 + 0;4,40,5,137 = 9;9,23,5,93$$

This last result is the true heliocentric longitude of the planet.

For completeness, brief calculations for the same data for the other two outer planets, Jupiter and Saturn, are as follows.

Jupiter

To find the particular day for Jupiter:

24806 + 3964 = 28770 ÷ 4332 = 6 rem. 2778

The mean slow longitude of Jupiter:

27 × 2778 = 75006
Dividing this result to obtain the mean longitude:

75006;0,0,0,0 ÷ 4332 = 17;18,51,5,49 (361)

Subtracting the birth-sign for Jupiter:

17;18,51,5,49 - 12;0 = 5;18,51,5,49

No subtraction of half a circle is necessary, and so now convert from lunar mansions to zodiacal signs:

5 × 60 + 18 = 318
318 ÷ 135 = 2 rem. 48

The index of 2 indicates in the table a total value of 20 nāḍī and a coefficient from the next row of 3. So, for the interpolation:

3 × 0;48,51,5,49 = 0;146,35,3,147
0;146,35,3,147 ÷ 135 = 0;1,5,6,330
0;20 + 0;1,5,0,330 = 0;21,5,0,330

As no half-circle was subtracted, the correction is subtracted from the mean slow longitude of Jupiter, to derive the true slow longitude:

17;18,51,5,49 - 0;21,5,0,330 = 16;57,46,4,80

Saturn

To find the particular day for Saturn:

24806 + 6286 = 31092 ÷ 10766 = 2 rem. 9560

The mean slow longitude of Saturn:

27 × 9560 = 258120

Dividing this result to obtain the mean longitude:

258120;0,0,0,0 ÷ 10766 = 23;58,31,4,1790 (5383)

Subtracting the birth-sign for Saturn:

23;58,31,4,1790 - 18;0 = 5;58,31,4,1790

No subtraction of half a circle is necessary, so now convert from lunar mansions to zodiacal signs:

5 × 60 + 58 = 358
358 ÷ 135 = 2 rem. 88

The index of 2 gives from the table a total value of 37 nāḍī and a coefficient from the next row of 6. So, for the interpolation:

6 × 0;88,31,4,1790 = 0;531,10,1,5357
0;531,10,1,5357 ÷ 135 = 0;3,56,0,2472
0;37 + 0;3,56,0,2472 = 0;40,56,0,2472
As no half-circle was subtracted, the correction is now subtracted from the mean slow longitude of Saturn, to derive the true slow longitude:

23;58,31,4,1790 - 0;40,56,0,2472 = 23;17,35,3,4701 (5383)

Geocentric longitude of the outer planets

The next step in the calculation effectively takes into consideration the motion of the Earth around the Sun. This involves finding a correction that will be applied to the slow (heliocentric) longitude of the planets in order to yield the fast (geocentric) longitude.

First, a calculation is needed for the mean longitude of the Sun at the end of the solar day under consideration. (The figure derived in chapter one is at the end of a lunar day and so a new calculation is needed.) The figure that is derived here is actually given two different names depending on its use.

For the current purposes, calculating for the outer planets, it is called the step index for the three wrathful planets (*drag gsum rkang 'dzin*), and is the basis for the correction that is going to be applied to the heliocentric position of the outer planets, due to the motion of the Earth. Their heliocentric position is also the same as their mean position from the point of view of the Earth, as the Earth is within their orbits.

For the two inner planets the same quantity will be used in a different way, as it represents the mean position of the planet from the point of view of the Earth, which is the same as that of the Sun. Their orbits are within the orbit of the Earth. For these two planets their heliocentric position is taken as the step index.

This terminology is clearly equivalent to the use of the two terms 'deferent' and 'epicycle' in Ptolemaic theory. The mean motion of the planet from the point of view of the Earth is equivalent to the deferent, the longer of the two cycles, and the step index is equivalent to the epicycle.

The calculation is simple, and is given by Chenrab Norbu in two ways. In the first, take the general day (in our example, 24,806) and multiply this by 18,382. This gives a result of 455,983,892. This then has an epoch value of 458,672 subtracted from it to yield a result of 455,525,220. This number is then divided by 6,714,405, and the remainder from this calculation is used in the next step. This calculation can be represented as:

$$(24806 \times 18382 - 458672) \div 6714405 = 67 \text{ rem. } 5660085$$

This remainder of 5,660,085 represents that part of the full circle the Sun has travelled since last passing the first point of Aries, with the full circle measured in 6,714,405 fractional units. This is very similar to the first part of our calculation for the planets' longitudes.

The calculation continues by multiplying this number by 27 and placing the result (this yields 152,822,295) in the mansion position of a longitude value. This is then divided all the way through by 6,714,405, multiplying the next step by 60, and so on. The least significant fractional unit used is 149,209. Writing this out in full, the calculation proceeds downwards:

152822295 ÷ 6714405 = 22 rem. 5105385
5105385 × 60 = 306323100 ÷ 6714405 = 45 rem. 4174875
417485 × 60 = 250492500 ÷ 6714405 = 37 rem. 2059515
2059515 × 6 = 12357090 ÷ 6714405 = 1 rem. 5642685
5642685 × 149209 = 841939386165 ÷ 6714405 = 125393 rem. 0

Or in brief:

152822295;0,0,0,0 ÷ 6714405 = 22;45,37,1,125393 (149209)

This result then, is the step index for the outer planets, which is the mean solar longitude at the end of the solar day.

The second method given is easier to represent. Here, using the same least significant fractional units, multiply the general day by the longitude value 0;4,26,0,93156, and then add the result to the value of 25;9,20,0,97440:

24806 × 0;4,26,0,93156 + 25;9,20,0,97440 = 22;45,37,1,125393 (149209)

The first of these longitude values represents the mean (solar) daily motion of the Sun, and the second the mean longitude of the Sun at the epoch.

This result can now be used to determine the true longitude of the outer planets from the point of view of the Earth. It is going to be necessary to use both the longitude of the planets and the mean solar position. As the units of the least significant fractional parts of these are different, it is first necessary to adjust one of them to make them compatible.

The one that is adjusted is the mean solar longitude, which has a lowest fractional part of 149,209. That for Mars is 229. The fraction from the solar longitude is first multiplied by 229, and then divided by 149,209. The quotient becomes the new fifth fractional place—with the same units of that of Mars, and the remainder becomes a new sixth place, with units of 149,209. The mean solar longitude is 22;45,37,1,125393 and so the conversion is:

125393 × 229 = 28714997
28714997 ÷ 149209 = 192 rem. 66869

This gives the new value of the mean solar longitude as:

22;45,37,1,125393 —> 22;45,37,1,192,66869 (229,149209)

The next step is an operation that should by now be familiar. After a first calculation, an index and a fractional part are used to calculate a correction, and this will then be applied to the heliocentric longitude of the planet to give the true longitude from the Earth.

The first step is to subtract the longitude of the planet from that of the Sun:

22;45,37,1,192,66869 - 9;9,23,5,93,0 = 13;36,13,2,99,66869

Mars				
Index	Total	Coefficient	Total	Index
1	24	24	0	0
2	47	23	24	13
3	70	23	47	12
4	93	23	70	11
5	114	21	93	10
6	135	21	114	9
7	153	18	135	8
8	168	15	153	7
9	179	11	168	6
10	182	3	179	5
11	171	11	182	4
12	133	38	171	3
13	53	80	133	2
0	0	53	53	1

Table 2-2

As in similar calculations, if this result is greater than a half-circle (13;30) then a half-circle is subtracted from it, making a note of whether this was done. In this example it is necessary, and gives a result of:

13;36,13,2,99,66869 - 13;30 = 0;6,13,2,99,66869

In this case the mansion and nāḍī figures are not converted into zodiacal signs and nāḍīs. Instead, the mansion figure itself is used as an index into a table and the rest of the value is used as the interpolation variable. The units given in the table are nāḍī. For example, on the left side of the table for Mars, an index of 6 mansions would indicate a correction to be applied to the heliocentric longitude of Mars of 135 nāḍī, or, 2;15.

Jupiter				
Index	Total	Coefficient	Total	Index
1	10	10	0	0
2	20	10	10	13
3	29	9	20	12
4	37	8	29	11
5	43	6	37	10
6	49	6	43	9
7	51	2	49	8
8	52	1	51	7
9	49	3	52	6
10	43	6	49	5
11	34	9	43	4
12	23	11	34	3
13	7	16	23	2
0	0	7	7	1

Table 2-3

The next index value of 7 mansions would indicate a correction of 153 nāḍī. The difference between these two is 18, and is found in the coefficient column, in the same row as the index value 7. This value of 18 is a number of nāḍī, and is multiplied by the remaining parts of the index—the number of nāḍī of the index, and optionally also the pala and breaths. These are fractions of a mansion, and so a division by 60 must be made. This is most easily done after the remaining part of the index has been multiplied by the coefficient from the table.

Saturn				
Index	Total	Coefficient	Total	Index
1	6	6	0	0
2	11	5	6	13
3	16	5	11	12
4	20	4	16	11
5	24	4	20	10
6	26	2	24	9
7	28	2	26	8
8	28	0	28	7
9	26	2	28	6
10	22	4	26	5
11	17	5	22	4
12	11	6	17	3
13	3	8	11	2
0	0	3	3	1

Table 2-4

The tables (Tables 2-2 to 2-4) used for the three outer planets are more complicated than the tables used in previous calculations and need some explanation. The tables are considered to have four quadrants—two on either side. In the upper left quadrant the total value is increasing from zero as the index increases, and then in the lower left quadrant the total decreases back to zero. In a similar way on the right-hand side, in the lower right quadrant the total increases as the index increases, and then decreases to zero in the upper right quadrant.

Continuing with the example of Mars, the index into the table is the result of subtracting the heliocentric longitude of Mars from the mean longitude of the Sun. As the longitude of the Sun increases faster than that of Mars, the index that results from subtracting Mars from the Sun increases through time.

So, a few days after the time when the Sun and Mars are in conjunction, when their longitudes are the same, the difference between their

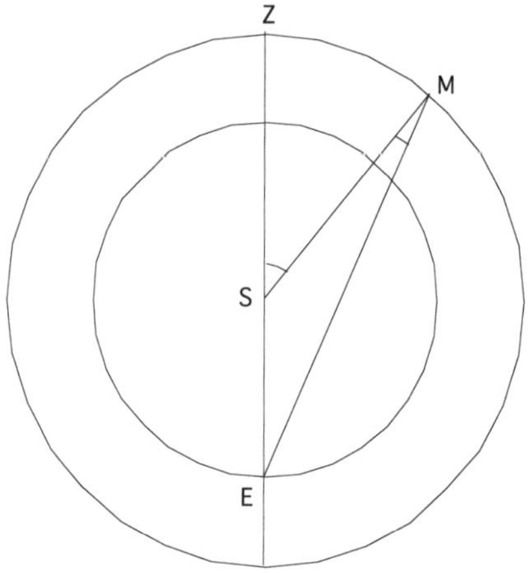

Figure 2a

longitudes yields a result of zero mansions and some number of nāḍī. This does not require the subtraction of half a circle, and so this result remains unchanged. We therefore enter the left-hand side of the table, at the top. Having not been visible around the time of conjunction with the Sun, Mars is now seen again briefly, rising just before the Sun. As the weeks pass, Mars rises increasingly early.

Some weeks later, as the index increases, Mars reaches a position similar to that shown in the diagram in Figure 2a.

In this diagram, the Sun (S) is in the centre, and the orbits of the Earth (E) and Mars (M) are shown approximately as circles, seen from the north. Longitude increases anti-clockwise around the diagram. For the sake of clarity, in this and diagrams illustrating the other quadrants of the table, I shall keep the Earth at the bottom of the diagram. What matters here for describing the calculations are the relative positions of the Sun, the Earth, and Mars.

In reality, of course, the Earth is rotating in its orbit around the Sun in an anticlockwise direction, but travelling faster in terms of angular speed than Mars. The point Z is marked for ease of describing the angles, and is the position Mars would occupy when in conjunction with the Sun, on the far side of the Sun from the Earth.

In Figure 2a, the longitude of the Sun is indicated by the direction ES, the heliocentric longitude of Mars by the direction SM, and the geocentric longitude of Mars by the direction EM. It can be seen that in this quadrant, and also the next, the longitude of geocentric Mars is moving ahead of (i.e., is greater than that of) the heliocentric Mars. For this reason the motion of Mars in this half of the table is called progressive.

The difference between the longitude of the Sun and Mars is shown by the acute angle ZSM, with a value here of something like 3 or 4 mansions.

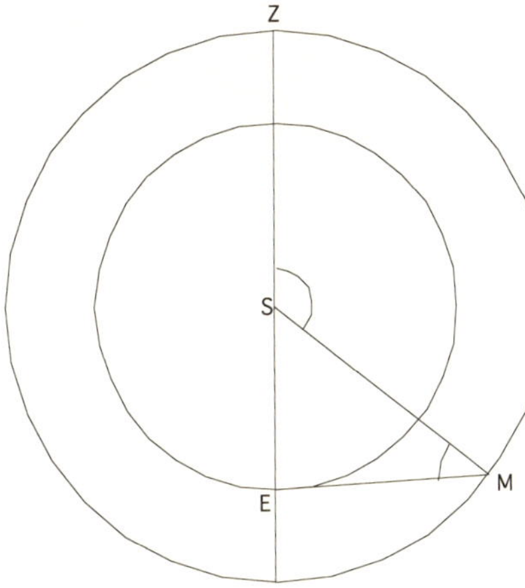

Figure 2b

In the table, an index of 3 mansions would give a total correction of 70 nāḍī, or 1;10 lunar mansions, as the amount that needs to be added to the heliocentric longitude of Mars to yield the geocentric longitude. This difference is indicated by the acute angle SME.

The four quadrants are said to entail the planets exhibiting different kinds of motions. In this upper left quadrant the motion is called fast (*myur ba, śīghra*).

Around conjunction with the Sun, Mars is invisible, and has been travelling (from the point of view of its geocentric longitude) at its fastest speed. In this first quadrant after conjunction Mars becomes visible again, rising in the east shortly before the Sun. At first it moves quickly relative to the Sun, but its speed gradually slows down during this quadrant.

Approximately five months later, Mars arrives in a position such as that illustrated in Figure 2b. Again, the longitude of the Sun is the direction ES, the (heliocentric) longitude of Mars is direction SM, and the geocentric longitude of Mars the direction EM. The difference between the longitudes of the Sun and Mars, the angle ZSM, now has a value of something like 10 mansions.

In the table, this is now in the lower left quadrant, and an index of 10 mansions would give a total of 183 nāḍī, or 3;3 mansions, as the amount that needs to be added to the heliocentric longitude of Mars for the geocentric longitude. Again, this difference is indicated by the angle SME.

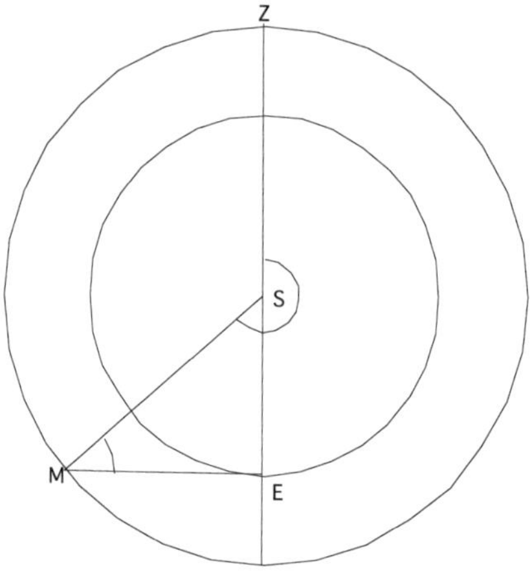

Figure 2c

The motion in this lower left quadrant is called slow (*dal ba, manda*). During this quadrant, Mars continues to slow down, and in fact, later on in this quadrant (when the index figure reaches a value of about 12 mansions), it appears to turn back on itself and to start to travel backwards in the Zodiac when viewed from the Earth. In the west, this apparent backwards travel is usually called retrograde motion, although there seems to be no specific Tibetan term for this kind of motion. (I'll come back to this point.)

Moving forward another few months, Mars arrives at a position similar to that in Figure 2c. Here, the difference between the longitude of Mars and the Sun is now the reflex angle ZSM, with a value of something like 17 mansions. For such a value a subtraction of half a circle is required, and the index would therefore become 3;30. This is now in the lower right quadrant of the table, and this index would indicate a total of around 180 nāḍī, or 3;0 mansions, as the value which needs now to be subtracted (as indicated by the subtraction of a half-circle) from the heliocentric longitude of Mars.

This difference is again the angle SME, but as now the geocentric Mars is moving behind the heliocentric Mars, for this reason the motion of Mars represented in this quadrant of the table, and also the next, is called regressive.

Of the four motions, the motion in this particular quadrant is called reversing (*'khyogs po, vakra*). When Mars enters this quadrant it is still travelling backwards, and retrograde motion ceases—the planet appears to stop before starting to travel forwards once more—when the index has a value of about 1;30. So, from the point of view of the Earth, Mars starts the quadrant travelling backwards, stops, turns direct, at first moving forwards very slowly, and then gradually picks up speed.

Finally, after another few months, Mars is in a position similar to that in Figure 2d. Here, the difference between the longitude of Mars and

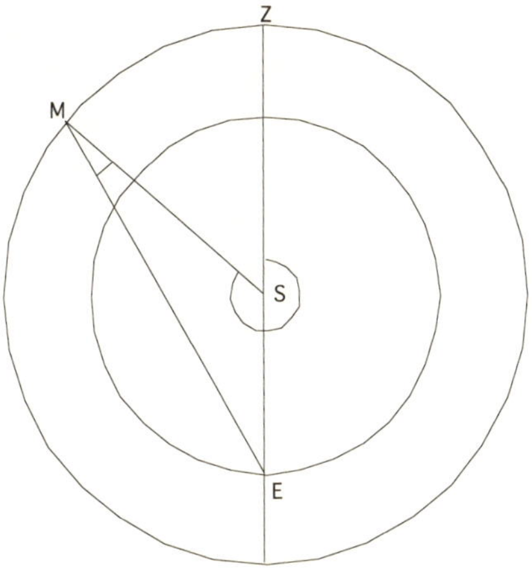

Figure 2d

the Sun is again the angle ZSM, with a value of something like 23 or 24 mansions. Again, a subtraction of half a circle is required, and this yields a value of 10 or 11 for the index. This is now in the upper right quadrant of the table, and the index gives a total of around 80 nāḍī, or 1;20 mansions, as the value which needs to be subtracted (the angle SME) from the heliocentric longitude of Mars.

In this quadrant, the geocentric Mars is still behind the heliocentric Mars, but is rapidly gathering speed and, after it is last seen, setting in the West just after the Sun, it will catch up with the heliocentric Mars, overtaking it at conjunction between the Sun and Mars, when Mars leaves this quadrant and enters again the upper left quadrant. In this upper right quadrant the motion is called advancing (*'byung ba, nirgama*).

If we now look back at the terminology for these four quadrants, it can be seen that their names are probably historical, and originally applied to the motion of the planet at the point of entering the quadrant.

When the Sun and Mars are in conjunction, at the crossover point between the two upper quadrants, Mars is travelling at its fastest, and it is clear how the motion here could be called fast. Later, at the point between the two left-hand quadrants, Mars is slowing down rapidly, and will soon turn retrograde. The motion at this point is therefore called slow.

At the point where the planet moves between the two lower quadrants, when Mars is in opposition to the Sun, it is in retrograde motion, and travelling backwards at its fastest. The term 'reversing' would well apply here, and in fact 'retrograde' is probably the best translation for the original use of the term vakra here, but in the Kālacakra and other later Tibetan literature, this term is applied to the whole of the lower right quadrant, through which the motion of Mars is retrograde only part of the time. The use of this and the other three terms here seems to have changed from the original intention.

Finally, at the junction between the two right-hand quadrants, Mars is accelerating rapidly, and the motion here is therefore called advancing.

Getting back to the calculation, if the subtraction of a half-circle has not been necessary, this is when the planet is moving ahead of its heliocentric position, and it is necessary to use the index on the left of the table, and also the left-hand total column. If the subtraction had been necessary, this would indicate that the planet is moving behind its mean heliocentric position, and it is necessary to use the right-hand two columns.

Also, in the case where the planet is moving behind its heliocentric position (if a half-circle had been subtracted) it is necessary to make an adjustment to the mansion and nāḍī values. 30 is added to the nāḍī figure, carrying up to the lunar mansion figure if necessary. For example, if the lunar mansion is 7 and the nāḍī 40, this addition results in new figures of 8 and 10. This addition is done in all cases, except when the mansion figure is zero and the nāḍī figure is less than 30.

The purpose of this adjustment is effectively to invert the index values. For motion ahead, the first half of the table, the index counts in whole lunar mansions, and ends with a half. For motion behind, the index count starts with the half a mansion incomplete, and so the count slides along by half a mansion. There is a further calculation later for the two half periods, where the value derived is doubled, effectively making the two half periods each count as a whole. These two half periods both refer to the coefficient in the bottom row of the table—53 in the case of Mars. These adjustments make the table—at least the indexing into the table—symmetrical.

In the example, the index, after subtraction of a half-circle, had become 0;6,13,2,99,66869. The mansion figure is zero, and the number of nāḍī 6. This latter is used as the interpolation variable. The subtraction of a half-circle was needed, and so reference needs to be made to the right side of the table.

The total figure for an index value of 0 is given next to it, and here equals zero. This is because Mars has just passed the point of opposition to the Sun. It may seem odd that the index value of zero is at the top of the table. The point is that this is in the first step which concludes with a total of 53—this is at the bottom of the table, where one might expect. The table could easily be rewritten with the zero at the bottom, and would perhaps make more sense that way. I have reproduced it here in the same way that it is drawn in the "Essence of the Kalkī" and other texts.

The necessary coefficient (which is a number of nāḍī) is given in the row next to that including the index figure. In this example, this refers to the bottom row of the table, and so the coefficient needed is 53.

The previous adjustment of sliding along the index figures was not done with the current example because it is in the half period at the beginning of this side of the table—the index figure is zero and the number of nāḍī (6) is less than 30. It is therefore necessary also to multiply by a factor of 2 to determine the correction. This yields:

$$53 \times 6 \times 2 = 636$$

This is a number of nāḍī, and now has to be divided by 60. This yields: 0;10,36. The mansion figure after the earlier subtraction of a half-circle gives the steps and total values of the correction to be applied, and the number of nāḍī has just been used as a variable to interpolate between two steps.

To be more accurate, other fractional parts, pala, breaths, etc., would be used as well. In fact, Chenrab Norbu describes using the whole of the index after the mansion figure. Both simple and complex methods seem to be in use by Tibetan practitioners, and following Chenrab Norbu, the calculation becomes:

$$53 \times 2 \times 0;6,13,2,99,66869 = 0;659,41,0,7,75291$$

There is no need to round up to the mansion value, as the next step is to divide through by 60:

$$0;659,41,0,7,75291 \div 60 = 0;10,59,4,23,3742$$

This is the intermediate correction, and this now has to be added to, or subtracted from, the total figure. If the current index refers to the part of the table where the total values are increasing, this intermediate correction is added, and if the totals are decreasing (on the right-hand side, index values of 7, 8, 9, 10, 11, 12 and 13) then it is subtracted.

As the current example is in the first part of the right-hand side of the table, where the total figure is increasing as the index increases, the intermediate correction is added. In this example this is trivial, as the total is zero, giving a correction of:

0;10,59,4,23

In that calculation, the lowest fractional part was dropped as it is no longer needed. If the value had been greater than half of 149,209, the next place would have been rounded up to 24.

This final correction is now applied to the heliocentric position of Mars, and reference has to be made back to the original creation of the index, and whether or not a half-circle was subtracted. In this case it was, and the geocentric Mars is moving behind the heliocentric Mars, and so it is necessary to subtract. The final figure for the geocentric longitude of Mars becomes:

9;9,23,5,93 - 0;10,59,4,23 = 8;58,24,1,70

I shall now briefly describe the equivalent calculations for the geocentric longitudes of Jupiter and Saturn.

Jupiter

The first step is to adjust the lower unit of the step index for the wrathful planets:

22;45,37,1,125393 (149209)

125393 × 361 = 45266873
45266873 ÷ 149209 = 303 rem. 56546

This gives the conversion as:

22;45,37,1,125393 = 22;45,37,1,303,56546 (361,149209)

Subtracting the slow (heliocentric) longitude:

22;45,37,1,303,56546 - 16;57,46,4,80 = 5;47,50,3,343,56546

No subtraction of a half-circle is needed, and in the left-hand side of the table an index of 5 refers to a total value of 43 and a coefficient of 6:

6 × 0;47,50,3,223,56546 = 0;287,3,3,257,40858

0;287,3,3,257,40858 ÷ 60 = 0;4,47,0,130,95180

0;43,0,0,0,0 + 0;4,47,0,130,95180 = 0;47,47,0,130,95180

As there was no subtraction of a half-circle, this correction is now added to the heliocentric longitude, to derive the geocentric longitude:

16;57,46,4,80 + 0;47,47,0,130 = 17;45,33,4,210

Saturn

To adjust the lower unit of the step index:

125393 × 5383 = 674990519
674990519 ÷ 149209 = 4523 rem. 118212

This gives the conversion as:

22;45,37,1,125393 = 22;45,37,1,4523,118212 (5383,149209)

Subtracting the heliocentric longitude:

22;45,37,1,4523,118212 - 23;17,35,3,4701 = 26;28,1,3,5205,118212

Subtraction of a half-circle is required:

26;28,1,3,5205,118212 - 13;30 = 12;58,1,3,5205,118212

As this refers to the right-hand side of the table, the index values have to slide along half a step:

12;58,1,3,5205,118212 = 13;28,1,3,5205,118212

In the right-hand side of the table an index value of 13 refers to a total value of 6 and a (decreasing) coefficient of 6:

6 × 0;28,1,3,5205,118212 = 0;168,9,5,4319,112436

0;168,9,5,4319,112436 ÷ 60 = 0;2,48,0,5365,41663

0;6,0,0,0,0 - 2,48,0,5365,41663 = 3,11,5,17,107546

As the subtraction of a half-circle was required, this correction finally has to be subtracted from the heliocentric longitude, to derive the geocentric longitude:

23;17,35,3,4701 - 0;3,11,5,17,107546 = 23;14,23,4,4684

Heliocentric longitude of the inner planets

In finding the positions of the inner planets, I shall take Venus as the main example in calculations, and then give a brief description of the calculation for Mercury.

The calculation for Mercury and Venus starts by determining the mean longitude from the point of view of the Sun, and again it is first necessary to find the particular day for each planet. The method is essentially the same as with the outer planets, and a value for each planet is added to the general day, and then the total is divided by another value to leave a remainder. The only difference is that with Mercury the general day is first multiplied by 100, and for Venus it is multiplied by 10. This is needed to give greater accuracy, as the orbital periods of Mercury and Venus are so short compared to those of the outer planets.

The values used are:

		Add:	Divide by:
Mercury	×100	4639	8797
Venus	×10	301	2247

For Venus, this gives a result of:

24806 × 10 + 301 = 248361 ÷ 2247 = 110 rem. 1191

The calculation then continues as with the outer planets, and a full circle of 27 lunar mansions is multiplied by the particular day, and then divided by the period (of 2,247). The lowest fractional part for Mercury is also 8,797, and for Venus 749 (a factor of 2,247). For Venus this gives:

27 × 1191 = 32157

32157;0,0,0,0 ÷ 2247 = 14;18,39,5,269 (749)

This result of 14;18,39,5,269 is here called the step index for the two peaceful (inner) planets (*zhi gnyis rkang 'dzin*), and this is where this part of the calculation stops. Unlike the calculation for the heliocentric longitude of the outer planets it is not necessary here to make an adjustment for the ellipticity of the planet's orbit. Instead, an equivalent adjustment will be made using the earlier result for the mean position of the Sun, which is equal to the mean geocentric position of the inner planets.

Geocentric longitude of the inner planets

The value derived earlier for the mean longitude of the Sun was 22;45,37,1,125393, and in this calculation it is referred to as the mean value for the slow longitude of the two inner planets. This is because the planets appear from the Earth to swing either side of the Sun, and so their mean longitude, from the point of view of the Earth, is the same as that of the Sun. Interestingly, when describing the motion of the inner planets, Pawo Tsuklag makes the comment in his "Treasury of Jewels," (Tlkuntu, p. 149) that it is "as though they circle around the Sun."

This mean longitude now needs to be corrected for the ellipticity of the orbit, and this correction is exactly the same in type as the one used for the heliocentric, or slow longitude of the outer planets.

First, it is necessary to subtract from the mean slow longitude the value for the longitude of the planet's birth-sign.

The values used (in mansions and nāḍī) for the inner planets are:

Mercury: 16;30
Venus: 6;0

Subtracting for Venus, this yields:

22;45,37,1,125393 - 6;0 = 16;45,37,1,125393 (149209)

A half-circle is subtracted if necessary, and this is needed with the present example of Venus:

16;45,37,1,125393 - 13;30 = 3;15,37,1,125393

As with the outer planets, it is necessary to convert from lunar mansions to zodiacal signs, and so the mansion value is now multiplied by 60 and the result added to the nāḍī. The result of 195 is divided by 135 (the number of nāḍī in a zodiacal sign), yielding a quotient of 1 and a remainder of 60:

$3 \times 60 + 15 = 195$
$195 \div 135 = 1$ rem. 60

The value of 1 is the index into the table given below for Venus, and the remainder is the figure to use for the interpolation variable.

The tables of values for Mercury and Venus are given in Tables 2-5 and 2-6.

Mercury		
Index	Coefficient	Total
1	10	10
2	7	17
3	3	20
4	3	17
5	7	10
0	10	0

Table 2-5

Venus		
Index	Coefficient	Total
1	5	5
2	4	9
3	1	10
4	1	9
5	4	5
0	5	0

Table 2-6

The last three units of the earlier subtraction are now added to the remainder from the division by 135. This gives the full interpolation variable as 60,37,1,125393, and this is now multiplied by the coefficient from the table. The index is 1, and so the coefficient, taken from the next row, is 4. This gives:

$$4 \times 0;60,37,1,125393 = 0;242,29,1,53945$$

This now has to be divided by 135 to derive the intermediate correction, as a number of nāḍī, etc.:

$$0;242,29,1,53945 \div 135 = 0;1,47,4,94346$$

The index of 1 indicates a total value of 5, and as this is in the first part of the table where the total value is still increasing, the intermediate correction needs to be added to the total:

$$0;5,0,0,0,0 + 0;1,47,4,94346 = 0;6,47,4,94346$$

Finally, as the original subtraction of half a circle was needed, this correction is added to the mean slow longitude:

$$22;45,37,1,125393 + 0;6,47,4,94346 = 22;52,25,0,70530$$

This figure, which is based on the mean longitude of the Sun, is called the true slow longitude for Venus.

The method that is used here is essentially the same as with the outer planets, but there is a difference in the way the basic quantities involved—the longitude of the Sun, and the heliocentric longitude of the planet concerned—are used.

The algorithm for the true geocentric longitude of the planet starts at the point when the planet, on the far side of the Sun from the Earth, is in conjunction with the Sun. Mercury and Venus can also be in conjunction when they are between the Sun and the Earth, but they are retrograde at this time. Conjunction when on the far side of the Sun is called superior conjunction and when between the Sun and the Earth, inferior conjunction. At the point of superior conjunction, the planets are moving at their fastest speed from the point of view of the Earth.

From that point, the planet then moves through the four quadrants, first exhibiting fast motion, then slow, etc. The variable that determines which quadrant the planet is in is the difference in longitude between the Sun and the planet.

It is easier for the mathematics if this quantity starts as a small positive value and increases through the quadrants to a full circle.

With the outer planets, as the Sun is moving faster than the mean heliocentric planet, a small positive value results immediately after conjunction if the longitude of the planet is subtracted from that of the Sun. This value then increases to a full circle as the planet moves through the four quadrants.

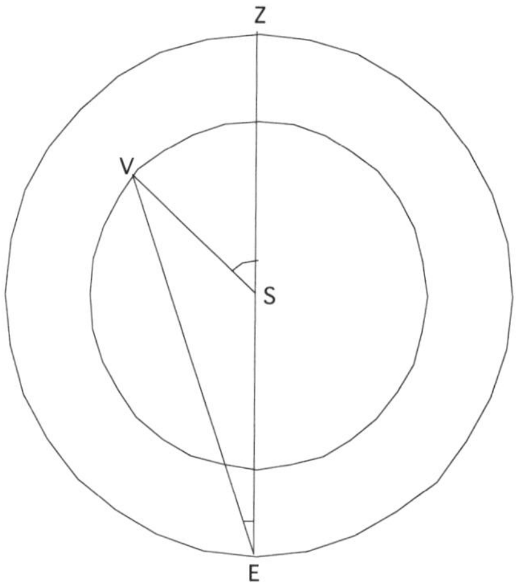

Figure 2e

With the inner planets the reverse is the case, and the heliocentric planet is moving faster than the Sun. So the same mathematical behaviour results if instead the Sun is subtracted from the heliocentric longitude of the planet, remembering, of course, that in this instance the longitude of the Sun is adjusted as it is taken here as the slow longitude of the planet.

The use of the term 'step index' is understandable from this point of view. With both outer and inner planets the quantity that determines the position—the relevant step—within the quadrants is the step index minus the slow longitude—how far the step index has advanced beyond the slow motion, since conjunction.

These differences with the inner planets are best understood by means of the Figures 2e to 2h.

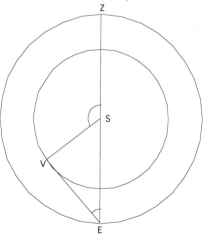

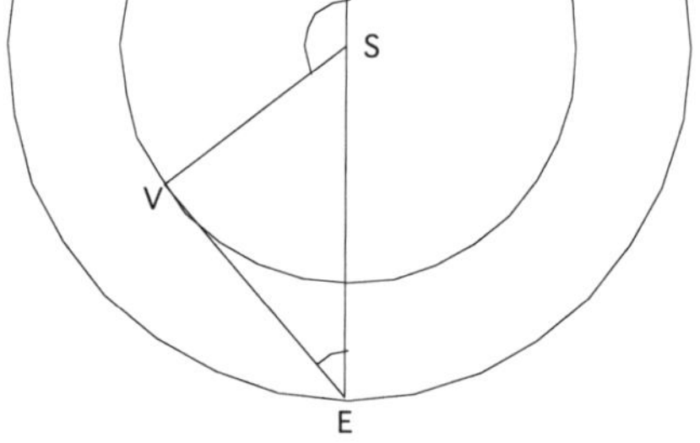

Figure 2f

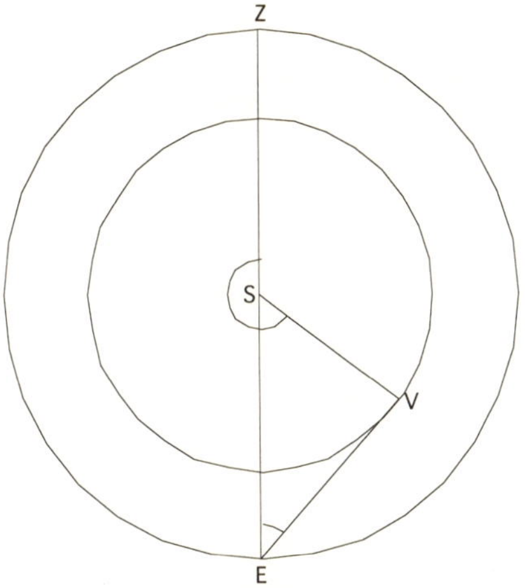

Figure 2g

In Figure 2e Venus is shown in a position relative to the Earth and the Sun as it would be a short while after its superior conjunction with the Sun. After that conjunction, up until shortly before its inferior conjunction, Venus will be seen from the Earth as an evening star in the west, just after the Sun has set. This is the other way around from the outer planets which are seen soon after conjunction rising in the east shortly before the Sun. The longitude of the Sun is indicated in the diagram by the direction ES, the heliocentric longitude of Venus by the direction SV and the geocentric longitude of Venus is given by the direction EV.

In this quadrant and the next, the longitude of geocentric Venus is moving ahead of the mean Venus, which coincides with the Sun.

The difference between the heliocentric longitude of Venus and that of the Sun (equal to the mean geocentric longitude of Venus) is shown by the acute angle ZSV, with a value here of something like 3 or 4 mansions.

In the table, an index of 3 mansions would give a total of 75 nāḍī, or 1;15 lunar mansions, as the amount that needs to be added to the mean longitude of Venus to yield the true geocentric longitude. This difference is indicated by the acute angle SEV. Just as with the outer planets, this first upper left quadrant represents from among the four motions the planet's fast motion.

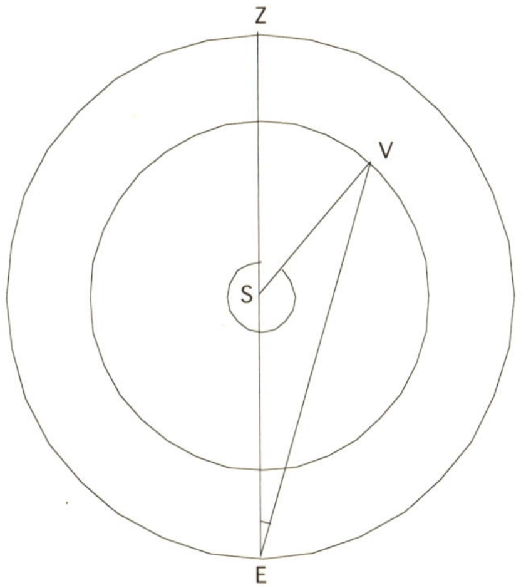

Figure 2h

The next three quadrants follow a similar pattern to those of the outer planets. Figure 2f represents the planet's slow motion in the lower left quadrant, shortly before it goes retrograde a little while before its inferior conjunction with the Sun and is no longer visible.

After that conjunction the planet enters the lower right quadrant, Figure 2g, with the planet exhibiting reversing motion. A little way into this quadrant retrograde motion ceases, and the planet goes direct again. It is now moving behind the mean geocentric position, and the amount that needs to be subtracted from the mean position, to give the true geocentric position is indicated by the angle SEV.

Finally, the planet exhibits the advancing motion of the upper right quadrant, represented by Figure 2h. In this and the previous quadrant the planet is seen as a morning star in the east, shortly before the Sun rises.

Continuing with the calculation, we can now determine the final correction that is required to find the true geocentric longitude of the inner planets. As with the outer planets, before the slow longitude of the planet can be subtracted from its step index, the least significant figure for the slow longitude must first be adjusted in the same way as was done for the solar longitude with the outer planets.

As the lowest fractional part for Venus is 749 and the slow longitude is 22;52,25,0,70530, the adjustment that is needed is:

70530 × 749 = 52826970 ÷ 149209 = 354 rem. 6984

This gives the new value as 22;52,25,0,354,6984 (749,149209).

This value for the slow longitude of Venus can now be subtracted from its step index:

14;18,39,5,269,0 - 22;52,25,0,354,6984 = 18;26,14,4,663,142225

Notice that a full circle had to be added to enable the subtraction. It is now necessary to check if a half-circle needs to be subtracted and note the fact. In this example the subtraction is needed, and so the index becomes:

18;26,14,4,663,142225 - 13;30 = 4;56,14,4,663,142225

Mercury				
Index	Total	Coefficient	Total	Index
1	16	16	0	0
2	32	16	16	13
3	47	15	32	12
4	61	14	47	11
5	74	13	61	10
6	85	11	74	9
7	92	7	85	8
8	97	5	92	7
9	97	0	97	6
10	93	4	97	5
11	82	11	93	4
12	62	20	82	3
13	34	28	62	2
0	0	34	34	1

Table 2-7

In the next part of the calculation the mansion figure is used as an index and the rest of the value as an interpolation variable, in just the same way as was done with the outer planets, using similar tables (Tables 2-7 and 2-8).

In this example, as there was a need to subtract a half-circle, Venus is moving behind its mean position (the mean positions as defined here, the adjusted solar mean, and not the heliocentric mean position of Mercury), and the index is used in the right-hand side of the table. It is first therefore necessary to make a correction to the mansion and nāḍī figures, sliding the index along as before. As the mansion figure is not zero and the nāḍī figure is not less than 30, simply add 30 the nāḍī figure, and carry over to the mansion figure if necessary. The index becomes:

4;56,14,4,663,142225 + 0;30 = 5;26,14,4,663,142225

Venus				
Index	Total	Coefficient	Total	Index
1	25	25	0	0
2	50	25	25	13
3	75	25	50	12
4	99	24	75	11
5	123	24	99	10
6	145	22	123	9
7	167	22	145	8
8	185	18	167	7
9	200	15	185	6
10	208	8	200	5
11	202	6	208	4
12	172	30	202	3
13	83	99	172	2
0	0	73	83	1

Table 2-8

From the table, the index of 5 refers to a total figure of 200. This is decreasing, and the coefficient from the next row is 15. So, taking the fractional part of the index—everything below the mansion figure—the coefficient is multiplied by the interpolation variable:

15 × 0;26,14,4,663,142225 = 0;393,42,1,222,44449

It is then necessary to divide all the way through by 60:

0;393,42,1,222,44449 ÷ 60 = 0;6,33,4,165,147463

This result is the intermediate correction which then needs to be subtracted from the number of nāḍī given in the total column:

0;200,0,0,0,0 - 0;6,33,4,165,147463 = 0;193,26,1,583,1746

This result should be adjusted by rounding the nāḍī to mansions and dropping the last fractional part as it is no longer needed: 3;13,26,1,583

This is the correction which needs to be applied to the planet's slow longitude. As the earlier subtraction of a half-circle was needed, the correction is subtracted:

22;52,25,0,354 - 3;13,26,1,583 = 19;38,58,4,520

This, finally, is the true geocentric longitude of Venus.

Mercury

I shall now describe in brief the equivalent calculation for Mercury.

To find the particular day:

24806 × 100 + 4639 = 2485239 ÷ 8797 = 282 rem. 4485

27 × 4485 = 121095

121095;0,0,0,0 ÷ 8797 = 13;45,55,4,4802 (27,60,60,6,8797)

Subtract the birth-sign from the mean slow longitude:

22;45,37,1,125393 - 16;30 = 6;15,37,1,125393 (149209)

No subtraction of a half-circle is needed. Convert from lunar mansions to zodiacal signs:

6 × 60 + 15 = 375
375 ÷ 135 = 2 rem. 105

From the left-hand side of the table an index of 2 indicates a total of 17 and a coefficient of 3:

3 × 0;105,37,1,125393 = 0;316,51,5,77761 (149209)

0;316,51,5,77761 ÷ 135 = 0;2,20,4,145364

0;17,0,0,0 + 0;2,20,4,145364 = 0;19,20,4,145364

As no subtraction of a half-circle was required, this correction is subtracted in order to find the true slow longitude:

22;45,37,1,125393 - 0;19,20,4,145364 = 22;26,16,2,129238

In order to adjust the lower unit of this figure:

129238 × 8797 = 1136906686 ÷ 149209 = 7619 rem. 83315

= 22;26,16,2,7619,83315 (8797,149209)

The true slow longitude is now subtracted from the step index:

13;45,55,4,4802 - 22;26,16,2,7619,83315 = 18;19,39,1,5979,65894

Subtraction of a half-circle is needed:

18;19,39,1,5979,65894 - 13;30 = 4;49,39,1,5979,65894

That subtraction indicates that the index refers to the right-hand side of the table, and so it is necessary to slide along half a step:

4;49,39,1,5979,65894 => 5;19,39,1,5979,65894

From the table, the index of 5 refers to a total figure of 97 and co-efficient of 0. The correction needed is therefore trivial, and is:

1;37,0,0,0,0

As the subtraction of a half-circle was needed, the correction needs to be subtracted from the slow longitude in order to yield the true geo-centric longitude:

22;26,16,2,7619,83315 - 1;37,0,0,0,0 = 20;49,16,2,7619,83315

Times for planetary longitudes

Earlier, it was stated that the time for which the longitudes of the planets were being calculated was the very end of the solar day during which the current mean lunar day completed. These example calculations have been for the new Moon, which fell on Wednesday 1st March. In the main calendar calculations for that day, the following values were derived:

Mean Weekday:	4;39,28,2,230	True:	4;21,24,2,32
Mean solar longitude:	22;44,6,1,41	True:	22;50,31,2,4

The weekday values of 4 indicate that the day is a Wednesday, and the other figures give the time in nāḍī, pala, etc., measured from 5 AM Local Mean Solar Time.

During the calculations for the planets another value was derived for the mean solar longitude. It should be clear that the planetary positions have been calculated for the same time as the mean Sun reached that position, as the same count of solar days was used to make each calculation. The value used was: 22;45,37,1,125393 (149209)

This mean value is greater than that derived at the time of mean new Moon, and so obviously occurs later. It is simple to check the consistency of these calculations by determining just how much later.

It is first necessary to change the lower fractional unit of the value arrived at for the time of mean new Moon so that it is compatible with that for the planetary calculation. The two fractional units are 67 and 149,209, and as 67 × 2227 = 149209, all that is needed is to multiply by 2,227. The conversion becomes:

22;44,6,1,41 (67) = 22;44,6,1,91307 (149209)

Subtraction can now yield the distance the mean Sun has moved between mean new Moon and the end of the solar day:

22;45,37,1,125393 - 22;44,6,1,91307 = 0;1,31,0,348086

So, how long does it take for the mean Sun to move this far? The mean movement of the Sun in one solar day is: 0;4,26,0,93156 (149209). (This value was used when calculating the mean Sun for the planets.)

Reducing the distance moved and the mean daily motion to their lowest fractional parts:

Movement:	0;1,31,0,348086 = 81502200
Daily motion:	0;4,26,0,93156 = 238230720

Therefore, the time taken for the mean Sun to move the distance calculated is 81502200/238230720 parts of one whole solar day. To find the time that this represents, all that is needed is to multiply one day by that fraction, first multiplying by the numerator, and then dividing by the denominator.

81502200 × 1;0,0,0,0 = 81502200;0,0,0,0

81502200;0,0,0,0 ÷ 238230720 = 0;20,31,3,477 (707)

This calculation is precise and leaves no other remainder as 707 is a factor of the divisor 238,230,720. This time difference can now simply be added to the time for the mean new Moon, to confirm the time for which the planetary calculations were relevant:

0;20,31,3,477 + 4;39,28,2,230 = 5;0,0,0,0

This is what was expected. The mean new Moon occurred on a Wednesday, and so the planetary calculations were for the very end of that solar day—i.e., the beginning of the Thursday.

It should be remembered that it can happen that the true weekday is different from the mean weekday.

For example, if the true weekday had been 4;1,0,0,0 it would be quite possible for the mean weekday to be something like 3;58,0,0,0. The first of these referring to a Wednesday, and the second to a Tuesday. In that case, the planetary calculations would have given positions for the very end of the Tuesday and not the Wednesday. However, the weekday check at the end of the general day calculation described in chapter one would correct for this.

Accuracy of the calculations

In assessing the accuracy of these calculations there are four main components that need to be considered: the mean motion of the planets, best represented by their periods, the mean positions at some suitable epoch, the longitude of the aphelion, or birth-sign, and the step functions that adjust the true slow and fast longitudes. The periods of the planets given in these calculations and the respective equivalents from modern calculations are, in solar days:

	Tibetan	**Modern**
Mercury	87.97	87.968
Venus	224.7	224.695
Mars	687	686.93
Jupiter	4332	4330.60
Saturn	10766	10746.94

We shall see in chapter six that the Tibetan planetary calculations were derived from an old Indian system using sidereal measurement, and for this reason the modern figures given here are sidereal. Tropical periods would be slightly less. The reason for this is that the tropical zodiac is moving backwards relative to the sidereal zodiac, the fixed stars, and so a planet reaches the same place in the tropical zodiac a little earlier than in the sidereal. According to my own calculations, this difference for Mercury would only be about a minute, and for Saturn about 12 days.

There are two valid ways of comparing the mean positions of the planets. The first is to take the actual mean positions and compare with those derived from modern figures in a tropical zodiac. For the primary epoch of the Phugpa system, the beginning of the month Caitra in 1447, the end of the solar day of Thursday 16th March 1447, the respective figures, all converted into degrees of longitude, are:

	Phugpa	**Modern**	**Difference**
Mercury	194°794	219°576	-24°782
Venus	316°903	351°265	-34°362
Mars	9°956	27°827	-17°871
Jupiter	159°640	170°895	-11°255
Saturn	107°639	127°015	-19°376

The other way of looking at this data is to compare the difference between the mean position of each planet and the Sun. The geocentric position of the planets is determined by calculating this difference, and it is also independent of the zodiac being used. For the same epoch, the following figures (planet–Sun) result:

	Phugpa	**Modern**	**Difference**
Mercury	212°578	216°908	-4°33
Venus	334°687	348°597	-13°910
Mars	27°74	25°159	+2°581
Jupiter	177°424	168°227	+9°197
Saturn	125°423	124°347	+1°076

It is also worth making that last comparison for a more recent epoch, such as the new Moon at the beginning of Caitra, 1987 (the start of the most recent 60 year prabhava cycle). This is the end of the solar day of Monday 27th April 1987 (mean new Moon was on the Tuesday, but I am taking the data for true new Moon here). The following figures result:

	Phugpa	**Modern**	**Difference**
Mercury	339°273	342°830	-3°557
Venus	280°879	286°068	-5°189
Mars	59°923	52°778	+7°145
Jupiter	352°955	333°937	+19°018
Saturn	224°056	219°533	+4°523

As one would expect, the accumulated errors are mostly increasing with time.

The next quantity to compare is the position of the aphelion of the planets' orbits. The figures for the epochs of 1447 and 1987 are:

1447	**Phugpa**	**Modern**	**Difference**
Mercury	220°	248°86	-28°86
Venus	80°	303°78	+136°22
Mars	126°67	145°89	-19°22
Jupiter	160°	185°45	-25°45
Saturn	240°	262°23	-22°23

1987	Phugpa	Modern	Difference
Mercury	220°	257°.26	-37°.26
Venus	80°	311°.39	+128°.61
Mars	126°.67	155°.83	-29°.16
Jupiter	160°	194°.13	-34°.13
Saturn	240°	272°.81	-32°.81

Similar reductions in these errors would be seen if the aphelion positions were compared relative to the Sun, as was done with the mean planetary longitudes. However, the important point with the aphelion data is that the Tibetan system does not consider that the aphelion of a planet is moving, and so the errors will increase steadily. The one exception with a decreasing error is Venus, which anyway has a huge error to start with. The reason for this is discussed in chapter six.

The best way of judging the accuracy of the slow longitude step functions is the method that was used in chapter one for the comparison for the Sun. The step functions are equivalent to the first trigonometric term in the series for the heliocentric position of the planet and the best comparison to make is with the maximum value this term can take—i.e., the coefficient of the trigonometric term compared with the maximum total value in the step function.

The shape of the functions is dependent solely on the maximum value, and if that maximum in one of the step function tables is in error by, say 10 per cent, then all the other total values will be in error by the same amount—correct of course to the nearest integer value. Adapting the data from "Astronomical Algorithms" (Meeus, p. 413, etc.), and converting to nāḍī, the figures for the five planets are:

	Step function	Modern
Mercury	20	105.7
Venus	10	3.5
Mars	50	48.1
Jupiter	23	25.0
Saturn	43	28.6

These errors are surprisingly large, and almost certainly reflect the fact that these algorithms are based on very old methods and that the data here is difficult to observe. We should expect greater accuracy with the fast motion step functions as the variable true longitude of the planets is much easier to observe.

As with the slow longitude functions the best way to assess the accuracy of the fast longitude step functions is to compare their maximum values. The shapes of the functions are all essentially the same, and that for Mercury is shown in Figure 2i. The values given in the Tibetan texts are represented by the solid line, and values calculated using trigonometry based on mean radii are shown by the dotted line. There are differences in their shapes as the position of the maximum varies depending on the relative sizes of the orbits, but this need not be of concern here.

The original step function values and the modern figures for comparison are based on simple trigonometric relations between the orbits of the Earth and the planet concerned.

For example, referring to Figure 2a, given the value of the angle ZSM, which is the step index minus the slow longitude of the planet, and

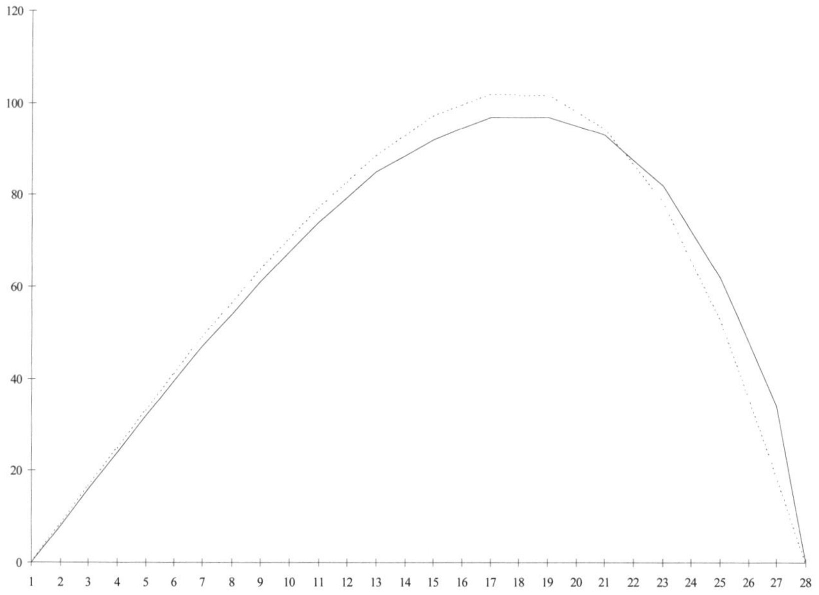

Figure 2i

given the ratio of the radii of the planets' orbits, simple trigonometry produces the angle SME, which is the correction that needs to be applied to the slow longitude of the planet. Very similar calculations produce the equivalent result for the inner planets.

In these calculations the planetary orbits are approximated as circular. The accuracy of the Tibetan calculations is limited here, as the eccentricity of the orbits is not properly taken into account. However, the comparison is useful as this calculation embodies the largest component of the many factors that determine the true geocentric longitude of the planets. It is from that point of view equivalent to the first trigonometric term in the heliocentric calculation in that it is the next component to consider once the heliocentric positions have been calculated.

These calculations depend on one factor alone, the relative radii of the orbits of the planets. For comparison purposes I have taken the data for the planetary radii as given in the "Explanatory Supplement to the Astronomical Almanac" (ESAA, p. 704). As before, all results are converted into nāḍī.

The maximum values for the corrections derived from the step functions are:

	Step function	**Modern**
Mercury	97	101.9
Venus	208	208.1
Mars	182	184.4
Jupiter	52	49.6
Saturn	28	27.0

The complete table for Mercury, the least accurate in the Tibetan system, is given in Table 2-9.

As expected, these data are significantly more accurate than the step functions used to adjust the slow longitude of the planets. The shapes of these functions are also clearly derived from the simple trigonometric calculation that was described above. With the exception of a couple of apparent errors, the figures in the step functions are derived directly from the same trigonometry as would be used in basic (pre-)Ptolemaic epicycle theory. If they were based on observation or some different theory, it would be very unlikely that they would match so very closely the shape of the functions as derived from epicycle theory.

Index	Step function	Modern
0	0	0.0
1	16	16.7
2	32	33.1
3	47	48.9
4	61	63.7
5	74	77.1
6	85	88.5
7	92	97.1
8	97	101.9
9	97	101.6
10	93	94.4
11	82	78.5
12	62	52.9
13	34	18.8

Table 2-9

CHAPTER III

Rāhu and Eclipses

The next major astronomical feature that needs to be considered is not in fact a real planet, but is treated as such. This is usually known by its Sanskrit name, Rāhu (*sgra gcan*). This is equivalent to the nodes of the Moon's orbit, the places where the Moon crosses over the plane of the ecliptic during its path around the Earth. As there are two such places Rāhu has two components, known as the Head (*gdong, vaktra*) and Tail (*mjug ma, puccha*). The first of these is the ascending node, where the Moon crosses the ecliptic travelling northwards. The Tail is the descending node. Another name often used for the Tail is Kālāgni (*dus me*).

Rāhu serves two purposes in the Tibetan astronomical system. It has astrological significance when it is treated as a planet in its own right, but more importantly for the calendar, it is also the indicator of eclipses. An eclipse, solar or lunar, can only occur when the Sun is near one of the nodes, which occurs approximately every six months, and so the position of Rāhu is calculated for the moments of exact new and full Moons, the two times in each month when eclipses are possible.

There are many different stories about Rāhu, who in mythology is considered to be a demon that swallows the Sun or Moon at the time of eclipse. Such descriptions are often found in Tibetan literature, but interestingly, Pawo Tsuklag (Tlkuntu, p. 281) makes it quite clear that language such as "the Sun and Moon are eaten by Rāhu and then escape" is not being literal, but poetic or descriptive.

One difference between Rāhu and the real planets is its direction of motion. From the point of view of the Earth, the zodiac is moving from east to west—rising in the east and setting in the west, completing a little more than a whole circle each day. But the planets all move across the zodiac from west to east. (They also of course rise in the east and set in the west, but relative to the zodiac, their mean motion is from west to east.)

Rāhu does the reverse of this, and moves "backwards" through the zodiac signs and lunar mansions, from east to west. In Tibetan texts (e.g., Rigthig, p. 37) this is often called motion to the right. For an observer in the northern hemisphere, looking at the ecliptic in the southern sky, an object moving from east to west would indeed be travelling towards the right. Relative to the zodiac, the mean motion of the Sun and Moon and the normal five planets is to the left from this point of view. Rāhu is the only one to travel towards the right.

As with other calculations, the determination of the position of Rāhu starts with the true month, the value of which in the example month (starting 2nd March 1995) is 840.

To this month has to be added an epoch value of 187, and then the total is divided by 230, taking the remainder. This is multiplied by 30, and then for the full Moon add 15, and for the new Moon (the new Moon at the end of the month for which the calculation is being performed) add 30. This calculation is clearly deriving a number of lunar days that have elapsed during a current Rāhu cycle. For the example month the calculation gives:

840 + 187 = 1027 ÷ 230 = 4 rem. 107
107 × 30 = 3210

3210 + 15 = 3225
3210 + 30 = 3240

These two results then have to be multiplied by 0;0,14,0,12 (23). This is the motion of Rāhu in one lunar day, and the calculation yields:

Full Moon: 3225 × 0;0,14,0,12 = 12;37,10,2,14
New Moon: 3240 × 0;0,14,0,12 = 12;40,41,4,10

These values are not for the actual position of Rāhu, but for his Source (*rtsa ba*), respectively for the full and new Moons during the month concerned. This is a device to make the main calculation similar to those that have been used for the planets—the Source moves through the zodiac from west to east, just like the real planets.

These values for the longitude of the Source now have to be subtracted from a whole circle in order to derive the position of the Head of Rāhu. Once this has been done, a half-circle is added to the Head in order to determine the longitude of the Tail.

The Head:

Full Moon: 27;0,0,0,0 - 12;37,10,2,14 = 14;22,49,3,9
New Moon: 27;0,0,0,0 - 12;40,41,4,10 = 14;19,18,1,13

The Tail:

Full Moon: 14;22,49,3,9 + 13;30,0,0,0 = 0;52,49,3,9
New Moon: 14;19,18,1,13 + 13;30,0,0,0 = 0;49,18,1,13

There are variations in the texts on these calculations. If all one is doing is checking for eclipses, the only data that are needed are for full and new Moons. In this case, a more simple method could be used in which one would multiply by two after adding the epoch value of 187, and then divide by 460 instead of 230.

The remainder from this would be a count of fortnights, and one would add to it a value of one for the full Moon on the 15th of the month, and two for the following new Moon. The resulting values would then each be successively multiplied by 27, 60, etc., each time dividing by 460. This would yield longitude values for the Source for the times of full and new Moons. Lochen Dharmaśrī gives this type of calculation in his "Golden Chariot" (Nangser, p. 207, etc.).

The point here is that the period of Rāhu is taken as an exact number of lunar months, 230, equivalent to 6,900 lunar days.

The other method given above, multiplying by 30 after the division by 230, is useful not only for eclipse predictions, but also for finding the position of Rāhu on any lunar day (by adding the value of that lunar day, instead of 15 or 30). This might be needed for astrological purposes, and is not normally included in Tibetan calendars.

This cycle of 230 lunar months for Rāhu might at first seem unusual as it is close to, but not equal to one of the famous eclipse cycles such as the Saros (223 lunar months) or the Metonic (235 lunar months). But it is not intended to be a cycle that matches up with other periods as these two do. For example, the Metonic cycle is dependent on the fact that 19 tropical years is almost exactly the same as 235 synodic months.

This value of 230 months is simply the period of Rāhu, and using the figure for the Tibetan length of the synodic months from chapter one, equals 29.5305870 × 230, or 6792.04 solar days. A modern figure for the tropical period of the Moon's nodes is 6798.4 solar days. Because Rāhu moves to the right through the ecliptic, its sidereal period is a little longer than the tropical (unlike the planets where the reverse is the case), and by my calculation the sidereal period is 6793.5 solar days, quite close to the Tibetan figure.

Prediction of eclipses

The prediction of eclipses might seem at first sight a relatively simple affair, as the key criterion is that if the nodes of the Moon's orbit are sufficiently close to the Sun and Moon at the time of full or new Moon, then an eclipse can occur. The closer the nodes are to the Sun and Moon, then the greater will be the magnitude and duration of the eclipse.

However, there are many complications involved. For a start, the distances between both the Sun and the Moon and the Earth are constantly changing. This changes the sizes of the shadows of the Earth and the Moon, and thereby the characteristics of eclipses. The speeds of the bodies in their orbits also vary with the distance—slowest angular speed at greatest distance—and this affects the duration and timing of eclipses.

The timing of eclipses will obviously affect their visibility—if a total solar eclipse occurs when it is night in your part of the world, you simply will not be able see it.

Finally, although lunar eclipses can be seen from any part of the Earth from which the Moon is visible, solar eclipses are quite different, and their characteristics vary considerably depending on the observer's location. If a total solar eclipse is visible from one place on the Earth, just a couple of hundred miles away to the north or south the eclipse will be partial, and two or three thousand miles away it may not even be visible at all, even though the Sun is clearly to be seen.

The Kālacakra literature on which the Tibetan calendar is based makes very little mention of eclipses and how to predict them. As with some other subjects, such as astrology, it expects the reader to have a knowledge of these matters from standard Indian works on the subject. It is said by some that eclipse prediction was explained properly in the Kālacakra Mūlatantra, but we cannot be certain that this was so, or even if this text ever actually existed. The Vimalaprabhā itself states why little attention is paid in the literature to eclipse prediction, with the comment that "this is well known in other karaṇas."

Whether the Mūlatantra existed or not, it would appear that the Tibetans did not receive any thorough eclipse prediction methods from India. This is surprising, as such material should have been available to them. See for example the reasonably sophisticated methods given by Varāhamihira in his *Pañcasiddhāntikā* (Pañca, chapters 6 to 11), written approximately 500 years before the Tibetans were translating this type of material from Sanskrit.

In the absence of any such inherited methodology, what they have done is to base their methods on the little information available in the Kālacakra literature, and then adjust and refine this in the light of observation and experience. However, no theory for the curvature of the Earth and the tilting of the Earth's axis has been incorporated into all this, and so their attempts have been much more successful with lunar eclipses than with solar, as one might expect.

For these reasons, although the basic methods described in the various texts are the same, there are many variations in the details, and in the following I shall follow the broad principles, but indicate the differences where they are important or interesting.

One important aspect of the Tibetan eclipse prediction methods is that they clearly found at some point inaccuracies in the method, and decided to apply a correction. Lunar eclipse observations should have made it relatively easy to determine this correction, but this process appears not to have been sustained systematically through the centuries, making yet further accumulation of errors inevitable.

In his great commentary on the Kālacakra Tantra, "The Illumination of the Vajra Sun," Mipham's frustration at the state of Tibetan eclipse prediction is made clear (MiKal, chapter 1, p. 369). He mentions that eclipses occur when not predicted, and even when predicted, some do not occur. He makes some of the sharpest comments on this subject that can be found in the Tibetan literature, and discusses the need to take into consideration geographical location when examining solar eclipses.

He makes the point that Chinese methods are often superior to those in use in Tibet, and lamenting that he will not find the time to investigate this more properly, he urges others to do so.

In looking at these methods of eclipse prediction, as lunar eclipses are much easier to predict than solar, I shall start with them.

Lunar eclipses

With both solar and lunar eclipses, there is a standard set of seven characteristics that are predicted by the Tibetan methods, and I shall follow this scheme, except for the last subject of astrology. These are to determine the conditions for an eclipse, its magnitude, duration, timing, direction, colour, and astrology.

Conditions

As Rāhu moves so slowly around the ecliptic, once every 18 and a half years, eclipses can occur approximately every six months—when the Sun and Moon are close to the nodes. So one starts looking for eclipses approximately six months after the last one that was predicted or observed.

For both solar and lunar eclipses, it is necessary to find the distance between the relevant body—the Sun or Moon—and the nearest of either the Head or the Tail of Rāhu. I shall call this the node-distance. For lunar eclipses, it is the Moon that is important. So, of the Moon's longitude and whichever of the nodes it is close to, the greatest longitude has the least subtracted from it.

Some texts point out that it is only worth doing this if the Moon and one of the nodes either lie in the same or adjacent lunar mansions, and this is easily checked from their longitudes. This is certainly the best way of making a quick assessment, as if the separation between the Moon and the nearest node is more than one mansion, no eclipse is possible.

There are four possible combinations here, depending on which quantity is subtracted from which, and they are considered differently when determining the characteristics of the eclipse. These will be referred to quite often, and so I shall represent them in the following simple form, with the hyphens indicating subtraction:

Head-Moon
Moon-Head
Tail-Moon
Moon-Tail

Whichever it is, the size of the difference obtained is then examined. Here we encounter the first, rather surprising, difficulty. In the "Essence of the Kalkī," Chenrab Norbu (Rigthig, p. 32) describes two such calculations. He states that the first is according to the work of Sangje Gyatso (Baidkar) and the second the work of Dharmaśrī (Nangser). Dharmaśrī was writing around the same time as Sangje Gyatso. Their respective epochs are 1681 and 1687.

In the first method Chenrab Norbu says that one should use the karaṇa true solar longitude and find the difference between this and the nearest node. (It does not actually matter if one uses the solar or lunar longitude. At full Moon they are exactly 180° apart, as are the nodes. The result will be the same.)

In the second method he describes first subtracting a value from the relevant node to determine a result that he calls the unerring determinant (*bslu ba med pa'i gzer*). The difference is then found between this and the longitude of the Sun or Moon from the siddhānta calculations.

The description of the karaṇa calculations is in chapter six, but it is interesting to notice here that the siddhānta calculations are being used to generate the main calendar, and yet for eclipse prediction they are apparently found to be wanting. Chenrab Norbu is effectively saying that one should either use the karaṇa calculations or correct the siddhānta.

He is right in assigning these two different methods to the texts that he quotes. In the "White Beryl" (Baidkar), Sangje Gyatso describes using the karaṇa longitude for the Sun (or Moon), and in the "Golden Chariot" (Nangser), Dharmaśrī applies a correction to the siddhānta longitude of the Moon, adding to it 32 nāḍī. Curiously, for solar eclipses, he adds a value to the longitude of the Sun equivalent to nine fortnights of the motion of Rāhu, i.e., 0;31,41,4,10 (23). I can only presume that this is for some simplification of a calculation.

Nine fortnights is equivalent to 135 lunar days, and given the mean motion of Rāhu in a lunar day that was used above, this would yield:

$$135 \times 0;0,14,0,12 = 0;31,41,4,10\ (23)$$

Chenrab Norbu actually says that instead of adding the correction to the longitude of the Sun or Moon, it should be subtracted from the node. It makes no difference which way around it is, as the key factor is to find the difference between either the Sun or Moon and the nearest node. The value Chenrab Norbu gives is also 0;31,41,4,10, although he uses this for both lunar and solar eclipses, which is what one would expect from Dharmaśrī.

Unfortunately, Dharmaśrī does not give detailed reasoning for his correction, and neither does he describe why the corrections for lunar and solar eclipses are slightly different. Logic says that they should be the same. All he does say is that village astrologers in general state that for predicting lunar eclipses karaṇa calculations are more effective than siddhānta. He adds that this correction is similar to the one he describes for adjusting karaṇa calculations for the solar longitude and bringing them in line with the siddhānta system.

In that discussion, he considers the correction needed up to the time of his epoch in 1681 from the epoch of 1027. This is when the Kālacakra system is said to have been introduced into Tibet, and is also a key date given in the Kālacakra Tantra. (In fact, Dharmaśrī considers 1027 to be the true epoch of the Kālacakra Tantra. More about this in chapter six.)

In his correction to the karaṇa Sun, he subtracts from the solar longitude at his epoch the value of 0;34,3,1,3. Now, for eclipse prediction, he is effectively telling us to reverse this, and add to the lunar or solar longitude about 31 or 32 nāḍī.

The logic appears to be this. It must have been observed by the Tibetans that although the siddhānta calculations gave more reliable results in general, perhaps for the time of day of events, and so forth, as far as eclipse predictions were concerned, the otherwise supposedly inaccurate karaṇa calculations were better at determining if an eclipse was due to occur.

Regardless of the actual values of the longitudes of the Sun and the nodes at any time, throughout the centuries the crucial difference between the solar longitude and the nodes in the Tibetan calculations was progressively getting less accurate when compared to modern calculations.

In fact, the siddhānta calculations were straying from reality more quickly than the karaṇa, and by the time of the epoch for which Dharmaśrī was writing, the measure of "Sun-node" in the karaṇa system was just over 2° too great, but in the siddhānta system (of the Phugpa tradition) it was just over 6°.5 too little.

So, adding a correction to the longitude of the Sun (or subtracting the same from the node) would increase the quantity "Sun-node." This quantity is too small in the siddhānta calculations, and the gap has been getting progressively larger. If the Phugpa siddhānta calculations are worked back to 1000 CE, then the value of Sun-node is 0°.35 too large. By 1500 it was 4°.75 too small, and by 2000, 9°.77 too small.

Similarly, the difference between the solar longitude as determined by the two systems has been changing. In 1000 CE they were almost exactly the same, correct to 0°.01. By 1500 the siddhānta Sun was 5°.58 less than the karaṇa Sun, and by 2000, the siddhānta Sun was 11°.58 less.

The amount Dharmaśrī adds to the longitude of the Sun, 32 nāḍī, is equivalent to just over 7°, which would have made at the time of his epoch (1681) the "Sun-node" quantity about one-third of a degree too great, instead of over 6° too little. It would in fact be more accurate than using the karaṇa calculations, and this must explain why this method became the preferred system.

In fact, by the time of Chenrab Norbu's epoch of 1927, the karaṇa and corrected siddhānta calculations would have been roughly equally accurate, with the karaṇa "Sun-node" being just over a couple of degrees too great, and the corrected siddhānta value, marginally more accurate at just less than a couple of degrees too little. Clearly, any historical data available to Chenrab Norbu since the time of Dharmaśrī would have shown the corrected siddhānta method as generally more reliable than the karaṇa.

This explains why we see Chenrab Norbu using exactly the same correction as Dharmaśrī. The latter made clear that his correction was needed due to errors accumulated over time, and yet over two hundred years later, when further errors would certainly have accumulated, Chenrab Norbu applies the exact same correction. Not enough time had elapsed for the corrected siddhānta calculation to stray far enough away from reality for this to be readily detectable by the Tibetans.

A surprising thing is that the Tibetans did not see here a need permanently to adjust their calculations for the nodes. That would have been a logical step to take, given that in general they considered the siddhānta longitude of the Sun to be accurate. It would have made sense to consider that if the karaṇa solar longitude needed to be corrected, then perhaps the longitude of Rāhu from the karaṇa needed a similar correction. I have not come across any discussion in the literature about this, but the fact that Dharmaśrī's correction is equivalent to a whole number of lunar days' motion of Rāhu suggests that perhaps he was thinking along these lines.

A possible reason for not making a correction to Rāhu in the basic calculations is that the period of Rāhu is given in the Vimalaprabhā (under the discussion of chapter 1, v.38; see chapter five for a translations of this) in a quotation from the Mūlatantra during the description of siddhānta values. If this period was indeed considered a siddhānta value, then it would have been thought accurate and not in need of correction.

Another point worth mentioning here is that there is no such correction made in the Tsurphu tradition of calculation. The main text (Kongleg) that I have used for this tradition is by Jamgon Kongtrul, and at the time of his epoch of 1852, the value in the calculations for "Sun-node" was just three and a half degrees too little. In previous centuries it had been more accurate, and in fact, in 1447 when the Tsurphu siddhānta calculations were started, the "Sun-node" value was only about half a degree too great. For most of the time, this would have seemed quite accurate enough.

Both the Phugpa and Tsurphu calculations use the same count of months derived from the Kālacakra Tantra to determine the longitude of Rāhu, and so the difference here is due to the difference in the longitude of the Sun in the two traditions. In the Tsurphu tradition the mean longitude of the Sun is greater than that in the Phugpa by 0;21,31,2,4. (There is also a small difference in the mean weekday, and hence in the time for which the Sun's mean longitude is given, but this is very small and is not relevant to the comparison here.)

One additional problem that I have not found discussed in the Tibetan literature is the poor granularity of the determination of the longitude of Rāhu. given that the value is given as a whole number of months in a cycle of a total of 230 months, this gives a maximum accuracy for the longitude of Rāhu of as much as 1°.56. This is bound to have a negative impact on all eclipse calculations.

To get back to the determination of a lunar eclipse, whether or not the Phugpa siddhānta correction has been applied, the figure that has been derived of the difference between the longitude of the Moon and the nearest node is examined. Chenrab Norbu simply states that if this node-distance is less than 50 nāḍī, then there will certainly be an eclipse.

Kongtrul says essentially the same, but Sangje Gyatso (Baidkar 1, p. 59) gives more details. He lists four different eclipse types, depending on which node was closest to the Moon, and whichever longitude was the greater of the node or the Moon. He states that an eclipse will occur if the node-distance is less than the following values of nāḍī.

Moon-Head:	57
Head-Moon:	50
Moon-Tail:	45
Tail-Moon:	50

There are a couple of problems here. First, a couple of pages later Sangje Gyatso gives a much more detailed analysis of the magnitude of eclipses, and clearly the extreme when the magnitude is zero is also the limit for eclipses to be visible. Taking the figures he gives there, and converting them to decimal nāḍī for comparison, we find the following:

Moon-Head:	55.75
Head-Moon:	50.75
Moon-Tail:	50.75
Tail-Moon:	45.75

I suspect that these figures are more correct—in other words, would have been found more reliable in his day—than the ones he gives earlier, for the following reason. He is using the karaṇa calculations here, and we know that for the few centuries before his time, the karaṇa value for the "Sun-node" was a little too great, by an average of a little less than one degree.

You would expect then that observations would have shown that the limits for eclipses when a node was subtracted from the Moon would have to be somewhat larger values than when the Moon was subtracted from a node. That is exactly what we see in the second set of figures, and the size of the differences—a little over one degree—is about right.

However, both sets of figures show an eclipse by the Head of Rāhu as more likely than one by the Tail. There is no immediately obvious explanation for this asymmetry.

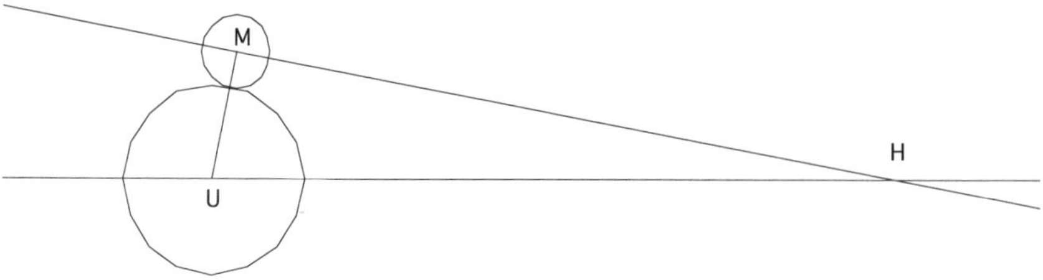

Figure 3a

It is worth looking now at the kind of figures we would expect from the modern theory of the motion of the Sun and Moon. The numbers used by the Tibetans to detect eclipses are clearly the extreme values for the difference between the longitude of the Moon and the nearest node. In Figure 3a, the horizontal line represents the ecliptic, and the line at an angle to it (the angle has been exaggerated for clarity) is the path of the Moon.

The point H is a node. If the diagram is considered to be from the point of view of the Earth, with north to the top, then H is the Head of Rāhu, the ascending node. As longitude increases from right to left, this would be a situation in which the longitude of the Head would be subtracted from that of the Moon, which is moving from right to left. The other three possible eclipse situations would be mirror images of this diagram. We need only consider the one here, as the basic geometry is the same for all.

The Moon is the smaller circle with centre M, and the umbral shadow of the Earth is the larger circle with centre U. The umbra is the shadow within which the Sun is completely obscured by the Earth, and the penumbra is the larger area where the Sun is only partially obscured. The penumbra is not shown in the diagram.

The point U is called the antisolar point, as its position on the ecliptic is exactly opposite the centre of the Sun. In the diagram the Moon is shown at the extreme position for visibility of an eclipse, where it just grazes the shadow as it passes. If H and U were any closer together, then at least part of the limb of the Moon would pass through the Earth's shadow, and there would be an eclipse.

One minor point of approximation here is that I am not going to take into consideration the time taken for the Moon to pass the point shown, and reach opposition with the Sun. Exact opposition will occur when the point M is directly above the point U (when their longitudes are the same). The distance moved by the point U in that time is tiny, and will not significantly affect the distance HU, which we are going to determine.

I am using the following data for this calculation. All values are mean.

Radius of Earth:	6.378136×10^6 m
Radius of Sun:	6.96×10^8 m
Orbital radius of Moon:	3.844×10^8 m
Orbital radius of Earth:	1.49598×10^{11} m

These values give the radius of the umbral shadow at the mean distance of the Moon as 4.606×10^6 m. It is necessary (ESAA p. 429) to introduce a correction to this due to the Earth's atmosphere, by increasing the value by one fiftieth. This gives the radius of the umbra as 4.698×10^6 m, which equates to 42.01 minutes of arc, as viewed from the Earth.

Given that the radius of the Moon at mean distance subtends an angle of 15.54 minutes of arc at the Earth, the distance MU is given by:

$$15.54 + 42.01 = 57.55$$

Given also that the inclination of the Moon's orbit to the ecliptic is 5°.1454, simple trigonometry determines HU, the node-distance, to be 641.701 minutes of arc. This equates to 48 nāḍī 7.7 pala.

If we take into account the variability of the distance of the Moon from the Earth—its orbit has an eccentricity of 0.0549—then we can determine extreme values for the visibility of eclipse at the apogee and perigee. Respectively, these yield 46 nāḍī 42.4 pala, and, 49 nāḍī 37.5 pala.

The second of these is very close to the figure given by Chenrab Norbu and Kongtrul, 50 nāḍī, and the mean of the figures given by Sangje Gyatso, 50.5 nāḍī.

Magnitude

There are two terms in use in English for the maximum fraction of a body that is hidden by shadow during an eclipse: 'obscuration' and 'magnitude.' The obscuration is a measure of the fraction of the surface that is obscured, and magnitude is the fraction of the diameter of the body that is obscured.

For example, if at maximum lunar eclipse the shadow of the Earth covers half the diameter of the Moon—the edge of the shadow crossing the very centre of the Moon, then the magnitude is 0.5. The obscuration will be less than this due to the curvature of the Earth's shadow.

Strictly speaking, in western terms the definition of magnitude is a little different for solar and lunar eclipses, but we can ignore this for the present purpose. Given the essentially linear nature of the Tibetan calculations, I have used the term 'magnitude' here, and I understand this to be the fraction of the diameter of the relevant body obscured or in shadow at the time of maximum eclipse. This seems to fit the intention of the Tibetan authors correctly.

Chenrab Norbu gives a simple means of determining the magnitude of a lunar eclipse. He states that the nāḍī value of the node-distance is divided by 5, and then this is used as an index into the following table.

Index	**Magnitude**
1	Total
2	Total
3	Total
4	Almost total
5	About 5/6th
6	2/3rds
7	1/2
8	1/3rd
9	1/6th
10	1/8th

Clearly, he considers that if the difference between the Moon and the node is less than or equal to 15 nāḍī, then the eclipse will be total. Kongtrul gives a similar, but slightly different set of figures. He simply says that one examines the node-distance, rather than dividing first by 5. Up to 20 nāḍī and the eclipse is total, and for other values:

Node-distance	**Magnitude**
25	5/6th
30	2/3rd
35	1/2
40	1/3rd
50	1/5th

He concludes by saying that magnitudes of one-fifth or one-sixth are difficult to observe and that one needs to be cautious in estimating them.

Dharmaśrī also divides the node-distance by 5, and then gives basically the same figures as Chenrab Norbu, although he treats the numbers as ranges. For example, he states: "If the result is between 0 and 4, i.e., a remainder of less than 20, this means that the eclipse will be total. If the result is from there up to 5, i.e., a remainder of less than 25, then all but one-sixth will be eclipsed."

He also describes something of the origin of these figures. He quotes the Vimalaprabhā, which gives a very approximate set of figures (this is commenting on Kālacakra Tantra, chapter 1, v. 86). It says that the limit for visible eclipse is 60 nāḍī, and that if the difference is zero then the eclipse will be total. If the difference is half of 60, then the magnitude will be half. These are very rough approximations, and Dharmaśrī explains that the figures used in practice are based on the (accumulated) experience of previous people.

Sangje Gyatso goes into much greater detail than these other writers, and covers a nuance that they do not even attempt—to compensate for the varying distance of the Moon from the Earth, although of course he did not explain it in the same way as I shall now describe it.

He states that one should perform the same calculation with the anomaly as is done when calculating the step function to correct the weekday. Take the anomaly value and add to it 15. This is the value of the lunar day for full Moon. As before, the result is then divided by 14 and both the quotient and the remainder are preserved. The results fall into four quadrants:

If the quotient is even and the remainder is 7 or less, then this is called fast motion. If the remainder is greater than 7, this is slow motion.

If the quotient is odd, and the remainder is 7 or less, then this is reversing motion, and if the remainder is greater than 7, this is advancing motion.

The use of this same terminology as is used for the motion of the planets is problematic here, and one needs to be careful for two reasons. First, as before, I am using the term 'anomaly' here to express the Tibetan usage. However, the western definition of anomaly is the distance of the Moon from its perigee—the point when it is closest to the Earth. The Tibetan (and ancient Indian) usage is with respect to the apogee, the point when the Moon is furthest away from the Earth.

When the (Tibetan) anomaly has a value of zero, the Moon is at its apogee, at its furthest away from the Earth, and therefore travelling at is slowest speed.

Secondly, the names of the quadrants seem wrong. As with the planets, the names given to the four quadrants really apply to the points of entering those quadrants. So to call the entry to the first quadrant "fast," when the Moon is furthest from the Earth, seems exactly the wrong way around. However, the term is not referring to the Moon. The phenomenon being considered is caused by the variable motion of the Moon, but these calculations are actually adjusting the weekday.

The true weekday (the time of an exact lunar day) moves forwards and backwards from the mean. When the Moon is travelling slowly, the length of the lunar day is increasing, and the time of the lunar day within the weekday is increasing—moving forwards, or getting later.

So, in the first half of the table, when the quotient is even, the Moon starts off travelling at its slowest, but the length of the lunar day is increasing at its fastest. This is therefore called fast motion. When the anomaly reaches the middle of the first half of the table, the Moon has speeded up and is travelling at its mean speed; the increase in the length of the lunar day has decreased to zero, and the lunar day is now about to start getting shorter. This is therefore called slow motion, as the time of true weekday starts to move backwards, or earlier, when compared to the mean.

At the beginning of the second half of the table, when the quotient is odd, the Moon is at its perigee, travelling at its fastest. At this point the length of the lunar day is decreasing at the greatest rate, and in the weekday calculation the calculated correction starts to be subtracted from the mean weekday. This point, when the true weekday starts to be earlier than, or behind, the mean weekday, is called reversing motion.

Finally, in the middle of the second half of the table, the Moon has slowed down and is again travelling at its mean speed. The length of the lunar day has reached its minimum, and they now start to get longer again. This is therefore called advancing motion.

What impact does all this have on lunar eclipses? The umbral shadow of the Earth that the Moon passes through during an eclipse is a narrow cone, and the further away the Moon is from the Earth, the smaller will be the cross section of that shadow, and also the apparent size of the Moon. So, the further away the Moon, the closer the Moon will have to be to the node for an eclipse to occur. The difference is small, but it was presumably noticed by the Tibetans, and Sangje Gyatso attempts to take this into consideration.

In effect, he considers 16 types of eclipses. He takes each of the four that were described earlier, depending on which node the Moon was nearest, and which value was subtracted from which. He then gives (some, not all) different figures for each of these, for each of the four quadrants.

He describes that one first has to convert the difference found between the node and the Moon to pala. This is done by multiplying the number of nāḍī in the node-distance by 60 and then adding to the number of pala. The resulting value is then divided by 15, and the quotient that results is used as an indicator of eclipses. His full set of figure is given on the next couple of pages

For Moon-Head:

At slow motion, below 83, total eclipse
At reversing motion, below 81, total
At advancing motion, below 79, total
At fast motion, below 77, total

From 84 to 92, 1/15th will not be eclipsed
From 93 to 101, 2/15th
From 102 to 110, 3/15th, or 1/5th
From 111 to 119, 4/15th
From 120 to 129, 5/15th, meaning 2/3rd is eclipsed

From 130 to 138, 6/15th
From 139 to 147, 7/15th
From 148 to 159, at slow motion, half is eclipsed
to 157, at reversing motion, half
to 155, at advancing motion, half
to 153, at fast motion, half
From 160 to 168, 7/15th is eclipsed
From 169 to 178, 6/15th is eclipsed
From 179 to 187, 1/3rd
From 188 to 196, 4/15th
From 197 to 205, 3/15th
From 206 to 214, 2/15th
From 215 to 223, 1/15th is eclipsed

For Head-Moon:

At slow motion, below 77, total eclipse
At reversing motion, below 75, total
At advancing motion, below 73, total
At fast motion, below 71, total

78 to 86, 1/15th will not be eclipsed
87 to 95, 2/15th
96 to 104, 3/15th, or 1/5th
105 to 113, 4/15th
114 to 122, 5/15th, meaning 2/3rd is eclipsed
123 to 131, 6/15th
132 to 140, 7/15th
141 to 151, at slow motion, half is eclipsed
149, at reversing motion, half
147, at advancing motion, half
145, at fast motion, half
152 to 158, 7/15th is eclipsed
159 to 166, 6/15th is eclipsed
167 to 173, 1/3rd
174 to 181, 4/15th
182 to 189, 3/15th
190 to 196, 2/15th
197 to 203, 1/15th is eclipsed

For Moon-Tail:

At slow motion, below 72, total eclipse
At reversing motion, below 70, total
At advancing motion, below 68, total
At fast motion, below 66, total

73 to 81, 1/15th will not be eclipsed
82 to 90, 2/15th
91 to 99, 3/15th, or 1/5th
100 to 108, 4/15th
109 to 117, 5/15th, meaning 2/3rd is eclipsed
118 to 126, 6/15th
127 to 135, 7/15th
136 to 147, at slow motion, half is eclipsed
145, at reversing motion, half
143, at advancing motion, half
141, at fast motion, half
148 to 155, 7/15th is eclipsed
156 to 163, 6/15th is eclipsed
164 to 171, 1/3rd
172 to 179, 4/15th
180 to 187, 3/15th
188 to 195, 2/15th
196 to 203, 1/15th is eclipsed

For Tail-Moon:

At slow motion, below 67, total eclipse
At reversing motion, below 65, total
At advancing motion, below 63, total
At fast motion, below 61, total

68 to 76, 1/15th will not be eclipsed
77 to 85, 2/15th
86 to 95, 3/15th, or 1/5th
96 to 105, 4/15th
106 to 115, 5/15th, meaning 2/3rds is eclipsed
116 to 124, 6/15th

125 to 133, 7/15th
134 to 145, at slow motion, half is eclipsed
    to 143, at reversing motion, half
    to 141, at advancing motion, half
    to 139, at fast motion, half
146 to 150, 7/15th is eclipsed
151 to 155, 6/15th is eclipsed
156 to 161, 1/3rd
162 to 167, 4/15th
168 to 173, 3/15th
174 to 178, 2/15th
179 to 183, 1/15th is eclipsed

Sangje Gyatso concludes this long list by saying that eclipses when the magnitude is less than 1/15 are very difficult to observe.

He also mentions, in a rather incomplete manner, that the time of year can make a difference, and he mentions particularly the equinoxes. In fact, according to the Tibetan system, the Sun is at its apogee (when the Earth is at aphelion) when it is at the beginning of Cancer. This is when it is at its furthest from the Earth, and at that time, the cone of the Earth's shadow would be stretched a little, making lunar eclipses marginally more likely. The reverse is the case in the winter when the Sun is at the beginning of Capricorn, and lunar eclipses are a little bit less likely.

He does not go into this in detail presumably because the effects are small and difficult to observe, and also the coincidence of the apogee with the beginning of Cancer is not accurate, and this may have caused problems in analysing any observed effects.

Between the four main different types of eclipse one sees the same asymmetry as before, but the figures relative to the different motions of the Moon are not quite what should be expected.

One would expect eclipses to be least likely to occur when the Moon is furthest from the Earth, during fast motion. The figures here agree with this. However, eclipses should be most likely when the Moon is nearest to the Earth, during reversing motion. This is not the case, and the numbers for slow and reversing motions are the reverse of what one would expect, although one would also expect slow and advancing motions to have the same likelihood of eclipse.

Unfortunately, Sangje Gyatso gives no theory as to why the numbers follow the pattern that they do, and one has to conclude that it is a result of the particular characteristics of the eclipses that were observed over a period of time.

We should now compare the modern theory of the motion of the Sun and Moon with the data given here, and examine the limits of total lunar eclipse.

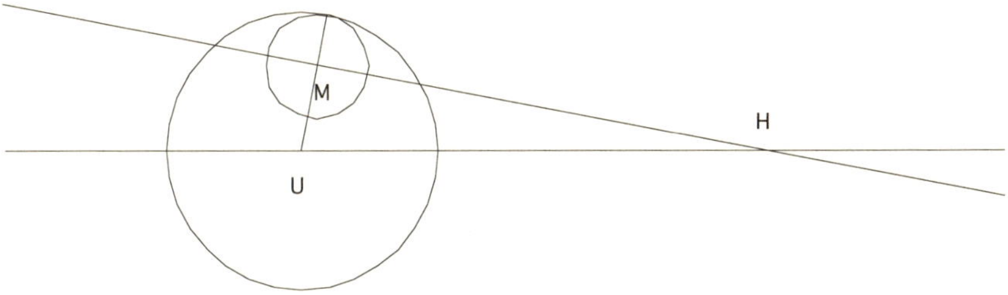

Figure 3b

In Figure 3b the Moon is at a point where it is briefly just fully obscured by the Earth's shadow. The variation here due to the distance of the Moon is not as great as for the earlier example of the limit of a low magnitude eclipse. The reason for this is that as the Moon gets nearer to the Earth, the size of the shadow at the Moon's distance is slightly larger, but so also is the apparent diameter of the Moon.

In the example of the extreme for a low magnitude eclipse (see Figure 3a) the two increased values are added together to give the distance MU—the increases are therefore added together.

For the current situation of total lunar eclipse, the two values are subtracted one from the other. The smaller apparent size of the Moon changes by a greater ratio than does the size of the shadow, and the increases tend to cancel each other out. Using basically the same trigonometry as before, the extreme values for the distance RU are:

Perigee: 22 nāḍī 7.7 pala
Apogee: 22 nāḍī 4.2 pala

If the calculation given by Sangje Gyatso is now applied, converting these values to pala, and then dividing by 15, the result is, to the nearest decimal:

Perigee: 22 nāḍī 7.7 pala —> 88.5
Apogee: 22 nāḍī 4.2 pala —> 88.3

The variation here is tiny, and although the values are close to those given by Sangje Gyatso for Moon-Head eclipse, his figures vary far too much. In fact, his range of values of six is exactly the same as he gives for a half magnitude lunar eclipse. This is not right.

We can also compare the situation of a half magnitude eclipse. This is a simple case where the point M, the centre of the Moon, lies on the edge of the umbral shadow. The path of the Moon makes a tangent to the circle of the shadow, and the calculation is simple.

Performing the necessary trigonometry, and then converting to the units given by Sangje Gyatso, the results are:

Perigee: 35 nāḍī 52.6 pala —> 143.5
Apogee: 34 nāḍī 23.3 pala —> 137.6

Now, these figures are much closer to the figures given by Sangje Gyatso, with a range the same as his to the nearest whole number. It can probably be inferred from this that, not knowing the actual physics and geometry involved in a lunar eclipse, he assumed that the variation for total and half-magnitude eclipses should be the same.

Duration

Chenrab Norbu deals with the magnitude and duration of an eclipse together, using the same calculation. That was to divide the node-distance by 5, and then use the quotient that results as an index into a table. In his table he has different figures for the duration (time expressed in nāḍī and pala) for an eclipse by the Head and Tail of Rāhu:

Index	Duration for Head	Duration for Tail
1	16;0	15;0
2	16;0	15;0
3	16;0	15;0
4	15;48	14;38
5	13;20	12;20
6	11;0	10;0
7	8;0	7;20
8	5;20	5;0
9	2;40	2;30
10	2;0	1;52,3

The other writers have very similar methods. Kongtrul basically has the duration ranging up to 12 nāḍī, and this is calculated by subtracting the node-distance from 60 and then dividing by 5.

Dharmaśrī has the same values as Chenrab Norbu, and the only difference is that he gives the values depending on the magnitude of the eclipse. He does add that the difference in the duration of eclipses by the Head and Tail are based on people's experience—therefore not based on any information in the Tantra or Vimalaprabhā.

As before however, Sangje Gyatso adds an extra twist. He gives the range of duration up to 15 nāḍī for a total eclipse, 7 1/2 nāḍī for an eclipse with magnitude half, and so forth, but he also says that there is a difference depending on the Moon's anomaly. He says that during slow and advancing motions, there is no change in the duration of a lunar eclipse, but during fast motion the eclipse has a duration 30 pala longer and starts earlier, and during reversing motion the eclipse duration is 40 pala shorter, with the eclipse starting 20 pala later.

At the beginning of the fast motion quadrant the Moon is at apogee, its furthest away from the Earth. It is therefore travelling at its slowest speed. This would mean that it would take a little longer to pass through the Earth's shadow, giving an eclipse a longer duration. At its furthest distance it also has a slightly smaller shadow to pass through. However, the proportional change in the shadow size is much smaller than the change in speed, and the net effect is certainly for the duration of the eclipse to increase.

Exactly the opposite applies at the beginning of the reversing motion quadrant when the Moon is at its closest to the Earth, travelling at its fastest speed, and the duration of an eclipse is shorter. At the beginning of the slow and advancing quadrants, the Moon is at its mean distance from the Earth, and so the duration has its mean value—there is no change from the values given.

There is one surprising fact about the figures given for the duration of an eclipse, and that is that they are too great by quite a large margin. In the previous sections I have used the Moon's umbral shadow to perform comparison calculations, and I have derived figures often very close to those in use by the Tibetans. They are clearly referring to the umbra as well.

However, applying a modern understanding to this, taking the mean value of the umbral shadow radius to be 41.19 minutes of arc, and the mean apparent radius of the Moon to be 15.54 minutes of arc, the mean maximum duration of an eclipse can be calculated. From the point of first contact with the umbral shadow, the Moon has to travel the entire diameter of the shadow before it starts to leave the shadow, and then travel its own diameter fully to leave the shadow. The total distance it will travel is given by:

$$2 \times 42.01 + 2 \times 15.54 = 115.1 \text{ minutes of arc}$$

If the length of the synodic month (from new Moon to new Moon) is taken to be 29.53059 solar days, in one synodic month the Moon travels, relative to the Sun or the antisolar point, a full 360°. This means that it travels relative to the shadow 12.1907 minutes of arc per nāḍī of time:

$$\frac{360 \times 60}{29.53059 \times 60} = 12.1907$$

At that speed, in order to travel 115.1 minutes of arc, the Moon will take 9.4 nāḍī. This is nothing like the Tibetan figures.

However, if we consider the penumbra, and take its mean radius as 74.63 minutes of arc, the distance travelled by the Moon becomes:

$$2 \times 74.63 + 2 \times 15.54 = 180.34 \text{ minutes of arc}$$

The time taken to travel this distance will be 14.8 nāḍī, almost exactly the same as the Tibetan figures. I have not come across any terms in these discussions in the Tibetan materials that would seem to differentiate between the umbra and penumbra, but it seems logical that at least as regards the duration of the eclipse, this is relative to the passage of the Moon through the penumbra.

If true, this is very surprising, because normally penumbral lunar eclipses are not observable, as the darkening of the Moon's disk is very slight. Perhaps high up on the Tibetan plateau, before the days of industrial pollution, that was not the case. This is very speculative, and I only offer it as a possibility because the numbers match quite well. However, there is a similar, in fact even greater, difference between the Tibetan figures for solar eclipse duration and those derived by modern methods. These cannot be explained in the same way at all.

Timing

In some ways this is trivial, as the Tibetan calculations consider the maximum of an eclipse to occur at the exact time of full Moon. In reality, the maximum is at that time when the centre of the Moon is nearest to the axis of the Earth's shadow, but this makes only a small difference which is not considered in the Tibetan calculations. Half of the duration of an eclipse is called the semiduration, and this length of time before maximum is the moment of first contact with the umbra, the start of the eclipse, and this length of time after maximum is the moment of last contact, the end of the eclipse.

However, many texts discuss the need to go into more detail. One of the main factors that need to be considered is that the length of day and night varies throughout the year, and a lunar eclipse will only be visible if it occurs at night. This needs therefore to be considered by subtracting the time of sunset from the time of maximum eclipse.

Many of the Phugpa texts also discuss subtracting the time of the previous full lunar day in order to determine the length of the 15th lunar day, at the end of which the full Moon occurs. This results in a value between 54 and 64 nāḍī, and this quantity is used to look up a figure in a table, of nāḍī and pala, that is then added to the time of full Moon.

Length of lunar day	Addition
54	0,0
55	1,0
56	1,30
57	2,0
58	2,30
60	3,0
61	3,30
62	4,0
63	4,30
64	5,0

In this list a value for a lunar day length of 59 is not given. This calculation does not seem to be necessary, and according to Lochen Dharmaśrī has been derived from observations rather than the theory. One possible reason for the perceived need for this correction is the error in the timing of mean weekday for new and full Moons in the Phugpa calculations. This may have resulted in observed eclipses occurring later than was predicted by the calculations.

At the time that the Phugpa calculations were being developed, the mean weekday values that were used were too little, by just over eight nāḍī. In other words, for greater accuracy eight nāḍī should be added to the time of mean full Moon when determining the timing of eclipses. This value is quite close to the maximum given for this correction, and I have not been able to find any more convincing explanation for these numbers.

The basis of all these estimates for the timing of the maximum of the eclipse is best summed up by Jamgon Kongtrul (Kongleg, p. 259). He states that one should subtract from the lunar day longitude (the weekday figure of nāḍī, pala, etc.) the length of the day (tables are given in most

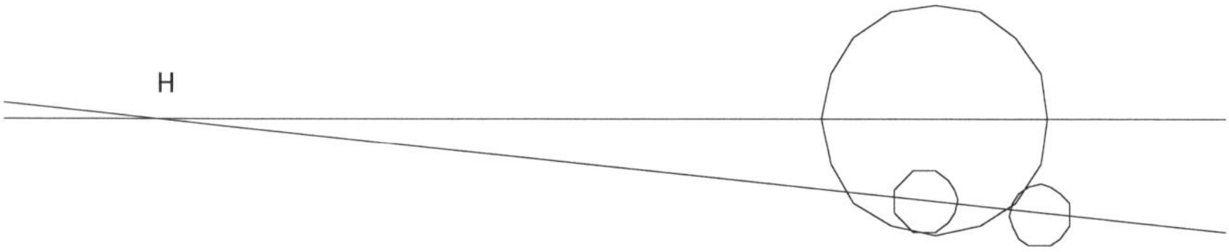

Figure 3c

texts for the length of day and night throughout the year), and then count from the beginning of darkness, the remaining number of nāḍī until the eclipse. He also states that if lunar day longitude is too small, then the beginning of the eclipse will not be visible—in other words it will occur during the daytime.

Direction

For the direction, all the relevant Tibetan texts give basically the same details, describing the direction from which the shadow of the Earth is first seen to touch the Moon. The four types of eclipse mentioned earlier are here categorised into two pairs with similar characteristics. The first pair is Head-Moon and Moon-Tail. The direction will vary according to the time of the occurrence of the eclipse, and these two are represented at midnight respectively in Figures 3c and 3d.

Both of these diagrams represent the view to an observer in the northern hemisphere, looking due south. North is therefore to the top of the diagram, and east is to the left. As in Figures 3a and 3b, the ecliptic—the path here of the centre of the Earth's shadow—is horizontal, parallel to the southern horizon, and the other line crossing it is the path of the Moon. The larger circle represents the shadow of the Earth, and the Moon, which is travelling towards the left, is shown in two positions, just after first contact with the shadow, and then at maximum eclipse. H is the Head of Rāhu and T is the Tail.

Both diagrams are shown near the limits of total eclipse as it is at these limits that the direction of the eclipse is also at its limits. It is clear in both diagrams that the first part of the Moon that is obscured by shadow is the upper left, which in these diagrams is the north-east direction from the centre of the Moon.

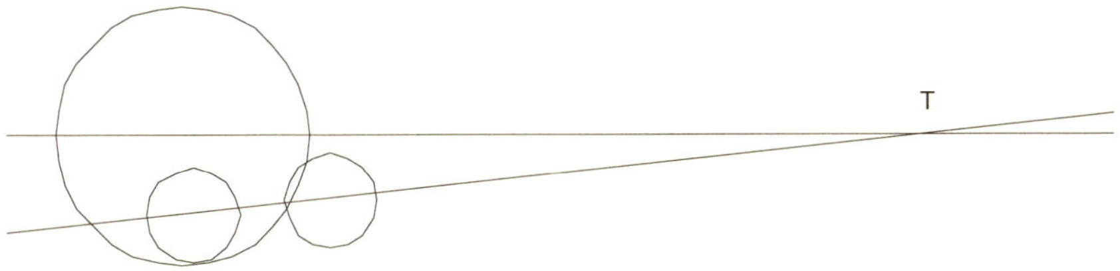

Figure 3d

In the left hand diagram of Figure 3e the Head-Moon eclipse is shown early in the evening, with the Moon not far above the eastern horizon, perhaps an hour or two after it has risen. The observer is looking a little north of east, and the ecliptic is oriented quite steeply compared to the horizon. In this diagram east is now approximately downwards, with north to the left, and the first part of the Moon to be touched by shadow is in the north from the point of view of the Moon. The orientation for Moon-Tail is almost identical.

In the right hand diagram of Figure 3e the same Head-Moon eclipse is shown very late at night, with the Moon not far above the western horizon, perhaps an hour or two before setting. In this diagram west is approximately downwards, with north to the right, and so the first part of the Moon to be eclipsed is in the east from the point of view of the Moon. Chenrab Norbu states here that the direction is east of north-east, which would suggest a steeper inclination of the ecliptic than shown in Figure 3e. The actual inclination will vary according to the time of year and the observer's latitude. I have chosen an example inclination for these diagrams of 60° as an average for Tibet. It will vary throughout the

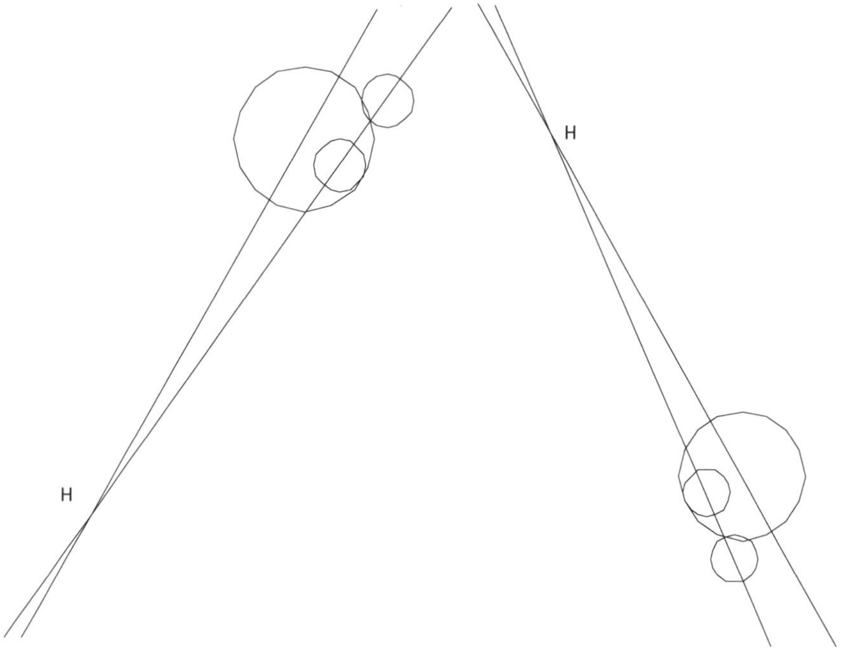

Figure 3e

year through a range 23° either side of this figure. Again, the geometry for a Moon-Tail eclipse is essentially the same as for Head-Moon.

The other pair of eclipses is represented at midnight in the upper diagram of Figure 3f for Moon-Head and the lower diagram for Tail-Moon. In both cases the first part of the Moon to be touched by shadow is now the south-east, the lower left side of the Moon in the diagrams.

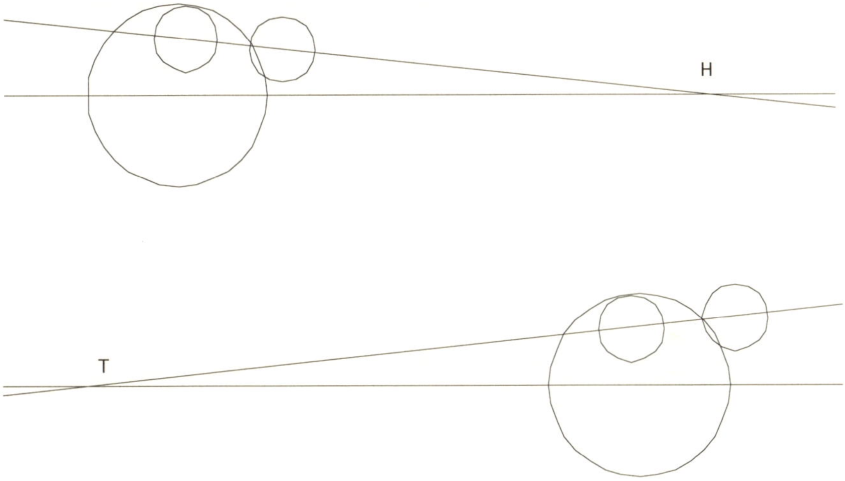

Figure 3f

In the evening (Figure 3g, left diagram), shortly after Moonrise, the direction will be more towards the east (Chenrab Norbu says due east) and in the early hours of the morning (Figure 3g, right), shortly before the Moon sets, the direction will be south of south-east.

Finally, there is the case of a maximum eclipse, when a node coincides with the centre of the earth's shadow. This is represented at midnight for an ascending node (Rahu's Head) eclipse in Figure 3h. The direction is almost exactly along the line of the ecliptic and is therefore from the east. In the evening it will be from the north-east and in the early hours of the morning from the south-east. The geometry for an eclipse by the Tail will be almost identical.

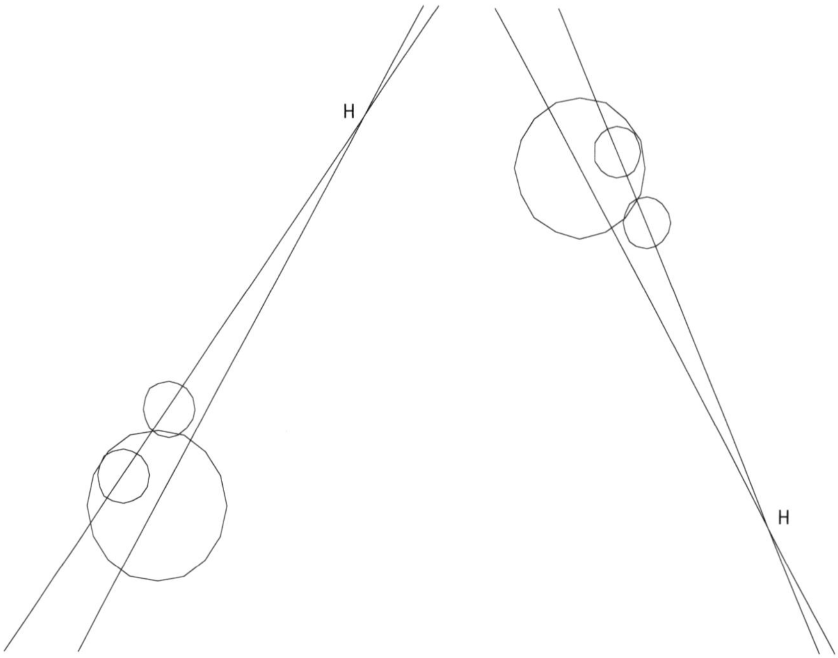

Figure 3g

Colour

All writers agree that for a lunar eclipse by the Head of Rāhu the colour will be dark red and by the Tail, light red. The Moon is still visible during a total eclipse because some light from the Sun refracts in the Earth's atmosphere and lightly illuminates the Moon. Just as refracted sunlight at dawn or dusk is predominantly red, so is the light that reaches the Moon in this way during eclipse.

Kongtrul (Kongleg, P. 260) likens the colour of a total eclipse to that of molten iron, and adds that at the extremes of the night, soon after sunset and shortly before dawn, the colour is smoky. A very similar comment to this is found by Varāhamihira in his *Pañcasiddhānta* (Pañca, p. 165). However, Varāhamihira does not describe differences in colour between Head and Tail eclipses, and there is no immediately obvious reason why there should be such differences.

For a partial eclipse it is said that the colour will be darker, the degree of darkening depending inversely on the magnitude of the eclipse.

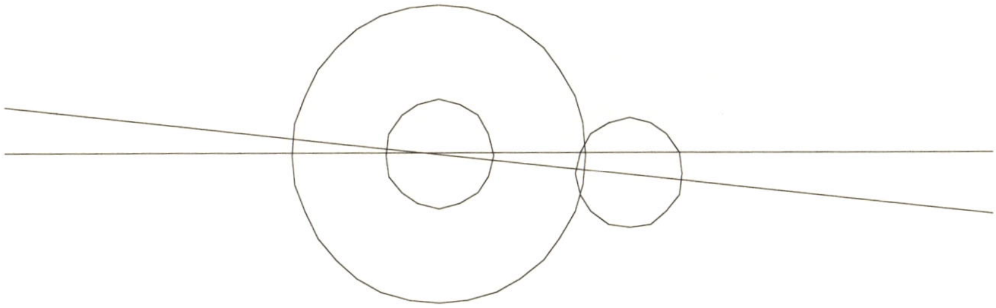

Figure 3h

Lochen Dharmaśrī (Nangser, p. 256) correctly points out that this is due to contrast. Because the part of the Moon that is in shadow is right next to the part that is still illuminated, by contrast it appears much darker, although the actual illumination within the shadow is the same as in a total eclipse.

It is further said that if the eclipse occurs with the Moon in the lunar mansions of either Mṛgaśiras or Ārdrā, then the colour will be the same as the colour of the sky (blue, according to Kongtrul, who also adds Rohiṇī to the list, making three consecutive lunar mansions). Such eclipses will occur in the 11th Tibetan month, late November or early December.

Solar eclipses

The basic device used in the Tibetan determination of solar eclipses is the same as that with lunar eclipses—the difference between the position of the eclipsed body (here, the Sun, taken at new Moon) and the nearest of the two nodes. However the situation is much more complex, and the results far less reliable.

Chenrab Norbu states that one should take the siddhānta new Moon true solar longitude, the corrected Head or Tail, depending which is nearest, and subtract the smaller figure from the larger.

Clearly, the same correction applies to solar eclipses as with lunar eclipses. He then describes the possibilities for the four types of eclipse. If the Head was subtracted from the Sun and the node-distance is less than 50 nāḍī there will certainly be an eclipse.

If the Sun was subtracted from the Head and if the node-distance is less than five nāḍī, then it is said that there can be an eclipse but this position is called the contrary position (*go log*) for the Head and an eclipse should not occur.

If the Tail was subtracted from the Sun and the node-distance is less than eight nāḍī, then this is the contrary position for the Tail, but an eclipse is possible.

If the Sun was subtracted from the Tail and the node-distance is less than 40 nāḍī, there will certainly be an eclipse.

In these figures—those given by other writers are very similar—there is the same asymmetry that was present with lunar eclipses where an eclipse by the Head of Rāhu was somewhat more likely than an eclipse by the Tail. With these figures for solar eclipses, however, there is another factor—these two types of eclipse which are called contrary, Head-Sun and Sun-Tail.

The best way to understand these differences is to estimate using modern theory the numbers one might expect for observations of eclipses made from Tibet.

Solar eclipses are much more complex to predict than lunar. The reason for this is that the position of the observer on the Earth makes a significant difference. For proper total eclipses—those that are not annular—the shadow of total eclipse on the surface of the Earth is usually only a few tens of miles across. The shadow—known as the penumbra—under which a partial eclipse is seen is much larger, and is in diameter on average just a little larger than the radius of the Earth.

So it is quite possible for a total solar eclipse to be visible, say, in the southern hemisphere, with a partial solar eclipse of varying magnitude to be visible throughout the southern hemisphere, but no eclipse at all visible in the north, except perhaps near the equator.

There is no component of the Tibetan calculations for eclipses that corrects for an observer's position on the Earth. However, the numbers used in attempting to predict eclipses are clearly based on observations in the northern hemisphere, and are asymmetrical largely because of this.

Although they were not devised with this intention in mind, as geographical position is not considered, the basic calculations are effectively relative to the centre of the Earth. For a total solar eclipse to be visible in the northern hemisphere, at the time of new Moon (conjunction with the Sun) the Moon will need to be somewhat to the north of the line between the centres of the Earth and the Sun. (From the point of view of the centre of the Earth, and therefore the basic calculations, the Moon will need to be slightly to the north of the Sun for its shadow to fall in the northern hemisphere.)

For the Moon to be north of the Sun at the time of conjunction there are two possibilities. It will either have just passed the ascending node (Head), travelling northwards, and therefore the longitude of the Sun and Moon (which are the same at conjunction) will be a little greater than that of the node. The other possibility is that it will be shortly before the descending node (Tail), travelling southwards, and the longitude of the Sun will be a little less than that of the node.

In the first of these instances the Head will be subtracted from the Sun, and in the latter the Sun will be subtracted from the Tail.

There are extreme positions possible, when the Moon is even further to the north, and the observer sees the Moon just touch the Sun, creating an eclipse of small magnitude. The other extreme is in the opposite direction, and the Moon might well be further south to such an extent that it is actually south of the Sun at the time of conjunction (from the point of view of the centre of the Earth).

In that case the two possibilities will be different from before. If the Moon is close to the ascending node (Head), it will need to be just behind the node, so that it is south of the Sun, travelling northwards, shortly before crossing the node. The other possibility is that it will have just passed the descending node (Tail), travelling south. In the first of these instances the Sun will be subtracted from the Head, and in the other the Tail will be subtracted from the Sun.

These give the four possibilities mentioned in the texts. In order to estimate the position of the nodes for these combinations, it is best first to determine the position the Moon would have to be in for a total solar eclipse to be visible in the northern hemisphere.

In addition to the fact that the orbit of the Moon is inclined at an angle to the ecliptic, the equator of the Earth makes a varying angle to the ecliptic, the maximum values being just over 23°. This inclination will have a significant effect on the visibility of solar eclipses, but it can be ignored it for the present purpose.

The Tibetan system of eclipse prediction is very simple, and to understand the numbers it uses one can safely deal here with averages, and consider the average situation where the Sun lies in the plane of the Earth's equator. This actually only happens twice each year, at the equinoxes. I

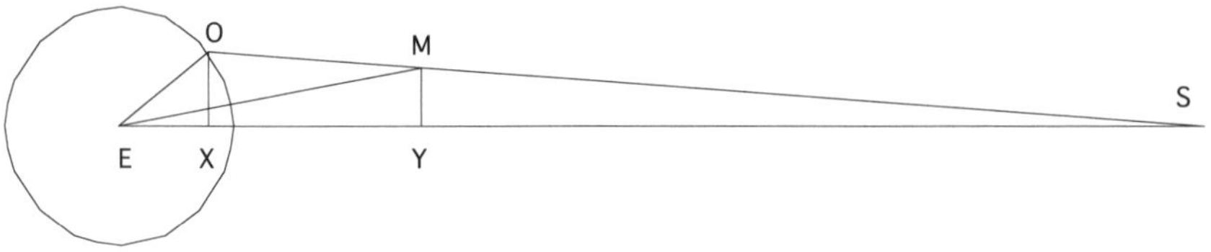

Figure 3i

am also going to ignore the time of day and the small differences between the timing of maximum eclipse and true new Moon.

Taking the position of Lhasa as a typical site for observations, Figure 3i represents—it is not to scale—the positions of the Sun and Moon relative to the Earth at the time of a total solar eclipse. E is the centre of the Earth and O is the observer's position on the surface of the Earth—the surface shown as a circle, with north to the top. M is the centre of the Moon and S the centre of the Sun. A total solar eclipse is visible at O because O, M, and S lie in a straight line. The angle OEX is the latitude of the observer and it is necessary to find the angle MES, the angular distance the Moon is north of the Sun.

Taking the latitude of the observer to be that of Lhasa, 29°6 north, the angle MES calculates as 0°47.

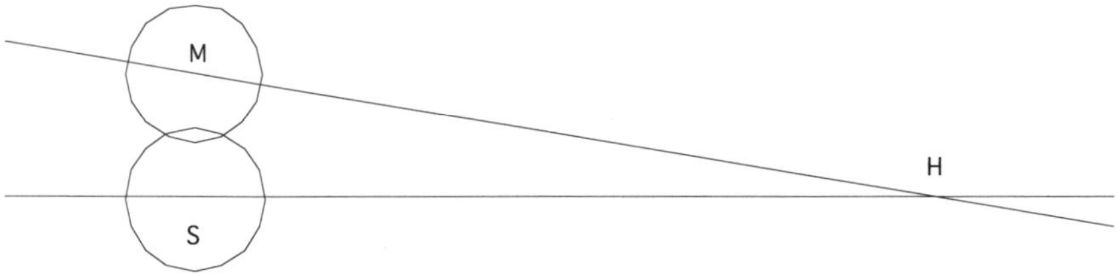

Figure 3j

The case when the longitudes of the Sun and Moon are a little greater than that of the ascending node—this is called eclipse by the Head, and the Head is subtracted from the Sun—is represented in Figure 3j, from the point of view of the centre of the Earth. North is to the top, and the disks of the Sun and Moon are represented as two circles. The horizontal line through the diagram is the ecliptic, the path of the Sun. Both the Sun and Moon are travelling from right to left in the diagram—ecliptic longitude increases from right to left.

The line at an angle to the ecliptic is the path of the Moon, and this passes through H, the point of intersection of the Moon's path with the ecliptic. This point is the ascending node, the Head of Rāhu. As before, the angle of inclination of the Moon's orbit has been exaggerated here for clarity, but the relative sizes of the disks of the Sun and Moon, and their distance apart are to scale, sizes taken being average values.

The centre of the Moon in the diagram, M, is 0°.47 north of the centre of the Sun, S. This is the position determined for a total solar eclipse to be visible in Tibet. Simple trigonometry, given that the angle of inclination of the Moon's orbit is 5°.15, yields the distance SH, the difference in longitude between the Sun and the node—in this instance, Sun-Head. This works out to 5°.20, or 23 nāḍī and 24 pala.

The case where the eclipse is by the Tail, and the Moon is heading south at conjunction, just before reaching the Tail, or descending node, is a mirror image of this situation, and would yield the same numerical result. In other words Tail-Sun would be equal to 23 nāḍī 24 pala.

It is now simple to adjust the calculations to derive the extreme positions where eclipses are just visible from the point O in Figure 3h. Considering a point north of O by a distance equal to the radius of the penumbra—taken as 3,535 kilometres—gives the distance between the Sun and the Head as 11°.04, or 49 nāḍī 40 pala.

Moving to a point 3,535 kilometres to the south of O actually takes it south of the line ES, and so this situation gives us the two possibilities when the Sun is subtracted from the Head, and when the Tail is subtracted from the Sun. The distance of the node in these instances turns out to be 0°.63, or 2 nāḍī 51 pala.

To summarise, these estimated values and the values given by Chenrab Norbu and other writers, are:

	Estimate	**Rigthig**	**Baidkar**	**Nangser**	**Kongleg**
Sun-Head	49,40	50	52	45 (50)	40
Tail-Sun	49,40	40	40	40	40
Head-Sun	2,51	5	5	5	5
Sun-Tail	2,51	8	7	8	8

The figures for the estimates are given in nāḍī and pala, the other figures only in nāḍī. The value of 50 in brackets is given because Lochen

Dharmaśrī gives 45 nāḍī as his determinant, but states that eclipses are possible up to values of 50 nāḍī.

The values I have estimated here are certainly close to those used by the Tibetans—and presumably developed by them by observational trial and error. At least these estimates satisfactorily explain the so-called contrary positions for solar eclipses, but it is also noticeable that the Tibetan figures are asymmetrical—50 and 40, instead of say, 45 and 45—and mine are not.

The situation is very similar to that with lunar eclipses, and it is most likely that this asymmetry is due to the error in the Phugpa difference between the position of the nodes and either the Sun or Moon. As with lunar eclipses, that error allows larger values for the node-distance when a node is subtracted from the Sun than when the Sun is subtracted from a node. As the Tsurphu figures for the Sun-node are more accurate, the figures quoted by Kongtrul for Sun-Head and Tail-Sun do not show this asymmetry except for the southern eclipse extremes.

There are many other factors that affect these figures, and the intention here has been to illustrate the principles underlying these Tibetan calculations. In fact, the estimated figures would be closer to the Tibetan ones if I had chosen as an average observation point places somewhat south of Lhasa—north-eastern India, for example.

As mentioned previously, the inclination of the equator of the Earth to the ecliptic would further complicate the calculations. During the winter, because of the north pole tilting away from the Sun, the observer in Lhasa would be further to the north of the line connecting the centres of the Earth and the Sun. This would increase the values for Sun-Head and Tail-Sun, and reverse those for Head-Sun and Sun-Tail. In fact, such eclipses would not be visible from Lhasa, and the southern extreme would be north of the line connecting the centres of the Earth and Sun.

Put another way, one extreme would be high values of Sun-Head and Tail-Sun, and the other extreme would be low values of the same. Total eclipses would have values roughly half way between these extremes.

During the summer, the North Pole tilts towards the Sun, bringing Lhasa further south in relation to the line connecting the centres of the Earth and Sun. This would lower the figures for Sun-Head and Tail-Sun, and increase those for Head-Sun and Sun-Tail, making them almost equal in value, but not quite. This means that close to the summer solstice, and only near that time, eclipses of Head-Sun and Sun-Tail will be almost as likely as eclipses of Sun-Head and Tail-Sun.

For much of the year, around winter time, only eclipses by the Head when the value of the longitude of the Sun is greater, and eclipses by the Tail when the Tail is greater, will be visible from Tibet. Eclipses when the Sun is subtracted from the Head or when the Tail is subtracted from the Sun are only likely in the summer, they are rare in spring and autumn, and they are not possible at all—i.e., not visible from Lhasa—in winter.

Chenrab Norbu makes a very similar point when he says that the experience of previous astronomers has shown that from shortly before the spring equinox until shortly after the autumn equinox, predicted eclipses do occur, but between these times, i.e., during winter, they need more investigation—in other words, they are less likely to occur.

Another factor that I have not considered here is that the varying distance between the Sun and the Earth, and between the Moon and the Earth, would change the sizes of the shadows and therefore some of the values in the example calculations.

Magnitude

The most straightforward method for determining the magnitude of a solar eclipse is given by Chenrab Norbu. Referring only to the two non-contrary types of eclipse he states that if the Sun is eclipsed by the Head of Rāhu, for values of the node-distance of 22 or 23 nāḍī, the eclipse will be total, and if the eclipse is by the Tail, then for values of 19 or 21 the eclipse will be total. For values greater or less than these, the magnitude will progressively decrease.

The figures he gives for total eclipse agree closely with the figures I derived as estimates for a total eclipse visible in Tibet—23 nāḍī and 24 pala. The average of the figures given by Chenrab Norbu here is 21. Again, this suggests a somewhat more southerly location than Lhasa, at a latitude of 26° or 27°.

Other writers attempt to go into more detail than this, giving calculations for the eclipse magnitude. As with lunar eclipses, Sangje Gyatso (Baidkar 1, p. 66) gives a similar calculation, but with different figures, for each of the four eclipse types. He starts by stating that the magnitude of an eclipse is measured in terms of 1/12 parts, so a result of 6 in the following calculations would mean a magnitude of one-half. All of these calculations start with the distance in nāḍī between the Sun and the relevant node.

For a Sun-Head eclipse, he states that the node-distance should be subtracted from 60, the result multiplied by 12 and then divided by 60. It is not clear to me why he simply does not give a division by 5. The result of this has to be adjusted by adding certain values:

if the result is 4 or more, add 3
if 3, add 2
if 2, add 1
if 1, add nothing.

The final result is the magnitude of the eclipse. For Head-Sun the node-distance is first adjusted. If it has a value of 7 or less, then 10 is added to it, if it is more then 5 is added. Then it is subtracted from 60 and multiplied by 5 and divided by 60. Then additions are made to yield the final magnitude:

if 4 or more, add 3
if 3, add 2
if 2, add 1
if 1, add nothing

For Tail-Sun, subtract the node-distance from 54 and then multiply by 12 and divide by 60. He also adds that if the remainder from the division is greater than 30, then the quotient should be rounded up. He seems to make this suggestion only for the present Tail-Sun eclipse. Then, as before:

if 4 or more, add 3
if 3, add 1
if 2, add 1
if 1, add 1

Finally, for Sun-Tail, if the node-distance is 7 or less, adjust it by adding 20, and if it is greater, add 15. Then, subtract from 60, multiply by 12 and then divide by 60. Then:

if 4 or more, add 3
if 3, add 2
if 2, add 1
if 1, add 1

Sangje Gyatso is clearly scaling the numbers to match the different ranges of values of the node-distance that are expected to indicate eclipses. But there are two problems with his method. It yields total eclipse for very small values of the node-distance and it does not have a maximum value either side of which magnitude decreases.

His method is much more similar to that for lunar eclipses, and he may have been trying to fit solar eclipses into a similar pattern.

Kongtrul's method is more simple, but along the same lines and therefore suffers from the same problems. He states that the node-distance is divided by 5. If the result is 0, 1 or 2, then the eclipse is total. Other values give the following magnitudes:

3 - 7/8
4 - 5/6
5 - 1/2
6 - 1/6
8 - 1/8

For contrary eclipses, the value of the node-distance is not divided by 5 but used directly, with the value 5 indicating an eclipse of magnitude half. He states that lower values can indicate a total eclipse but these are difficult in the contrary cases.

Kongtrul also gives an alternative calculation, as follows. Subtract the node-distance from 60 and divide the result by 5. The quotient will lie in a range up to 12, and yields both the magnitude and duration of the eclipse, total eclipse being indicated by values of either 11 or 12.

In the case of contrary eclipses, if the eclipse is by the Head then first multiply the node-distance by 5, if by the Tail multiply by 4. Then subtract from 60 and continue as before.

Duration

Most writers give a simple method for the determination of the duration of a solar eclipse. Magnitude is measured as a fraction of 12 parts, and for each part the duration of the eclipse is one nāḍī. An eclipse of magnitude half will therefore have a duration of 6 nāḍī and a total eclipse 12 nāḍī.

However, as was the case with the duration of lunar eclipses, estimates using modern methods are quite different. Using the same mathematics as with lunar eclipses, in order to travel from first contact, through a total solar eclipse to last contact, the Moon needs to move through both its own apparent diameter and that of the Sun.

Taking mean values, the radius of the Moon is 15.54 minutes of arc and that of the Sun 15.99. For an eclipse of maximum magnitude, the Moon therefore needs to move a distance of:

$$2 \times 15.54 + 2 \times 15.99 = 63.075 \text{ minutes of arc.}$$

The figure I derived earlier for the apparent speed of the Moon, relative to the Sun, was 12.1907 minutes of arc per nāḍī of time.

To travel 63.075 minutes of arc the Moon will therefore take 5.17 nāḍī, a much smaller figure for the maximum duration of a solar eclipse than that given in the Tibetan texts.

The relationship that for each part of the magnitude the duration is one nāḍī explains why Kongtrul states in his alternative calculation for the magnitude of the eclipse that the division by 5 yields both the magnitude and duration.

He also gives an alternative calculation for the duration. For values of the node-distance up to and including seven, add 10, and for higher values add 5. Subtract the result from 60 and then multiply by 12. Divide by 60 and the quotient is the length of duration of the eclipse in nāḍī.

Given that Kongtrul considers non-contrary eclipses to occur only for values of the node-distance up to 40, the range of values that his calculations can yield for the duration of a solar eclipse is from 3 to 10 nāḍī.

Timing

The method for determining the timing of a solar eclipse is given in most texts as basically the same as that described for use with lunar eclipses.

However, Lochen Dharmaśrī adds an interesting point. He states that for the time of maximum eclipse—effectively the same time as true new Moon—the experience of previous astronomers had shown that 4 nāḍī should be added to the weekday value for the time of new Moon. He adds that this should be adjusted for the variable length of the lunar day in the manner that was described for lunar eclipses.

The value for the mean weekday in the Phugpa system is inaccurate, and at the time that Dharmaśrī was writing, it was short by 8.3 nāḍī. In other words, in order to find the true time of new Moon from the Phugpa calculations, 8.3 nāḍī should be added to the figures produced by the calculations. This is larger than the amount described by Dharmaśrī, but his informants had clearly observed the discrepancy due to the weekday error.

Direction

With lunar eclipses, the direction from which the eclipse starts was given for an eclipse at midnight and then at the extremes of early evening and shortly before sunrise. For solar eclipses the direction is given for midday and then at the extremes of early morning and late afternoon.

The directions should all be approximately the reverse of those given for lunar eclipses. For example, with Tail-Moon and Moon-Head lunar eclipses, the Moon approaches the Earth's shadow from the west, and somewhat to the north. Therefore the first limb of the Moon to enter the Earth's shadow is in the south-east, from the point of view of the Moon.

For a solar eclipse, the direction is determined relative to the Sun, and in a similar situation with the Moon approaching the Sun from the west and somewhat to the north, the first limb of the Sun to be obscured by the Moon will be in the north-west, from the point of view of the Sun. These two possibilities, Sun-Head and Tail-Sun, are represented in the upper and lower diagrams in Figure 3k. As before, both diagrams illustrate the view to an observer looking south around midday, with north to the top.

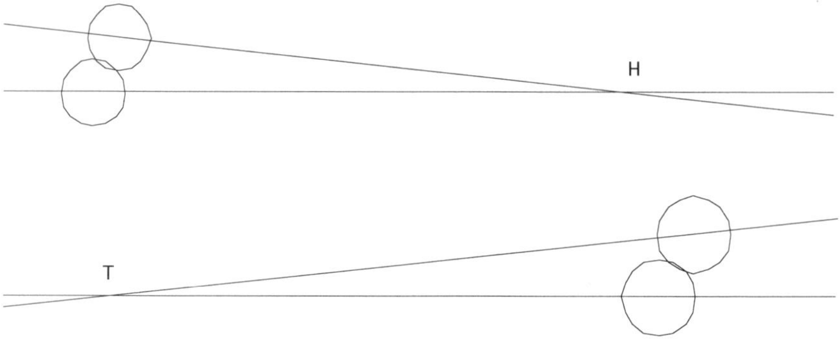

Figure 3k

The upper and lower diagrams in Figure 3l illustrate Head-Sun and Sun-Tail eclipses in which the first part of the Sun to be obscured is in the south-west. Between these two extremes, for total eclipses, the Moon will approach the Sun from almost due west.

Surprisingly, the authors I have consulted on this—Chenrab Norbu, Sangje Gyatso, Lochen Dharmaśrī, and Jamgon Kongtrul—all give a different set of combinations. If the longitude of the Sun is subtracted from either the Head or Tail of Rāhu, then the direction is north-west, and if Rāhu is subtracted from the Sun, then the direction is south-west. Somehow, the directions of the Head-Sun and Sun-Head eclipses have become swapped around in the Tibetan texts. I am not sure when this happened, but the fact that all these writers give the same error indicates the degree to which they depend on each other, or on some earlier common source.

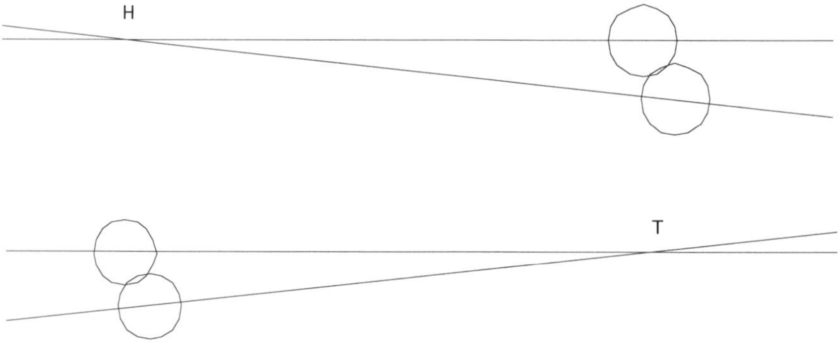

Figure 3l

They all agree that for an eclipse that would start from the south-west at midday, if it occurs early in the morning it will be more to the south, and in the late afternoon, more to the west.

There is not complete agreement regarding an eclipse that would start from the north-west at midday. Chenrab Norbu states that in the morning the direction would be nearer north, and in the afternoon, nearer west. These are clearly the wrong way around, and Kongtrul points out that for a Tail-Sun eclipse, in the morning it would be from the west and in the afternoon from the north. He gives the same directions as Chenrab Norbu for Head-Sun, but writes in a note that it appears that it should be the same as Tail-Sun.

Colour

The main point expressed by all writers regarding the colour of a solar eclipse—by this is meant the colour of the obscured part of the Sun—is that the colour varies due to contrast depending on the magnitude, the fraction of the Sun that is obscured.

If the magnitude is small, then the brightness of the Sun makes the obscured part seem black or deep blue. For larger magnitude eclipses the colour is more red, Kongtrul likening it to copper for a total eclipse. Chenrab Norbu states that eclipse by the Head of Rāhu is a darker red then one by the Tail.

Again, as with lunar eclipses, the comment is made that when the eclipse occurs over the lunar mansions of Mṛigaśiras or Ārdrā, the colour is the same as the sky, light blue.

Interestingly, Chenrab Norbu adds a word of caution, and describes how eclipses of magnitude 2 or 3 (parts out of a maximum of 12) are difficult to observe. He advises a potential observer not to look directly at the Sun because this can damage the eyes. Instead, they should arrange a non-white vessel containing clear water, undisturbed by the wind, and observe the Sun's reflection in the surface of the water.

Tibetan observations of eclipses

Eclipses have clearly been a most problematic area for the Tibetan calendar makers, particularly solar eclipses. The confusion described earlier regarding the direction of initial obscuration of solar eclipses can probably be explained by the simple fact that the Tibetans had very little observational data that made sense to them, in the absence that is, of a theory of eclipses that takes into consideration the curvature of the Earth and the tilt of its axis.

The estimates that I made of the circumstances of eclipses matches the Tibetan data quite closely, but these estimates ignored two important factors which affect the distance of the observer from the line between the centres of the Earth and the Sun, a distance which is crucial to the nature of a solar eclipse. This distance changes as the tilt of the Earth's axis moves around throughout the year, relative to the direction of the Sun, and also as the observer's position moves around the axis during the day.

These two factors mean that the circumstances of solar eclipses vary greatly from the mean values in my estimates. Solar eclipses are rare enough in themselves, but solar eclipses occurring at times close to the equinoxes are even more rare, and only at those times will the circumstances of the eclipse come close to these estimates. This did not go unnoticed by Tibetan astronomers.

Add to this the fact that the Tibetan calculations for the Sun, Moon, and Rāhu contain errors, and one can understand the very difficult nature of the task the Tibetans had in accounting for the eclipses that they observed.

Unfortunately, no systematic records survive of eclipse observations, and in the material I have been consulting I have only found mention of very few eclipses.

For example, when criticizing another's (Zhonnu Pal, see chapter six) calendrical calculations, Norzang Gyatso (Padzhal, p. 446) cites a total lunar eclipse that took place on 26th January 1469. He states that these other calculations gave the longitude of the Moon at the predicted time as 10;11, in the lunar mansion Pūrvaphalgunī, but that the Moon was instead clearly to be seen in the mansion Āśleṣā.

Eclipses make good data points for astronomers, and this is an example of how the position of the Moon was observed in order to work back to the longitude of the Sun, from which the Moon's longitude is calculated. But it also demonstrates that even though Norzang Gyatso used a version of the Kālacakra method for defining the longitude of the Sun using solstice determination, he did not understand the difference between what we now call tropical and sidereal zodiacs.

Chenrab Norbu points out that it is said that whenever the siddhānta 15th or 30th lunar days are omitted, then eclipses are not seen. He goes on to say that even though this is explained, sometimes such eclipses are observed. His comment should only apply to solar eclipses, as when the lunar day is omitted, full or new Moon occurs just before sunrise, and so such a solar eclipse would not be visible, but the restriction of the invisibility of solar eclipses when new Moon falls during the night is not limited only to omitted days.

He states that the methods of eclipse prediction generally work, but with some exceptions. He then cites two of these.

The first was a solar eclipse shortly after midday on the 30th day of the 5th month in the Wood-Dog year of 1814. This was 17th July, and in the siddhānta calendar the 30th lunar day was not omitted, but in the karaṇa calendar it was.

Chenrab Norbu states that in the provinces of U and Tsang (central Tibet) the eclipse was total, day became like night, and the stars were visible. In the province of Kham in eastern Tibet, the maximum magnitude was half.

However, he also states that the Moon was eclipsed on the night of the 22nd of the 8th month in the Water-Sheep year of 1823. This was 26th September, around the time of third quarter, and as lunar eclipses can only occur at full Moon, it is puzzling to consider just what phenomenon caused Chenrab Norbu's informants to consider that one took place during that night.

Epoch data

This description of eclipse predictions based on the position of Rāhu completes the discussion of the main calendrical calculations from the "Essence of the Kalkī" by Chenrab Norbu. In chapter six I shall describe some other calculation systems, and so this is a good point at which to recap the epoch data from Chenrab Norbu's work, including the main calendrical data from chapter one, the general day and the five planets from chapter two, and Rāhu from the present chapter:

Epoch: Friday 1st April 1927. Julian day: 2424972.

True month:	m × 1;2	+ 0;55 (1,65)
Mean weekday:	M × 1;31,50,0,480	+ 6;57,53,2,20 (707)
Anomaly:	M × 2;1	+ 13;103 (28,126)
Mean Sun:	M × 2;10,58,1,17	+ 25;9,10,4,32 (67)
General day:	+2,+178	
Mars:	157	
Jupiter:	3964	
Saturn:	6286	
Mercury:	4639	
Venus:	301	
Rāhu:	187	

CHAPTER IV

The Tibetan Almanac

In the previous chapters I have described most of the calculations used to produce the Tibetan calendar. I use the word "calendar" to refer to two things: the system, including the necessary algorithms and calculations, that determines the start and duration of years, months, and days; and also the structure that this system produces.

This structure is presented in booklets which are produced for each year. These are more properly called almanacs, and contain the calendar itself, listing the months, days, lunar days, planetary positions, eclipses, and so forth, together with historical information, important festivals, some astrological prognostications, particularly for the year concerned, and a large amount of symbolic information that is overlaid on the structure formed by the calendar.

In this chapter I shall describe much of this information and how it is presented in an actual almanac. Many of the raw numbers that have been derived in the previous chapters are usually reproduced in an almanac, but in this chapter I need mainly to describe the symbolic information that is added to them. This information is taken from both Chinese and Indian Buddhist systems, two systems that have effectively been synthesized by the Tibetans. There are also some details that appear to have their origins in ancient Tibet.

Covering the astrological content is beyond the scope of this current work, and so I shall not describe the prognostications and similar material to be found in an almanac. That is really a separate study in its own right. However, the symbolic information, and there is a significant quantity of it, is on the border where the strictly mathematical calendar ends, and astrology begins. It is also covered in some detail in most Tibetan texts on the calendar, including those that do not cover interpretative astrology (*'bras rtsis*).

Most Tibetan almanacs published today have the same overall structure that has been in use for hundreds of years. Major textbooks on the subject contain a specification of the contents of an almanac, and in this chapter I shall mainly follow the description given by Jamgon Kongtrul

(Kongleg, p. 378ff.), although I shall not go into the level of detail that he does—I will restrict myself to the most important features. Naturally, I shall also be relying on several almanacs, published both in Tibet and northern India.

Almanac contents

Typically, there is first a section several pages long containing information relevant to the year as a whole, then sections dealing with each month at a time. For each month there is at least one page containing information specific to the month, and then four or five pages covering details for each day at a time.

The yearly information always starts with an introduction which consists of a few verses in praise of deities associated with the calendar or teachers in the tradition, and which usually includes some verses wishing good fortune.

The first main section consists of a listing of historical information, starting with the earliest data. Then there is a list of several key attributes for the year concerned, usually followed by planetary data, sketching the movements of the five planets throughout the year. This starts a collection of data that is a listing of prognostications for the year from many different sources, a prominent feature of which is usually a drawing and description of the "Earth Ox" for the year.

The next most common feature is a large table with information for a basic level of yearly predictions for the current year for each of the years of the sixty-year cycle. Finally, the yearly information concludes with many minor calculation results, including data regarding the change of year, positions of certain of the earth-lord (*sa bdag, bhūmipati*) demons, and so forth.

Modern almanacs are quite extensive, and contain most of the list just described, but I have seen older ones—going back to the early nineteenth century—that contain very simplified lists of yearly information, covering just a page or two. In the descriptions that follow I shall try to pick what appear to be the most important components of the almanac.

Yearly information

The title of a typical Tibetan almanac will usually contain at least one, and often two names for the year for which the almanac is produced.

There are two issues that should first be considered regarding years—how they are enumerated, and when the new year is considered to start.

The Tibetans use two methods for enumerating their years, one from India and one from China, and they are based on different sixty-year cycles.

There are in fact two main systems in use in India, but they have the same origin in the cycle of Jupiter. In this system, the Jovian year that is current at the beginning of a solar year gives its name—and qualities—to that solar year.

The point is that the period of Jupiter is just less than twelve years, and considering its mean motion, it spends about four days less than a solar year in each zodiacal sign. These periods of time are called in Sanskrit saṃvatsara, which simply means a year, but for the current purpose it is best to refer to them as Jovian years.

Quite why the twelve year cycle of Jupiter became enlarged to a sixty-year cycle is not clear, but there is a list of sixty names applied to these Jovian years, and the name of the Jovian year that is current at the beginning of each solar year is applied to that solar year. Clearly, there will be times when a Jovian year begins very shortly after the beginning of a solar year, and ends just before the end of the solar year. In that case, the Jovian year advances by two in the course of a single solar year, and the Jovian year that starts and finishes within the solar year is said to be expunged. (See Sewell, pp. 32–37 for a fuller description of this cycle.)

This process is very similar in principle to the methods described in chapter one for lunar day numbers and other qualities applying to weekdays. That which is in effect at the beginning of the weekday applies to the whole weekday.

The expunging of years takes place on average every 85 or 86 years, and clearly this is more a cycle of sixty year-names rather than a cycle of sixty years.

This system is still in use in northern India. In the south there is an almost identical system, with the one difference that from about the beginning of the 9th century CE, no years have been expunged. The southern, or Teliṅga, system is therefore no longer properly a Jovian system, but is simply a regular sixty-year cycle. Naturally, the southern naming of the years is now considerably out of step with the northern.

It is this southern system that is used by the Kālacakra Tantra, and this raises the interesting, but small, possibility of a link between the

Kālacakra system and southern India. A further hint at such a link lies in the fact that the Vimalaprabhā states that the Buddha taught the Kālacakra Mūlatantra at the famous great stūpa of Dhānyakaṭaka, in Amarāvatī, southern India.

The sixty-year cycle is generally known by the name of the first year of such a cycle, Prabhava (*rab byung*). A particular beginning of a sixty-year prabhava cycle is mentioned in the Kālacakra Tantra, and it is in this year, 1027, that the Kālacakra is said to have been taken to Tibet, although some sources state that this happened two or three years earlier. Tibetan years are counted from 1027 in terms of numbers of cycles plus the year concerned. The most recent cycle started in 1987, and so the year 1989, the third in this cycle, would be referred to as the year Śuklata in the 17th prabhava cycle. (See Appendix 1 for a full list of the names of the sixty years.)

The prabhava cycle has to be quoted to identify a year properly, and even though these Indian names for the years are quoted in many texts, they are rarely used alone. Nearly always a year is identified by its name from the Chinese sexagenary cycle. 1989 would more fully be called the year śuklata, Earth-Snake of the 17th prabhava.

The Chinese system is a combination of two cycles, the first of which is not apparently based on any astronomical phenomena, and the second of which is similarly based on the cycle of Jupiter.

The first cycle has ten components, usually translated as the ten celestial stems (*gnam gyi rtsa ba, tīan gān* 天干). The Tibetan word *sdong po* is also used (e.g., Kongleg, p. 292). This has more of the meaning of the trunk of a tree than the term *rtsa ba*.

It is often said that the names of the individual stems are not translatable into English. This is because their origins and early meanings are now largely lost (See Needham 2, p. 396). They appear to have been the names of the days in an ancient (Shāng dynasty, c. 1600–1045 BCE) ten day week, to which the attributes that are now associated with them were later added.

These attributes are the five elements, each paired with the qualities yin (*yīn* 阴) and yang (*yáng* 阳). These two very well known Chinese terms are translated into Tibetan in two ways, respectively as 'female' (*mo*) and 'male' (*pho*), or 'understanding' (*shes rab, prajñā*) and 'method' (*thabs, upāya*). The five elements are wood, fire, earth, iron, and water.

These are combined together in pairs, yielding Wood-male, Wood-female, Fire-male, Fire-female, etc. The Tibetans rarely use the original Chinese names for these stems (although Jamgon Kongtrul makes frequent use of Chinese terms such as these transliterated into Tibetan); instead they use Tibetan equivalents to Wood-male (*shing-pho*), and so forth.

The second cycle is that of the twelve earthly branches (*sa'i yan lag, dì zhī* 地支). These are the familiar twelve animals, sometimes wrongly referred to as the Chinese zodiac: the Mouse, Ox, Tiger, Rabbit, Dragon, Snake, Horse, Sheep, Monkey, Bird, Dog, and Pig.

These stems and branches are combined together. The animals Mouse, Tiger, Dragon, Horse, Monkey, and Dog are considered male and so are only combined with the male stems, and the other animals are combined with the female stems. The first year of the Chinese cycle is three years before the prabhava cycle, and starts with Wood-male-Mouse. In the most recent cycle this corresponded to 1984. The following year was Wood-female-Ox, followed by Fire-male-Tiger, and then Fire-female-Rabbit.

This was 1987, the first year of the 17th (Tibetan) prabhava, and all prabhava cycles start with the Fire-Rabbit year. Because every one of these years has the female stem, often it is simply written Fire-Rabbit. The Tibetans nearly always use the Indian sixty-year cycle when quoting dates, and merely note the fact that the Chinese cycle starts with the Mouse year.

The next point to cover is the start of the year, and although Tibetan new year has been fixed for some time now, when they were devising their calendar they certainly had plenty of possibilities from which to choose in both the Indian and Chinese systems.

In chapter one, when describing the months I simply referred to them by number, and stated that the year started with month number one. Strictly speaking, this numbering system is known as the Mongolian month (*hor zla*). This goes back to the time when Drogon Chogyal Phagpa visited Mongolia in the 13th century CE, and decided to set the Tibetan new year to the same as the Mongolian. It was decided to number the months accordingly.

Later, following the example of the Chinese almanac and combining it with the existing system of years, months, days, and double-hours in Tibet, Yungton Dorjepal created the first Sakya almanac, and used this numbering system. His almanac became the main model for the later development of Tibetan almanacs.

There had been several traditions in India for the timing of new year, including more than one in the Buddhist sūtra traditions. The Kālacakra system talks in terms of three types of start to the year.

Two of these depend on specific months. In common with most Indian systems, Kālacakra identifies the months by the names of the lunar mansion in which, on average, the full Moon is seen for the month in question. (The fit is only approximate, but this is a convenient way of naming the months.) They are also defined by the zodiacal sign that the (mean) Sun enters during the month. (If the Sun does not change sign, then the month is intercalary.) Naturally, the lunar mansion that gives its name to the month is opposite in the zodiac to the sign that defines the month, as at full Moon the Sun and Moon are in opposition.

Regarding new year, in the first definition the Kālacakra system identifies (see chapter one) the beginning of the zodiacal sign of Cancer as the birth-sign of the Sun, and this is where it is considered to have been at the beginning of time. For this reason the month Pūrvāṣāḍhā, numbered by the Tibetans as the 6th Mongolian month, during which the Sun enters Cancer, can be considered as the beginning of the year.

The second Kālacakra new year definition is with regard to the solar year, and is the time when the Sun enters the sign of Aries, the first sign of the zodiac. There is a calculation (see chapter five) given in the Kālacakra Tantra for determining the day on which this occurs for each year, and an interpretation of this calculation is perpetuated in modern almanacs.

Finally, the main Kālacakra new year definition specified the month of Caitra as the first of the year. This is the month during which the Sun enters Aries, the beginning of the zodiac, and is also the month during which the Buddha is said to have taught the Kālacakra Mūlatantra.

There were some other variations, particularly in what is said to have been the original intentions of the Mūlatantra. For example, it is said that in the Mūlatantra the beginning of each month was the waning fortnight (*mar ngo*), immediately following full Moon. In the Tantra as it existed when translated into Tibet, the waxing fortnight (*yar ngo*) started each month, following new Moon.

Strictly speaking, the waxing fortnight starts the day after new Moon, and culminates with full Moon. The waning fortnight follows, culminating with the day of new Moon, the very last day of the month.

The month of Caitra as the first of the year is still acknowledged in the Tibetan system. In the calculation in chapter one for the true month count, the count was made from the third month of the Tibetan calendar, and this is the month Caitra. Most Tibetan almanacs start with the third month of the year, and work through to the second month of the following year. From the point of view of the calculations the Tibetans take Caitra as a nominal new year, but this is not the accepted beginning of the civil year.

In a short modern work on the Tibetan calendar (Lithsh, p. 21) Tsewang Lhamo cites four different Chinese traditions for the month that starts the year, stating that the modern Chinese calendar is known as the "xià lì" (夏曆) after the ancient Xià (夏) dynasty (2025 to 1070 BCE). The modern system, the new year definition of which dates from the Han dynasty, starts the year with the month of the Tiger, as did the almanacs in the Xià dynasty.

Tsewang Lhamo also states that when the Chinese system of astrology was introduced into Tibet (seventh century CE) by Kongjo, the Chinese wife of the Tibetan King Songtsen Gampo, the month taken then as the beginning of the year was also Tiger. There were subsequent changes, but the new year has been settled since Drogon Chogyal Phagpa visited Mongolia and the Mongolian numbering was adopted for the months. The Mongolian new year also starts with the Tiger month.

The situation is complicated somewhat by the fact that although the two main calendrical systems in Tibet, the Phugpa and Tsurphu, agree that the first Mongolian month is the start of the year, and that this is identified with the Indian month of Māgha, they do not agree on the Chinese month with which this is identified. The Tsurphu tradition identifies the first Mongolian month as Tiger (the third earthly branch), but the Phugpa identifies the first month as Dragon, making the 11th Mongolian month the Tiger. They both identify this Tiger month as the first month of spring.

Phugpa almanacs also state that the start of the 11th month is the correct Chinese new year (*lo 'go 'khrul med*), a practice to which Tsewang Lhamo (Lithsh, p. 23) quite strongly objects. Given that in the 15th century when the Phugpa calculations were started the start of the 11th month fell between the middle of November and the middle of December, these objections seem perfectly valid.

I should point out that there was one Chinese calendrical system, that of the Xià dynasty, which did align the Tiger month with what one would call in this context the 11th month—the month during which the winter solstice occurs. However, this was the exception rather than the rule, and as the Xià dynasty came to an end with the eclipse of 1070 BCE, it was hardly contemporary with the development of the Phugpa tradition. It has been normal in Chinese calendars for the first earthly branch (Mouse) to be associated with the winter solstice, the 11th Mongolian month, thereby associating the third earthly branch with the 1st month. The third earthly branch is Tiger.

These two main Tibetan traditions have very similar calculations, and so their new years usually fall on the same day, and during the last few hundred years this has more often than not coincided with the same new Moon at the beginning of the Chinese year (plus or minus a day due to different calculations for the timing of true new Moon).

The Chinese year is properly fixed to the tropical zodiac, and so new year is always in the same period in the western calendar, falling in the range 21st January to 21st February inclusive. Because of inaccuracies in the Tibetan calculations, the start of new year is gradually drifting later relative to both the western and Chinese calendars.

When these two traditions were started in the 15th century CE, their new years usually coincided with the Chinese, and when they did not, they fell a month earlier. When their dates for new year differed from each other, the Phugpa would be one month later than the Tsurphu, and so tended to coincide with the Chinese new year a little more often. The situation now is that when they differ from the Chinese new year they are a month later, and it is the Tsurphu system that somewhat more often coincides with Chinese new year.

It certainly seems to have been the original intention for the Tibetan new year to fall at the same new Moon as the Chinese, and this seems best expressed in the Tsurphu tradition (and others, except the Phugpa) by the identification of the first month with the month of the Tiger. When they agree on the new Moon at the beginning of the year, which they usually do, the Tsurphu calendar identifies the same month as Tiger as do Chinese calendars.

Of course there is one difference between the Tibetan and Chinese systems in that the Tibetan month follows the Indian systems and starts on the day following new Moon. With the Chinese system the first day of the month is the new Moon day itself.

One final difficulty here is that the relationship between the Chinese months and the Indian months is not synchronised properly. If the third Tibetan month is the month Caitra, when the Sun enters Aries, you would expect the first month to be the month when the Sun enters Aquarius. But the Tiger month as defined in the Chinese system is the month in which the Sun enters Pisces instead. (The Dragon month, which the Phugpa tradition puts at new year, is defined by the Chinese as the month during which the Sun enters Taurus.)

The reason for this discrepancy is that around the time that the Phugpa and Tsurphu traditions were created, their value for the longitude of the Sun was nearly 20° less than would be given by the tropical zodiac on which the Chinese system and the western calendar are based. In trying to reconcile the Chinese and Indian Kālacakra month and new year definitions—which should not be particularly difficult as their definitions are so similar—most Tibetan calendar makers had an extra difficulty due to their solar longitude being significantly inaccurate.

They clearly did not understand this properly, and so were unable to correct it. This error is increasing, and it is for this reason that the Tibetan new year is slowly drifting later relative to the seasons and the Chinese and western calendars. (See chapter six for a further discussion of this.)

In fact, some recognised the problem, and the famous Indian expert Paṇḍita Vimalaśrī, and others such as the translator Shongton, pointed out that in India and Kashmir the months named Caitra, and so forth, occurred one month before they did in the Tibetan calendars. This advice was noted by the Tibetans (for example, Padzhal, p. 33) but apparently ignored by most of them. As Shongton was translating in the 13th century CE the problem is clearly an old one and predates the Phugpa and Tsurphu calendars.

Historical information

The first main section of yearly information in a Tibetan almanac is a listing of historical information. This starts with the earliest data, giving for each event the year in terms of the Chinese element and animal, and the count of years up to the year for which the almanac is calculated.

Naturally, the Chinese year identifications for years before 1027 have been worked out retrospectively by the Tibetans, and they have not been immune from errors. While compiling and checking the list of historical information that is in Appendix 2 at the back of this book, I found very few errors in data since 1027, but significantly more for the previous years. One difficulty also lies in the fact that the Indians, from whom many of these data came, were not as interested as the Tibetans in correct chronological information, and took far less care with it.

In the calculation examples in earlier chapters I have used 1995 as an example. In a Phugpa almanac for that year, the birth of the Buddha is given as the Earth-Monkey year, 2,955 years before the year of the almanac. This works out to 961 BCE, taking into account the fact that in the western calendar there is no "year zero."

There are three distinct categories of historical information presented in this list, and it is convenient for our present purposes to deal with these separately. These are dates associated with the life of the Buddha, dates associated with the land of Sambhala and the acts of its kings, and finally, normal historical data dealing with the kings of Tibet, important events in Tibet, and the birth or activities of important teachers. The dates associated with Sambhala and normal Tibetan historical data are given in Appendix 2.

The main focus of these three categories is the development and spread of the teachings of Buddhism, and so this whole subject is usually called "Account/calculation of the teachings" (*bstan rtsis*).

There are many different traditions for the timing of the life of the Buddha in Tibet, and these mostly place him some time before the period suggested by the work of most modern historians. The most commonly accepted date for the birth of the Buddha in areas south of Tibet is that given in the Theravada system, 624 BCE, about three hundred years later than the date given in the Phugpa system.

However, these different traditions agree closely on the relative timing of the events in the life of the Buddha. The best comparative discussion on this subject that I have seen is by Mipham (MiKal 1, p. 358 ff.) and I shall follow his example and take the Phugpa tradition as a reference point. According to that tradition, the key points in the life of the Buddha occurred at the following times:

962 BCE, Earth-Sheep: On the evening of the 15th of the month of Āṣāḍha, the Buddha entered the womb of his mother. He stayed in the womb for nine whole months and 23 days.

961 BCE, Iron-Monkey: On 7th of the month of Vaiśākha, having completed 10 months in the womb, the Buddha was born at Lumbini.

933 BCE, Earth-Mouse: In his 29th year, the Buddha observes suffering in the world and renounces his royal life, leaving the palace.

927 BCE, Wood-Horse: Having practised meditation for six years, in his 35th year, at the time of the lunar eclipse on the 15th of the month of Vaiśākha, the Buddha achieved full enlightenment in what is now known as Bodhgaya. In the original descriptions of the Phugpa tradition (Padzhal, p. 83) details are given for this date based on the Phugpa calculations. This enables the identification of the date as Sunday, 17th March 927 BCE.

A month later, on the 4th of the month of Āṣāḍha, the Buddha teaches for the first time, the so-called first turning of the Wheel of the Dharma, in the deer park at Varanasi.

881 BCE, Iron-Dragon: In his 81st year, on 15th of the month of Caitra, the Buddha revealed the Kālacakra Mūlatantra.

On the 15th of the following month of Vaiśākha, the Buddha passed into Nirvāṇa.

There are other details regarding the life of the Buddha that can be included in an almanac, but most often these are the ones that are given.

Mipham lists nine other timings given by previous teachers for the Nirvāṇa of the Buddha, ranging from three years later than that given by the Phugpa, to 406 years later.

One of these places the Nirvāṇa 337 years later than the Phugpa, in 544 BCE. Mipham says that this system was followed by the highly renowned Indian Kālacakra experts Abhayākara and Śākyaśrībhadra (also known as the Kashmiri Pandit Śākya Śrī), and also the Nepali translator Namkha Zangpo (*nam mkha' bzang po*). Interestingly, this timing agrees with the southern Theravada chronology, and places the birth of the Buddha in 624 BCE.

Mipham also describes different views on the year in which the Buddha taught the Kālacakra. For example, he cites Buton (*bu ston*) as giving the teaching of Kālacakra in 879 BCE, the year before the Nirvāṇa. Others held the view that the Kālacakra was taught during the year following the Enlightenment. (See Grönbold for a discussion of the subject of the timing of the life of the Buddha.)

Mipham concludes his discussion of the different views regarding the timing of the life of the Buddha by giving the chronology according to the Tsurphu tradition, as follows:

958 BCE, Water-Pig: The Buddha enters the womb of his mother.

957 BCE, Wood-Mouse: The birth of the Buddha on the 8th of the month of Vaiśākha. (Note that the Phugpa tradition has the 7th of the same month, four years earlier.)

923 BCE, Earth-Dog: Enlightenment.

878 BCE, Water-Sheep: Teaching of Kālacakra, followed a month later by Nirvāṇa.

Mipham goes on to state that the Tsurphu tradition is in accordance with the count of years given in the Kālacakra Tantra, although as we shall see the match is not perfect.

Certainly, trying to match historical information obtained from India with the timings (if taken literally) given in the Tantra, would have given the early Tibetan writers considerable difficulty. The timings given in the Tantra refer to the activities of the kings of Sambhala following the Nirvāṇa of the Buddha, and lead right up to 1027 CE, when the Kālacakra teachings were introduced into Tibet.

The key points are these (see chapter five for the discussion of this chronology in the Vimalaprabhā):

600 years after the Nirvāṇa is the time of the Sambhala king Yaśas. After his reign of 100 years starts a period of 800 years, after which is the time of the barbarian, the development of Islam. 403 years later is the start of the prabhava cycle that is relevant to the Tantra. Also, 182 years after the time of the barbarian is the calculation epoch for the Tantra, when the king Aja reformed (or perhaps developed) the calendar.

In chapter five I describe how we can derive three of these dates fairly easily. The timing of the barbarian is two years later than would be expected, 624 CE, instead of 622. The epoch of the Tantra is 806, and the relevant prabhava cycle started in 1027. Working backwards, 1,400 years before 624 takes us to 877 BCE.

As we have seen, the Tsurphu tradition places the Nirvāṇa in 878 BCE, and it is fair to say that the Tsurphu system comes closer than any other to fitting the data in the Tantra. The round numbers given of a period of 600 years, then 100 years followed by another 800 years suggests that perhaps these periods are more symbolic (or approximate) than literal, but the Tibetans have tried to take them literally and fit them into the chronology.

The Vimalaprabhā gives a list of the dharma-kings of Sambhala, each of whom is said to have reigned for a period of 100 years. These were then followed by a list of 25 kalkī-kings, all of whom are considered to reign for 100 years, except for the tenth (Samudravijaya, 182 years) and the 11th (Aja, 221 years). (See chapter five for some further explanation of the origin of the kalkī line.)

However, these numbers of years are not given in the Vimalaprabhā, only the names of the kings. The only one to whom we can unambiguously assign a date as being within his reign is Aja, and that date is the Tantra epoch of 806. It is usually assigned to the first year of his reign.

Counting back from his time gives the start of the reign of Samudravijaya as 624. Before him were the seven dharma-kings and nine kalkī-kings, with each reigning for 100 years. This makes the start of the reign of the first king, Sucandra, who is said to have requested the Kālacakra teachings from the Buddha, 977 BCE.

According to Karma Ngelek Tendzin, one of the main writers of the Tsurphu tradition, Sucandra died in 877 BCE, the year following the Nirvāṇa of the Buddha, and his son Sureśvara ascended the throne. This would have Sucandra reigning for 100 years.

600 years later, 277 BCE, is the time of the first kalkī, Yaśas; he reigns for 100 years, and then a further 800 years brings us to 624 CE, the "year of the barbarian," at the same time as which is said to have started the reign of Samudravijaya.

Ngelek Tendzin simply states the value of 900 years, the 100 years of Yaśas and the 800 given in the Tantra, without breaking it down into further detail.

The reasonings for many of these differences in the traditions are not properly explained, at least in the texts that survive to this day. The basic information on which the chronology of the life of the Buddha is based comes from sūtras such as the Lalitavistara and the Sūryagarbha together with their various commentaries, but the information is scant and open to multiple interpretations, as is the little information about the Sambhala kings.

Regardless of all these differences, the main data for the Buddha's life as found in modern almanacs comes from either the Phugpa or Tsurphu traditions as given above. The three categories of historical information are merged together in an almanac and presented with the earliest item—usually the entry of the Buddha into the womb of his mother—coming first.

Another important year that is sometimes seen is that of the enthronement of the first Tibetan king, Nyatri Tsenpo (*gnya' khri btsan po*) in 127 BCE. Counting from that year gives a Tibetan royal date, sometimes used in almanacs. In this system, the Tibetan year starting early in 2006 CE is considered to be year 2133.

Symbolic information

After the historical data just described, the almanac then usually includes a short section that gives symbolic attributes and similar data for the year concerned. In fact, most of the rest of what follows in the almanac is based on what I am loosely calling symbolic information. Essentially this is a set of various attributes derived from both Indian and Chinese systems, and applied to the years, months, and days. (Subdivisions of a day are mentioned, but the almanac user needs to derive most of this, if it is needed.)

Most of these attributes come from the Chinese system of astrology. There is much more available from the Indian Kālacakra system than is actually used in Tibetan almanacs. For example, there is a set of vowels and consonants, and multiple combinations of these, that are used in Kālacakra as the basis for its symbolism. This symbolism links the outer world, which includes the cycles of the planets, months, days, and so forth, with the inner world of the seeds, winds, and channels, and with the maṇḍala and deities of the Kālacakra system of practice (see chapter five for some further details on this).

This is a complex system of symbolism, arguably the most integrated and comprehensive such system Buddhism has produced, and yet it hardly merits more than a mention in modern Tibetan almanacs. Perhaps the main reason for this is that the Tibetans had a history of using the Chinese system for at least three hundred years before the Kālacakra was introduced to Tibet, and they have tended to stay with this, presumably because of having felt comfortable with it.

Whatever the reason, this system of Kālacakra symbolism is described in textbooks on the calendar, and so it is something I need to include here. However, there are attributes from India that are included in Tibetan almanacs, and these are the five components that form the basis of the whole calendar structure—the calculations for which were covered in chapter one.

Before detailing how these Indian and Chinese attributes are applied to the components of the calendar, we should first consider the basic symbolism of both the Kālacakra and Chinese systems.

Kālacakra symbolism

The basis of the Kālacakra system of symbolism is the Sanskrit alphabet, and I should first describe this. The alphabet consists of vowels and consonants that are changed and combined in various ways. A modern textbook on Sanskrit grammar would give a list of 25 consonants, to which a few others are added in a separate classification. The Kālacakra system is a variant on the standard grammatical system, and classifies the consonants in the following way:

	hard	hard aspirate	soft	soft aspirate	nasal	hard spirant
Velar	ka	kha	ga	gha	ṅa	ḥka
Palatal	ca	cha	ja	jha	ña	śa
Retroflex	ṭa	ṭha	ḍa	ḍha	ṇa	ṣa
Dental	ta	tha	da	dha	na	sa
Labial	pa	pha	ba	bha	ma	ḥpa

For the terms hard and soft, voiceless and voiced are often used. Also guttural is sometimes used instead of velar, and cerebral instead of retroflex. Notice that all the consonants are considered to have the simple vowel "a" inherent within them. This can become changed to other vowels.

The two spirants, ḥka and ḥpa are old aspirants (*jihvāmūlīya* and *upadhmānīya*) that have long fallen from use, but are used symbolically in Kālacakra. Strictly speaking, they each represent the respective aspirant followed by the consonant ka or pa, each treated here as one spirant. The aspirant that is still in use is the visarga, and this is transliterated as "ḥ." This makes a common ending to many Kālacakra syllables, as does the anusvāra, written "ṃ," which indicates that the vowel inherent in the syllable is nasalized.

There are several ways of categorising the vowels. A modern Sanskrit textbook would usually list five basic vowels: a, i, ṛi, u, and ḷi. (Also, a modern textbook would almost certainly not print the "i" that I have shown with ṛi and ḷi. I am using these as they make pronunciation somewhat easier for people not familiar with Sanskrit. I am also ordering them in the same way as found in most of the Kālacakra literature.)

Each of these vowels can be lengthened, and the long vowel is represented in transliteration by a bar over it. The long vowels are therefore: ā, ī, ṛī, ū, and ḷī. The last of these never occurs in Sanskrit, but is needed for Kālacakra symbolism.

These vowels can also undergo changes known as gradation, which implies successive strengthening of the vowels. These grades are known as guṇa and vṛiddhi. For the basic vowels, the Kālacakra system often adds a sixth in the form of aṃ, and their respective grades are:

Normal:	a	i	ṛi	u	ḷi	aṃ
guṇa:	a	e	ar	o	al	aḥ
vṛiddhi:	ā	ai	ār	au	āl	āḥ

One final classification that we need to consider is the interchange between the standard five vowels and their respective semi-vowels. Again, the Kālacakra list is different from a standard Sanskrit list, which would normally only include the middle four of each of the following groups:

Vowel:	a	i	ṛi	u	ḷi	aṃ
Semi-vowel:	ha	ya	ra	va	la	haṃ
Long vowel:	ā	ī	ṛī	ū	ḷī	aḥ
Long semi-vowel:	hā	yā	rā	vā	lā	hāḥ

In the relationship between the different things that are categorised in the outer and inner worlds, and the symbolism of the maṇḍala and deities of Kālacakra, these vowels and consonants, together with further combinations of them, are used to indicate the category to which something belongs. The syllables represent the quality or combinations of qualities inherent in the things being categorised.

We have seen that there are groups of four (taking the standard Sanskrit analysis), five and six sets of vowels, and the consonants are arranged in six groups of five. There are therefore many permutations possible of combinations.

A simple example that will have an immediately obvious relationship to the calendar is the combination of the 30 consonants, in six groups, with the twelve short and long vowels. These come to a total of 360, and are associated in the outer world with the 360 lunar days of the year, and in the inner world with 360 channels in the joints of the limbs, hands, and feet. In the triple maṇḍala they are associated with the 360 deities of the lunar days in the body palace, and in the chief deity Kālacakra, with the knuckles of his 24 hands (three to each finger).

Before moving on to describe more of the things that are symbolised, I should introduce some of the main structures discussed by Buddhism. An important concept in Buddhist theory that is central to Kālacakra symbolism is the five skandhas. These are form (*gzugs, rūpa*), sensation (*tshor ba, vedanā*), interpretation (*'du shes, saṃjñā*), response (*'du byed, saṃskāra*) and consciousness (*rnam shes, vijñāna*). These are components in the process of perception, and Buddhism describes this overall structure as that which is conceptually clung to as the self.

To give a very brief description of these, form is the physical structure of the sense organs and sense objects. The combination of these two produce sensations, which are then subject to interpretation, given names, associations, and so forth. The mind then produces a response to the situation, and there is a consciousness of the whole experience. As is often the case with Kālacakra, that standard list from Buddhism is increased in the Kālacakra system by the addition of a sixth skandha, awareness (*ye shes, jñāna*).

In the impure, unenlightened state, they are described in that way, but when purified, they are represented by five buddhas, or six in the case of Kālacakra. There are also other groupings of factors within sentient experience that are treated in a similar manner. These include such things as the senses, organs, and main bodily activities. Also in these lists are the five elements. The usual list is of space, wind, fire, water, and earth, but in Kālacakra the list is often extended by the addition of the sixth element of awareness, also known as the "empty element."

Another related set of concepts is that of the five emotional defilements (*nyon mongs, kleśa*) that drive the actions of beings. The pure awareness is considered to be obscured, and when the obscurations are removed, the result is the pure state of enlightenment. There are usually considered to be two types of obscurations, conceptual and emotional. The main conceptual obscuration is the perception of the five skandhas as a self.

The emotional obscurations are the five defilements of bewilderment (*gti mug, moha*), desire (*'dod chags, rāga*), aversion (*khong khro, dveśa*), pride (*nga rgyal, māna*) and jealousy (*phrag dog, īrṣyā*).

In the pure state these become transformed into five (pure) awarenesses, or five aspects of pure awareness. Aversion is transformed into the reality awareness (*chos dbyings ye shes, dharmadhātujñāna*); bewilderment the mirror-like awareness (*me long ye shes, ādarśajñāna*); desire the distinctness awareness (*so sor rtog pa'i ye shes, pratyavekṣaṇajñāna*); pride the equality awareness (*mnyam nyid ye shes, samatājñāna*) and jealousy becomes the accomplishing awareness (*bya ba grub pa'i ye shes, kṛityānusthānajñāna*).

The emotional defilements are said to be caused by the activities of the elements, which themselves are associated with the five skandhas. In the pure state the five (or six) elements are represented by the consorts of the buddhas mentioned earlier.

In this way there is a complex set of relationships between the things entailed in human experience, both externally and internally, and the description of these factors in the pure state of enlightenment. Very often the symbols that are used to describe that pure state are employed in the meditation practices of Kālacakra—the goal is utilised to progress on the path.

These are the main factors that are to be dealt with in the description of the ground, path, and goal of Kālacakra, and very near the beginning of the Vimalaprabhā commentary to the Kālacakra Tantra these basic categories of things are set out, together with the set of syllables that symbolise them.

As is often the case with Buddhist symbolism, the two fundamental principles of method and understanding (also mentioned earlier as translations of the Chinese principles of yang and yin) are represented in Kālacakra by the syllables e and vaṃ.

There are two other syllables that have a similar function in Kālacakra, and these are more specific to the Kālacakra system itself.

These are haṃ and kṣa. Pema Karpo (Pktant, 80) states that all vowels arise from haṃ, or vaṃ, and all consonants from kṣa, or e.

Being in essence understanding, the syllable e has the nature of emptiness, and being method, vaṃ has the nature of non-conceptual compassion. It is a fundamental point that all things can be categorised as either method or understanding. This is the first, or top level of categorisation, and there are also three- and fourfold classifications very commonly used, but for the purpose of understanding the symbolism used in astrology, the five- and sixfold classes are more useful.

These two main syllables are both considered to have the nature of two further groups of syllables: vaṃ, the five "letters of great emptiness" (*stong pa chen po yi ge lnga, pañcākṣaramahāśūnya*), which are the vowels: a, i, ṛi, u, and ḷi; and e, the six "letters of empty potential" (*thig le stong pa yi ge drug, binduśūnyaṣaḍakṣara*), which are the six consonant groups: ka, ca, ṭa, ta, pa, and sa.

The relevance of five- and sixfold classifications to astrology is easy to understand. There are 60 (2×5×6) nāḍī in a solar day, 30 (5×6) lunar days in a month, just more than 12 (2×6) months in a year, 12 signs in the zodiac, and so forth.

Kālacakra describes six groups of six factors in human experience. The six skandhas are the first group, followed by the elements, senses, sense objects, bodily organs, and activities. In the pure state, these are represented by various groupings of deities within the Kālacakra maṇḍala.

Mipham (MiKal 1, 66) states that "The pure state of the six groupings within the thirty-six skandhas and elements, when awareness and consciousness are counted together are known as the five 'great letters of emptiness,' indicating the five awarenesses. When the elements of awareness and consciousness are treated separately, they are known as the six 'letters of empty potential'."

In the pure state, each of these groupings become:

6 skandhas	6 buddhas
6 elements	6 consorts
6 senses	6 bodhisattvas
6 objects	6 bodhisattvās
6 organs	6 wrathfuls
6 activities	6 consorts of the wrathfuls

Looked at another way, each of these groups (represented by the consonants) is divided into six different classes, known by symbolic names such as Vajra, Sword, and so forth. These are associated with the vowels and the elements, the fivefold classification, as shown in Table 4-1.

	Earth	Water	Fire	Wind	Space
	ḷi	u	ṛi	i	a
Vajra	ka	kha	ga	gha	ṅa
Sword	ca	cha	ja	jha	ña
Jewel	ṭa	ṭha	ḍa	ḍha	ṇa
Wheel	pa	pha	ba	bha	ma
Lotus	ta	tha	da	dha	na
Knife	sa	ḥpa	ṣa	śa	ḥka

Table 4-1

Taking the list of the six "letters of empty potential," we have the arrangement shown in Table 4-2. The buddhas, Vairocana and so forth, represent the purified skandhas. Each of these is associated with a particular colour, number, and direction—very similar to ideas we shall see later in the Chinese astrological symbolism. A full list would include the other groups of deities as the pure forms of the senses, organs, and so on.

Vairocana	Ratnasambhava	Amitabha	Amoghasiddhi	Akṣobhya	Vajrasattva
Yellow	Red	White	Black	Green	Blue
5	3	4	2	1	6
ta	ṭa	pa	ca	ka	sa
West	South	North	East	Above	Below
Form	Sensation	Interpretation	Response	Consciousness	Awareness
ḷi	ṛi	u	i	a	aṃ
Earth	Fire	Water	Wind	Space	Awareness
ḷī	ṛī	ū	ī	ā	a
Body	Eyes	Tongue	Nose	Ears	Intellect
al	ar	o	e	a	aṃ
Odour	Tastes	Forms	Textures	Reality	Sounds
āl	ār	au	ai	ā	āḥ
Rectum	Hands	Legs	Voice	Vagina	Penis
la	ra	va	ya	ha	haṃ
Speech	Motion	Grasping	Defecation	Orgasm	Urination
lā	rā	vā	yā	hā	haḥ

Table 4-2

In one sense, the sixfold classification is an extension of the fivefold. The main associations of the five "letters of great emptiness," their symbols, directions, elements, and awarenesses, are as follows:

Curved knife	Club	Visarga	Tilaka	Plowshare
a	i	ṛi	u	ḷi
Centre	East	South	North	West
Space	Wind	Fire	Water	Earth
Reality	Accomplishing	Equality	Distinctness	Mirror-like

When this is extended to a sixfold classification, both the classes of Akṣobhya and Vajrasattva are associated with the reality awareness.

We can also include here some astrological correspondences, first in the sixfold classification.

In the following list are the six classes, together with the zodiac signs, skandhas, and associated activities:

ka	Capricorn	consciousness	killing
ca	Aquarius	response	killing
ṭa	Pisces	sensation	expulsion
pa	Aries	interpretation	coercion
ta	Taurus	form	controlling
sa	Gemini	awareness	increasing
sa	Cancer	awareness	pacification
ta	Leo	form	pacification
pa	Virgo	interpretation	increasing
ṭa	Libra	sensation	controlling
ca	Scorpio	response	coercion
ka	Sagittarius	consciousness	expulsion

The planets are more usually associated with the fivefold classification, as follows:

Space	Fire	Water	Wind	Earth
a	ṛi	u	i	ḷi
Kālāgni	Sun	Mars	Jupiter	Saturn
ā	ṛī	ū	ī	ḷī
Rāhu	Moon	Mercury	Venus	Comet

These correspondences, and the extensions to them that can be produced by linking with the six classes of consonants, are not necessarily those that are used in practical astrology—although some are. Notice, for example, that the activities are associated with the zodiac signs in a symmetrical pattern.

This is because these activities are associated with the zodiac signs according to the planets that rule them. For example, pacification is associated with the signs ruled by the Sun and Moon, Leo, and Cancer; increasing is associated with the signs ruled by Mercury, and so forth, through Venus, Mars, Jupiter, and Saturn, arguably the most negative of all the planets, and therefore associated with killing.

However, the correspondences given here are those associated with the maṇḍala of Kālacakra and the meditation practices, and as we shall see later, the definitions of the months.

Chinese symbolism

The Chinese system is often referred to as elemental calculation or divination (*'byung rtsis*) as its basis is an analysis of the relationships that form between various cyclic attributes and the elements associated with them. The list of elements is not quite the same as that in Indian systems, and so they cannot be compared exactly, but there are strong similarities.

It is worth mentioning here the somewhat unsatisfactory nature of translating the Chinese term wǔ xíng (五行) by 'five elements.' As Needham points out (Needham 2, p. 244) the term implies movement, and that the elements are "five powerful forces in ever-flowing cyclical motion, and not passive motionless fundamental substances."

There are two words in use in Tibetan that could perhaps be translated respectively as transformation (*'byung ba*) and constituent (*khams*). The latter is the one that is also mostly used for the elements in reference to Indian systems (*pañcadhātu*). Keeping to these speculative translations, Tsewang Lhamo (Lithsh, p. 102) refers to the "constituents of the four or five transformations as the basis" of Chinese elemental calculation, and then defines 'transformation' as the "main cause of the creation and destruction of all constituted phenomena."

On the next page Lhamo continues: "The main functions of the material particles of the transformations are: the constituent of earth causes completion, the constituent of water combines together, the constituent of fire brings maturation and the constituent of wind causes movement."

Clearly, distinctions are being drawn between substances and processes, and as it as yet unclear how best to draw these distinctions in English, and because it matters little for the present work, I shall continue with the word 'element.' However, it should be born in mind that for a deeper understanding of the Chinese system, not just is a better word than 'element' needed, but two terms are in fact required.

The attributes that are involved in elemental divination are cyclic, and in addition to the elements consist of three main groups. These are the twelve animals that were mentioned earlier, together with the eight trigrams (*spar kha brgyad*, bā guà 八卦) and nine numbers (*sme ba dgu*, jiǔ gōng 九宫), known in the west mainly from the famous book of Chinese divination, the I Ching. Together with the elements, particularly in the form of the celestial stems, but not exclusively so, these cycle through the years, months, days, and double-hours, and the various interactions between them, in particular between the elements associated with them, give rise to astrological prognostications.

I shall only touch briefly on the history of this system, but this subject and its history is the one aspect of Tibetan astrology that has been described comprehensively in English, in the work by Gyurme Dorje entitled "Tibetan Elemental Divination Paintings" (Gyurme). In that work he mainly follows the writings of Sangje Gyatso (Baidkar) and Lochen Dharmaśrī (Zlazer).

Similarly, my main sources have also been Sangje Gyatso, but also Karma Ngelek Tendzin (Nyernag) and Mipham Gyatso (Miptsug). The content of all these works is very similar, but with differences of emphasis or interpretation. There are also the two excellent modern works, by Lhamo Tsultrim (Rdelgre) and the large five volume work on general Tibetan astronomy and astrology, the "Compendium of Tibetan Astronomy," edited by Jampa Trinle (Tsrikun).

All of these sources describe a mythical turtle from which the attributes such as the trigrams are derived or understood. The origin of the myths associated with the turtle go back to the time when turtle and bone divinations were performed in China—bones and turtle shells were heated until cracks appeared in them, and prognostications divined from the shapes of these cracks.

According to Edward Shaughnessy, this practice dates back at least to the Shāng (商) dynasty (c. 1600–1045 BCE), and later evolved into the divination procedures of the I Ching. Later in the same work he translates one of the legends of the creation of the trigrams by the sage, or emperor, Fú Xī (伏羲). He is often described as mythical, but recent archaeological discoveries in China suggest that he was in fact a historical figure. Fú Xī is said to have studied the heavens, the earth, the animals, and his own body, and then "first made the eight trigrams in order to penetrate the virtue of spiritual brightness and to categorise the real characteristics of the ten-thousand beings" (Mawangdui, p. 205).

Another legend has it that Fú Xī was offered by a subject a golden turtle, and the patterns on the turtle inspired him to devise the eight trigrams (Gyurme, p. 16). Yet another about him does not mention a turtle, but states that "he lived near the sea and it was he who saw the sea-horse Hai-ma-fa-tu (*hǎi mǎ fù tú* 海马负图) emerge from the sea with a circle on his back, which came out of chaos; from this came the yin and yang, in the form of two fishes; from these sprang the four seasons and then again the eight diagrams and then the sixty-four Kwa. From the eight diagrams came the five elements according to the book of divination." (Chinrec, Vol 3, no 2, July 1870, p. 41.)

As far as modern usage is concerned, the texts talk about several different turtles, partly from the point of view of a cosmology describing the world, and also as a means of understanding that world. Mipham (and I am also following Lhamo Tsultrim in this description) describes two aspects to reality, that which is the basis of all things, and is beyond analysis, and that which constitutes the world of erroneous appearance, that gives rise to all the experiences of beings entailing both benefit and harm and therefore things that should be adopted and things that should be avoided. (These are the things that are to be calculated by astrology.)

From the cosmological point of view, there are described three turtles (however, see Gyurme, p. 46, for the "turtle of exegesis," and also for a more extensive description of the following). The first of these is the natural (or naturally existent) turtle (*gnas pa'i rus sbal*). This is identified with dharmadhātu, the pure nature of reality, which is beyond analysis and calculation.

From the natural turtle arose the material turtle (*chags pa'i rus sbal*). From the breath of the natural turtle arose the green disk of the element of wind; from its saliva arose the disk of the element of water and from its flesh arose the great golden ground, together with Mount Sumeru, the (four) continents and minor continents, oceans and mountains, all of these together constituting the material turtle.

From the contact between these two turtles, there then arose the existent turtle (*srid pa'i rus sbal*), with its head facing south, its tail north, and its limbs in the intermediate directions. From the various parts of its body arose the six classes of beings of the three worlds, together with the planets, stars, trigrams, numbers, yearly cycles, earth-lords, nāgas (*klu*) and demons of disease (*gnyan*). Clearly, the material turtle is the physical world, and the existent turtle the animate world.

In order that beings could understand the world described by these turtles, the bodhisattva Mañjughoṣa emanated as a youth from a growth on a Trisha (unidentified) tree at Mount Wu Tai (*ri bo rtse lnga, wǔ tái shān* 五台山) in China. He then manifested the turtle of emanation (*sprul pa'i rus sbal*), or the great golden turtle, in the manner of, or representing, the existent turtle.

We are actually given, at least in Phugpa texts, a precise date for this event. This is said to have happened on a Saturday, the 15th of the Tiger month, the month of Mārgaśīrṣa (*mgo zla*) (this is the Phugpa definition of the Tiger month, not the Chinese), in the Wood-male-Mouse year, which calculates to 837 BCE.

This moment is said to have been taken as the start of the cycles, and so it should be a Wood-Mouse day that is the 15th of the Tiger month at the start of this Wood-Mouse year. It must be the case that this date was calculated retrospectively, but I have not been able to find a match using the Phugpa calculations.

Mipham says that everything is calculated on the basis of the body of this turtle of emanation. Its head faces south, and tail north. Its right lung is to the east, left to the west, its limbs point in the intermediate directions and it is lying on its back.

These basic directions indicate the main elements—to the east is wood, the south fire, west iron, north water, and in the intermediate directions earth. Karma Ngeleg adds that the turtle's veins and ligaments make possible the element of wood; from its body heat comes fire, from its flesh earth, from its bones iron, and from its blood water.

Another text (Lithsh, p. 115) tells us that the turtle is shot through with an arrow, the shaft of which penetrates its right lung on the eastern side, indicating the element wood; blood pours from its mouth in the south (presumably as a consequence of being shot with the arrow) indicating the element fire; the arrowhead sticks out from its left lung on the western side indicating the element of iron; it is urinating from its rear on the north side indicating the element of water; and its four limbs are clutching at the ground, indicating the earth element in the intermediate directions.

The elements have the following characteristics, shapes, colours, and numbers associated with them:

wood	growth	elliptical	green	1
fire	combustion	triangular	red	2
earth	stability	square	yellow	3
iron	hardness	semi-circular	white	4
water	dampness	circular	deep blue	5

Sangje Gyatso (Baidkar 1, 236) has for the numbers associated with the elements: wood 1, earth 2, water 3, fire 4 and iron 5.

Sangye Gyatso gives quite a long list of associations with the elements. After all, one aim of the Chinese philosophers was to categorise all things according to the principles of yin and yang and the elements.

One more association worth mentioning here, particularly with regard to predictive astrology, is with different types of diseases. Sangje Gyatso lists them as follows: wood, stiffness and rigidity in muscles and tendons; fire, fever and headaches; earth, heavy, debilitating illness; iron, general pain and bone problems; and, water, illnesses of cold and the lower body.

There are quite extensive descriptions—particularly by Sangje Gyatso—of the various other astrological factors arising from the body of the turtle. In brief, the eight trigrams arise from the eight consciousnesses of the turtle, the nine numbers from its nine orifices, the eight planets arise from its eight great fangs and the twenty-eight lunar mansions from its spinal vertebrae. The twelve animals are considered to be the offspring of the trigrams. Arranged on the underside of the turtle—it is lying on its back—the eight trigrams are considered to be in the following arrangement:

Direction	**Tibetan**	**Chinese**	**Western**	**Element**
South	li	lí (离)	Clinging	fire
South-west	khon	kūn (坤)	Receptive	earth
West	dwa	duì (兑)	Joyous	iron
North-west	khen	qián (乾)	Creative	sky
North	kham	kǎn (坎)	Abysmal	water
North-east	gin	gèn (艮)	Keeping Still	mountain
East	zin	zhèn (震)	Arousing	wood
South-east	zon	xùn (巽)	Gentle	wind

The western names that I have used are the familiar ones from Wilhelm's translation of the "I Ching."

Similarly, the twelve animals are arranged in a clockwise fashion around the body of the turtle, in the following directions:

Upper East	Tiger
Lower East	Rabbit
South East	Dragon
Upper South	Snake
Lower South	Horse
South West	Sheep
Upper West	Monkey
Lower West	Bird
North West	Dog
Upper North	Pig
Lower North	Mouse
North East	Ox

Mouse, Tiger, and so on are considered male, and Ox, Rabbit, and so on are considered female.

The nine numbers are said to be like birthmarks on the turtle, and have the following associations with colours, elements, and directions:

1 White	iron	North
2 Black	water	South-west
3 Deep blue	water	East
4 Green	wood	South-east
5 Yellow	earth	Centre
6 White	iron	North-west
7 Red	fire	West
8 White	iron	North-east
9 Red	fire	South

They are usually depicted in a square, as:

SE		S		SW
	4	9	2	
E	3	5	7	W
	8	1	6	
NE		N		NW

As we have seen, all these attributes are associated with the five elements, and the outcome of meetings between the elements of the various attributes is determined by the five possible relationships between them. The simple case is of an element meeting itself, and the other four relationships form two pairs: mother and son; and friend and enemy.

Taking the five elements in the following order: wood, fire, earth, iron, and water; moving in that order are sons, and reverse order, mothers. For example the son of wood is fire, the son of fire is earth, and the son of water is wood. Similarly, the mother of fire is wood, and so on.

It is also said that grandmothers are enemies and grandsons friends. This yields another order: wood, earth, water, fire, and iron. In this order the friend of wood is earth, the friend of earth water, the enemy of earth wood, and so on. These relationships are the basis of most of the calculations and prognostications of elemental divination.

When these calculations are performed, it is traditional to use small pebbles to indicate the result. These form a simple scoring measure of how good or bad a particular combination is. The best is three white pebbles and the worst is two black. So, when an element meets its mother, such as earth meeting fire, the score will be three white. This might occur when the main element for the year in which a person was born—known as the power element—was earth. If the element for the current year under consideration is fire, then earth is meeting its mother, and the score would be three white. The full list is as follows. When an element meets its:

Mother: 3 white
Friend: 2 white
Son: a pair of black and white
Enemy: two black
When earth or water meet themselves: 1 white
When fire, iron or wood meet themselves: 1 black

In texts, a small circle is used to represent a white pebble and a small cross a black pebble. Considering all the possible combinations, we have the following, in which an element represented in the left column meets the element indicated in the top row:

	Wood	Fire	Earth	Iron	Water
Wood	x	ox	oo	xx	ooo
Fire	ooo	x	ox	oo	xx
Earth	xx	ooo	o	ox	oo
Iron	oo	xx	ooo	x	ox
Water	ox	oo	xx	ooo	o

The main use of these combinations in an almanac is with regard to the years, and as we shall see, a table is usually included showing for any year which elements meet which in the current year and the resultant pebbles. Naturally, a user of the almanac can go into much more detail and consider also the elements of the months, days, and double-hours.

There is one final attribute type that we should consider before returning to the description of the almanac contents. This is the list of the twelve phases (*dar gud bcu gnyis, shí èr shèng shuāi* 十二盛衰), a concept that expresses the fact that the cycles being represented are not qualities that simply turn on or off, or switch from one to another, but that go through periods of growth followed by decline. These are in the following list, together with, in the right-hand column, Needham's (Needham 2, p. 250) original translations from the Chinese:

Conception	dbugs len	to receive breath
Gestation	mngal gnas	to be in the womb
Physical completion	lus rdzogs	to be nourished
Birth	btsas pa	to be born
Ablution	khrus byed	to be bathed
Clothing	gos gyon	to assume the cap and girdle
Work	las byed	to become an official
Maturity	dar ba	to flourish
Decline	gud pa	to become weak
Illness	na ba	to become ill
Death	shi ba	to die
Entombment	dur zhugs	to be buried

The six from "physical completion" to "maturity" are considered good, and the other six bad.

As the cycles progress, the elements move through these phases, and so we have for the twelve months the following: the element wood is conceived (literally, takes breath) in the first autumn month, Monkey; the element fire in the first winter month, Pig; the element iron in the first spring month, Tiger; and the elements earth and water are both conceived in the first summer month, Snake.

These cycles are not only applied to the months, but also to the years, days, and double-hours. Karma Ngeleg (Nyernag, p. 69) also adds the phases of the trigrams, stating that Tiger and Rabbit are conceived at Zin; Horse and Snake at Li; Bird and Monkey at Dwa; and the other animal signs are conceived at Kham. A similar description is given in other texts, but it is not clear how this would work in practice.

Yearly attributes

Following the list of historical information there then usually follows a short list of information specific to the year for which the almanac is drawn up. This will usually include a count of years relative to the time the Buddha's teachings are predicted to last, usually given as ten sets of five hundred year periods. This can simply be given as a count of years since the Nirvāṇa of the Buddha, or, and this is more usual, as a count of years within the current five hundred year period. This is sometimes followed by the time remaining—the number of years left from the total of five thousand.

Next, the names of the year are given, from both Indian and Chinese systems. The most usual forms of these are given in the table in Appendix 1.

In the example I have been using for calculations of 1995, the names of that year would be given as Wood-female-Pig from the Chinese cycle, and Yuvika (*na tshod ldan*) from the 17th sixty-year prabhava cycle. If the almanac were from the Tsurphu tradition, 1995 is 2,872 years since the Nirvāṇa of the Buddha as given in that tradition, which would place it as the 372nd year in the sixth 500 year period of the teachings, leaving the teachings a further 2,128 years still to exist.

After these names of the year, the next items given are usually four factors that are very important for Chinese elemental predictions. These are the elements associated with four different areas in the life of a subject. Each year has a specific element associated with each factor, and when an astrological examination is performed, those elements from the natal year are compared with those in the year under consideration. Many almanacs give charts covering several pages to help with this kind of analysis.

These four factors are power (*dbang thang*), life (*srog*), body (*lus*) and fortune (*klung rta*). I translate them by these particular terms because of the aspects of life about which they are used for prognostication, as described by Mipham and others.

The power factor is associated with wealth, food, children, and so forth. Control could also be a good translation for this in the sense that we talk in English of the resources a person controls. The life factor is concerned with the life itself, and risks to it, whether through illness, accident, danger, natural causes, etc. The body factor is concerned with physical health, well-being, and illnesses. Naturally, somebody with conflicts regarding both the life and body factors at the same time would be considered perhaps to be in mortal danger through ill health.

Finally, the fortune factor is concerned with the progress of one's activities and work. Will there be obstacles, or will things flow smoothly? The use of the word "fortune" does not of course imply any random luck, as all these indications are determined, from the point of view of Buddhist theory, by the previous actions of the subject of any astrological examination. Those actions in previous lives are considered to cause the person to be born at a time and place that will give them experiences and opportunities appropriate to those actions, and astrology simply identifies these various circumstances.

The power element is the one we have seen already as part of the ten celestial stems. These are the elements associated with the twelve animals to identify the years. The current Chinese cycle commenced in 1984 with the year of the Wood-Mouse, followed by Wood-Ox and then Fire-Tiger. Those elements are the respective power aspect elements for those years.

The life factor elements are also easy to understand. I described earlier the arrangement on the turtle of the twelve animals. Tiger and Rabbit are to the east and this direction is associated with the element wood. That element is then the life factor element for Tiger and Rabbit years. Similarly, Snake and Horse are to the south, as is the element of fire; Monkey and Bird are to the west, as is the element iron; and Pig and Mouse are to the north, as is the element water. The four remaining animals, Dragon, Sheep, Dog, and Ox, are in the intermediate directions, as is the element earth.

The body elements are much more difficult to describe, and there are two methods given for their derivation, although they both yield the same results.

In the first, given by Mipham (Miptsug p. 566), the elements that make up the usual list of five, fire, earth, iron, water, and wood, are associated with five of the trigrams, respectively Li, Khon, Dwa, Kham, and Zin. These are listed in the order in which they appear in the usual arrangement of the trigrams (this is leaving out the trigrams associated with 'extra' elements such as mountain, etc.), in a clockwise direction. This list is used for counting, in a clockwise direction, and so if we reach the end of the list we then count from the beginning again.

The twelve animals are arranged into three groups of four. For Ox, Sheep, Horse, and Mouse, we count from the trigram Zin. For Dragon, Snake, Dog, and Pig, we count from the trigram Dwa. For the remaining four of Tiger, Rabbit, Bird, and Monkey, we count from the trigram Kham.

We count around the trigrams until we hit the one which has the element associated with it that is the same as the power element of the year concerned, and we count using the list: iron, water, fire, earth, wood.

A few examples are in order. For a year of the Ox we count from Zin, the element of which is wood. So, for a Wood-Ox year, we count one, i.e., iron, and we are already in the place of wood, and so iron is the body element for that year.

For an Earth-Ox year, we count iron, water, fire to reach the place of Khon, earth, and so fire is the body element.

Finally, for a Water-Ox year, we count iron, water, fire, earth, wood to reach the place of Kham, water, and so wood is the body element.

For an example from the next group, for a Dragon year we count from Dwa, and so for an Iron-Dragon year, we count iron, are already in the place of Dwa, iron, and so iron is the body element.

For a Fire-Dragon year, we count iron, water, fire, earth to reach the place of Li, fire, and so earth is the body element.

As an example from the third group, for a Tiger year we count from Kham, and so for a Fire-Tiger year, we count iron, water, fire to end up on Li, fire, so the body element is fire.

Finally, for an Iron-Tiger year, we count iron, water, fire, earth, wood to end up at Dwa, iron, so the body element calculates as wood.

The second method for determining the body elements is well described by Jigme Namkhai Dorje (Brasrat p. 9). The animal signs are taken in the same three groups of four, but this time each group is associated with a particular element. Wood is associated with Mouse, Horse, Ox, and Sheep; water with Tiger, Monkey, Bird, and Rabbit; and iron with Dog, Dragon, Pig, and Snake.

For any year this element is compared with the power element for the year, and the relationship between the two examined. If they are the same element, then the body element is iron; if the power element is the mother, then the body element is wood, if the power element is the son the body is water, if the enemy then earth, and if the friend then fire. Karma Ngelek Tendzin describes these relationships with the words: "The mother collects wood, and the son draws water, the enemy digs earth, and the friend fans the fire."

For example, for the Fire-Rabbit year, Rabbit is in the group associated with the element water. The power element fire is the friend of water, and so the body element for the year is fire.

The elements for the fortune factor are more straightforward. The animals are grouped into four groups of three. For Tiger, Horse, and Dog, the fortune factor element is iron; for Mouse, Dragon, and Monkey it is wood; for Bird, Ox, and Snake it is water; and for Pig, Sheep, and Rabbit it is fire.

Some almanacs also add a fifth factor, known as the spirit factor (*bla*). The element for this is simply determined: it is that which is the mother of the element for the life factor.

Together with these factors, another important attribute is the number associated with the year from the set of nine numbers in Chinese symbolism. The so-called "central number" is the main one for the year, and these simply count in reverse order through the years. For example, the value for 1995 was 5 Yellow, for 1994 6 White, and so forth.

These numbers are also associated with the attributes of body, life, and power. The main number is the one for body, counting up four places from it (in terms of years, not numbers) is that of life, and four below it is power. So, for a native born in the year 1995, the body number, also called the 'birth number,' will be 5 Yellow, the life number will be 2 Black, and the power number 8 White. As these other two are very easily determined, only the central number is given in most almanacs.

Yearly prognostications

The yearly information that I have described so far has been neutral, without any particular interpretation or meaning. In the usual structure of Tibetan almanacs most, although not all, of what follows in the yearly information contains much that is astrological interpretation. As I explained before, I intend not to describe most of this, mainly because covering the interpretative side of the Tibetan calendar properly would increase the size of the present work several times.

Much of this material is based on Indian sources, and appears to go back at least as far as Varāhamihira, in the sixth century CE. Some of this material is said by Tibetan sources to be taken from a text called the "Mirror Teaching Time" (*dus bstan me long*), and the only comment I have seen regarding authorship attributes this to Varāhamihira. Some of this material as it is presented in works such as the "White Beryl" (Baidkar, chapter 18) compares very closely with other writings of Varāhamihira (see for example, Bṛhat chapter 19).

Following on from the yearly attributes given above, the next pieces of information presented in an almanac are one or more of the various lords of the year, together with the lunar mansion for the year.

Each of these is given with a short sentence describing the main relevant prognostication for the year. (The calculation for one of these is given in chapter five, and the exact values calculated are often given in tables towards the end of the almanac's yearly information, as are such details as planetary positions at key points in the year, and so forth.)

There then follow several other sections from Indian astrology, the largest of which deals with the five planets and their movements throughout the year. This will give details of the main characteristics of the planets' motion—main positions, when they change from one motion to another, and so forth—together with any resultant prognostications.

Earth Ox

After the other shorter sections from Indian astrology, the almanac generally then returns to the Chinese system. Of usually three diagrams used to depict information for the year, by far the most important, and one that is often described in texts and commented upon, is that of the Earth Ox (*sa glang*), also known from modern Chinese sources as the Spring Ox (*niú chūn* 牛春).

Earth Ox diagram from the 2003 almanac of the Tibetan Institute of Medicine and Astrology in Lhasa, Tibet.

This is a diagram symbolising certain aspects of the new year. In this is depicted an outdoor scene including an ox and his herder, together with a dragon in the sky. An almost identical diagram is found in Chinese almanacs (*tōng shū* 通书), although the only ones I have seen do not contain the dragon, but the Sun instead.

It is a pity that it is only in recent years that modern printing methods have enabled the use of colour in creating these diagrams, as colour is a key feature of the symbolism employed in the diagram. However, the Chinese did not limit the use of the Spring Ox to almanacs, and would often make physical representations for use at new year festivals, when colour could be fully exploited. The following description is based mainly on the "Essence of the Kalkī" (Rigthig, p. 119).

The colours are used to represent the elements of certain aspects of the new year, and these are: wood, green; fire, red; earth, yellow; iron, white; and water, blue or black. Banda Gelek adds (Bgglang, p. 211) that the wood element can also be represented by blue.

The colour of the head of the ox is determined by the power element for the year concerned. This is the element of the celestial stem for the year. The life element—the element of the earthly branch—for the year gives the colour of the body of the ox, and the body element for the year gives the colour of its belly.

These factors repeat throughout the sixty-year cycles, and so will be the same for every particular year in each sixty-year cycle. For this reason, some textbooks draw up a table giving the colours of the head of the ox, its body, and so forth, for each year of the sixty-year cycle. See, for example, the "White Crystal Mirror" (Citsmel, p. 13).

Spring Ox diagram from a Taiwanese almanac for the Water-Sheep year, 2003.

A different table is required for other factors in the diagram as these depend on characteristics of the solar day during which the first spring minor term is passed. This is the first of the list of 24 solar terms, called 'Beginning of Spring,' and in the Chinese tropical zodiac system refers to the Sun passing the point 15° Aquarius, on approximately 5th February. This is the new year as far as the Chinese solar calendar is concerned, and from this point of view, the first point of Aries, the vernal equinox, is not the beginning of spring, as some maintain, but the middle. The beginning of spring is approximately three fortnights earlier—or 45° in terms of the motion of the Sun, each of the solar terms being separated by 15°.

The important factor is the solar day during which the Sun passes this point, and the elements for that solar day are needed. See later in this chapter for a description of how these elements are derived.

The power element for the day of the beginning of spring gives the colour for the horns, ears, and tail of the ox, the life element gives the colour of the four limbs, and the body element the lips. Some sources, particularly Chinese, add to the lips the hooves of the ox.

If the year is male then the mouth of the ox is open and the tail wags to the left, and for a female year the mouth is closed and the tail wags to the right.

Regarding the herdsman, the life element of the first day of spring gives the colour of the herdsman himself, the enemy of that element gives the colour of his clothes, and the enemy of that element the colour of his belt. (This latter is also the son of the life element.)

The body element of the first spring day determines the disposition of the herdsman's boots. If the body element is iron then he wears the left boot and the right one is tied to the left side of his belt. If wood, he wears the right boot and the left one is hanging from the right side of his belt. For the water element he wears both boots (as this indicates much travel). For the fire element, which indicates little travel, he wears neither. In this case they seem usually to be tied to his waist, or, as Banda Gelek describes it, placed on the ground in front of him. For the earth element he leaves his boots aside—they are depicted sitting aside on the ground or not depicted at all (this indicates no travel).

If the first day of spring is one of Tiger, Monkey, Pig or Snake, then the herdsman is depicted as an old man; for Mouse, Horse, Bird or Rabbit he is in the prime of life; for Dog, Dragon, Ox or Sheep he is youthful.

Regarding his hair (which is long, and arranged in two bunches), this is determined by the life element of the first spring day. (The "Essence of the Kalkī" has here the body element, but it also gives this for the boots, and so one of them would seem to be a mistake. Banda Gelek gives life element here and body element for the boots.)

For a life element of iron, the two bunches of hair hang down, forwards in front of his ears. For wood, they are both behind his ears. For water the right bunch hangs behind his ear and the left is in front; fire is the reverse of this. (One source, Citsjam, has these two the other way around. This appears to be a mistake.) For earth, both bunches are bound up to the right and left of his head.

The tail of the whip held by the herdsman is determined by the animal sign of the first spring day. If this is Tiger, Monkey, Pig or Snake then it is made from hemp; if Mouse, Horse, Bird or Rabbit, it is made from cotton thread; and if Ox, Sheep, Dog or Dragon, it is made from silk thread.

If the first spring day is before the 27th (or 25th, according to Banda Gelek) of the 12th (Mongolian) month, then the herdsman is in a hurry and walks in front of the ox. If it is after the 5th of the first month then he is slow, and the herdsman follows the ox. If the day is between the 27th (or 25th) of the 12th month and the 5th of the first month, then this is balanced, and the herdsman travels with (i.e., beside) the ox. If the year is male then he is on the right of the ox, and if female on its left. (Three different Tibetan texts agree on this, Rigthig, Tsrikun, and Bggsert, but I have seen at least one Chinese source with them the other way around.)

Counting from the first lunar day of the first (Mongolian) month, up to when there occurs a day of Ox or Dragon, then that number of days gives the number, respectively, of oxen and dragons (the numbers are written underneath or on the drawn animals in the Earth Ox diagram). For example, if the first lunar day of the first month is Tiger, the 3rd Dragon, and the 12th Ox, then this implies 3 Dragons and 12 Oxen.

The form of the Ox is a full span (*'dom*) in size and square in shape, symbolising the four seasons. His tail is in length a cubit (*khru gang*) and two inches (*tshon*), symbolising the twelve double-hours of the day (I have also seen this given as the twelve months of the year). The herdsman is in height three cubits and six inches, symbolising the 360 (lunar) days. The whip is two cubits and four inches in length, symbolising the 24 solar terms.

These details are studied in various ways to give prognostications for the year. For example, if the main colour in the drawing is green, then this will indicate the element wood and strength in the growth of trees, crops, and so forth, but sluggishness in men and livestock, and illnesses due to the wind element. A predominance of black will indicate cloudy weather and much rain, lustrous flowers and illnesses of cold, phlegm (*bad kan*) and wind.

The ox represents the replenishment of the fertility of the soil, and the dragon is considered the deity of the weather, drinking water from the ocean and delivering it from its mouth as rain. The relative numbers of these two therefore give indications regarding the fertility of the soil and the weather.

Two other diagrams commonly given after the Earth Ox are the 'farming cycle' (*so nam 'khor lo*), and the 'plough cycle' (*thong gshol 'khor lo*). Both of these depict the relative positions of the lunar mansions entered by the Sun and Moon, and yield prognostications relevant mainly to the weather and agriculture.

Rāhu and eclipses

Another discrete section is usually given over to eclipses that are predicted for the year. This lists the main circumstances of the eclipse, the timing, magnitude, colour, and so forth, as well as the lunar mansions in which the Sun and Moon will be found. It will usually also contain some diagram illustrating the maximum of the eclipse. Perhaps surprisingly, there is usually little in the way of predictions given in this section.

Yearly tables

These tables are produced in just about all modern almanacs, and fill usually around six or seven pages. They are intended to aid the job of making prognostications for an individual for the current year. One table is short and is the same every year. This lists the twelve animal-signs for the years, and for each one gives a list of nine weekdays and mansions that when encountered are either auspicious or inauspicious. These are the spirit, life, and adversary (*gshed*) weekdays, and the spirit, life, power, obstacle (*keg*), demon (*bdud*), and adversary mansions.

Some of these follow understandable relationships between the elements associated with them.

For example, for a Tiger year the life element is wood. This is what might be considered the natural element of the Tiger, and is also the element associated with Thursday. Therefore Thursday (5) is the spirit weekday for the Tiger year. The friend of this life element is earth, and this is also the element associated with Saturday, and so Saturday (0) is the life weekday for Tiger. The enemy of the life element is iron, which is associated with Friday, and so Friday (6) is the adversary weekday of Tiger.

	Mouse	Ox	Tiger	Rabbit	Dragon	Snake
Spirit weekday	4	0	5	5	1	3
Life weekday	3	4	0	0	4	6
Adversary weekday	0	5	6	6	5	4
Spirit mansion	19	16	4	10	2	12
Life mansion	5	13	26	26	23	11
Power mansion	2	11	8	11	16	5
Obstacle mansion	25	1	13	25	7	7
Demon mansion	9	7	11	14	8	8
Adversary mansion	22	4	1	17	10	5

	Horse	Sheep	Monkey	Bird	Dog	Pig
Spirit weekday	3	6	6	6	2	4
Life weekday	6	2	5	5	4	3
Adversary weekday	4	5	3	3	5	0
Spirit mansion	16	7	7	13	8	1
Life mansion	11	0	0	8	26	7
Power mansion	5	1	1	24	4	10
Obstacle mansion	19	19	8	2	10	25
Demon mansion	4	4	4	10	2	2
Adversary mansion	26	26	16	23	11	11

Similarly, for the Mouse year, the life element is water, Wednesday (4); its friend is fire, Tuesday (3); and its enemy is earth, Saturday (0). Most of the weekdays can be analysed in this manner, but not all.

[illegible]	1	2	3	4	5	6	7	8	9	10	11	12	13	14	15	16	17	18	19	20
[illegible]	o	oX	oX	o	oo	oo	o	XX	XX	o	ooo	ooo	o	oX	oX	o	oo	oo	o	XX
[illegible]	X	X	oo	oo	XX	XX	oX	oX	ooo	ooo	oo	oo	XX	XX	X	X	ooo	ooo	oo	oo
[illegible]	o	o	oX	oX	oo	oo	XX	XX	ooo	ooo	o	o	oX	oX	oo	oo	XX	XX	ooo	ooo
[illegible]	X	XX	oo	oX	X	XX	oo	oX	X	XX	oo	oX	X	XX	oo	oX	X	XX	oo	oX
[illegible]	X	oX	oX	X	oo	oo	X	XX	XX	X	ooo	ooo	X	oX	oX	X	oo	oo	X	XX
[illegible]	[illegible]	[illegible]	[illegible]	[illegible]	[illegible]	[illegible]	[illegible]	[illegible]	[illegible]	[illegible]	[illegible]	[illegible]	[illegible]	[illegible]	[illegible]	[illegible]	[illegible]	[illegible]	[illegible]	[illegible]
[illegible]	[illegible]	[illegible]	[illegible]	[illegible]	[illegible]	[illegible]	[illegible]	[illegible]	[illegible]	[illegible]	[illegible]	[illegible]	[illegible]	[illegible]	[illegible]	[illegible]	[illegible]	[illegible]	[illegible]	[illegible]
[illegible]	X	o	o	o	o	o	o	o	X	X	o	o	o	o	o	o	X	X	X	o
	o	oX	o	o	o	o	o	Xo	X	o	o	o	o	o	[illegible]	Xo	o	Xo	o	o

First page of the sexagenary table from the 2003 Lhasa almanac.

The next table is for the whole sexagenary cycle and gives attributes that apply for the current year for people born in each of the sixty years of the cycle.

There are usually eight rows of attributes given, for each of the sixty years arranged in columns. This arrangement is very similar to charts that are used by Tibetan astrologers for their calculations. On those charts the various attributes are represented for each year, together with their element, and then starting from the subject's natal year, the astrologer counts forward to the year under consideration, and then places white and black pebbles to indicate the auspicious or inauspicious meetings between the elements. There is much more to the work than this, but the tables given in almanacs are to aid this first level of astrological investigation.

The first row of the sexagenary table gives headings for the columns: the names of the sixty years, the relevant age in the current year of one born in that year, and the central number for the birth year.

The next five rows of the sexagenary table give the results of the combinations of the elements of the five factors mentioned earlier, for life, body, power, fortune, and spirit. As described before, the results are given in terms of pebbles, with a small circle representing a white pebble and a small cross a black pebble.

As an example, take the case of a person born in the year 1949, Earth-Ox, and calculate for 1995, Wood-Pig. The elements are as follows:

	Life	Body	Power	Fortune	Spirit
Earth-Ox	Earth	Fire	Earth	Water	Fire
Wood-Pig	Water	Fire	Wood	Fire	Iron

In Earth-Ox the life element is Earth and in Wood-Pig, the life element is water. As water is the friend of earth, the result is two white pebbles (oo).

For the body element we have fire meeting fire, and so the result is one black pebble (x). For the power element we have earth meeting its enemy wood, and so the result is two black pebbles (xx). For fortune we have water meeting its friend fire, and so the result is two white pebbles (oo). Finally, for spirit we have fire meeting its friend iron, and so the result is again two white pebbles (oo).

The next attributes given in the sexagenary table are best described as progressed attributes. I am using this word from western astrology by way of contrast with the previous five attributes in which a natal element meets one in the current year. With the progressed attributes, something starts in the year of birth, and then counts or cycles up to the year under consideration.

The sixth row in the table contains two such attributes, the so-called 'reverse-year' (*log men*) for both men and women (sometimes these are given in two separate rows). If the subject is a man, to determine the reverse-year take the son of the power element of his natal year, and combine this with Tiger, and then count forwards in the sexagenary cycle for the age of the subject. If the subject is female, take the mother of the natal power element, combine with Monkey, and then count backwards in the cycle.

So, for the previous example of a subject born in the Earth-Ox year, for a target year of Wood-Pig, the subject's age in the target year would be 47—remembering that in this method of counting (usually called inclusive counting) the age of the subject is one during the calendar year of birth, two during the next year, and so forth. The son of the element of earth is iron, and so the count starts from Iron-Tiger. Counting forwards we reach in the 47th place in the cycle, Fire-Mouse.

If the subject is female, using the same natal information, the mother of the earth element is fire, and so the count starts from Fire-

Monkey. Counting backwards to the 47th place (counting Fire-Monkey itself as the first place) we find Iron-Dog.

In almanacs, very often the element associated with the reverse-year is omitted, and just the animal signs are given.

In the next row of the sexagenary table, three items are given. These are the progressed trigrams for men and women, and the progressed central number—which is the same for both men and women.

The main descriptions of how to calculate the progressed trigram differ somewhat. The common element is that for men one starts from the trigram Li and counts clockwise, and for women the count starts from Kham and continues anticlockwise. However, many texts describe jumping diagonally when reaching a count of ten, from one corner of the normal arrangement of the trigram to its opposite.

Zon	Li	Khon
Zin		Dva
Gin	Kham	Khen

For example, with a man, starting from the trigram Li in the first year, the second year is Khon, and we return to Li in the ninth year, and then again Khon in the tenth. The count then jumps diagonally to the trigram Gin for the 11th year, Zin for the 12th, and so forth, arriving at Zon in the 21st year. There is then another diagonal jump to Khen for the 22nd year.

Not all the texts make it clear that a jump is made every time ten is counted, although as before, Namkhai Dorje (Brasrat p. 10) does spell this out unambiguously.

However, some texts comment that the main method that is actually used in practice does not involve diagonal jumping, and this is certainly the case with most almanacs, in which the count simply proceeds steadily, clockwise from Li for men and anticlockwise from Kham for women.

The progressed central number also has two gender-specific methods of counting, but these are dependent not on the gender of the subject, but on that of the natal year. For female years the count is clockwise, and for male years anticlockwise. In each case the count starts with the central number in the middle of the appropriate square arrangement. The count then moves to the east—to the left in the relevant diagrams—and then in the appropriate direction, until completing a full circle and returning to the centre again on the count of ten. The process then repeats.

Take the example of the Water-Bird year, 1993. This is a female year with the central number of seven. The second year entails the step to the east, and so the first progressed number is five, then moving clockwise the next is six, then two, until at age nine, one is reached. The count then moves back to seven in the centre, and so on.

3	8	1
2	4	6
7	9	5

8	4	6
7	9	2
3	5	1

1	6	8
9	2	4
5	7	3

2	7	9
1	3	5
6	8	4

4	9	2
3	5	7
8	1	6

6	2	4
5	7	9
1	3	8

7	3	5
6	8	1
2	4	9

9	5	7
8	1	3
4	6	2

5	1	3
4	6	8
9	2	7

There is a difference here from the trigrams in that every subject has a natal-central number determined by the year of birth, and the progressed count starts from there. But the count for the progressed trigram starts at either Li or Kham—this is the same for all subjects, depending only on their gender.

Earth		Fire			Earth
	Dragon	Snake	Horse	Sheep	
Wood	Rabbit			Monkey	Iron
	Tiger			Bird	
	Ox	Mouse	Pig	Dog	
Earth		Water			Earth

There is such a thing as the natal-trigram, but it is not used in this calculation of the progressed trigram. It is used for other purposes, and is simply calculated—for any subject it is the progressed trigram of the subject's mother in the year of the subject's birth. There are many such factors used in the analysis of a subject's horoscope that depend upon the subject's father or mother, but clearly these are very specific and cannot be represented in a general almanac.

The final row of the sexagenary table consists of two minor rows, containing pebble representations of nine-sign (*dgu mig*) and tomb-sign (*dur mig*) calculations. By comparing almanacs from different authors for the same years one quickly realizes that although there is general agreement, there are some differences in the calculations that are used. There are actually several different methods and each almanac presumably contains those that its author considers the most important.

There are three main kinds of nine-signs, or multiples of nine: for the count of years, the progressed trigrams and progressed numbers. For the count of years, the multiples of nine are simply the ninth, eighteenth, etc., years. For the progressed trigrams these are the years when for a man the trigram Li is reached, and for a woman the trigram Kham. For the progressed numbers, these are the years when one comes to one's own birth-number.

These three methods are called calculations based on a single, or solitary, sign (*rkyang pa'i dgu mig*). The next most important method entails the use of combined signs (*khug pa'i dgu mig*), but before describing this I need first to introduce the basic concept behind the tomb-signs. This is associated with the twelve phases of growth and degeneration.

For example, as was stated earlier, the element wood is conceived, the first phase, in the first autumn month, Monkey. In the diagram of the twelve animals, this is the uppermost of the two animals in the western sector (north is to the top). Moving around in a clockwise direction, the element moves through the phases, and in the seventh and eight positions, Tiger and Rabbit, the respective phases are work and maturity. These could arguably be said to be equivalent to the prime of life, and these two animals have wood as their natural (life) element.

Continuing around the cycle, the final phase, entombment, is reached in the S.W. sector, with the animal sign of the Sheep. The Sheep is therefore said to be the tomb-sign for the element wood.

Similarly, the element fire starts from the Pig, and its tomb-sign is the Dog; iron starts from the Tiger and its tomb-sign is the Ox. And both earth and water start from the Snake, with their tomb-sign being the Dragon. In this way the animal signs in the four intermediate directions, each with the natural element of earth (into which people are buried or entombed), are known as the four tomb-signs.

In the combined nine-sign method, one counts through the sexagenary cycle backwards, with a starting point that depends on the year of birth. So, for people born in the Pig, Mouse, or tomb-sign years (Ox, Dragon, Sheep or Dog), the count starts from Wood-Mouse.

For those born in the Tiger or Rabbit years, the count starts from Fire-Rabbit; for the Horse or Snake years, from Iron-Horse; and for the Bird or Monkey years, from Water-Bird.

With the correct starting point one then counts backwards until the tomb-sign of the natal power element is reached. The pattern is the same for all animal signs, and the first tomb-sign reached in this way is at age nine, and then at subsequent increments of twelve, i.e., ages 21, 33, etc.

These are the basic results that are given for the nine-signs in most almanacs, although sometimes others are also given. In the almanac published by the Institute of Medicine and Astrology (*sman rtsis khang*) in Lhasa for the Water-Sheep year 2003, small circles, representing white pebbles, are given for most birth years, indicating the absence of a nine-sign. However, for some years a cross is given representing a black pebble.

For example, three consecutive years each get a black pebble for 2003—Wood-Ox 1985, Fire-Tiger 1986 and Fire-Rabbit 1987. In 1985 the central number was 6 as it also was in 2003; in the year count, 2003 was the eighteenth year from 1986, and counting from 1987, the progressed trigram for men in 2003 was Li and for women Kham.

The natal year Water-Pig 1983 also has a black pebble associated with it as a result of the combined sign calculation. The tomb-sign of the element of Water is the Dragon, and counting backwards from Wood-Mouse, after nine years (1991) Fire-Dragon is reached, and after a further 12 years (2003) Wood-Dragon. For further details on nine-sign calculations, see "Tibetan Elemental Divination Paintings" (Gyurme, pp. 115 & 249, etc.).

The main method used for calculating the tomb-signs depends on the life element for the natal year in combination with the progressed trigram.

For example, if the natal life element is wood, the relevant tomb-sign amongst the animals is the Sheep, in the S.W. intermediate direction. This is also the position of the trigram Khon.

Similarly, for a natal life element of fire, the tomb-sign is the Dog, in the N.W. together with the trigram Khen; for iron, the tomb-sign is the Ox, in the N.E. together with Gin; and for the earth and water elements, the tomb-sign is the Dragon, in the S.E. together with Zon.

As there are two methods of progressing the trigrams, one for men and the other for women, different results need to be indicated in the table.

For example, for the year Water-Horse 2002 in the 2003 almanac, the life element of the Water-Horse year was fire. This element has the tomb-sign trigram of Khen, and the progressed trigram from natal Water-Horse to Water-Sheep year is for men Khon and for women Khen. So, for this year a tomb-sign needs to be indicated for women. The convention is to place a pebble to the left for men and to the right for women, and so in this case the entry will be a white pebble on the left together with a black pebble on the right, indicated by a small circle and a cross.

For the year Fire-Mouse 1996, the natal life element was water, and the relevant trigram Zon. The progressed trigram for men in the Water-Sheep year was Zon, and so the entry placed is a cross on the left and a circle on the right.

In a year for which no tomb-sign needs to be indicated, either the position is left blank, or a single circle is placed.

Another tomb-sign calculation employing four types is also used in this row of the sexagenary table. For each natal year this produces four results in each sixty-year cycle: the major and minor own-tombs, and the major and minor enemy-tombs. The calculation for these is somewhat similar to that used for the combined nine-sign method, with a starting point that depends on the year of birth.

For natal years of Tiger or Rabbit, the counting starts from the Rabbit; for Horse or Snake from the Horse; for Bird or Monkey from the Bird, and from Mouse, Pig or the four tomb-signs, from the Mouse. In each case the starting point animal is combined with the power element of the natal year.

One counts backwards until one reaches particular tomb-sign years with either the same power element as the natal year, or its enemy.

So, for natal Tiger or Rabbit:
the same power element Sheep year is the major own-tomb;
the same power element Ox is the minor own-tomb;
the enemy power element Sheep is the major enemy-tomb;
the enemy power element Ox is the minor enemy-tomb.

Similarly, for natal Horse or Snake:
the same power element Dog year is the major own-tomb;
the same power element Dragon is the minor own-tomb;
the enemy power element Dog is the major enemy-tomb;
the enemy power element Dragon is the minor enemy-tomb.

For natal Bird or Monkey:
the same power element Ox year is the major own-tomb;
the same power element Sheep is the minor own-tomb;
the enemy power element Ox is the major enemy-tomb;
the enemy power element Sheep is the minor enemy-tomb.

For natal Mouse, Pig or tomb-sign:
the same power element Dragon year is the major own-tomb;
the same power element Dog is the minor own-tomb;
the enemy power element Dragon is the major enemy-tomb;
the enemy power element Dog is the minor enemy-tomb.

I'll describe as examples the four years that calculate to these results in the 2003 calendar.

From Earth-Snake 1989, Water-Sheep (2003) is the 15th year. The count starts in Earth-Horse, and the count of 15 years results in Wood-Dragon. As the enemy of earth is wood, this indicates the minor enemy-tomb. (The minor enemy-tomb year is the Water-Sheep year 2003, not Wood-Dragon, which merely indicates the tomb-sign.)

For Water-Pig 1983, a count of 21 years starts from Water-Mouse and leads to Water-Dragon, and this therefore indicates the major own-tomb.

For Earth-Pig 1959, a count of 45 years starts from Earth-Mouse and leads to Wood-Dragon, and Wood being the enemy of Earth, this therefore indicates the major enemy-tomb.

Finally, for Water-Snake 1953, a count of 51 years starts from Water-Horse and leads to Water-Dragon, and this therefore indicates the minor own-tomb.

There is a regular pattern to these calculations, and in any almanac the four years that calculate for one of these four tomb-signs are on counts of 15, 21, 45 and 51 years.

The earth-lords

Another yearly table that is included in most modern almanacs shows the positions of some of the various earth-lords for the year. There are a large number of these beings mentioned in the texts (over 400), and for a more extensive analysis of them see "Tibetan Elemental Divination Paintings" (Gyurme, p. 120, etc.).

As Sangje Gyatso points out (Baidkar 1, p. 218), these and other factors are produced by the discursive activity of the minds of beings, but are considered to have very physical effects. Their positions change, and there are different groups of them associated with the changes of the years, months, days, and double-hours.

According to their characteristics and their respective positions they are considered to have an effect on most aspects of life: health, prosperity, journeys, undertakings such as marriage, and so forth. As a simple example, a particular earth-lord residing in the north might make it dangerous to make a journey in that direction. Naturally, if such a journey has to be undertaken, then certain rituals will be prescribed to avert the negative influence.

Most almanacs reproduce a diagram listing the positions of the main earth-lords for the particular year. A minority also add monthly tables showing the changes of other earth-lords during the months.

Sangje Gyatso gives brief descriptions of these main earth-lords, most of whom are members of the court of King The-se (*the se rgyal po, tài suì* 太岁). In the following list the numbering is that given in the modern Beijing edition of the "White Beryl."

1. King The-se. He wears royal clothes, is red-yellow in colour and blazing with light. He sits in a grand pose on a golden throne, holding a copper (sometimes said to be iron) garuḍa.

2. Queen Mother The-chim. She is deep red in colour, wearing a white silk long-sleeved dress, holding a flask in the right hand and a mirror in the left. She is depicted seated, with the right leg extended.

3. Queen Hang-ne. She is white in colour, holding a golden flask.

Diagram showing the location of the earth-lords in the 12 directions for the Wood-Monkey year, 2004.

4. Prince Te-se. He is red in colour, holding in his right hand a golden casket and in the left an iron whip. He wears a jacket of fine red silk and has a vest of white silk over his shoulders.

5. Minister Tsang-kun. He sits on a multicoloured turtle, wearing ministerial costume. He is light red in colour, blazing with light and dressed in red silk. In his right hand he holds a crystal staff and in the left a jewelled flask.

6. Astrologer Se-wa. He is red-yellow in colour and in the guise of a priest. On his head is a "hat of existence" (this is sometimes simply called a black hat, and is commonly worn in ritual dances associated with the protective deities); in his right hand he holds a silken-arrow adorned with a yellow silk streamer, and in the left a magical mirror.

7. Royal dog-keeper yellow Hang-phen. He is red-yellow in colour and blazing with light, dressed in blue silk, holding in his hands a sack of diseases and a lamp (depicted in the right).

8. King's Treasurer Se-ji. He is white in colour, with a human body, a tiger head, and spotted leopard's tail. He carries a mouse-topped victory banner.

9. Bodyguard Se-shar. He is terrifying and dark-red in colour. He wears armour and rides a galloping water-buffalo, holding a sword and shield.

10. The royal mount Se-wa. He has the body of a horse and the head of a man, is radiant yellow in colour, carrying in his hands golden turquoise ladles.

11. The royal groom Se-u. Yellow in colour, he wears armour and rides a horse. He is depicted holding a sword and shield.

12. Timekeeper Se-ja. Red-yellow in colour and blazing with light, he has a human body, a bird's head, and wings of copper and iron. Vicious in nature, in his right hand he holds a trumpet and in the left a phurpa (ritual dagger).

An example of one of the earth-lords, time-keeper Se-ja, from the "White Beryl."

13. Seating arranger Se-wa. Light green in col-

our, he holds in his hands a wooden seat-frame.

14. The official. He is red in colour and holds a red lance (shown in the right hand) and a banner.

15. The sweeper Se-lo. Blue in colour, he carries a brush.

16. The King's dog, black Hal-chi. He has a human body with a dog's head and the tail of a snake. Black in colour, he has iron wings and holds a flag-lance.

Another earth-lord example, the King's dog, black Hal-chi.

26. Princess Kar-sham. Brilliant white in colour and beautiful, dressed in red silk, she holds in her hands a white-silver mirror.

27. Her husband, Bal-te. He is a young man, light yellow in colour, blazing with light. Dressed in blue waterproof silk, his right hand reaches for a golden arrow, and his left raises a silver bow.

28. Red General Wang-ging. Dressed in armour, he holds a bow and arrow. His anger blazes like fire, and he is accompanied by a retinue of planets and earth-lords.

29. General Tsangkun. Red in colour, he is dressed in armour and helmet and holds a red lance and a banner.

30. Assistant Tsang-kun Che-wo. Deep blue in colour, he is depicted naked except for a tiger skin.

31. Dog-headed Tsang-kun. He is the colour of eye-medicine (black), has a human body with a dog's head and carries a jewel.

32. The advisor Phe-u. No description of him is given in the "White Beryl," but he is depicted in a drawing in that text as human and dancing.

33. The black earth-lord Zin-phung. He rides a bull, has a scorpion head, and holds a sword in his right hand and a noose in the left.

34. The earth-lord Pi-ling. He is depicted naked, with a tail, riding a horse, and carrying a black pennanted lance. He is said to be extremely

fierce, although only the size of a thumb, with his horse the size of a mouse.

35. The eleven ministers of the earth-king. Said to be riding horses and carrying weapons.

There is a much longer list of the main earth-lords that cycle through the months. Sangye Gyatso lists 64 of these, but this is not exhaustive. There are also others that cycle through each of the years, months, days, and double-hours, such as the male and female Black Sky-dog (*gnam khyi nag po*), and the twelve Hidden Gods (*gab pa'i lha bcu gnyis*). In general, however, it is the group led by King The-se that is mainly featured in almanacs.

Monthly information

After all the information and tables has been presented for the year as a whole, an almanac then contains a section for each month of the year. Each of these sections starts with general information for the month concerned, followed by a table, spread usually over three or five pages, of the 30 lunar days in the month, containing the daily information.

The general information for the month starts with the basic identifiers for each month, and some of these are different in the Phugpa and Tsurphu traditions.

Although I have in my possession one example that starts with the first Mongolian month, most Tibetan almanacs do not start at civil new year, but with the 3rd Mongolian month of the year. The reason for this is that the 3rd month is identified in the Phugpa and Tsurphu traditions with the Kālacakra month of Caitra, and as we saw earlier, this was considered the beginning of the Kālacakra year.

The main identifiers given for each month are those from the original Kālacakra system, together with their seasonal names. The year is divided into the usual four seasons, each of three months each, qualified respectively as early-, mid- and late-. In the Phugpa tradition the third Mongolian month is identified with the Kālacakra month of Caitra, late-spring, being the month during which the Sun enters the sign of Aries.

In practice, Phugpa almanacs state that the identification of the third month with Citrā (the 13th lunar mansion) is approximate, and that more accurately the full Moon falls in the lunar mansion of Svātī (14).

This reflects the Phugpa calculations in which the full Moon does indeed fall in the mansions numbered 13, 14 or 15, showing that the calculations are offset from the original definitions. According to those original Kālacakra definitions, the full Moon in the month of Caitra would most often fall in mansion 13 (Citrā), but also in either 12 or 14. A similar "accurate" mansion association is given for each of the other months.

The next most important identification is with the Chinese months. As mentioned earlier, the months in the Phugpa tradition do not agree with the actual Chinese calendar, and the 3rd Mongolian month is identified as the Chinese month of the Horse, mid-summer. This means that the usual first month of the Chinese year, Tiger, early-spring, is identified with the 11th Mongolian month.

The full list of these associations of the months in the Phugpa tradition is as follows (the month numbering is Mongolian):

	Kālacakra			**Chinese**	
1	Māgha	Early-spring	Aquarius	Dragon	Late-spring
2	Phālguna	Mid-spring	Pisces	Snake	Early-summer
3	Caitra	Late-spring	Aries	Horse	Mid-summer
4	Vaiśākha	Early-summer	Taurus	Sheep	Late-summer
5	Jyeṣṭha	Mid-summer	Gemini	Monkey	Early-autumn
6	Āṣāḍha	Late-summer	Cancer	Bird	Mid-autumn
7	Śrāvaṇa	Early-autumn	Leo	Dog	Late-autumn
8	Bhādrapada	Mid-autumn	Virgo	Pig	Early-winter
9	Āśvina	Late-autumn	Libra	Mouse	Mid-winter
10	Kārtikka	Early-winter	Scorpio	Ox	Late-winter
11	Mārgaśīrṣa	Mid-winter	Sagittarius	Tiger	Early-spring
12	Pauṣa	Late-winter	Capricorn	Rabbit	Mid-spring

In the Tsurphu tradition the identifications are somewhat different. The first month is still considered to be the Kālacakra month of Māgha, when the Sun enters Aquarius, and is considered to be the early-spring month.

However, Karma Ngelek Tendzin states that the first month is early-spring for Tibet and China, but that it is late-winter from a Kālacakra point of view. Jamgon Kongtrul associates the months with a list of six seasons that are given in the Kālacakra system. The names I use for these are adapted from the normal (but rather ancient) use of these in India: winter, spring, summer, rains, autumn, and pre-winter. I consider a couple of these to be marginally more meaningful than translating the Tibetan terms that are used.

There are two months to each of these six seasons, and Kongtrul gives the first and second Mongolian months as early- and late-winter, the third and fourth months as early- and late-spring, and so forth.

The important point with the Tsurphu tradition is that with the first month identified as early-spring for both Tibet and China, it is also assigned as the Chinese month of the Tiger, in line with actual Chinese calendars. It is important to bear in mind that much other symbolic information from the Chinese system depends upon the animal assigned to the month, and that these factors are therefore also out of step between the Phugpa and Tsurphu traditions.

It should be pointed out that some almanac writers—there seems to be no general rule about this—do not adhere completely to the above associations between the Chinese, Indian, and Tibetan months, but instead describe Chinese intercalary months as they would appear in a Chinese almanac. As intercalary months in the Chinese calendar occur at different times to those in the Tibetan traditions, although much of the time the associations given above will apply, there will be many months where they are out of synchronisation by one month.

In a note about another monthly feature, Jamgon Kongtrul refers the reader to the way this is presented in a Chinese almanac, if this information is available. There are Tibetan translations of the calculations for the Chinese calendar, and these could be used for this purpose, but the ones that I have obtained are fairly recent. It is not clear if such calculations would have been used two or three hundred years ago.

As with the years, the Chinese month animals are also associated with the ten celestial stems; i.e., an element plus one of the two genders. Also, as with the years, the elements appear in pairs, alternately male then female, associated with the male and female animals.

Once the element for the first Chinese month, Tiger, has been determined, that is male, and the following month, Rabbit, has the same element, but female. The son of this element for the first two months becomes the element for the next two, Dragon and Snake, and the son of that element is associated with the next two months, and so on, as with the cycle of years. This is the case for both the Phugpa and Tsurphu traditions.

Where they differ is in the method for determining the element for the Tiger month. As an example, I shall take the year 1995 that was used in the example calculations. Phugpa Tibetan new year fell on the 1st March that year. However, that is not the start of the year from the point of view of the Phugpa interpretation of the Chinese calendar. That was two months earlier, with the 11th Mongolian month that started on 2nd January 1995—later than usual due to an intercalary month late in 1994.

The 11th Mongolian month is the Tiger month in the Phugpa tradition, and this is the one needed here, the start of the Chinese year as interpreted in the Phugpa system. 1995 was the year of the Wood-female-Pig, and so the son of wood, which is fire, becomes the element associated with the 11th and 12th months. The 11th month was therefore Fire-male-Tiger, and the 12th month Fire-female-Rabbit. The son of fire is earth, and this is associated with the next two months. The 1st month was therefore Earth-male-Dragon, and the 2nd month Earth-female-Snake. And so on.

The Tsurphu new year in 1995 fell a month earlier than the Phugpa, on 31st January. For the Tsurphu calendar that was the start of the 1st Mongolian month, the month of the Tiger. Tsurphu texts describe two methods for determining the element associated with the first month. The first of these is the same as that used in the Phugpa tradition, and is part of a general rule regarding elements: The son of the year element gives that of the (first) month; the son of the month gives the day, and the son of the day gives the double-hour.

However, this does not seem to be much in use. The second method is used in almanacs, and consists of the following rule. (This method is also given in Phugpa texts, but in my experience not used in Phugpa almanacs.) Given the celestial stem for the year, the element of the first month of the year is given by:

Year	**First Month**
Wood-Male	Fire-Male-Tiger
Earth-Female	Fire-Male-Tiger
Wood-Female	Earth-Male-Tiger
Iron-Male	Earth-Male-Tiger
Fire-Male	Iron-Male-Tiger
Iron-Female	Iron-Male-Tiger
Earth-Male	Wood-Male-Tiger
Water-Female	Wood-Male-Tiger
Fire-Female	Water-Male-Tiger
Water-Male	Water-Male-Tiger

In the example of 1995, a Wood-female-Pig year, the 1st month was Earth-male-Tiger, and the 2nd was therefore Earth-female-Rabbit. The son of earth is iron, and so the 3rd month was Iron-male-Dragon, and the 4th month Iron-female-Snake. And so on.

Also in the Chinese system are the nine numbers and eight trigrams. Monthly trigrams are not given in either Tsurphu or Phugpa almanacs, and only Tsurphu almanacs give a number for the month. These run sequentially, duplicating at intercalary months, and are derived from a simple calculation. The following is from Jamgon Kongtrul (Kongleg, p. 274).

Take the elapsed years since the epoch (1852), multiply by 12 and add the elapsed months. Add 4 to this result, and divide by 9. Subtract what remains from 10, replacing zero with a 1 if necessary. The result is the number for the month.

To take the example of 1995, the first month has to be considered as 10 months after Caitra of the previous year. The calculation becomes:

$1994 - 1852 = 142 \times 12 = 1704$
$1704 + 10 = 1714$
$1714 + 4 = 1718 \div 9 = 190$ rem. 8
$10 - 8 = 2.$

The number for the 1st month of the year, Tiger, was therefore 2 Black. The numbers count downwards, and so that for the 2nd month, Rabbit, was 1 White, for the 3rd month 9 Red, and so forth.

Another group of symbols associated with the months is common to both Phugpa and Tsurphu traditions.

In the following table, the first two columns give the Mongolian month number and the zodiac sign associated with it. The third column gives the twelve links of dependent origination. These are very old Buddhist concepts that describe the chain or cycle of causality that perpetuates normal cyclic existence. They are well known from their depiction around the rim of paintings of the "Wheel of Life" which expresses the Buddhist view of the different states into which beings are born and the causes of these different experiences. These twelve links are particularly important in Tibetan astrology as they cycle through the months and the lunar days.

The fourth column is a list of the six activities from the Kālacakra Tantra. These are a classification of the various activities that ensue from enlightenment, but in this instance they are more a classification of the activities that are best suited to or gain most success in a particular month. Pacification of illnesses, defilements, anger, etc.; increase of life, merit, wealth; control of resources and abilities; coercion, aversion or expulsion, and destruction of negative influences and evils.

The last column gives the monthly position of the empty flask. This is a concept from Chinese astrology, and in Tibetan texts is usually included in the section devoted to geomantic influences, such as the earth-lords, King The-se, and so forth, mentioned above.

1	Aquarius	Consciousness	Killing	west
2	Pisces	Name and form	Expulsion	north
3	Aries	Senses	Coercion	east
4	Taurus	Contact	Controlling	south
5	Gemini	Sensation	Increasing	west
6	Cancer	Attachment	Pacification	north
7	Leo	Grasping	Pacification	east
8	Virgo	Involvement	Increasing	south
9	Libra	Birth	Controlling	west
10	Scorpio	Old age and death	Coercion	north
11	Sagittarius	Misperception	Expulsion	east
12	Capricorn	Response	Killing	south

Karma Ngelek Tendzin (Bumzang, p. 239) describes there as existing four flasks in each of the cardinal directions, and that any time, one of these is empty (unfortunately, he does not say of what). The direction in which the empty flask lies is indicated by the zodiac sign in which the Sun is to be found at any time, and it is this that gives the association with the months. However, most almanacs give in the monthly information the dates for the position of the empty flask.

For example, when the empty flask is in the east due to the Sun being in Aries, the dates for the Sun's entry into Aries and then Taurus are given. This is usually in the form of a comment such as "from the 12th of the current month to the 14th of the next, the empty flask is in the east." This information is easily derived from the daily longitude of the Sun.

Among other information that is commonly given for each month are the relevant solar terms that occur during the month (see chapter one), the relative length of day and night, and some general information about the dates of the movements of some of more important among the earth-lords during the month.

Other dates that are given are for particular commemorative days, such as the day of the birth of the Buddha, or festivals that occur during the month. The daily data is presented in small boxes, and as this does not give enough room for this type of information, it usually has to be included with the monthly data. See Appendix 2 for a list of the most typical of these commemorative days.

A few almanacs also give diagrams for the positions of the earth-lords for each month, similar to those given for the year, although involving only those earth-lords that move from month to month. The diagrams for these purposes are given together with the yearly diagrams in works such as the "White Beryl" by Sangje Gyatso. Such texts also give details and diagrams for the changing positions of some earth-lords through the days and double-hours. This kind of information is not given in almanacs, apart from the days of the movements of some of the most important of these earth-lords.

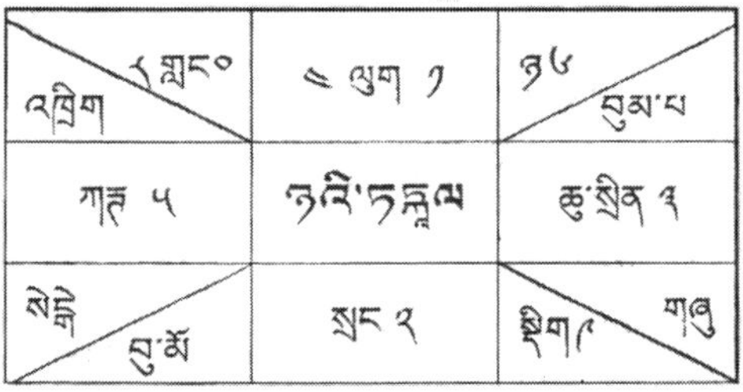

Chart of planetary positions for the full Moon day of the Water-Sheep year, 2003

Most almanacs give in some form the positions of the five planets and Rāhu for both full Moon and new Moon for each month. At a minimum, two small charts are given showing the relative positions of the planets at daybreak on those two days. These are the Tibetan equivalent to horoscopes drawn up by astrologers in the west and elsewhere.

The diagram is divided into 12 sectors, known as houses (*gnas mal*), each of which is occupied by one of the zodiac signs. The name of the relevant sign is written in its sector, and the square sector to the top is known as the first house, or ascendant (*dus sbyor, lagna*). The usage here is somewhat different from that in the west in that the whole of the sign that is rising above the eastern horizon is considered the first house. The next house in order, the triangular sector immediately to the left of the first house, which is under the horizon, is the second house, and so on.

The planets are indicated by their index numbers: 0 for Saturn, 1 for the Sun, and so on. The Head of Rāhu is given the index 8, and the Tail 9. In a more full version, the slow and fast motion longitudes for all five planets and Rāhu will be given in a small table for both full and new Moons. An astrologer needing the position of the planets for a day other than full or new Moon, will either use these figures and derive values by a method of interpolation, or calculate them from first principles.

Daily information

There are 30 lunar days in each month, and so the daily information is given in tables in which usually either 6 or 10 days fit on each page, although strictly speaking, each box contains the data for a solar day, numbered according to the lunar day in effect at daybreak. When a lunar day is duplicated, then the box in the table for that day is either divided into two or the whole row in which it sits has its entries shrunk in size.

There are two sets of information in each entry box. The first is at the top, and is a set of key words, including some numbers, indicating the main attributes for the day. These words indicate the information required in the briefest possible form. At the bottom of the box is a group of numbers. There are usually between four and six sets of these, and they are longitudes relevant to the five components of the calendar. In addition, recent calendars printed both inside of Tibet and in India also include in the bottom right corner the western date for the day concerned. Increasingly, these are given in western numerals.

A page of daily information from the 2003 Lhasa almanac, for lunar days 1 to 6 of the 2nd month of the Wood-Monkey year, 21st to 27th March 2004. In the lower row, the lunar day in the middle is duplicated over two weekdays, taking up the middle two boxes.

The row of figures at the bottom of each entry are best described first. They are nearly always expressed in three significant terms (sometimes two in older almanacs), and so the true weekday derived in the example calculation in chapter one, 4;21,24,2,32, would be expressed as the three numbers 4, 21 and 24, written one on top of the other, with the 4 at the top.

The true weekday is the first of the group of numbers given. The second is usually the longitude of the Moon, not that derived at the exact time of the true lunar day, but the longitude adjusted to the time of mean daybreak. The next set of three figures is the longitude of the Sun, as calculated for the time of exact lunar day. The fourth set of figures is the longitude (using the term somewhat loosely, as in Tibetan usage) for the yoga, calculated as the sum of the previous two, the longitude of the Moon at daybreak and the Sun at true lunar day.

Many almanacs give just these four figures, although I have seen examples with none at all, and some with just two sets of figures (for the weekday and Moon).

The most common practice nowadays is to include a set of six figures. In this case the fifth is rather surprising, and is the longitude of the Moon at daybreak, calculated using the karaṇa calculations as given in the Kālacakra Tantra (see chapters five and six for explanations of these calculations). I have not found any comment in the Tibetan materials explaining why this should be considered necessary in an almanac.

The final set of figures is the mean longitude of the Sun, expressed in terms of zodiacal signs, zodiacal days (equivalent to degrees) and 60th parts of a zodiacal day, usually referred to as (zodiacal-)nāḍī. No value zero is given for the zodiacal sign, and 1 is assigned to Aries, 2 to Taurus, and so on. This is easily calculated from the longitude of the Sun as derived in the five components of the calendar.

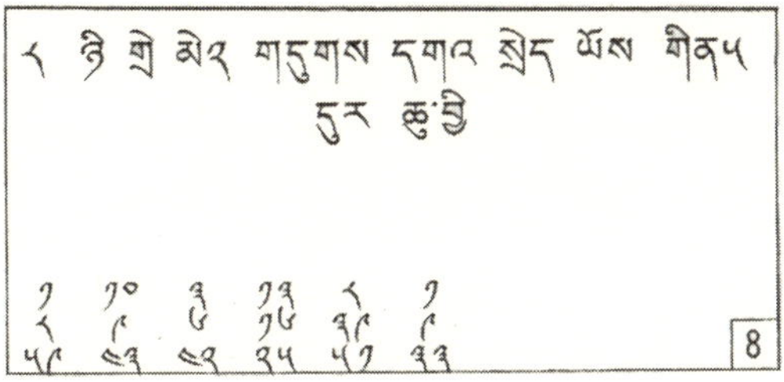

Daily information for the 8th of the 4th month, Water-Sheep year, 2003. The western date (8th June 2003) is indicated in the bottom right corner.

When a lunar day is duplicated, all of these figures are given for each day, but when a lunar day is omitted, this is not necessary. In such a case, usually only two sets of figures are given. The first is the weekday value for the lunar day concerned (this is the time at which the lunar day that is omitted ends, shortly before daybreak) and the longitude of the Sun at that time, the exact time of lunar day change.

The data given at the top of the daily box starts with the lunar day value—the lunar date—in the top left corner. This is followed by the name of the weekday concerned. When a lunar day is omitted it still has a box, but no weekday name is given, and when a lunar day is duplicated, two successive weekday names are given in consecutive boxes.

The next words in a daily box describe in varying details certain yogas, or conjunctions. The word "yoga" occurs frequently in Indian astrology to indicate the combinations of planets with lunar mansions or signs of the zodiac, or combinations of planets together in one house, and so forth. Here, the most important use is the combination of the elements of the weekday and the lunar mansion. They are therefore referred to as elemental yogas (*khams kyi sbyor ba*, or, *'byung 'phrod*).

See Appendix 1 for the elements associated with both the weekdays and the lunar mansions. To give one example, if on a Saturday (element earth) the lunar mansion at daybreak is Rohiṇī (also earth), then this indicates the first of the following ten yogas. In this list they are given with their Tibetan, Sanskrit, and English names for each element combination.

Earth + earth:	dngos grub	siddhi	accomplishment
Water + water:	bdud rtsi	amṛita	nectar
Earth + water:	lang tsho	yauvana	youth
Fire + fire:	’phel ’gyur	pragati	progress
Wind + wind:	phun tshogs	saṃpanna	excellence
Fire + wind:	stobs ldan	balayukta	powerful
Earth + wind:	mi phrod	alābha	deficiency
Water + wind:	mi mthun	pratikūla	discord
Earth + fire:	sreg pa	dahana	burning
Fire + water:	’chi ba	maraṇa	death

This first combination of earth with earth, the accomplishment-yoga, is considered highly auspicious, and is beneficial for achieving one’s goals, building forts, buying land, and so forth.

These yogas are clearly considered important, as they are among the most common items listed in almanacs for daily information. In fact, I have one calendar example that lists only these yogas in addition to the basic weekdays and lunar dates.

These yogas are usually described simply by writing the names of the two elements next to each other, and if they are the same, then the element name is given together with the numeral 2. Sometimes the name of the yoga can also be given.

There is another list of 28 yogas, not between the elements of the weekdays and mansions, but the weekdays and mansions themselves (*’phrod ’byor*). To judge by the frequency of their use in almanacs, they are not as important as the 10 elemental yogas given above.

On most days the lunar mansion changes at some point, and many almanacs indicate the time of this change, the new lunar mansion that the Moon enters, and the new yoga that results from this change. The time is easily calculated by interpolation using the true weekday value and the Moon’s longitude, and is represented in terms of the double-hour during which the change occurs plus a numeral from 1 to 5. As there are 12 double-hours during the day, and 60 nāḍī in each solar day, then there are exactly five nāḍī in each double-hour. It is the nāḍī that is represented by the numeral. For example, if a lunar mansion change occurs 8 nāḍī after daybreak, this is in the third nāḍī of the second double-hour, Dragon.

The next item in the list is often the name of the yoga from the five components, the longitude for which is given at the bottom of the daily box. It would make sense for the change in this yoga to be given as well, but in practice I have not seen this done, perhaps because of the limits on the amount of information that can be presented.

The following item is usually the name of one of the twelve links of dependent origination. There are two methods for assigning these, and fortunately they use the same list. In the method used in the Phugpa tradition, the links are associated with the solar days and start with the solar day during which the definition point for the month concerned occurs.

The link that is associated with the month itself is applied to the solar day during which the mean Sun passes the definition point. This is the first day in a cycle of solar days that continues until the day before the mean Sun passes the next definition point. From that first day the links then progress in order for a full cycle of twelve.

Forward fortnight	**Reverse fortnight**
1 Misperception	1 Misperception
2 Response	2 Old age and death
3 Conciousness	3 Birth
4 Name and Form	4 Involvement
5 Senses	5 Grasping
6 Contact	6 Attachment
7 Sensation	7 Sensation
8 Attachment	8 Contact
9 Grasping	9 Senses
10 Involvement	10 Name and form
11 Birth	11 Consciousness
12 Old age and death	12 Response
13 Consciousness	13 Birth
14 Name and form	14 Involvement
15 Senses	15 Grasping
(31) Contact	(32) Attachment

Table 4-3

As an example, take the 11th month, for which the associated link is Misperception. The definition point for that month in the Phugpa system is 18;36, and the day during which the mean Sun passes that point is counted here as day 1 and has Misperception associated with it. Day 12 therefore becomes Old age and death. For the next three solar days, numbered 13, 14 and 15, those links that were associated with days 3, 4 and 5 are repeated, in this example these are Consciousness, Name and form, and Senses.

According to the "White Beryl" there can be between 28 and 32 solar days before the next definition day, and these each have to be treated differently.

If there are 31 days before the next definition day, then the next link—the one falling on the 16th day is Contact. In Table 4-3 this is marked with the number 31 in brackets, as this link is omitted when there are less than 31 days to fill.

Either way, the next day is considered to be the start of what could be called a reverse fortnight, and the first link, the one associated with the month, is repeated here. The links then progress backwards for a full cycle of twelve, and on the reverse fortnight's days 13, 14 and 15, those links that fell on days 3, 4 and 5, are repeated. In the current example these would be Birth, Involvement, and Grasping.

If there are a full 32 days to be filled, then the link indicated by 32 in brackets is included next. In this instance an extra link is added both in the middle and the end of the cycle.

For periods when there are only 28 days for links to be applied, both those indicated as day 15 are omitted, and when there are 29 days, the second of these, which would otherwise be the 30th, only is omitted.

A similar system is described in the Tsurphu tradition, and this uses the same list as above, but cycling through the lunar days, starting with the first lunar day in a month having the same link as the month itself. Similarly, days 13, 14 and 15 are repeats of the links from days 3, 4 and 5, but as the links are applied to the lunar days, no extra links need to be added.

After describing this system, Karma Ngelek Tendzin (Bumzang, p. 193) mentions another method in which the cycle of links starts with the day during which the Sun enters a new zodiac sign, and this is clearly the origin of the method used in the Phugpa tradition. The definition points of the months in the original Kālacakra system are the entry of the Sun into the zodiac signs.

The next items in the daily information are details from the Chinese symbolic system, and here there are differences between the Phugpa and Tsurphu traditions as well as some differences between the various calendar makers in those systems. The Chinese information can be associated with both the lunar days and the solar days, and the easiest way of describing the difference is to say that the Phugpa tends to use mainly the lunar day information, and that the Tsurphu tradition uses the lunar information less, with more emphasis on the solar data. However, both solar and lunar data are described in textbooks from both traditions.

To cover the lunar data first, four items are included, one of the 12 animals, associated with an element, together with a trigram and one of the nine numbers. Each of them only requires a definition of the one for the first lunar day of the month as they then cycle through the lunar days without interruption or jumps.

For odd numbered months, and this applies to both the Phugpa and Tsurphu traditions, the animal associated with the first lunar day is Tiger, the next is Rabbit, and so forth. For even months the first lunar day is Monkey, the second Bird, and so forth.

With the years and the months the element combined with the animals are doubled—two water years, followed by two wood years, and so on. There is no doubling of the elements with the lunar days (although there is with the solar days which will be described later). Continuing the pattern with the relationship between the years and the months, the son of the element associated with any month is applied to the first lunar day of that month. That element's son is then applied to the next day, and so on.

In the earlier example of 1995 in the Phugpa tradition, the 11th month of the previous year was Fire-male-Tiger. The son of fire is earth, and so the first lunar day of that month was Earth-Tiger. The second lunar day was Iron-Rabbit, the 3rd was Water-Dragon, and so forth.

In the Tsurphu tradition the only difference is that the Tiger month is the first Mongolian month and not the previous 11th. Most calendars, from both traditions, only give the animal and do not mention the element.

There are four different groupings for the cycling of the trigrams through the lunar days. For the months Tiger, Horse, and Dog, the first lunar day has the trigram Li; for the months Rabbit, Sheep, and Pig it is Zin; for Dragon, Monkey, and Mouse it is Kham; and for Snake, Bird, and Ox the trigram is Dwa. They cycle in the usual order, and so for a Tiger month the second lunar day is Khon, the third Dwa, and so forth.

For the nine numbers there are three groupings. For the months Tiger, Snake, Monkey, and Pig, the first lunar day is 1 White; for Rabbit, Horse, Bird, and Mouse, it is 4 Green; and for Dragon, Sheep, Dog, and Ox it is 7 Red. The numbers cycle forwards, and so for a Tiger month, the 2nd lunar day is 2 Black, the 3rd is 3 Deep blue, and so forth.

When a lunar day is omitted, just these three items of information are given in its box, together with the figures for the weekday value and the longitude of the Sun. When a lunar day is duplicated, as the animal, trigram, and number apply to two consecutive solar days, they are usually only listed in the first of the two relevant boxes.

The solar day information, which is usually the last regular data given in the daily boxes, is mostly independent of the calendar itself, and except for one item is not calculated on the basis of any astronomical information. Just as the weekdays cycle through the solar days without interruption, so do the sexagenary cycle of element-animal pairs, trigrams, numbers, and, lunar mansions.

Phugpa texts give a method for determining these attributes that uses the general day count that was needed for planetary calculations. Epoch day values are added to this, and then the results are divided by 12, 10, 8, and 9, respectively to determine the cyclic animal, element, trigram, and number.

The count for the animals starts at 0 for Rabbit, 1 for Dragon, etc. For the elements, results of 1 and 2 are for fire, 3 and 4 for earth, 5 and 6 for iron, 7 and 8 for water, and 9 and 0 for wood. These values yield the power elements for any particular day, the elements for the other factors (body, etc.) can then be derived from the same sexagenary cycle as is used for the years.

The count for the trigrams starts at 1 for Li, 2 for Khon, etc. For the nine numbers, the result of the calculation is subtracted from 10, and if the result was initially 0, the final result is given as 1.

The "White Beryl," the "Essence of the Kalkī," and the "Compendium of Tibetan Astronomy" (Tsrikun) all give the same results for the new year new Moon day in 1995, 1st March. The numerical results and the attributes they represent are:

Element:	6	Iron
Animal:	0	Rabbit
Trigram:	4	Khen
Number:	6	4 Green

These values could be taken as epoch values for calculation taking 1st March 1995 as an epoch. As I am comparing six different texts here, it is clearer to give their results for one particular day rather their individual epochs.

In the Tsurphu tradition, Kongtrul does not give such a calculation for the trigrams and numbers, but he gives a similar system for the element, animal, and lunar mansion. (It should be born in mind that this has no relationship with the actual lunar mansions and the position within them of the Moon, just as the days of the week have no relationship to the movements of the planets after which they are named.)

His method also uses the general day calculation and divides by 420 after adding an epoch value. Reference is then made to a lookup table. The results this method yields for the animal and element agree with the Phugpa methods, and the lunar mansion that his method gives for the 1st March 1995, is Uttarabhādrapāda.

The numbering is different with the Chinese list of 28 mansions, and taking Citrā as number 0, Uttarabhādrapāda is number 13. In his text on this subject (Kongleg), when writing about the Chinese list of mansions, Kongtrul usually writes the names of the mansions in Chinese transliteration, Uttarabhādrapāda being "dbi'i." See Appendix 1 for a list of the Chinese lunar mansion names. Tsurphu calendars also follow this convention.

Two Tibetan texts on Chinese calendar calculation, the "Cloud of Offerings Pleasing Mañjuśrī" (Citsjam) and the "White Crystal Mirror" (Citsmel), both give calculations for all of these attributes, the first from the winter solstice epoch during the most recent Fire-Tiger year, 23rd December 1986, and the second text from the first day of that year, 11th January 1986.

Apart from an apparent error with the trigram in the first of these texts, their results agree with a combination of the attributes derived from the Phugpa and Tsurphu sources.

Tsurphu calendars use these calculations for the solar attributes, except for the nine numbers. The method for these is based on the occurrence of the solstices, and is very similar in principle, although not exactly the same, as the method used in modern Chinese almanacs. The solstices needed are the true ones, not hypothetical times based on old Tibetan observations and the longitude of the Sun, and so reference is made here by the Tibetan calendar makers either to Chinese calculations or almanacs. Once the days of the solstices are known, the method is easily described.

The numbers cycle in opposite directions in the two halves of the year, each change taking place on the first Wood-Mouse (solar) day after the solstices. After the winter solstice, the first Wood-Mouse day becomes 5 Yellow, the next is 6 White, and then the numbers cycle forwards. This continues until the first Wood-Mouse day after the summer solstice, to which is assigned 4 Green. The next day is 3 Deep blue, and the numbers then continue cycling backwards until the next winter solstice.

The above represents the majority of the attributes listed in the daily information. In addition, most almanacs give the movements on certain days of various classes of earth-lords. For example, the days of the arrival and return of nāgas, the movements of the eight classes of demons, the days when the sky-dog searches for food, and so forth. Space does not allow any details of these here, as this whole subject—the movements of the earth-lords through the years, months, days, and double-hours—is really a large, and necessarily separate, study in its own right.

Chapter V

The Kālacakra Tantra and Vimalaprabhā

As was explained briefly in the first chapter, the main definitions of the Tibetan calendar and the calculations used to derive it all come from an Indian Buddhist source: the Kālacakra Tantra. In this chapter I translate the relevant section from both the Tantra and its important Indian commentary, the Vimalaprabhā.

The Kālacakra system is said to have been taught by the Buddha and preserved for hundreds of years in the land of Sambhala, until it was finally taken to India, in the 10th or early 11th century CE.

According to the great Tibetan tantric expert Tāranātha (Takhist, p. 8): "On the full moon of the month Caitra in the year following his enlightenment, at the great stūpa of Dhānyakaṭaka, the Buddha emanated the maṇḍala of 'The Glorious Lunar Mansions.' In front of an audience of countless buddhas, bodhisattvas, viras, ḍākinīs, the twelve great gods, gods, nāgas, yakṣas, spirits, and fortunate people gathered from the 960 million villages north of the river Śītā, he was requested by the emanation of Vajrapāṇi, the king Sucandra, to teach the Tantra."

Tāranātha continues: "Some teachings were taken to other human realms, and the Dharma king Sucandra wrote the tantras in textual form in his land of Sambhala. He composed the Explanatory Tantra in 60,000 verses to the Mūlatantra of 12,000."

It is said that the teachings of Kālacakra were propagated in Sambhala for many centuries, with a succession of righteous kings teaching and writing about Kālacakra. Most of these kings are said to have reigned for a hundred years each. After seven generations, it is said that a king called Yaśas, an emanation of the bodhisattva Mañjuśrī, united the Brahmin Ṛiṣis living in his kingdom into the Vajra caste; in other words converted them to Buddhism as protection against the coming Islamic invasions.

Tāranātha states that: "As in this way the Ṛiṣis of different castes were brought into the single caste of the Vajrayāna, from the time of Yaśas onwards, these kings were called Kalkī kings, meaning of one caste."

Yaśas is also important for another reason. He wrote the Kālacakra Laghutantra, which summarises the meaning of the Kālacakra Mūlatantra that is said to have been the original text taught by the Buddha. If it ever existed, only short quotations (many are to be found in the Vimalaprabhā) now remain of the Mūlatantra, but the Laghutantra has survived in both the original Sanskrit, and Tibetan translations.

The next of the kings was the emanation of Avalokiteśvara, Puṇḍarīka. He composed the commentary on the Laghutantra, called the Vimalaprabhā. This also survives in both Sanskrit and Tibetan, and part of it is the subject of this chapter.

A few generations after Puṇḍarīka came another king of importance to our subject, the 11th Kalkī, Aja. He is said to have corrected the karaṇa calculations and re-established the calendar. Unfortunately, no record survives of exactly why he did this, or what methods he used. It is clear that the Kālacakra writers considered the calendrical methods in general use in India to have become corrupted over time, and it seems that for this reason, instead of relying on the inaccurate work of others, Kalkī Aja established a corrected Kālacakra calendar.

We are given a date when Aja is said to have established his calendar, or at least the date he used as his epoch, 806 CE, and according to Tāranātha it was during his time that the Kālacakra teachings were taken to India. This might seem rather early, as most of the historical individuals who can be identified and dated that had dealings with the Kālacakra system were no earlier than the tenth century, but most Tibetan sources give the reign of Aja as lasting until 1027 CE.

Like most of the texts known as tantras, the Kālacakra concerns itself mainly with meditation and the Buddhist path. However, many of the tantras include other subjects of use or concern to Buddhist practitioners, and the Kālacakra Tantra is a natural home for the description of a Buddhist calendar.

The subject matter of the tantra can be analysed in three main ways. First, there is the division of the text of the tantra itself into five chapters.

The first chapter deals with some general introductory material, particularly symbolic information that is relevant to the whole work, and then with the external physical world. This includes a discussion of the cosmology, or world view, of Kālacakra. It then discusses astronomy, describing the calculations and definitions of the calendar itself, and some aspects of astrology.

There is no such thing as "Kālacakra astrology" as such, although I have heard many references to such a subject. The Kālacakra system accepts the basics of general Indian astrology, but corrects some points that are considered wrong. In particular, it adds its own very rich and detailed symbolism, which permeates the whole Kālacakra system, making it, as I suggested in the previous chapter, arguably the most integrated system of tantric symbolism that Buddhism has produced.

The second chapter is concerned with the inner world. It describes the processes of conception, gestation, birth, illness, and death. In particular, it describes the vajrakāya, the Kālacakra view of the structures and processes that constitute a human body and mind. These are described in terms of channels in the body, with particular centres (*'khor lo*, *cakra*) of multiple channels. Winds with different functions pass through these channels, emanating from seeds (*thig le*, *bindu*) located within some of the centres.

These are described from the point of view of the body and how it exists, and this entails many ideas relevant to medicine. The winds and channels are also described from the point of view of tools or methods used in meditation. The actual meditation practices are given mainly in the fourth chapter. As with the first chapter, the description of the inner world is permeated by the rich symbolism of Kālacakra, thereby providing correspondences between the outer and inner worlds.

The third chapter concerns the entry onto the Kālacakra path of practice. This entails initiation or empowerment by a teacher (*bla ma*, *guru*), and so the discussion starts with the characteristics of the teacher, and then moves on to the preparations for the initiation. These include preparing the site and drawing a powder maṇḍala, representing the divine palace that is imagined in meditation as the abode of the deity Kālacakra. In the initiation itself, known as the "seven empowerments raising the child," the student is introduced to this maṇḍala palace, reborn within it as the deity Kālacakra, and brought symbolically to maturity.

The fourth chapter deals with the meditation practice of the Kālacakra system. As with other tantras, there are two components to this, known as the generation process and the perfection process. In the generation process meditation, the practitioner imagines arising as the deity Kālacakra inside the maṇḍala palace, surrounded by all the deities of Kālacakra's retinue. The tantra describes the main triple Kālacakra maṇḍala of body, speech, and mind, containing a total of 636 deities.

The processes of conception, gestation, birth, and growth to maturity, described in the second chapter, are purified by the generation process meditation, with the practitioner arising from contemplated emptiness as the deity Kālacakra, the radiation of the deities of the retinue, empowerment of the deities, and so forth. There are many steps in the process when performed in its full form.

The perfection process of Kālacakra meditation is known as the six yogas, and is intended for those who have gained proficiency in the generation process. This set of practices should not be confused with the well know six doctrines of Nāropa, which hold a similar status within the Cakrasaṃvara Tantra cycle.

Just as the generation process purifies the processes of being born into and developing in the world, the perfection process could be said to be purifying the processes of cognition and action within the world, processes that for normal beings are characterized by error, or misperception.

These practices start devoid of any imagined forms, calming and concentrating the mind, with the intention of stopping the movement of the winds conceived as moving in the right and left channels in the body. Once the winds have been calmed in this way, they return to the central channel, are brought further under control with breathing exercises and meditations in which the channels, winds, and seeds are imagined.

Once the winds are controlled, they return into the seeds from which they originated—the process that entangles us in the world has been turned back to its origins. The practices then culminate with the well-known Tummo (*gtum mo*, *caṇḍālī*, inner heat) and similar meditations, with the winds and seeds now in the practitioner's control. (This is necessarily a very brief description of what are amongst the most complex and sophisticated meditation practices developed within Buddhism.)

The subject of the fifth chapter is awareness, and this deals with the results of the Kālacakra practices. The purification of aspects of the mind and body are described in terms of deities in the Kālacakra maṇḍala, but the chapter deals with much more than this, including the activities that result from realization, the benefits to other beings, and so forth.

To recap, these five chapters deal with: the outer world, the inner world, initiation, practice, and awareness. Another classification common to many tantras can also be applied here, that of ground, path, and goal.

In simple terms, the ground is the description of the state that humans find themselves in and the processes involved, and this includes the potential in human existence to overcome the causes that create suffering. The ground is therefore the subject of the first two chapters of the tantra, dealing with the outer and inner worlds.

The path is the path of practice, of purifying the state known as cyclic existence and developing the potential for enlightenment. The path is the subject of the third and fourth chapters of the tantra, on initiation and practice. The goal is clearly the subject of the fifth chapter, on awareness.

A third classification is peculiar to the Kālacakra system, and this is into outer, inner, and other. Outer Kālacakra is the description of the physical world from the first chapter, inner Kālacakra is the inner world described in the second chapter, and other Kālacakra is everything else, everything other than normal worldly concerns—the path and goal of Kālacakra as described in the last three chapters.

The highly integrated nature of the symbolism, taking in the outer world and the cycles of the years, months, and so forth, is not the only feature that makes the Kālacakra system, as I wrote earlier, a natural home for a Buddhist calendar. The other main feature is the relationship of the Kālacakra with the concept of time itself.

The Sanskrit word *kāla* means time, and *cakra* means cycle or wheel, so Kālacakra is often translated as either 'cycle of time' or 'wheel of time.' Mipham (MiKal 1, p. 27) gives an interesting explanation of the word Kālacakra:

"That which is called time (*kāla*) is vajra-time, the three times (of past, present, and future) equal in timelessness, characterized by unchanging great bliss, and because this generates the wheel (cycle, *cakra*) of everything consisting of the skandhas, elements, senses (and so forth), free from obscuration, is called 'wheel of time.'

"All things in all directions and times are created and destroyed, appearing as a result of their (interconnecting) causes and conditions; this process of change is called time, and entails all that is observable. As this time embraces all things it is called a wheel (of time). This term 'embracing' is not meant to imply some separate creator such as Īśvara, but the inseparableness of unchanging great bliss and emptiness possessed of all positive characteristics, the non-duality of time, the components, classes, and so forth."

Mipham is describing Kālacakra here from the point of view of the goal of the tantric path. It is time that enables the totality of experience, and when this has been purified by the path one experiences directly the equality of the three times, the indistinguishability of time and its contents, an experience that is personified by the image of the deity Kālacakra.

From a Kālacakra point of view, naturally one can talk in terms of outer time, inner time, and other, or awareness time. Outer time is the form or structure of time, the various appearances in nature. Inner time refers to the changes, in time, of the winds and elements in the body. Other time is the all embracing reality, the Kālacakra awareness of indivisible emptiness and great bliss, and the path used to achieve this state of realization.

Later in the same text (MiKal 4, p. 5) Mipham tells us: "We draw physical and mental distinctions in reality, between day and night, Sun and Moon, the vajra and the lotus, semen and blood, all classified as either method or understanding. The indistinguishable unity of the pair of method and understanding is called Kālacakra, and has the nature of great bliss."

He goes on to discuss the fact that the division into day and night is the basis of our measurement of time which is subdivided into further divisions, such as the cycle of the twelve rising signs, associated with the twelve aspects of dependent origination, which is the basis for the appearance of all of conventional reality, the birth and death of beings, and so forth. In this same discussion Mipham gives a famous quote from the Kālacakra Mūlatantra:

> All beings arise in time,
> Time continually consumes them all,
> Time is the Lord who possesses the vajra,
> Whose nature is that of day and night.

The rest of this chapter is a translation of the section of the Vimalaprabhā that comments on verses 26 up to the third line of verse 52 of the first chapter of the Kālacakra Laghutantra. This constitutes two complete sections of the commentary. The first consists of just verse 26, and the topic (number 13) covered in this section is entitled "the prophesy of the coming of Mañjuśrī." This deals with some of the history described above, particularly Kalkī Yaśas and the corruption of the calendrical systems, and serves as an introduction to the discussion of the calendar.

The next topic (14), covered in verses 27 to the third line of verse 52, is "siddhānta and karaṇa astronomy." This contains the definitions and calculations of the Kālacakra calendar.

These original texts are terse, and often not easy to read and understand even for native speakers. For this reason I have interspersed them together with comments, explanations, and sample calculations where relevant.

The verses of the tantra and commentary are indented on the left margin, the Tantra verses are also italicised, and verse numbers are given at the end of each verse in square brackets, starting with [26]. My comments and explanations are not indented at all. Structuring the text in this way will hopefully make it easier to read and understand.

13. The prophesy of the coming of Mañjuśrī

> *After this year, six hundred years, there will arise in Sambhala the appearance of the lord of men, Yaśas; Then after nāga hundred years, for certain, in the land of Mecca, the barbarian teachings will be established. At that time, people in the world will know the accurate brief karaṇas. All through the land the siddhāntas will be corrupted, in the effects of time. [26]*

> Now, I shall explain "After this year," and so forth, the prophesies of the Tathāgata regarding the appearance in Sambhala of Mañjuśrī, the arising of the barbarian teachings and the corruption of the astronomical siddhāntas, and the development of the brief karaṇas.
>
> Regarding, "After this year, six hundred years, there will arise in Sambhala the appearance of the lord of men, Yaśas," "this year" is referring to the year when the Tathāgata taught the Dharma (of Kālacakra). Six hundred years after that year, in Sambhala, north of the River Śītā, there will arise, Yaśas, as it says in the text,

> Mañjuśrī, the great Yaśas, his appearance, meaning that he will take a nirmaṇakāya body.
>
> "Then after nāga hundred years," means that nāga, eight, hundred years after the nirvāṇa of Yaśas, "for certain," meaning without doubt "in the land of Mecca, the barbarian teachings will be established." South of the River Śītā, in the land of Mecca with ten million villages, the demonic teachings of the barbarian Tajiks will be established.

This brief historical discussion is referring back to the time of the Buddha when the original Kālacakra Mūlatantra is said to have been taught. The importance of Yaśas most likely lies in the fact that he first taught the Kālacakra Laghutantra—the shortened version of which is being commented upon here. The Vimalaprabhā commentary, a section of which is translated here, is said to have been composed by Yaśas' successor in Sambhala, Puṇḍarīka.

Yaśas is also said to have foreseen the danger that the barbarians (Islamic invaders) posed to Indian culture, and tried to avert this. (For the Vimalaprabhā description of this activity of Yaśas, see Newman, 1987, p. 306 ff.)

The term I have translated (following John Newman—see Newman, 1998a) as "barbarian," mleccha, is usually considered to refer literally to somebody of indistinct speech, one who does not know Sanskrit—an outsider or foreigner. In this instance the "barbarian teachings" refers to Islam.

> "At that time," of the barbarians, "people in the world will know the accurate brief karaṇas." Regarding, "the siddhāntas will be corrupted," the Brahma, Saura, Yamanaka, and Romaka siddhāntas, these four will be corrupted and so (it is said that) the siddhāntas will be corrupted. "All through the land," "all" means that wherever in the land there are the heterodox siddhāntas, then there; "the land" refers to the land south of the River Śītā.
>
> It is not the case that the siddhāntas of the Buddhists in Sambhala and other lands will be corrupted.

The Vimalaprabhā is here starting its criticism of other Indian systems of astronomy, claiming that their understanding of the position of the Sun has become inaccurate. Indian systems use a sidereal zodiac—one defined by the fixed stars—and, as will become clear, the Kālacakra advocates a tropical zodiac, one that keeps step with the seasons, and where the definition of the entry of the Sun into Aries is the vernal equinox—the moment when day and night are of equal length.

> Regarding, "in the effects of time," the "effects of time" is a barbarian concept, and the effect is on the siddhāntas, the effect of time. In, "in the effects of time," the locative case is used instead of the ablative. As the siddhāntas will be corrupt, the words "accurate brief karaṇas" are like a mother's offer of sweets.

The identification of the cause of the corruption of the siddhāntas with Islamic influence is puzzling here, as current historical understanding is that during the relevant period there was a much greater influence by Indian astronomers on their Islamic counterparts than the other way around. It is tempting to speculate that the "effects of time" referred to as corrupting the siddhāntas—the results they produce becoming less accurate—is a reference to precession, a factor that was not taken properly into account by the Indian astronomers, but well understood in the Islamic world.

> Ultimately, the brief karaṇas, and so forth, of the heterodox are not accurate. And why? This follows from the described corruption of the siddhāntas. If the karaṇas, and so forth, were accurate, then the siddhāntas would not be corrupt, because even the karaṇas establish the (longitudes of the) planets.

One does not find an accurate Sun in karaṇas other than those in which an accurate determination with the shadow has been made of the day of the start of the northward passage. Without the accurate shadow for the northward passage, the solar longitude will not be accurate. If the solar longitude is not accurate, then as a result the lunar longitude will not be accurate. Similarly, as Maṅgala (Mars) and so forth are subtracted from the solar longitude, if the

> *solar longitude is not accurate then their longitudes will also not be accurate.*

The distinction between tropical and sidereal zodiacs is not spelled out here, but the intention is clear enough. If the longitude of the Sun is determined, thereby defining the zodiac, by reference to a shadow at the time of the solstice, this can only define a tropical zodiac. The actual definition occurs later in the text, during the commentary to verse 38.

It is interesting to note that the main Indian siddhāntas (Sewell, p.10) place the coincidence of the tropical and sidereal zodiacs at the beginning of the 6th century CE. I shall show later that the planetary calculations included in the Kālacakra Tantra almost certainly are derived from one of these siddhāntas, described by Varāhamihira with an epoch of 505 CE.

It is from that time that the Kālacakra would claim to have adhered to a correct, tropical, zodiac. Presumably one interpretation of the Kālacakra criticism of other Indian systems is that they misunderstood the nature of the zodiac, and confused it with the fixed stars.

I should point out that I use the term 'passage' here in a way slightly different from normal western usage. The meaning in the original texts is to divide the motion of the Sun in a year into two halves (*bgrod pa, ayana*), one when it is travelling towards the north, between the winter and summer solstices, and the other when it is travelling back towards the south. It seems reasonable to call these the northward and southward passages.

The normal western use of passage is similar, but in that case northern passage refers to the half of its orbit when the Sun is north of the Earth's equator—between the spring and autumn equinoxes.

The comment that the longitudes of Mars and the other planets are subtracted from the longitude of the Sun is a reference to the importance of the Sun in the calculation of the geocentric longitude of the planets.

> So, as their longitudes for the planets are not accurate, the planetary prognostications and horoscopes of the heterodox are pointless. Now, if women and children were able to determine movements of the planets from the siddhāntas, these children and others would quickly understand the planets.

Therefore, as a result of their jealousy, the evil heterodox thought, "If women, children, and others come to understand the movements of the planets, who will have respect for us? Therefore we should hide the siddhāntas and use the karaṇas of the Tantras." Having discussed this, they hid the siddhāntas and calculated the Tantra karaṇas.

So that such children and others would not be able to cope with these and would avoid them, not even wanting to hear the name of astrology, they created in the Tantras many different values for the counts of days, and complicated the karaṇas with the inclusion of the four motions, slow, fast, and so forth. And so, through the course of time, the karaṇa definitions became inaccurate; with these inaccurate the solar longitude is inaccurate, and with the solar longitude inaccurate, the longitudes of all the planets become inaccurate.

So, the evil heterodox arranged the karaṇas so that others would be unable to understand them, and through the course of time due to their harming others, they too have come to misunderstand them. For this reason, harming others is totally contradictory.

Now, the daily motion of the longitude of the planets will be explained.

14. Siddhānta and Karaṇa astronomy

The count of years since the epoch

To fire (3) sky (0) ocean (4) add (the years) since Prabhava; this establishes the year of the barbarian. The years since the lord of the barbarian less hand (2) snake (8) Moon (1), the remainder should be multiplied by Sun (12). Adding the months since Caitra, multiply the lower by age (4), and divide by sky (0) fire (3) Moon (1). The quotient is added to the upper, and lord of men, yields the true number of months. [27]

> Now is explained a little about the brief karaṇas, by "To fire sky ocean," and so forth. The definition for this Tantrarāja is transient, as after sixty years the definition needs to be re-established. Here, for the definition of the karaṇa, 600 years after the time of the Tathāgata is the time of Mañjuśrī, and 800 years from then is the time of the barbarian. 182 years after that time of the barbarian is the time of Aja, the time of Kalkī Aja who corrected the brief karaṇa.

In literature of this kind, numbers are represented by symbolic names. These texts were written in verse form, and such names would have made for better poetry and ease of memorization. The terms used usually reflect some known list or other quality that would be associated with the number concerned. Easily understandable examples are "hand" and "eye," both of which represent the number two.

Most of these symbolic names are for single numbers, although double digit values are sometimes used. For numbers greater than one digit, the individual numbers are to be understood "backwards." So, the present "fire (3) sky (0) ocean (4)" means four hundred and three, and "hand (2) snake (8) Moon (1)" one hundred and eighty-two. Again, I have decided here to follow John Newman (e.g., Newman, 1987, p. 538) and give in the Tantra verses the value of these symbolic numbers in brackets. This makes it much easier to follow the calculations that are being described.

> It is this time, after the year of the barbarian, that is the definition for the karaṇas.
>
> Regarding (the years) "since Prabhava," this refers to Prabhava, which is the beginning of (a period of) sixty years. The years since Prabhava are the years that have passed since prabhava until the present year, and this is the (number of) years since Prabhava.
>
> This is "added" to the value of four hundred and three and "establishes the year of the barbarian." Having taken this one year as the first, however many sixty-year cycles have passed, that many are added to the years

> since Prabhava. This year is well known to other karaṇas, just as the Sunday (is the first) of the weekdays.
>
> Adding this to the number four hundred and three establishes the year of the barbarian. The barbarian is Madhumatī, the incarnation of al-Rahman, teacher of the barbarian dharma, and guru and lord of the barbarian Tajiks.
>
> Regarding "The years since the lord of the barbarian less hand snake Moon," less hand snake Moon means subtract one hundred and eighty-two, and this is the year of Kalkin Aja in Sambhala. This now is the count of years for the brief karaṇa.

There are three dates described together here. The first (chronologically) is the time of the "year of the barbarian," and one would expect this to be the date of the start of the Islamic calendar, 622 CE. However, for reasons that will be soon be described, that date must instead be 624 CE, although it is not clear why what appears very much to be an Islamic date, is reckoned from two years after Hijra, the flight of Mohammed. (For an extensive discussion of this subject, and the dating of the Kālacakra epoch, see Newman, 1998b.)

The second date is the actual epoch of the Tantra calculations, and the third is the year from the point of view of which these calculations are being described. This latter date is said to be the year when the Kālacakra Tantra was translated into Tibetan, and is also the first year (Prabhava) of a sixty-year cycle. As the Vimalaprabhā itself states, this year is "well known," and we can easily place it at 1027 CE.

This would put the epoch as 806 CE (following the calculation given, 1027 - 403 + 182 = 806), and in fact, this is the only date that fits. This is, after all, an epoch for the calculation of a calendar, and the description of that calendar includes epoch positions for the Sun, Moon, and planets. The new Moon day of Tuesday 24th March 806 CE is the only date that provides a good fit to the astronomical arrangement described in the Tantra. For immediate years either side of 806 CE (I have done computerized searches through many more years than are needed—many dozens), the planetary positions on equivalent new Moon days are very different from those given in the Tantra.

The facts that the year 1027 CE is very well known and that 806 CE provides the only reasonable fit for the astronomical data leave little room for doubt over the epoch, although the question of the two year difference with the usual Islamic calendar remains unanswered.

One possible explanation lies in the fact that there were two methods of counting these cycles of sixty years in India, commonly known as the northern and southern systems. Up until a point early in the 10th century CE (see Sewell, Tables, xxxviii) both of these systems expunged years in order to keep the cycle in step with the motion of Jupiter—the origin of these cycles.

After that point, only the northern system continued to expunge years, and the southern system stopped doing so, and kept a regular count of sixty years. The Kālacakra system and subsequent Tibetan use of these cycles follow this same regular cycle of years.

As it happens, between the time of the start of the Islamic calendar and the critical date of 1027 CE there were five years expunged from the southern calendar and three from the northern—a difference of two years. It is easy to imagine a calculation reckoning 1027 CE in terms of Hijra, missing the difference between these two systems of sixty-year cycles, and producing a result of 403 years instead of the correct 405 years.

Another similar possibility arises from the fact that in both northern and southern systems there were two expunged years between Hijra and the Tantra epoch of 806 CE. Again, a miscalculation could have been performed regarding these two dates.

We have no proof that either of these happened, but they are far more likely than that the epoch was a date other than 806 CE. If that were the case, then the planetary positions given in the Tantra do not fit with the real positions at the epoch—no such match can be found—but do closely match the real positions on this particular day in 806 CE simply by chance. This is not at all likely!

Calculation of the count of months

> Regarding "the remainder should be multiplied by Sun," in order to derive the count of months, the count of years that remains from having subtracted one hundred and

> eighty-two, should be multiplied by twelve, and this produces the count of months.
>
> Regarding "Adding the months since Caitra," to that count of months, in order to derive the count of months to the present month, add the number of months to the current month since the month of Caitra.
>
> Regarding "multiply the lower by age," having the count of months in lower and upper places, in order to determine the extra months during the count of months, multiply the lower quantity by "age," meaning by four.
>
> Regarding "and divide by sky fire Moon," every thirty-two and a half months there is an extra (intercalary) month, when the Sun does not change (sign) before the new Moon, and therefore this is not counted. (The division by "sky fire Moon" implies a division by 130, four times thirty-two and a half.)
>
> Multiplying the quantity by four produces the fractional part. This fractional part that is multiplied by four: there is nothing needed (to be added) as there is nothing that is carried forward, and so the quantity to be divided is just multiplied by four.

This point is a little obscure, and I have translated it assuming that it is referring to the fact that for the epoch month the intercalation index is zero, and therefore no epoch value needs to be added to the fractional part in this calculation.

> Therefore, this quantity that is divided by the fractional part, from this arises the result of a quotient. "The quotient is added to the upper," means that the quotient is the number of extra months and this is added to the upper quantity, "and lord of men, yields the true number of months," for (calculating) the 30 lunar days of the current month.

The calculation now moves on to derive the count of the true month from the count of years from the epoch. This is very similar to the calculation given in chapter one, except that instead of multiplying the lower value by 2 and then dividing by 65, it is instead multiplied by 4 and then divided by 130. The reason for this is given as poetic, and has no bearing on the result.

In the notation used in chapter one, after first multiplying the year count by 12 and adding months since Caitra if necessary, we find the true month from the formula:

M × 1;4 + 0;0 (130)

Nothing is added here, no epoch value for the intercalation index. The reason for this is that the month we are calculating for is itself a delayed month. The relevant new Moon—on 24th March 806 CE—is at the end of an intercalary month. This, combined with the fact that on the preceding full Moon there was a total lunar eclipse—an excellent time for adjusting luni-solar calculations—may well provide part of the reasoning why this date was chosen as an epoch.

Also, on the day of the new Moon itself, there was a partial solar eclipse. According to my calculations this would have been visible from northern India at, and shortly after, sunrise. Another good data point for calendar makers. (Interestingly, and perhaps these two events had some symbolic significance, the full Moon on 8th March 806 CE was at maximum just around sunset in northern India—the Moon itself would have just been rising.)

The Tantra is said to be a discourse by the Buddha, and in the final comment "and lord of men, yields the true number of months," he addresses the king of Sambhala, Sucandra, who is said to have requested the Tantra from the Buddha. Similar comments are found many times throughout the text.

Calculation of the mean weekday

With the true month in three places, multiply the middle number by hand (2) summit (3). The quotient from dividing the base by six yields a deficit that is to be subtracted from the middle. To the top and the one beneath add eye (2) and thirty; then clearly from the latter sum is taken a sixtieth part, the quotient from which is added above and divided by sage (7) with the remainder being the weekday. [28]

> Now the definition of the month is explained: "With the true month in three places, multiply the middle number by hand summit."
>
> Here, having put the true month in three places, in order that the month (value) that is in the middle place produce the weekday nāḍī for each month, it is multiplied by hand summit, meaning, multiplied by thirty-two.
>
> "The quotient from dividing the base by six" means that the quotient from dividing the base (lower) figure by six "yields" for the middle figure "a deficit." As this is a deficit, it "is to be subtracted from the middle" figure.
>
> "To the top and the one beneath add eye and thirty; then clearly." This definition, in order to reduce Mars (Tuesday?) and so forth, and thereby develop Sun (Sunday?) and so on, the value of two weekdays is added to the upper figure, and thirty is added to the lower nāḍī quantity. So to the top and the one beneath are added "eye and thirty."

This mention of Mars and the Sun is the most obscure point in this whole calendrical section of the Vimalaprabhā. It occurs again during the calculation of the year change and some possible interpretations are given then.

> Regarding "from the latter sum is taken a sixtieth part," the basic quantity of nāḍī is divided by sixty, and the quotient from this becomes a count of weekdays, and the remainder becomes the quantity of nāḍī passed within the weekday.
>
> Regarding the "quotient from which is added above," the quotient from the division by sixty which is a count of weekdays, is added to the upper weekday quantity.

> Then, "and divided by sage," this value is divided by seven "with the remainder being the weekday."
>
> In this definition for the month, the weekday is placed as the upper quantity and underneath it is the count of nāḍī.

This calculation for the mean weekday is easily summarised by the following, given a true month value of M:

M × 1 + 2
M × 32 - X + 30
M ÷ 6 = X (any remainder can be used for greater accuracy)

Working from the bottom, the true month value is divided by 6, and this result is subtracted from the second line, the month value, after it has been multiplied by 32. The value of 2 is added to the top line, and 30 to the middle line. These represent the epoch value, in other words the value of the mean weekday at the mean new Moon of the epoch: 2;30,0.

The text then goes on to describe the need to divide by 60 and 7 where necessary to derive the final answer.

Another way of representing this formula is to see that the division by 6 on the third line is taking 10 pala away for each month. So, instead of the weekday change each month being 1;32,0 it is in fact 1;31,50. So, the calculation could be expressed as:

M × 1;31,50 + 2;30,0

It was usual just to keep the two figures for the weekday and nāḍī, the nāḍī written underneath the weekday figure.

Calculation of the anomaly

> *With two places, having added Sun (12) Moon (1), divide by season (6) Sun (12); the total from the addition of element (5) Is added to the upper sum, first multiplied by hand; dividing by eight and two is the anomaly. Multiply the middle of three places by Īśa (11); two is added to the result of dividing the lower by nine and quality (3), then subtracted from the middle; this is divided by nāḍī*

(60) and the result is an increment added to the upper quantity, by which two [29]

Has been multiplied; this is divided by mansions (27), and the remainder, lord of men, yields the longitude of the Sun, mansions, and so forth. To the weekday, add a weekday, and twice lord of men (16) to the nāḍī; to the lower anomaly, also add two; Two mansions and Rudra (11) nāḍī are the correct increment, and are to be added to the solar longitude; These (methods) produce the definitions for the months, and so it is said are added month by month. [30]

Now is explained the steps for the weekday, from "With two places, having added Sun Moon." With the true month in two places, add Sun Moon, or one hundred and twelve. This value of "Sun Moon" is from the point of view of the karaṇa and not the siddhānta.

Regarding "divide by season Sun," the lower count of months is divided by one hundred and twenty-six, and the quotient becomes an increment for the upper quantity. Then, "adding to the upper sum," and so that each month the count (advances by) two, this is "first multiplied by hand," and after this the addition is performed.

Regarding "the total from the addition of element," this is from the point of view of the karaṇa, but dividing by the season Sun fraction is siddhānta. The division by one hundred and twenty-six is due to the stepping of the Moon, and the increase in the count value by a count of one (every 126 months).

"Dividing by eight and two is the anomaly," means that dividing (the upper quantity) by twenty-eight yields the anomaly. As the quadrants are of seven weekdays, the divisor is twenty-eight.

Dividing by this divisor yields the weekday step for each month, and this is (placed) below the weekday's nāḍī. The remainder from dividing by the season Sun

> divisor yields the fractional part of the anomaly, and is placed below the anomaly.

Here is described the anomaly calculation, which is in just the same form as that given in chapter one. As described here, it would be represented:

$$M \times 2 + 5 + P = Y \div 28 = Q \text{ rem. } S$$
$$M + 112 = X \div 126 = P \text{ rem. } R$$

S and R are the anomaly. The values 5 and 112 are the epoch values for the anomaly, and here they are described as karaṇa values. They are for a particular moment in time, an epoch, and the siddhānta, the theory, provides the values 28 and 126 that are the same for all anomaly calculations.

Another way of representing this calculation would be:

$$M \times 2;1 + 5;112\ (28,126)$$

In the description it is mentioned that the anomaly is written below the weekday number of nāḍī. By this stage in the calculation, four numbers would be written one above the other. On top, the weekday value, next the weekday nāḍī, next the whole value for the anomaly, and finally the anomaly fractional part.

Calculation of mean solar longitude

> Now the definition of the Sun's mansion is explained, with "Multiply the middle of three places by Īśa," and so forth. The true month is put in three places, an upper, middle, and lower. The month value that is in the middle is multiplied by Īśa, by eleven. Multiplying by eleven is from the point of view of the karaṇa and not siddhānta.
>
> "Two is added to the result of dividing the lower by nine and quality," means that the lower quantity is multiplied by nine and quality, thirty-nine, and the result added to two—this addition of two is an addition for the karaṇa. "Then subtracted from the middle," means that

> this is a deficit for the middle quantity and is subtracted from it.
>
> "This is divided by nāḍī and the result is an increment," means that the middle quantity is divided by nāḍī, sixty, and the quotient becomes an increment for the upper quantity, the count of mansions. The remainder from dividing by sixty becomes the number of nāḍī of the mansion.
>
> This increment is "added to the upper quantity, by which two has been multiplied; this is divided by mansions," meaning that the result is divided by twenty-seven leaving a "remainder." "Lord of men" is an address, and "yields the longitude of the Sun, mansions, and so forth," means that the result is the count of mansions, and below it the count of nāḍī of the mansion.

This calculation is more complex than the previous one, and can be represented, where M is the true month count, as:

$$M \times 2 + P = \div 27 = T \text{ rem. } X$$
$$M \times 11 - (R+2) = N \div 60 = P \text{ rem. } Y$$
$$M \div 39 = R \text{ rem. } Z$$

First, the upper and middle figures of the month count are multiplied respectively by 2 and 11. The lowest value is divided by 39, the quotient that results (R) is added to 2, and the sum of these subtracted from the middle. This value of 2 is in fact the epoch value—the mean solar longitude at the mean new Moon. It is subtracted for simplicity. The actual epoch value of the mean solar longitude is 26;58, and it is easier to subtract 0;2 than add the full value. The result is the same.

The usual value for the mean motion of the Sun in one month in karaṇa calculations is 2;10,58,2,10 (13). Instead of multiplying by this, we are instead multiplying the month count by 2;11, and then subtracting one thirty-ninth of a nāḍī for each month. One thirty-ninth of a nāḍī is 0;0,1,3,3 (13), and if we subtract this from 2;11, we find:

2;11,0,0,0 - 0;0,1,3,3 = 2;10,58,2,10 (13)

Although this present calculation looked at first sight quite different from the type one would normally expect, it is in fact essentially the same. Our present calculation can now be represented as:

M × 2;10,58,2,10 + 26;58,0,0,0

In the text this multiplication by 11 is said to be for the karaṇa and not the siddhānta because the monthly mean motion of the Sun in the siddhānta is: 2;10,58,1,17 (67). The value 11 is not part of an epoch value, but of an approximation to the monthly mean motion, and for this reason is referred to as karaṇa.

As before, the epoch value (here a subtraction of 2) is also said to be from the point of view of the karaṇa.

Approximate calculations for later months

> Although it is not (completely) accurate, in order that children could understand an approximate definition for (further) months, "to the weekday, add a weekday," meaning that the value of one is added to the weekday place. "And twice lord of men to the nāḍī"; here, lord of men means sixteen, and so "twice lord of men to the nāḍī" means that thirty-two is added to the nāḍī position.
>
> "To the lower anomaly, also add two" means that the value two should be added to the anomaly which is underneath the nāḍī value. To the mansion place "two mansions and Rudra nāḍī," means that to the place of the mansion's nāḍī, as Rudra, eleven, nāḍī need to be added, "are the correct increment, and are to be added to the solar longitude," to the mansion, and so forth.
>
> For this reason, "these (methods) produce the definitions for the months, and so it is said are added month by month." Thus the Tathāgata predicted for the future that from the point of view of the definitions of the months, (these values) should be added for each month.

These are simplified calculations for successive months, thereby avoiding the need to repeat the same long hand calculation for each month. These are very simplified, and to the weekday value, for each successive month is added 1;32, and to the anomaly 2;0. It is surprising that the need to add the value one to the fractional part of the anomaly is not given in the text. Finally, for each month the value 2;11 is added to the solar longitude.

We can presume that the use of these approximate calculations was not encouraged because the unknown author of the old Indian text, the Kālacakra Anusāri Gaṇita (KBhaga, p. 61), states that they are for when one "becomes lazy (*le lo, alasa*) of calculating."

The reason for the inclusion of these calculations is probably political. The point is made that this Kālacakra system is even usable by children, in contrast to the Hindu siddhāntas that are considered gratuitously complex and elitist.

Table for calculation of the true weekday

For the lunar days there are addition, subtraction, and again addition, in the weekday, nāḍī, and steps; Dividing the anomaly by ocean (4) Moon (1) to yield even or odd, is the quadrant indicator of addition or subtraction. For zero, it is exactly zero; at thirteen the lunar step is five, eye (2) and Sun (12) both direction (10); At eleven (and) fire (3) is lunar day (15); at ten and ocean (4) the step is twenty less one. [31]

Now is explained the derivation from the definitions of the months of lunar days, and so forth. "For the lunar days there are addition, subtraction, and again addition, (respectively) in the weekday, nāḍī, and steps: Here, from the definition of each month, from the first waxing lunar day, from the first lunar day to the thirtieth at new Moon, for each of these there is addition, and subtraction, and again addition.

In the weekday place there is addition in order to derive each particular weekday. In the nāḍī place is subtraction, because by the month's fractional part the nāḍī are reduced. In the place of the anomaly there is again

> addition in order to determine the increments and decrements in the steps of the Moon.

The process that is being described here in rather awkward terms is of the preparation of the figures for determining the weekday values for the whole of a month. The calculation will be performed for each lunar day in turn, but first the mean values need to be prepared.

Going through the lunar days, for each one the weekday value will increase by one, but as the lunar days are slightly shorter than solar days, the nāḍī figure for the mean weekday will decrease. The anomaly is needed in order to adjust to the true weekday, and this increases each lunar day. Therefore there is for each lunar day an addition, a subtraction, and another addition.

> Regarding "Dividing the anomaly by ocean Moon to yield even or odd, is the quadrant indicator of addition or subtraction"; in the place of the anomaly, divide the anomaly by ocean Moon, fourteen, and if the result is even the quadrant indicator is of increments, and if the result is odd the quadrant indicator is of deficits.
>
> Here, even is a result of two or four, and no result (i.e., zero) is also even; odd is a result of one or three. There are no other results than these, because lunar day of thirty together with the (maximum) anomaly of twenty-seven gives fifty-seven, and this is not exceeded. Dividing this by fourteen yields a result of four.
>
> Whether there is addition or subtraction is to be understood by the quadrant indicator of even or odd results. Regarding the quadrant indicator, the lunar steps are in fourteen places with an upper group of seven steps and a lower reversed group of seven steps, each classified according to the qualities of earth, and so forth. The quadrant indicators are of either addition or subtraction.

This section describes the interpolation method for determining the semi-true weekday. The method is exactly as described in chapter one, with the difference that more simple calculations are performed here, whereas in chapter one we were dealing with the more detailed siddhānta figures.

The interpolation table that is used is exactly the same, and the next section describes first the figures in the total column and then the coefficient column.

> Regarding "for zero, it is exactly zero," if the remainder after dividing by fourteen is zero, then in that case, according to the karaṇa, the step indicator is also zero as there is nothing to be added or subtracted.
>
> "At thirteen the lunar step is five": if the remainder indicates step thirteen or one, this yields either an increment or deficit of five. Similarly, "eye and Sun both direction" means that for a remainder of either the second or twelfth steps there is an increment or deficit of ten.
>
> "At eleven (and) fire," meaning three, "is lunar day," or fifteen. "At" step "ten and ocean," meaning if the fourth step appears as a remainder, "the step is twenty less one."

Five and orifice (9) are twenty-two, season (6) and jewel (8) jina (24), and the seventh is twenty-five; Similarly, this is dependent on the solar steps, and so they will be used in addition or subtraction. Element (5) and element (5), arrow (5) and knowledge (4), fire (3), hand (2), 'having a hare' (1); these are the first section, and also the other. Dividing the anomaly by ocean (4) Moon (1) to yield even or odd, determines whether the coefficient should be added or subtracted. [32]

> "Five and orifice are twenty-two," refers to the fifth and ninth; "season," six, and "jewel," the eighth step, yields "jina," twenty-four. When the remainder indicates "the seventh," "twenty-five" nāḍī are added when even and subtracted when odd, due to the increase and decrease of the movement of the Moon.
>
> "Similarly, this is dependent on the solar steps, and so they will be used in addition or subtraction." This longitude of the lunar day is dependent on the solar steps; it is dependent in that a solar deficit is here also a deficit, and a solar increment is here also an increment.

This comment is making the point that the correction that will be derived later for the solar longitude will also be applied to the semi-weekday value. This was done in the calculations in chapter one, and is the reason that the term "semi-true" is used. To the mean weekday is first added the lunar step correction to derive the semi-true weekday, and then the solar step correction is added to yield the true weekday. These two corrections are needed because the weekday is dependent on the variable speed of both the Moon and the Sun.

The use of the term 'longitude' as a measure of time is not common in English, but it is known, and I use it here because the same word is used in Tibetan (*longs spyod*) and in Sanskrit (*bhoga*) for a measure of both angular distance and time.

The steps for the weekday correction

> Here, the lunar steps: "Element and element, arrow and knowledge, fire, hand, 'having a hare'; these are the first section, and also the other." Element means five. Then again element, so below that also five. Arrow means below that also five. Knowledge means below that a four. Fire means below that a three. Hand means below that a two, and 'having a hare' (a name for the Moon) means below that a step of one.
>
> Such are the steps in seven places. The other seven places are one, and so forth, the reverse of these, giving a total of fourteen steps, up to (the last of) five. In that way the lunar steps should be arranged in fourteen places.
>
> Regarding "Dividing the anomaly by ocean Moon to yield even or odd, determines whether the coefficient should be added or subtracted." Here, inspecting the result of having divided by fourteen; if the result is even, then the coefficient, five and so forth, is added, and if it is odd, then subtracted; if the remainder from the division was one, then the value of five nāḍī is taken.
>
> Two is that which is in the second place, together with ten. Three is in the third place, together with fif-

> teen. Four is in the fourth place, and together with four is one less than twenty.
>
> Five is in the fifth place, and together with three is twenty-two. Six is in the sixth place, and together with two is twenty-four. Seven is in the seventh place, and together with one is twenty-five.
>
> Then, the increase in the lunar steps is reversed, and if eight results, the previous seventh place is subtracted to yield the total of the other six places, twenty-four nāḍī, which is to be added or subtracted.
>
> Ninth, is the twenty-two nāḍī of the fifth step. Tenth is the twenty incomplete by one of the fourth step. Eleventh is the fifteen of the third step. Twelfth is the ten of the second step. Thirteenth is the five of the first step. Fourteenth is zero, and thus is the siddhānta definition.

The table that this has been describing is that of the weekday steps in chapter one.

> *There is a variable if there is a remainder, according to the division by season (6) and Sun (12). As this is also dependent on the Sun, the nāḍī from the solar quadrants are added or subtracted. That which is the product of knowledge (4) and the lunar day is an increment, and has a third of its value added. Season (6) mansions and three quadrants are a deficit, and are to be subtracted directly from the Sun's longitude. [33]*

> Regarding "There is a variable if there is a remainder, according to the division by season and Sun," here, regarding the term '(interpolation) variable' (*rgyu zhing yod pa, saccāra*), the remainder after dividing the lower fractional quantity in the anomaly by "season" and "Sun" (126), this is known as the interpolation variable.
>
> Whichever is the variable step that resulted from dividing the anomaly by 14, the one above it is the interpolation variable step, the one containing the anomaly fractional part. There exists the (true) weekday; and so

> therefore determine this in order to obtain what should be added or subtracted.
>
> Take that step and multiply by the remainder from the anomaly fractional part. The result of this is divided by one hundred and twenty-six and combined as was done before with the count of nāḍī.

This completes the calculation for the semi-true weekday. The terms that are found here are used in somewhat different ways in later Tibetan texts on the subject. The important point is that the step values (5, 5, 5, 4, etc.) that are added to produce the totals (5, 10, 15, 19, etc.) in the table are used to perform linear interpolation between steps.

For the interpolation, these step values are taken as coefficients that will be multiplied by the fraction of the step that is indicated by the remainder, if there is one, from the division by 126. Strictly speaking, that remainder divided by 126 is the interpolation variable that is multiplied by the coefficient, although in this calculation, as integer arithmetic is being performed, the division is performed last.

After making the point that the solar longitude correction needs also to be applied to the semi-true weekday, the text next describes the method and the interpolation table for that solar correction.

> "As this is also dependent on the (longitude of the) Sun," as before, "the nāḍī from the solar quadrants will be added or subtracted." This is siddhānta.

The steps for the solar longitude correction

> Now is explained the longitude of the Sun for each day. Regarding "That which is the product of knowledge and the lunar day is an increment, and has a third of its value added," the product of knowledge and the lunar day is a multiplication, and this product of knowledge and the lunar day becomes an increment in the nāḍī position of the (longitude of the) Sun. A third of this lunar day (value) that was multiplied is added, meaning that this increment is (also) added to the nāḍī position.

This calculation is describing how to determine, from the data for the new Moon, the solar longitude for different lunar days.

The motion of the Sun in one lunar day according to the karaṇa calculations is 0;4,21,5,9 (13). An approximate value is taken here of 0;4,20,0,0—in other words, four and one-third nāḍī. The calculation proceeds by writing the lunar day value down in two places. The first of these is considered to be a number of nāḍī and is multiplied by "knowledge" (4). The other value is then divided by 3, and the quotient—if there is one—is added to the number of nāḍī.

Naturally, more accuracy could be obtained by also considering the remainder to the division by 3, and converting this to a number of pala. This would be done simply by multiplying the remainder by 20.

The resulting value is added to the value for the mean longitude of the Sun at new Moon. This gives what is sometimes called the semi-true solar longitude (*nyi ma phyed dag*)—the mean longitude of the Sun at the exact time for the lunar day under consideration.

Some writers point out that this approximation partly makes up for the earlier error in the monthly calculation for the mean solar longitude. In that calculation, simply adding a value of 2;11 each month is too much, by 1/39th nāḍī. This amounts to 4 of the lowest fractional units each lunar day.

In the present calculation, a value of 0;4,20 is being added for each lunar day which is indeed less than the more correct karaṇa figure of 0;4,21,5,9. The difference is 0;0,1,5,9, which is equivalent to 152 of the lowest fractional units each lunar day. It is rather stretching the arithmetic to claim that these approximations in any way cancel each other out.

> Regarding "Season mansions and three quadrants are a deficit, and are to be subtracted from the middle of the Sun's longitude" in order accurately to determine the steps for the Sun, for each day the birth-sign of the Sun is subtracted from the solar longitude, to find the nāḍī, pala, and so forth, of the (interpolation) variable.

In the calculation for the stepping of the Sun, the individual steps are whole signs of the zodiac, and the interpolation variable is the longitude covered between any two steps. This quantity is derived in terms of nāḍī, pala, and so forth, as described here.

Others do not have an accurate Sun in their karaṇas. For this reason, from the longitude, (counted in) mansions from Aśvinī, is subtracted six mansions and three quadrants, or 45 nāḍī. In order for the solar steps to be accurate, three signs from Aries, and so forth, are subtracted, Cancer being the birth-sign (of the Sun).

Therefore "Season mansions and three quadrants are a deficit, and are to be subtracted directly from the Sun's longitude."

By longitude is meant the longitude of mansions, and so forth, and breaking down the Sun's longitude, subtracting directly means that mansions are subtracted from the mansion place, and nāḍī are subtracted from the nāḍī place.

The rest of the method is as for Mars, but the steps for the slow motion are taste (6) age (4) and 'having a hare' (1). Convert the longitude to nāḍī and then divide by arrow (5) quality (3) Moon (1) to yield a quotient and longitude; Due to the passage either an increment or deficit is applied to the Sun; others do not have this correct. For the Sun, time (3), taste (6), snake (8), and ten and Remover (11), Remover (11), Rudra (11), direction (10), nāga (8) and six, [34]

"The rest of the method is as for Mars" means that here the rest of the method for the Sun is to be understood as the same as for Mars, but the variable steps are different.

For the Sun, "the steps for the slow motion are taste, age, and 'having a hare'": "taste" is six, underneath it "age" is four, and underneath that "having a hare" is one. These are the first half, for three signs.

The last half is the reverse of this, with the fourth sign being one, the fifth sign four, and the sixth sign six, the motion here being the 'slow motion.'

It is surprising that this term 'slow motion' is used here, as there is no 'fast motion' for the Sun. However, as the text has stated, the method used for the Sun is the same as that for deriving the 'slow motion' of Mars and the other planets.

> Regarding, "Convert the longitude to nāḍī and then divide by arrow quality Moon to yield a quotient and longitude; Due to the passage either an increment or deficit is applied to the Sun; others do not have this correct," these words are of definitive meaning. Just as with Maṇgala (Mars), the (value for the) variable steps is converted to nāḍī and divided by arrow, quality, Moon, the number of nāḍī, one hundred and thirty-five, in a sign.
>
> The remainder is a number of nāḍī, and in the nāḍī position will become an increment. It can also become a deficit as a result of the passage (of the Sun). Due to the passage of the Sun, from Capricorn, and so forth, it will be an increment, and from Cancer, and so forth, it will be a deficit. Methods described in other karaṇas are not accurate from day to day.

The point here is that between the solstices the Sun is travelling slowly either towards the North, after the winter solstice, between the beginning of Capricorn and the end of Gemini, or towards the south, between the beginning of Cancer and the end of Sagittarius.

According to the Kālacakra Tantra, the birth-sign, or apogee of the Sun is at the very beginning of Cancer. This is when it is at its furthest from the Earth and travelling at its slowest speed. This figure is wrong, and the error rather confuses the situation.

At the time of the epoch of the Kālacakra Tantra, the position of the apogee was about 7°5 Cancer, and currently the value is about 17° Gemini.

However, the two processes mentioned here—the two passages of the Sun between the solstices, and the variable speed of the Sun—are not connected. The variable speed of the Sun depends on its anomaly—the distance from the perigee (which is on the opposite side of the orbit from the apogee). It does not depend at all on the position relative to the solstices and the two passages. The fact that around eight hundred years ago these two coincided clearly gave rise to this confusion, and the Kālacakra

Tantra therefore reads as if the variable speed of the Sun depends upon its position relative to the solstices.

At its apogee—here taken as the beginning of Cancer—the Sun is travelling at its slowest, and the true Sun coincides with the mean Sun. After it has passed that point, the Sun is gathering speed but moves behind its mean position as it is moving slower than the mean Sun. Therefore, the corrections that will be calculated will be subtracted (will be taken as a deficit) from the mean longitude. The true Sun catches up the mean Sun at its perigee, and from then on the corrections have to be added, as it overtakes and moves ahead of the mean.

> Here is explained the method described for the karaṇa: Regarding "For the Sun, time, taste," the deficit for Cancer is in the first half "time," or three nāḍī, and in the second half of Cancer it is "taste," six.
>
> Similarly, in Leo "snake," eight, "and ten." Similarly, in Virgo "Remover," eleven, and again "Remover," eleven. Then in Libra "Rudra," eleven, and "direction," ten. Similarly, in Scorpio "nāga," eight, "and six."

Regarding the 'Remover,' or Hara, it is unclear why the number 11 is associated with this form of Śiva who destroys all things. One possible reason is that he is sometimes considered to be one of the Maruts, and in some sources these are 11 in number. However, one list in which he appears numbers 12 members! (Daniélou, p.105)

Also, regarding the use of symbolic names for numbers, one limitation of the Tibetan translation is highlighted here. In the space of just eight verses, the same Tibetan word, *dus*, has been used to translate three different Sanskrit terms: yuga (age or aeon, 4), ṛitu (season, 6), and, kāla (time, 3, as in the three times of past, present, and future).

> *Fire (3) and space (0), which is the end of the passage, to the north and the south being increment and deficit. From the division of the changes of the months, this gives the longitude of the Sun through six months divided into half-months. To the Sun add the lunar day value and underneath multiply by taste (6), combined with the longitude of the day, By subtraction, yields the "marked by a hare." Lord of men, the yoga is the Sun and the Moon added together. [35]*

> Then in Sagittarius "fire," three, "and space," zero, at "the end of the passage." In the same way, through Capricorn, and so forth, these are increments, this all being for the karaṇa and not the point of view of the siddhānta.
>
> In that way, "From the division of the changes of the months, this gives the longitude of the Sun through six months divided into half-months."

The figures given here are unusual, in that for other interpolation methods—for example, for the weekday, the planetary longitudes, and so on—when a certain number of steps are given, the same number of totals are also given. Here, the steps are effectively divided into two, and yet their values do not provide any greater accuracy.

For example, the first step given, for the sign Cancer, was a value of six nāḍī. The first two totals given here are for the first half of Cancer, three, and the second half six. This is equivalent to saying that taking half months as steps, the first and second steps would both be three.

Then for the next sign, the step given is four nāḍī. Adding to the previous total, this gives a total for the first half of eight, and for the second ten. Again, this is simply dividing the step into two equal halves.

The third month is a little different, in that the total of eleven is arrived at in the first half of the sign, as if the first half-step were one, and the second zero. This is not unreasonable, as the rate of increase is slowing down dramatically at this point, and in fact theoretically becomes zero at the end of the third sign.

The figures for the fourth sign may look odd—the first and last sets of three signs should be symmetrical—but they are not. Given that the first half-step will be zero, the first total in the fourth sign is again eleven, and then as the second half-step has a value of one, and the totals are now decreasing, the second total is ten.

Similarly, the totals continue until we reach the last, the second total of Sagittarius, which has a value of zero. It is clear that these totals are for the middle and end of each of the signs, but it is not clear at all why they are given in this way.

The reason may simply be historical, and that the Indian values from which these Kālacakra figures are derived were originally given in the same format, perhaps to suit an old calculation method. For example, in the *Pañcasiddhānta*, Varāhamihira (Pañca, pp. 182, 183) gives a set of values for the same purpose, very similar in magnitude, and also for every 15°—every half a sign—although the signs themselves are not confused with the solar anomaly, as in the Kālacakra. See also Pingree (Pingree, p. 659 ff.) for a discussion of the possible origin of these figures, and chapter one for an analysis of their accuracy.

Calculation of the lunar mansion at change of lunar day

> Now is explained the longitude of the Moon (for successive lunar days). "To the Sun add" means that to the longitude of the Sun (at new Moon) is added "the lunar day value" and "underneath multiply by taste," that underneath this lunar day value also multiply it by six.
>
> "Combined with the longitude of the weekday" means combine with the nāḍī position of the longitude for the weekday, "by subtraction," and this yields the longitude of "marked by a hare" (the Moon).

The point of this method is to find the longitude of the Moon on successive lunar days, first at the precise moment of the lunar day change. The starting point is the longitude of the Sun, which was just corrected. As each lunar day the separation between the Sun and Moon increases by a fixed amount—this is how the lunar days are in fact defined—then we simply multiply that quantity by the lunar day number, and add the result to the longitude of the Sun at new Moon.

The separation between the Sun and Moon each lunar day is 12°, which is just less than a single lunar mansion: 0;54. This is six nāḍī less than a whole lunar mansion, and so the first step is to add to the solar longitude, the lunar day value taken as a number of mansions. It is then taken as a number of nāḍī multiplied by six, and then this new value is subtracted from the new longitude for the Sun. This yields the longitude of the Moon at the very end of the lunar day in question.

The final point made is that the longitude of the weekday is then subtracted from this. At first sight this is an odd thing to do, as the figures are of different quantities. The longitude of the weekday is a measure of time, the time from daybreak on the weekday in question when the lunar day ends. The longitude of the Moon at the end of the lunar day is an angular measure.

However, as the mean motion of the Moon in a single lunar day is about 58 nāḍī (angular), and the mean length of a lunar day is about 59 nāḍī (time), then clearly the Moon moves at an approximate average speed of one angular nāḍī per nāḍī of time. So, although the values are essentially incompatible, they are in this instance numerically equivalent, and subtracting the weekday longitude from the longitude of the Moon at the end of the lunar day yields the longitude of the Moon at daybreak, at the beginning of the weekday in question. As was the case in chapter one, this is the value that is needed for the calendar.

> "The yoga is the Sun and the Moon added together," means that the yoga is derived by adding together the longitudes of the Sun and the Moon.

> *For the karaṇa multiply the lunar day by eye (2), subtract Moon (1) and take the remainder of division by seven. To the true year add nāga (8) and multiply by space (0) sky (0) ocean (4), subtracting the result of multiplying by nāga (8); Divide by mountain (7) Moon (1) fire (3), multiplying by sky (0) taste (6) divide again by mountain (7), and so forth for nāḍī. Here the definition is two and thirty, for the weekday and nāḍī, in the month of the change of year. [36]*

> Regarding "For the karaṇa multiply the lunar day by eye, subtract Moon," eye is two, by which the lunar day value is multiplied, one is subtracted and "the remainder of division by seven" produces the karaṇa. The longitude of the weekday becomes the longitude.

This is a rather incomplete description of the calculation needed, and it would seem easier in practice not to a use a calculation, but a lookup table to determine the karaṇa. Perhaps the reason this description is so brief is that it is for completeness and theoretical purposes, rather than actual use.

The point is that there are exactly two karaṇa in each lunar day, and for that reason the lunar day value is first multiplied by two. There are four karaṇa that do not change, and a list of seven that rotate through the lunar days. The first half of the first lunar day is one of the constant karaṇa (the other three are the last three in any month) and then the following karaṇa are a repeating list of seven. So, to discount the first constant karaṇa, one is subtracted, and then to determine the position in the list of seven, the remainder is taken after a division by seven.

The method is clearly incomplete, and as this calculation is performed for daybreak, the amount of the current lunar day that has passed will need to be taken into consideration. This is determined from the longitude of the weekday, and this will also enable the determination of the amount of the current karaṇa that has passed. These points are presumably implied by the cryptic comment: "the longitude of the weekday becomes the longitude." This method is very similar to that given by Banda Gelek and cited in chapter one.

> These are the five components: the weekday, lunar day, lunar mansion, yoga, and karaṇa.
>
> Regarding these, the weekdays are Sunday (Sun), Monday (Moon), Tuesday (Mars), Wednesday (Mercury), Thursday (Jupiter), Friday (Venus) and Saturday (Saturn).
>
> The lunar days are from lunar day one up to fifteen.
>
> The lunar mansions are: Aśvinī, Bharaṇī, Kṛittikā, Rohiṇī, Mṛigaśirā, Ārdrā, Punarvasu, Puṣya, Aśleṣā, Maghā, Pūrvaphālgunī, Uttaraphālgunī, Hastā, Citrā, Svati, Viśākhā, Anurādhā, Jyoṣṭā, Mūlā, Pūrvāṣāḍhā, Uttarāṣāḍhā, Śravaṇā, Dhaniṣṭhā, Śatabhṛiṣā, Pūrvabhādrapadā, Uttarabhādrapadā, and Revatī, a total of twenty-seven.
>
> Similarly, the yogas are: Viṣkambha, Prīti, Āyuśmān, Saubhāgya, Śobhana, Atigaṇḍa, Sukarma, Dhṛiti, Śūla, Gaṇḍa, Vṛiddhi, Dhruva, Vyāghāta, Harṣaṇa, Vajra, Siddhi, Vyatipāta, Varīyan, Parigha, Śiva, Siddha, Sādhya, Śubha, Śukla, Brahma, Indra, and Vaidhṛiti, a total of twenty-seven.
>
> The latter half of the white lunar day one is Vava, the first and latter halves of two are Vālava and Kaulava, the first and latter halves of three are Taitila and Garaja, the first and latter halves of four are Vaṇija and Viṣṭi. Similarly, five has Vava and Vālava, six Kaulava and Taitila,

seven Garaja and Vaṇija, and the first half of eight is Viṣṭi.

The latter half of eight is Vava, the first and latter halves of nine Vālava and Kaulava, the first and latter halves of ten Taitila and Garaja, and the first and latter halves of eleven Vaṇija and Viṣṭi.

Then, the first and latter halves of twelve are Vava and Vālava, thirteen Kaulava and Taitila, fourteen Garaja and Vaṇija. The first half of the full Moon day is Viṣṭi and the latter half Vava.

The first and latter halves of the black lunar day one are Vālava and Kaulava, the first and latter halves of two Taitila and Garaja, and the first and latter halves of three are Vaṇija and Viṣṭi. Similarly, four has Vava and Vālava, five Kaulava and Taitila, six Garaja and Vaṇija, and the first half of seven is Viṣṭi. The latter half is Vava. Eight has Vālava and Kaulava, nine Taitila and Garaja, the first and latter halves of ten Vaṇija and Viṣṭi.

Similarly, eleven has Vava and Vālava, twelve Kaulava and Taitila, thirteen Garaja and Vaṇija, and the first half of fourteen is Viṣṭi, and this completes the progress of the seven (changing) karaṇa. Then, the latter half of black fourteen is Śakuni, the first half of new Moon Catuṣpada, and the latter half Nāga. The first half of white lunar day one is Kintughna, and the latter half is again Vava. This completes the (list of the) karaṇa and the five components.

Aśvinī, Bharaṇī, and the first quadrant of Kṛittikā are in Aries. In this way, nine quadrants are understood to constitute Aries and the other twelve signs.

Mars, Venus, Mercury, Moon and Sun, Mercury, Venus, Bhauma (Mars), Guru (Jupiter), Saturn, "Child of the Sun" (Saturn), and "Guru of the gods" (Jupiter); these respectively are the rulers of the signs, Aries and so forth.

> Now for the heterodox to be able to ascertain signs, the assignment of the letters is described. Here, when the natal chart and the vowels and consonants are not known, the Ṛiṣi examine the letters of the name according to this arrangement.
>
> a i u e are Kṛittikā. o va vi vu are Rohiṇī. ve vo ka ki are Mṛigaśirā. ku gha nga cha are Ārdrā. ke ko ha hi are Punarvasu. hu he ho ḍa are Puṣya. ḍi ḍu ḍe ḍo are Aśleṣā. ma mi mu me are Maghā. mo ṭa ṭi ṭu are Pūrvaphālgunī. ṭe ṭo pa pi are Uttaraphālgunī. pu ṣa ṇa ṭha are Hastā. pe po ra ri are Citrā. ru re ro ta are Jyoṣṭā. ye yo bha bhi are Mūlā. bhu dha pha ḍha are Pūrvāṣāḍhā. bhe bho ja ji are Uttarāṣāḍhā. ju je jo kha are Śravaṇā. khi khu khe kho are Abhijit. ga gi gu ge are Dhaniṣṭhā. go sa si su are Śatabhṛiṣā. se so da di are Pūrvabhādrapadā. du tha jha ña are Uttarabhādrapadā. de do ca ci are Revatī. cu ce co la are Aśvinī.
>
> These are the letters associated with the names of the twelve signs.

There are some differences in the letters given in some of these groups between the standard Tibetan translation of the Vimalaprabhā and the current Sanskrit edition (Vimala, 1, p. 86). The "White Beryl" (Baidkar 1, p. 97) agrees closely with the Sanskrit Vimalaprabhā, and I have therefore given the same letters here. The differences are probably due to variants in the Sanskrit manuscripts used by the Tibetan translators.

There is also quite a contradiction here. A list has been described of four letters for each of 28 mansions, giving a total of 112 letters or quadrants. However this has now been associated with the twelve signs of the zodiac, and yet this is only possible with a list of 27 mansions, when nine quadrants of mansions make up each zodiacal sign, with a total of 108 quadrants. Neither Khedrupje nor Mipham discuss this problem.

> The reasoning of the heterodox is hollow when they think that "with these letters the zodiac signs of beings can be understood and from that the good and bad re-

> sults that they experience." Ultimately, all good and bad (results) are determined by one's actions.
>
> Regarding this: "For all weekdays, lunar days, mansions and yogas, karaṇas, ascendants, and evil planets, good will result when virtue is practised. Beings born in the same moment will have different lives and different consequences; dependent on their individual actions, they will not have the same result. Because of battles, forest fires, and entrapment in fishing nets, many beings come to die at the same time. The virtues of beings create strong life, effort, power, and fortune, and their evils weaken life, effort, and power."
>
> This has been a brief account of the karaṇa of five components.

This quotation is said to be from the Kālacakra Mūlatantra, and constitutes a criticism of the literal manner in which primarily Hindu astrologers interpreted the weekdays, lunar mansions, and the rest. The logic that is presented is fairly simple, that beings born at the same time, with the same astrological signs, end up having very different fates, with different lengths of life, different degrees of happiness or misery, and so forth. Also, that many can have exactly the same fate—such as dying together in a forest fire—and yet have very different birth horoscope characteristics.

It should not be understood that the Kālacakra Tantra considers astrology to be meaningless, but that it should not be interpreted as rigidly and fatalistically as was so often the case in ancient India. The Buddhist view would be that a person's horoscope, dependent itself on that person's previous actions, would tell a great deal about their potential in the current life, but that their behaviour in this life is the main determinant of that future.

Definition of the change of karaṇa year

> Now is explained the definition for the change of the karaṇa year, from "To the true year add nāga...." "The true year" is the karaṇa year, and "add nāga" means eight is added; "multiply by space sky ocean" means to

> multiply by four hundred, and "subtracting the result of multiplying by nāga" means then to decrease this by subtracting the (original) result from adding eight to the karaṇa year.
>
> "Divide by mountain Moon fire" means to divide by three hundred and seventeen to produce the weekday value, and "multiplying by sky taste," multiply the remainder by sixty, for nāḍī, and divide by "mountain and so forth" to produce the "nāḍī."

After the addition of eight to the year count, this is multiplied by 400 and then subtracted from this is the original value obtained from the addition of eight. This is a simplified method of multiplying by 399. The result is then divided by 317. It is clear that this is an approximation to the average length of the solar year in terms of solar days.

The siddhānta value for the length of the solar year is 365;16,14,1,12,121 (13,707), and that for the karaṇa is 365;15,30,3,1209 (1277). The equivalent value being used here (364 is a multiple of seven) is:

$$364 + \frac{399}{317} = 365;15,31,1,121\ (317)$$

The calculation would therefore seem to be giving us a weekday and nāḍī value for the return of the Sun to the same point in the zodiac each year, and the addition of eight would seem to be an epoch value, as is needed for all such calculations. However, the next line also looks as though it contains an epoch value, and it is effectively described as such.

> "Here the definition is two and thirty, for the weekday and nāḍī"; this is in order to create the Sun (Sunday?) and so forth from the definition of Mars (Tuesday?) and so forth. To the weekday place two is added, and to the nāḍī place thirty, dividing by sixty, the quotient being weekdays and remainder weekday nāḍī.
>
> The remainder from dividing the weekday place by seven is the weekday, for "the month of the change of year."

As Buton rightly complains (Tskhaga, p. 224), the Vimalaprabhā commentary does not clearly explain this calculation, and none of the Tibetan commentators are able in my opinion satisfactorily to explain what is going on. For example, Lochen Dharmaśrī (Nangser, 198) says that the value 2;30 is added in order to correct for the accumulated error since the original epoch of the Kālacakra Tantra up to the epoch in 1027 CE, due to the difference between the approximate mean motion of the Sun used here, and that—considered accurate—in the siddhānta.

The numbers are close, but this seems more by chance than anything else. The approximate value used here for the length of a solar year is 365;15,31,1,121 (317). The value in the siddhānta is 365;16,14,1,12,121 (13,707).

Multiplying each of these by the 221 year difference between 806 and 1027, we get:

221 × 365;15,31,1,121 = 80722;10,1,5,113 (317)

221 × 365;16,14,1,12,121 = 80724;48,45,1,11,582 (13,707)

Taking these values to the nearest breath, it is clear that after 221 years, we would have to add to the approximate solar day value a difference of 2;38,43,3 in order to make it agree with the siddhānta calculation. Lochen Dharmaśrī performs this calculation as support for his view.

Khedrupje (KDkhas1, 572) makes a similar point, but relates it to the original epoch value as set by the originator of the Kālacakra karaṇa, Kalkī Aja. He says that the view offered by Buton (Tskhaga, p. 224) that the addition of 2;30 is the epoch value of the solar day for the year change is wrong, as the epoch value was given in a simple format by the earlier addition of eight to the true year. Indeed, that does seem to be an epoch value, and the result of calculating for the epoch year (806) gives a value for the day of year change as:

3;4,9,5,17 (317)

This is a Tuesday (Mars) and Khedrupje states that this would be the wrong day, and the correction of 2;30 is added because if it were not, then "the first day of Caitra would be defined as Tuesday, and so forth, and it is so that the first weekday Sunday, and so forth, appear."

This seems more reasonable than Lochen's analysis, except that in the calculations for that epoch year the new Moon at the beginning of Caitra does actually fall on a Tuesday (the first day of Caitra on the Wednesday), and the epoch value for the weekday at that new moon has been given earlier as 2;30. Intriguingly, the true weekday value for the new Moon turns out to be 3;4,45,4,8, but this in no way explains the addition of 2;30 described in the text.

None of this is particularly satisfactory, and I have not found it possible to make these year change calculations fit with any of the actual characteristics that would normally define a year. What seems most likely is that the entry of the Sun into Aries was the original intention here, but there is not clear agreement amongst the various commentators on even this point, and the figures, although close, do not actually fit. Other possibilities are that the figures for the year change are either based on observation, or are borrowed from another tradition and are not even based on the Kālacakra calculations.

I favour the latter explanation, and I have translated these curious phrases regarding Mars and the Sun in a literal manner, without unfortunately understanding their original intention.

> *The additions of weekday and nāḍī for Aries, and so forth, are the following twelve, respectively. Moon (1) mountain (7) element (5) knowledge (4) with quality (3) arrow (5) 'having a hare' (1), and mountain (7) Moon (1), for the third. Knowledge (4) fire (3) element (5) Moon (1) eye (2) with hand (2) age (4) knowledge (4) eye (2) for the sixth. Six and Moon (1) arrow (5) Moon (1) mountain (7) age (4) fire (3) with six Moon (1) knowledge (4) mountain (7) and world (3). [37]*

> Now are explained regarding the definition of the year, the additions for the moves (of the Sun) into Aries, and so forth, with "the additions of weekday and nāḍī for Aries, and so forth." The weekday and nāḍī for the weekday place and nāḍī place are "the following twelve, respectively."
>
> "Moon mountain element" means that "Moon," one, is added to the weekday place, and that "mountain element" fifty-seven, is added to the nāḍī place. Here, tak-

ing the definition of the year, which ever weekday results in the weekday place, on that weekday is the move into Aries. Whatever nāḍī results in the nāḍī place is the respective nāḍī; this is how it is understood in the karaṇa.

"Knowledge," a two syllable word, is used for reasons of poetics, means that knowledge, four, is added to the weekday place. "Quality arrow" means that fifty-three is added to the nāḍī place for the move into Taurus. "Having a hare" means one in the weekday place, and "mountain Moon" seventeen in the nāḍī place, "for the third" move into Gemini.

"Knowledge" means four in the weekday place, "fire element" means fifty-three in the nāḍī place for the move into Cancer. "Moon" is one for the weekday, and "eye with hand" is twenty-two in the nāḍī place for the move into Leo. "Age" means four in the weekday place, and "knowledge eye" is twenty-four in the nāḍī place, for the move into Virgo, "the sixth."

To the weekday add "six and Moon arrow" means fifty-one in the nāḍī place for the move into Libra. "Moon" means one for the weekday, and "mountain age" means forty-seven in the nāḍī place for the move into Scorpio. "Fire" is three in the weekday place, and "six Moon" means sixteen in the nāḍī place for the move into Sagittarius. "Knowledge" is four in the weekday place, and "mountain and world" means thirty-seven in the nāḍī place for the move into Capricorn.

Six with knowledge (4) and zero and zero eye (2) arrow (5) and the Sun reaches the state of Pisces. The increase and decrease through six months of day and night, is caused by the movement of the Sun. Ocean (4) life and fire (3) pala, this is the daily change in each passage. Towards the south, night is increasing, and when towards the snowy mountains of the north, day. [38]

> In the weekday place "Six," and "knowledge and zero," means four in the nāḍī place for the move into Aquarius. "Zero" means nothing to add in the weekday place, and "eye arrow" means fifty-two in the nāḍī place, and with this addition, "the Sun reaches the state of Pisces"; in this way should be understood the longitudes of the (monthly) changes for the karaṇa.
>
> These values for the moves are not found in the siddhānta.

These numbers are not consistent, and have clearly not been derived from the theory (siddhānta). Rather, they must be based either on observation or some other source.

The figures here give the weekday and nāḍī for subsequent sign changes. To understand them properly, we need to add integral multiples of seven weekdays to each.

For example, the first figure given is 1;57. Four weeks have to be added to this, so the figure becomes 29;57. The length of this first zodiacal month then is 29 weekdays and 57 nāḍī, and to determine the day and time when the next month starts we need to add that amount to the date and time found earlier for the year change.

The next figure given is 4;53, and eight weeks need to be added to this to give a figure of 60;53. This needs to be added to the time of year change to give the start of the third month, and gives the length of the second month as:

60;53 - 29;57 = 30;56

This is in fact 29;57 plus 59 pala. Continuing in this way, we can build up a table for all twelve months:

Tantra figure	Total	Month length	Compared to Buton figure	Compared to average figure
1;57	29;57	29;57	29;57+0	30;24-27
4;53	60;53	30;56	29;57+59	30;24+32
1;17	92;17	31;24	29;57+87	30;24+60
4;53	123;53	31;36	29;57+99	30;24+72
1;22	155;22	31;29	29;57+92	30;24+65
4;24	186;24	31;2	29;57+65	30;24+38
6;51	216;51	30;27	29;57+30	30;24+3
1;47	246;47	29;56	29;57-1	30;24-28
3;16	276;16	29;29	29;57-28	30;24-55
4;37	305;37	29;21	29;57-36	30;24-63
6;4	335;4	29;27	29;57-30	30;24-57
0;52	364;52	29;48	29;57-9	30;24-36

There are a couple of things to notice about this table. The first is that the length of a whole year is given as less than 365 days. The figure for a solar year correct to the nearest nāḍī would normally be 365;15.

Interestingly, Buton states (Tskhaga, p. 225) that the karaṇa month is 29;32 days long, and that this is not long enough for the Sun to complete a sign change. For this reason, 25 nāḍī are added for each month, and that then each month length is adjusted for the stepping of the Sun. He provides a list of these values, but does not derive them from the step tables—it seems he just subtracts from the figures given here, as I have done in the table.

The 25 nāḍī that he adds presumably come from the next section of the Vimalaprabhā, which talks of a "missing…twenty-five nāḍī each month."

He is certainly correct that the figures given here appear to have been adjusted for the variable speed of the Sun, but if so, it has not been done very well! If figures such as these were derived from the basic theory and the step tables for the Sun, then they would at least be symmetrical about a six month period, and these clearly are not.

Another puzzling point is that the first sign is said to be the change of the Sun from Pisces into Aries. This would mean that the year change point derived first is for the entry of the Sun into Pisces, and not Aries as one would expect. However, others interpret the "move into Aries" as the completion of the sign of Aries, or the Sun moving out of Aries, and into Taurus.

> Regarding "That which is the product of knowledge and the lunar day is an increment, and has a third of its value added," this loses a nāḍī in (the course of) a month, and so with (the monthly calculation) "Multiply the middle of three places by Īśa," the error is corrected and the solar longitude is accurate.

This is referring back first to the calculation (verse 33) for the mean solar longitude for individual lunar days.

In that calculation an approximation was used for the mean motion of the Sun in a lunar day. That value was 0;4,20,0,0, and in a whole month that would amount to:

$$30 \times 0;4,20,0,0 = 2;10,0,0,0$$

The actual karaṇa value for the monthly motion of the Sun is 2;10,58,2,10 (13), and so the calculation in verse 33, if carried on for a whole month, would fall short by just less a whole nāḍī of longitude, the nāḍī mentioned here.

The next comment quotes the original monthly calculation from verse 30, and makes the point that use of this calculation would correct errors that would otherwise accumulate if the daily figures were used.

> Through the course of a year, the daily longitude is accurate, apart from the measure of days of a solar cycle. Then for the following year, (one uses) another definition for the (sign) changes. For this reason, although for each year the solar longitude is (sufficiently) accurate going from one Caitra month to the next, from the point of view of (determining) successive karaṇa years the definition of the month is not completely accurate.

The point being made here is that in successive years the solar longitude is accurate when dealing with lunar months—the years starting with successive Caitra months. However, the data for the solar longitude for the months is not sufficiently accurate to determine the change of the zodiacal year, when the Sun moves into Aries.

Perhaps the reason that rather crude data has been given for the yearly and monthly changes of the Sun sign is to add force to the argument that is being developed here: that these calculations have a practical value over relatively short periods of time, but in the long term the only way of determining an accurate solar longitude is by solsticial observation.

> The solar longitude for each solar day is inaccurate, as it is missing each day four breaths and three pala. From one northward passage to the next, this amounts to a missing five solar days, which is twenty-five nāḍī each month. From one karaṇa change to the next karaṇa change, there are twenty-five nāḍī extra each month. In one year this is five extra days.

There is a curious discrepancy here between the Tibetan text and the currently available Sanskrit original (Vimala, 1, p. 88), which gives a quantity of "three breaths and four pala." The Tibetan translations of the Vimalaprabhā that I have seen, and subsequent commentators (Khedrupje, Buton, Mipham) use instead the value of "four breaths and three pala."

One can only presume that the translators either had Sanskrit texts with different content from those that survive today, or they assumed that Sanskrit texts that contain the phrase "three breaths and four pala" were in error. It is certainly not an unlikely type of error, particular as the units are written the other way around from what one would expect, and also the figure "four breaths and three pala" fits the next part of the description well.

Buton states that some Sanskrit texts did indeed contain "four breaths and three pala," and his analysis of these figures (Bujigle, p. 497) seems the most cogent. He says that the difference being cited here is between the mean longitude change of the Sun each solar day and each zodiacal day. The zodiacal day is simple, and is a measurement in terms of degrees of longitude. One degree of longitude is equal to 0;4,30,0.

The mean movement of the Sun on each solar day, to the nearest whole day (365) and approximated to the nearest breath, is given by:

$$27;0,0,0 \div 365 = 0;4,26,2$$

The difference between these yields "four breaths and three pala":

0;4,30,0 - 0;4,26,2 = 0;0,3,4

In the 365 days of a whole solar year, this difference between the zodiacal day and solar day data amounts to a longitude difference of:

365 × 0;0,3,4 = 0;22,18,2

If we then divide this by the speed of the Sun (the mean motion in a single day from the year change figures) we get a number of days, which, to the nearest breath is:

0;22,18,2 ÷ 0;4,26,0,78348 (115787) = 5;1,45,1

The comment regarding 25 nāḍī each month is easily understood, as:

5;1,45,1 ÷ 12 = 0;25,8,5

The exactness of the figures here seems not to be the most important point, as this section is really adding more evidence to an important view that is being presented—that none of these figures can be relied upon for the true solar longitude, and observation needs to be made in order to gain accuracy.

Siddhānta definitions

> In order to understand these omissions and additions, for ten days before the first month of the northward passage, the shadow of a gnomon should be carefully studied. That day from which the gnomon shadow shows the turn towards the north, that is the day of the Sun's change, with that weekday, that lunar day, that yoga, and that karaṇa.
>
> On that day the longitude of the Sun has twenty in the mansion place and fifteen in the nāḍī place, and this is the primary definition.

The Vimalaprabhā now starts to explain the key component of the Kālacakra siddhānta; the method of correcting the longitude of the Sun. The "day of the Sun's change" is the day of the winter solstice, and this is the crucial passage for the definition of the zodiac according to the Kālacakra system. The phrase "primary definition" leaves no room for doubt regarding its importance. The figure given of 20;15 corresponds exactly to the beginning of Capricorn, the position of the Sun at the winter solstice in a tropical zodiac.

As the perigee of the Sun is also considered in this system to be at zero degrees Capricorn, the stepping of the Sun is here zero, and so the longitude of 20;15, which is clearly a measure of the true Sun, can be directly applied to both the mean and true Sun.

The description here of finding the day of the solstice does not give the accuracy one would expect, and the more important point is clearly the definition of the zodiac. The author certainly expects the reader to be familiar with the techniques of gnomon analysis.

As the length of the midday shadow changes only very slowly on those days either side of the solstice, one would expect to take shadow measurements for a period of several days either side (at least ten), and use interpolation techniques to determine the time of the solstice. Given the materials likely to be available to the author, an accuracy of a few hours could probably be achieved. However, see the next chapter for the method the Tibetans used to apply this observation.

> With this definition, for each day of all the days of the Sun's period, apply this finding. Then, with the previously explained method, correct the steps of the Sun.

Clearly, the point is to correct the solar longitude, not just for one day, but also for the whole of the following year. How might this be done? A difference between the solar longitude derived from the karaṇa calculations and that determined by gnomon analysis will have been found, but this cannot be applied uniformly to the true Sun figures for the whole year. The mean Sun needs to be adjusted, and then the solar steps applied to determine the true Sun.

> Here follows the description from the Mūlatantra of the days, nāḍī, pala, and breaths of the period of the Sun, and the completion of the zodiac.

In order to perform these quite complex corrections—at least as complex as the original calculations for the karaṇa calendar—certain standard quantities and methods need to be available to the calendar maker, and these are now given from the siddhānta definitions in the Kālacakra Mūlatantra. This is done in the form of a quote from the Mūlatantra, describing these definitions. It is rather like a toolkit of the numerical parameters and methods needed in the calculations.

In this section on the siddhānta definitions, and particularly the following extract from the Mūlatantra, I have relied heavily on the explanation given by Pawo Tsuklag in his "Treasury of Jewels" (Tlkuntu, p. 203, etc.). This text is a commentary to an original work, the "Compendium of Astronomy," by the third Karmapa, Rangjung Dorje, that unfortunately now seems to be lost. However, it could be reconstructed, as Pawo Tsuklag appears to quote every single line of it.

The original text was written in verse, in the same metre as the Mūlatantra, and Rangjung Dorje quotes these verses from the Mūlatantra, interleaving between them his own verses offering further explanation where he felt it was needed. Pawo Tsuklag breaks the resulting extended set of verses into sections, and gives his own commentary and calculation results for each.

As he points out at the end of this section, the quotations from the Mūlatantra in Rangjung Dorje's text are from an earlier translation of the Vimalaprabhā than that available to Pawo Tsuklag (he was writing a little over two hundred years after Rangjung Dorje). He quotes both sets of verses, and these make for an interesting comparison. The earlier verses follow the structure of the Sanskrit original more closely, trying to replicate its grammar, but at the loss of some clarity. The later translation is not so literal and tries more to bring out the intended meaning.

The first quantity to be discussed is the period of the Sun, the time it takes for the "completion of the zodiac."

Period of the Sun in lunar days

> "Multiply one year by space (0) season (6) fire (3). In two places, multiply the lower by two. Dividing by sixty-five, add the result to the upper figure."

Given that a lunar year is defined as twelve lunar months, and a solar cycle as the time for the Sun to make a full circle of the zodiac, this calculation is using the fundamental relationship that 67 lunar years = 65 solar cycles. This is the relationship used to make the determination of the true month figure and to find intercalary months.

The calculation starts with the number of lunar days in a whole lunar year, 360, and this is increased by 2/65th in order to find the number of lunar days in a single solar cycle. This is a siddhānta relationship, and although it is used in the Tantra for the determination of intercalary months, it is not the basis of the karaṇa solar calculation.

The calculation starts by writing the number 360 down in two places. Multiply the lower value by 2 and divide by 65. The quotient is added to the upper figure to yield 371—the whole number of the result. The next couple of verses go on to find the fractional parts of the result.

360 + 11 = 371
360 × 2 = 720 ÷ 65 = 11 rem. 5

> "Then, multiply the remainder by sixty, and dividing again multiply the remainder below by sixty. Dividing again, carry below, and multiply the result by six. The result of dividing by sixty-five, lord of men, is the count of breaths, and again carry below."

The remainder (which was 5) is then multiplied by 60 and divided again by 65. The quotient is the number (4) of nāḍī of the result. The remainder of 40 is carried to the next line down, again multiplied by 60 and the result divided by 65. The quotient of 36 is the number of pala in the result, and the remainder (60) is carried to the next line down.

This is multiplied by 6 and again divided by 65. The quotient (5) is the number of breaths, and the remainder of 35 a number of 65 fractional parts of a single breath. In later Tibetan writings this is normally divided by 5 to give the final fractional part out of 13.

371
5 × 60 = 300 ÷ 65 = 4 rem. 40
40 × 60 = 2400 ÷ 65 = 36 rem. 60
60 × 6 = 360 ÷ 65 = 5 rem. 35

What this is actually doing is: 360 × 1 2/65, with a final result of: 371;4,36,5,7 (13). This is called the lunar day period of the Sun (i.e., the period of the Sun measured in lunar days).

Period of the Sun in solar days

> "The days, nāḍī, and pala are reduced to breaths and written in three places. Divide the bottom by mountain (7) space (0) mountain (7), and add to the middle figure. Divide that by sixty-four and subtract as a deficit from the upper figure. The result yields solar days, nāḍī, pala, and breaths. These being the completion of a cycle are the period of the Sun."

This calculation converts the solar period from lunar days to solar days, using the relationship used with the general day calculation in chapter one:

$$1 \text{ lunar day} = 1 - \left(\frac{1}{64} + \frac{1}{64 \times 707} \right) \text{ solar days.}$$

This is a siddhānta relationship, also given in verse 40 of the Laghutantra. Therefore the two crucial relationships from which can be derived the siddhānta mean motions for the weekdays and the Sun, are not only introduced here in this quote from the Mūlatantra, they are also both found in the Laghutantra.

First, the Sun's lunar day period, 371;4,36,5,7, is reduced to its smallest fractional part. Although the text actually says to reduce down to breaths, going one step further is the usual way this is described by later writers.

$$(((371 \times 60 + 4) \times 60 + 36) \times 6 + 5) \times 13 + 7 = 104198400$$

This number is the lunar day period in terms of the lowest fractional units. The formula is now applied to convert from lunar days to solar days.

Calculating from the bottom, upwards:

$$104198400 - 1630402 = 102567998$$

104198400 + 147381 = 104345781 ÷ 64 = 1630402 rem. 53
104198400 ÷ 707 = 147381 rem. 33

In the formula, the fractional part, the lowest two lines of this calculation, is subtractive, and so the final figure should be reduced by one, to give 102,567,997.

Pawo Tsuklag (Tlkuntu, p. 206) goes further, and describes subtracting the remainder of 53 from the division by 64 from 64, to yield 11, and then, reducing that by one, and subtracting the remainder of 33 from its divisor of 707, to yield 764. This is turning the original result into a normal fractional form, of:

102567997;10,764 (64,707)

The two fractional parts are not needed for what follows, but Pawo Tsuklag (Tlkuntu, 207) points out that their existence means that there is a slight inaccuracy in the following calculation. For more accuracy, these fractional parts would be taken into consideration (see, for example, Desi Sangje Gyatso, in Baidkar 1, p. 190).

This figure of 102,567,997 is now divided by the respective fractional denominators. As before, calculating from the bottom upwards:

21916 ÷ 60 = 365 rem. 16
1314974 ÷ 60 = 21916 rem. 14
7889845 ÷ 6 = 1314974 rem. 1
102567997 ÷ 13 = 7889845 rem. 12

This gives a result for the Sun's period in solar days as: 365;16,14,1,12 (13).

The last comment, that these figures "are the period of the Sun," means that these calculations have derived the period of the Sun in terms of the three types of day—zodiacal, lunar, and solar. The zodiacal day is trivial—there are 360 of them in a full cycle—and that was the starting point of these calculations.

Derivation of mean motions

> "Multiply one day by mansion (27), and similarly by sixty nāḍī; dividing by the period (365) of the Sun, yields the numbers of nāḍī per day. Further multiplying by sixty yields the pala, and by six the breaths."

For each of the different types of day, dividing the number of angular nāḍī in a full circle by the period of the Sun (i.e., a length of time), will yield the mean angular distance (*rtag longs*) covered by the Sun in one such day. The first line here is describing the number that needs to be used as the dividend in these calculations—the number of angular nāḍī in a full circle, which is:

$$1 \times 27 \times 60 = 1620$$

This is then to be divided by the period of the Sun in terms of the three different types of day. For each day, the first division will give the number of angular nāḍī covered, and if there is a remainder, this should be multiplied by 60 and then divided again to yield the number of angular pala. If there is still a remainder, multiply by 6 to derive the number of breaths, and so on.

Pawo Tsuklag (Tlkuntu, p. 208) gives the calculation for all three days, starting with the zodiacal day. It is easy to confuse zodiacal days with degrees, but the intention here is clearly to take them as a measure of time—the time taken for the mean Sun to cover one degree of longitude. There are 360 of these (the number of degrees in a full circle), and so, 1,620 has first to be divided by 360:

$$1620 \div 360 = 4 \text{ rem. } 180$$
$$180 \times 60 = 10800 \div 360 = 30 \text{ rem. } 0$$

So, the mean solar motion in a zodiacal day is: 0;4,30,0. This is a trivial result, and is simply the conversion of one degree of longitude into a measure of mansions, nāḍī, etc.

In order to determine the Sun's mean motion in a lunar day, the period in terms of lunar days must first be reduced to one number. The method described by Pawo Tsuklag (Tlkuntu, p. 208) is certainly neat, and uses the fact that the period of the Sun, 371,4,36,5,7 is actually the same as 371 1/13 lunar days. The period is written down in its five places, and each one is multiplied by 13. Working from the bottom upwards, dividing by each of the fractional parts in turn, each line produces a remainder of zero:

> 371 × 13 = 4823 + 1 = 4824
> 4 × 13 = 52 + 8 = 60 ÷ 60 = 1 rem. 0
> 36 × 13 = 468 + 12 = 480 ÷ 60 = 8 rem. 0
> 5 × 13 = 65 + 7 = 72 ÷ 6 = 12 rem. 0
> 7 × 13 = 91 ÷ 13 = 7 rem. 0

This means that 13 solar cycles are exactly equal to 4,824 lunar days. We can now divide by this number, but first of all the dividend (1,620) must also be multiplied by 13, to get a new dividend of 21,060. Divide through, working downwards, and the result is:

> 21060 ÷ 4824 = 4 rem. 1764
> 1764 × 60 = 105840 ÷ 4824 = 21 rem. 4536
> 4536 × 6 = 27216 ÷ 4824 = 5 rem. 3096
> 3096 × 13 = 40248 ÷ 4824 = 8 rem. 1656
> 1656 × 67 = 110952 ÷ 4824 = 23 rem. 0

This yields the mean solar motion in a lunar day as: 0;4,21,5,8,23 (13,67).

The fractional part of 67, which we find in the siddhānta solar calculations, comes from the value that we divide by, 4,824, which equals 67×72.

For the mean motion in terms of solar days there is no neat trick similar to the simple multiplication by 13 for lunar days. Instead, it is usual to make an approximation.

In the value we have for the solar period, 365;16,14,1,12 (13), we remove the last fractional part and then round up the number of breaths, to give: 365;16,14,2.

This approximated value for the solar period is equal to 365 2923/10800 solar days, and so we write this out in its four places, multiply each of them by 10,800, and then carry up from the bottom, again producing a single figure:

$365 \times 10800 = 3942000 + 2923 = 3944923$
$16 \times 10800 = 172800 + 2580 = 175380 \div 60 = 2923$ rem. 0
$14 \times 10800 = 151200 + 3600 = 154800 \div 60 = 2580$ rem. 0
$2 \times 10800 = 21600 \div 6 = 3600$ rem. 0

This figure of 3,944,923 can now be used as a divisor. As before, the dividend (1,620) must first be multiplied by 10,800, which gives a new dividend of 17,496,000. This is now divided by 3,944,923, working downwards:

$17496000 \div 3944923 = 4$ rem. 1716308
$1716308 \times 60 = 102978480 \div 3944923 = 26$ rem. 410482
$410482 \times 6 = 2462892 \div 3944923 = 0$ rem. 2462892
$2462892 \times 13 = 32017596 \div 3944923 = 8$ rem. 458212

This gives the approximate mean motion of the Sun in a solar day as: 0;4,26,0,8 (13).

Correction of solar longitude

> "This longitude is applied to the mansions, nāḍī, and so forth, of the Sun, every day from the solstice to the next solstice. By means of the described method, correct the stepping of the Sun; otherwise the karaṇa methods will never have an accurate Sun. If the longitude of the Sun is wrong, just like the branches of a tree with a rotten trunk, Mars and so forth which are subtracted from it will be in error."

This section is describing the correction that needs to be applied to find the true solar longitude. Although it is not as explicit as one would like, the sense is clear enough. A difference will have been found between the calculated longitude of the Sun and the true Sun by observation at the solstice. The correction needs to be applied, first to the mean motion of the Sun, and then the step function needs to be used in order to correct for the variable speed of the Sun. It is not good enough simply to apply a uniform correction to the previously calculated true Sun values, although the error would be very small.

The point is also made that in order to find the geocentric (fast) motion of the planets, a difference between the solar longitude and the planets' heliocentric (slow) motion is needed, and therefore this is also dependent on an accurate solar longitude. For this reason, the planets cannot be determined accurately unless the solar longitude is correct.

Naturally, the longitude of the Moon is also dependent on that of the Sun, and the mean motion of the Moon is the subject of the next verses.

The motion of the Moon

> "To explain the period of the Moon, as it traverses the whole zodiac, take as the Moon's longitude the nāḍī of a circle and the nāḍī of the Sun combined; the result of dividing by thirty is the Moon's longitude in nāḍī each day. With the Moon's daily nāḍī, pala, and breaths, completing all the nāḍī of a circle yields the period."

This section describes the mean motion for each lunar day of the Moon. At the time of a new Moon, the longitude of the Moon and the Sun are identical. When the next new Moon occurs, the Sun has moved through a distance of thirty times its mean lunar day motion of 0;4,21,5,8,23 (13,67). The Moon moves right around the whole zodiac before meeting the Sun again at new Moon, so its change in longitude is equal to the change in the Sun's longitude, plus a full circle.

The first step in this calculation is to multiply the lunar day motion of the Sun by thirty:

$$30 \times 0;4,21,5,8,23 = 0;130,58,1,3,20 \ (13,67)$$

It is easiest to leave the nāḍī value as 130 rather than rounding up to the mansion place. To this is then added the number of nāḍī (1620) in a full circle, to arrive at a figure for the mean distance travelled by the Moon in a full synodic month: 0;1750,58,1,3,20. This now has to be divided by 30 to determine the mean motion in a single lunar day:

$$1750 \div 30 = 58 \text{ rem. } 10$$
$$58 + 10 \times 60 = 658 \div 30 = 21 \text{ rem. } 28$$
$$1 + 28 \times 6 = 169 \div 30 = 5 \text{ rem. } 19$$

$3 + 19 \times 13 = 250 \div 30 = 8$ rem. 10
$20 + 10 \times 67 = 690 \div 30 = 23$

This gives the result of: 0;58,21,5,8,23 (13,67).

At this point Pawo Tsuklag (Tlkuntu, p. 213) gives a rather surprising calculation to determine the period of the Moon in terms of lunar days. The answer he derives is 27;45,21,3,0,11856 (13,17072), but there seems little benefit in such a result. It is also somewhat odd to see a whole lunar day subdivided into nāḍī that will be slightly shorter in duration than those that are sixtieth parts of a solar day.

However, some such calculation is clearly intended here, as calculations that complete "all the nāḍī of a circle" would indeed yield "the period" of the Moon. As this particular description comes to an abrupt halt, it is more likely that the intention of the text is to point out that having explained these basic methods for the Sun, the reader could now apply similar methods to derive whatever similar parameters are needed for the Moon, and later for the planets as well.

Motions of Rāhu and the planets

> "Six thousand and nine hundred days are the period of Rāhu."

This simple point could be misleading. The text reads as if the period of Rāhu is 6,900 solar days, but it is in fact that many lunar days. However, the next verses deal with the planetary periods, and these are measured in solar days.

> "For Maṅgala and the others, the periods are derived from their own motions. A day is multiplied by mansions, and divided by the period. The quotient yields mansions, and the remainder is multiplied by sixty and divided again by the period for nāḍī. Similarly pala, breaths, and period-fraction results are obtained. Each day for the planets, lord of men, having added just this, with the planetary periods, the planets are corrected."

The planetary slow motions are described in terms of their periods, counted in solar days. In order to determine the motion in a single solar day, one takes a whole circle of 27 (mansions) and divides by the period.

If a quotient resulted from this division, it would be a number of mansions, but the planetary periods are too long for this to happen. So, multiply by 60, and divide again by the period in order to derive, possibly, a quotient of nāḍī.

The calculation is carried down, and the last fractional part is some factor of the period itself.

> "When the planetary longitude is accurate, then in the monthly sector, determine the monthly longitude within the calculated motion."

This verse is referring to the slow motion, and the need to correct the mean longitude of the planets for their variable speed.

This is done with a step function, using interpolation within each step. There are six steps for each half-circle, and so they correspond, at least in size, to zodiacal months, and for this reason the term "monthly sector" is used. The "monthly longitude" is referring to the interpolation variable, the amount the planet has passed through the particular step it is in.

The point here is that having arrived at a correct mean motion of the planet, one then uses the step function to derive its true slow motion.

> "Having subtracted the motion from the Sun, correct with the Sun the month for the longitude in the sector where it (the planet) stands, and so with the months for Maṅgala and the others."

This verse is concerned with the next step in correcting the planets, their fast motion. In that calculation, for the outer planets the slow (heliocentric) position is subtracted from that of the Sun. A step function is then used, but this has 14 steps each half-circle. According to Pawo Tsuklag, the term 'month' is again used to refer to these steps, as the process is similar to that with the slow motion, where the steps were equivalent in size to zodiacal months.

> "The day when Rāhu enters, between the white and black junctures and the following days; this is when the Sun or Moon are defeated."

This verse is referring to eclipse detection, and the simple point is made that an eclipse, when "the Sun or Moon are defeated," can only occur when Rāhu, the node of the Moon's orbit, is present with the Sun and Moon. This can only occur between the beginning of the new or full Moon day and the beginning of the following day—in other words, at the time of new or full Moon. Full and new Moon are the junctures at the end of the white and black fortnights, respectively.

> "Having understood all of this, abandon the inaccurate longitudes in other siddhāntas and the other brief karaṇas."
>
> This has described the characteristics of the siddhānta from the Tantrarāja of the Paramādibuddha. As it says briefly in the Abridged Tantra (Laghutantra), "the siddhāntas will be corrupted," and this (Buddhist siddhānta) is not made clear in the Tantra.
>
> Why is this? When the heterodox see the Laghutantra, having seen the accurate longitude for the Sun, they would say "Our karaṇas also have an accurate Sun," and they would write it into their own karaṇas. For that reason, it is explained that it is not made clear.

This concludes the discussion of the Kālacakra siddhānta and the quote from the Mūlatantra. The Vimalaprabhā now returns to commenting on the tantra, continuing with the rest of verse 38.

Changes in the lengths of day and night

> Now is explained the increase and decrease of day and night. "The increase and decrease through six months" means that for that period, there is both increase and decrease (respectively) "of day and night," for both day and night. This "is caused by the movement of the Sun," the movement in the northward direction and the movement to the south.
>
> "Ocean life and fire pala, this is the daily change in each passage." This quantity is for the region between Kailash and the Himavat, and means that each day the increase and decrease are four breaths and three pala during each passage.

> "Each passage" is one hundred and eighty-two and a half days, and through that number of days of the (Sun's) passage "towards the south night is increasing," and, to "the north, day." The explanation for south of Kailash will be taught later.
>
> This quantity means that on the day of the change to the southward passage, the day is thirty-six nāḍī in length and night twenty-four. Similarly, at (the change to) the northward passage, one should understand that the lengths of day and night are reversed.

The numbers here do not quite fit together, and are very simplified. There is not a continuous rate of change in the lengths of day and night. Immediately after the winter solstice, when the length of night is greatest, the rate of increase in the length of day is very slow. It is at its fastest around the spring equinox, slowing down again near the summer solstice. The figures given for the daily change can only be approximate averages.

The rate of three pala and four breaths each day would account for a total change in the length of either day or night as 0;11,9,1, and not the twelve nāḍī as suggested by the text.

Incidentally, a maximum day length of 36 nāḍī would suggest a latitude of 33° or 34° north. This is a couple of degrees further north than Mt. Kailash, and passes through the eastern Himalayas and southern Kashmir.

Longitude of Rāhu

To the true month add eye (2) and Sun (12), multiply by eye (2) and for the lunar juncture add one; Divide by sky (0) season (6) ocean (4), multiply by sage (7) hand (2), and divide by sky (0) and so forth for mansions. Multiply the remainder by sixty, and from this derive nāḍī, multiplying again for pala, Subtracting the result from a circle yields the Head, and the Dark One's Tail by adding half of the mansions. [39]

> Now is explained the longitude of Rāhu in the lunar mansions. By "month" is meant the karaṇa month, and "add eye and Sun" is from the point of view of the karaṇa and not siddhānta. "Eye and Sun" mean that one

> hundred and twenty-two is added, and "multiply by eye" means that to derive the count of fortnights, multiply by two.
>
> By "for the lunar juncture add one," is meant that in order to find the longitude at full Moon one fortnight is added, and for the longitude at the (following) new Moon two fortnights are added, to the count of fortnights.
>
> Regarding "divide by sky season ocean," in order to determine the fortnightly longitude of Rāhu, divide by the fortnightly cycle of four hundred and sixty, "sky season ocean," and then "multiply by sage hand" the remaining fortnights.
>
> For the longitude in mansions, "divide by sky and so forth for mansions," means that mansions are derived by dividing by zero and so forth, the divisor of four hundred and sixty.
>
> Again, take the remainder, and "multiply the remainder by sixty, and from this," and dividing again by the divisor derive the "nāḍī." Similarly, "multiplying again" by sixty, and dividing by the divisor derive "pala." Multiplying by six and dividing again will yield breaths.

The calculation here is straightforward. Because of the need for eclipse prediction, and the fact that eclipses can only occur at new and full Moons, the position of Rāhu is calculated every fortnight, and not just every month. For this reason, after the epoch value ("from the point of view of the karaṇa") of 122 has been added, the month count is multiplied by two.

The base calculation is for the new Moon that is at the beginning of a month, but strictly speaking this occurs during the last full solar day of the previous month. Therefore, for the month under consideration one is added for the full Moon, and two for the new Moon.

The rest of the calculation should be clear. The divisor is 460, and repeated divisions and multiplications by 27, 60, and so forth produce a longitude.

> "Subtracting the result from a circle yields the Head": here, the remainder from the division by sky season ocean, that many mansions, and so forth, is subtracted from a circle, a circle of twenty-seven mansions, and this "yields the Head," the longitude in mansions, Aśvinī and so forth, of the Head.
>
> The "Dark One" (*mun can, tamin*) is Rāhu, and is the Dark One because of possessing darkness. The Dark One's "Tail by adding half of the mansions," means half of the mansions, thirteen and a half mansions, that number is added to the longitude of the Head to derive the Tail, meaning the longitude of the Tail.

There are two nodes of the Moon's orbit. The ascending node (Head) is the point where the Moon crosses the ecliptic when travelling northwards, and the descending node (Tail) when moving southwards. The nodes travel in the opposite direction around the zodiac to the Sun, Moon, and all the other planets, and so the derived longitude is subtracted from a full circle of 27 mansions in order to determine the longitude of the Head. The Tail's longitude is then derived by simply adding half a circle.

Daily longitudes of the planets

> *The month is multiplied by thirty, and together with the particular days divide by mountain (7) sky (0) mountain (7), Add to the middle of three places, and again divide by ocean (4) taste (6), subtract the result for the uncorrected solar days. Add mountain (7) season (6) one for the accurate day count, divide by mountain (7) nāga (8) season (6); Multiply the remainder by mansions for quotient, and then multiply by sky (0) taste (6) and divide again by mountain, and so forth, for nāḍī. [40]*

> Now is explained the count of solar days needed to determine the longitude in mansions of Maṅgala and the others. "The month" means the karaṇa month.
>
> For the number of solar days, (the month) "multiplied by thirty" yields days. That number of solar days, "together with the particular days" of the current month, is

> put in "three places." The lower place, "divide by mountain sky mountain," means divide by seven hundred and seven, and "add" the quotient to the "middle" place. That middle place, "again divide by ocean taste," and the "result" from this division by sixty-four, "subtract the result for the uncorrected solar days."
>
> Some say that to correct the fact that for all days the weekday is in excess, one weekday should be subtracted. This will result in the correct count of solar days.

This is the familiar calculation for converting a count of lunar days into a count of solar days. The final comment that some state that the count is not accurate and would need to have one subtracted from it refers to the fact that the fractional parts are subtractive and for complete accuracy need to be subtracted from the final count.

However, neither the Tantra nor the commentary give the correction method that is normally applied in practice—of adding a weekday epoch value, dividing by seven and then comparing the remainder with the current weekday. This correction is very important for accurate results, as the count derived moves in and out of step with the weekday values due to omitted and extra lunar days, due to the variable speed of the Moon.

Longitude of Mars

> Now, Maṅgala (Mars) is explained. "Add mountain season one" is from the point of view of the karaṇa and not siddhānta. Add one hundred and sixty-seven is meant by "add mountain season one."
>
> "For the accurate day count, divide by mountain nāga season"; this count of solar days is divided by the period of Mars, six hundred and eighty-seven days. "Multiply the remainder by mansions" means multiply by twenty-seven, and then dividing again by mountain nāga season (687), the "quotient" is mansions.
>
> "Multiply" (the remainder) by "sky taste," sixty, and divide again by "mountain, and so forth" (687), the quo-

> tient is "nāḍī." This yields the longitude of Mars, and the pala, and so forth, are derived as previously described.

The calculation here is again straightforward. As before, the epoch value that is added, of 167, is identified by being the "point of view of the karaṇa." The count is then divided by the period of Mars, 687, and then repeated multiplications by 27, 60, etc., and further divisions by 687 yield the mean slow motion longitude.

> Here, the longitudes of the planets are derived in five places. These are the sign place, the mansion place, the nāḍī place, the pala place, and the breath place, each one beneath the other.
>
> Any excess over six breaths in the breath place is not kept, and the quotient from dividing by six is carried to the pala. Any excess over sixty in the pala is not kept, and the quotient from dividing by sixty is carried to the count of nāḍī. Also the nāḍī are similarly carried to the mansions. Any excess over the two motions of the mansions, thirteen and a half, is not kept, and is placed in six-sign; so these are defined.

These last comments are somewhat surprising, and the value in having an extra place of "signs," where there are just two possible values, is not made clear. It might be connected with the notion that will soon be introduced about the progressive and regressive motions of the planets, but these are not centred symmetrically on the zodiac—they start at different places. The addition of this extra place also does not make the following calculations any easier; in fact it would slightly complicate them.

True Mars

> *For Mars, subtract nine and a half, and if this leaves a deficit, add a circle and then subtract. If there is a remainder from a half, half a circle should be subtracted, and the remainder from the subtraction is regressive. The mansions multiplied by sixty, together with nāḍī, this is then divided by element (5) fire (3) Moon (1); Whatever results for the slow motion gives increment or deficit when regressive or progressive. [41]*

Now Mars is explained. "For Mars, subtract nine and a half," means that here, making discrete (values of) the longitude in mansions, etc., of Mars, from one of these longitudes of Mars, in order to determine the birth-steps, subtract nine mansions, "and a half," meaning subtract thirty nāḍī from the nāḍī place.

This longitude of mansions from Aśvinī, and so forth, "if this leaves a deficit, add a circle and then subtract," means that the subtraction from this longitude of mansions from Aśvinī certainly needs to be performed.

However, if the subtraction of this quantity makes the quantity of the longitude negative, then a circle is added, and then the subtraction is performed. A circle is a total of twenty-seven lunar mansions, and adding this the subtraction is then performed.

"Half a circle should be subtracted" means that here, if there would be a remainder from subtracting half a circle, then it "should be subtracted," "if there is a remainder from a half," the remainder being the remainder from a half. "The remainder from the subtraction," this is "regressive." For the slow motion of all the planets, for regressive there is an increment and for progressive a deficit.

"The mansions multiplied by sixty, together with nāḍī," means that in order to determine the number of nāḍī the count of mansions is multiplied by sixty and has added to it the lower count of nāḍī. Then, in order to find the sign-step, this count of nāḍī is "divided by element fire Moon," one hundred and thirty-five, and "whatever results" is the sign-step. "The slow motion gives increment or deficit when regressive or progressive," and this is determined by examining the values that result.

Reality (25) eighteen and mountain (7) are the steps above and below for half a circle; The longitude is multiplied by the nāḍī and divided by arrow (5) quality (3) Moon (1), and the result, within that half circle, For the first half is to be accumulated, because of the stepping, for the second half is similarly to be subtracted. Having combined the portion into one quantity, depending on the planet's motion, either add to or subtract from the nāḍī. [42]

Regarding the stepping through the signs, "Reality," means that the first sign from birth is twenty-five, the second is "eighteen," and the third is "mountain," seven. These are the first three signs.

The terminology used here is a little different from that used in the Siddhānta section above, where the six steps in each half circle were described as monthly sectors. The cycle starts from the point in the zodiac which is the birth-sign of the planet, and is then divided into two halves, each of six equal sectors. These are therefore in size equal to zodiac signs or the motion of the mean Sun in a zodiacal month.

Then for the other half of the half circle, the fourth sign is seven, the fifth eighteen, and the sixth is twenty-five; these "are the steps above and below for half a circle."

"The longitude is multiplied by the nāḍī" means that the quotient from dividing the number of nāḍī by one hundred and thirty-five yields the traversed signs. This is the step (required) within the six steps.

Then, secondly, in order to find the part traversed, the remainder, the remainder of the nāḍī is multiplied by the nāḍī (of the step) and "divided by arrow quality Moon, and the result, within that half circle," the result obtained by multiplying the longitude by the nāḍī and dividing by one hundred and thirty-five, "for the first half is to be accumulated, because of the stepping," means until the planet has completed the first half. Below that, "for the second half is similarly to be subtracted," means that that longitude is to be subtracted for the latter half.

"Having combined the portion into one quantity," means that in the first half, because of the planet's sign, the step and whatever portion (of a step) there is

> combined into one quantity, and in the latter half, as the portion from the first half is subtracted in the latter half, the negative portion is combined into one quantity.

The language here is a little awkward, and the word I have translated as "portion" is indicating the fractional part of a step that is the result of the interpolation calculation. The step defines a certain number of nāḍī as a total, and another number of nāḍī as the step itself. The portion of the step is calculated by multiplying that number of nāḍī by the distance travelled (longitude) through the step, and then dividing by 135. This portion is then added to the total in the first half of the half circle, and subtracted in the second half. The resulting correction then has to be applied to the mean slow motion of the planet.

> By, "depending on the planet's motion, either add to or subtract from the nāḍī" is meant the two motions of the planets, regressive and progressive. Depending on these, either add or subtract. If regressive then add, and for progressive subtract.
>
> By "the nāḍī" is meant the planet's count of nāḍī and its longitude as a count of mansions. This is the definition for the slow motion of Maṅgala and the others, the correction for the birth motion by the method of movement through signs.

Fast motion

Then subtract Bhauma from the Sun, and also Guru and Ravija, for the fast motion. Similarly, from Saumya and Śukra, the Sun; for the fast motion progressive is defined as an increment. Here, the result of subtracting is the step, and the step the planet is traversing is multiplied by the remaining nāḍī; Dividing by sixty gives the planet's traversing step, and this is accumulated or removed. [43]

> Now the method for the fast motion is explained, with "Then subtract Bhauma from the Sun, and also Guru and Ravija, for the fast motion."
>
> "Then" means immediately after that, subtract the planet's longitude that has been corrected by the sign-

motion, from the longitude of the Sun. "Subtract Bhauma (Mars) from the Sun," means to determine the difference in longitudes, between the slow longitude and the Sun without its steps.

"Then" implies that "Guru" (Jupiter) is also subtracted, "Ravija" (Saturn) is also subtracted, "also," meaning in the same manner as with Mars. This is "for the fast motion."

Similarly, "Saumya," from the longitude of Saumya, meaning the longitude of Mercury, the Sun is subtracted. "And Śukra," from the longitude of Śukra (Venus), meaning the longitude of Śukra, "the Sun" is subtracted.

Here, it is defined that the higher planet is subtracted from the lower planet. For this reason, "from Saumya" and "Śukra" subtract "the Sun."

Regarding the fast motion, "for the fast motion progressive is defined as an increment," meaning that it is certainly defined for the fast method that progressive yields an increment, and that regressive yields a deficit.

From the remainder after having subtracted the longitude of the higher planets, (if necessary) subtract half a circle, and "here, the result of subtracting is the step."

The mansions of the remainder after having subtracted the longitude of the higher planets, produces the (step) mansion they are traversing, due to the planets' daily (change of) longitude.

This "step the planet is traversing" is associated with a number of nāḍī, and these nāḍī of the step the planet is traversing are "multiplied by the remaining nāḍī."

"Dividing by sixty gives the planet's traversing step, and this is accumulated or removed." By this is meant that just like before, for the first half it is accumulated and for the latter half removed.

In this verse the basic method is described to derive the fast motion of the planets. The language of the commentary—particularly in Tibetan—could be a bit clearer here. In fact the original lines from the Tantra seem more precise.

The point is that the difference between the longitudes of the mean Sun ("the Sun without its steps") and the heliocentric planet is calculated, half a circle is subtracted if necessary, and then the remainder is divided into steps. There are fourteen of these steps for each half circle, one is only considered to be a half, and so they are each exactly one lunar mansion, sixty angular nāḍī, in size. Just as the steps for the slow motion were one zodiacal sign each in size, so here they are one mansion each.

The whole number of mansions gives the total figure for the correction, and then the distance it has travelled in the "step the planet is traversing" is used as an interpolation variable and multiplied by the step's nāḍī value, and divided by the step size, sixty (nāḍī).

The interpolated correction is added to the total in the first part of the half-circle, and subtracted in the second.

> *Having combined the portion into one quantity, due to the motion of the planet, either add or subtract. For Bhauma the steps are jina (24) and so forth, in total an arrangement of elder (14) places. It should be understood that all the planets are reckoned in this same manner; leader of men, From Saumya and Śukra, Daymaker is subtracted, and yields accurate Saumya and Śukra. [44]*

> "Having combined the portion into one quantity, due to the motion of the planet, either add or subtract." By this is meant that for the fast motion, when progressive one adds, and when regressive subtracts, similarly to before, the quantity with added portion in the first half, and the quantity with negative portion in the latter half.
>
> "For Bhauma the steps are jina, and so forth," jina meaning twenty-four. This is in the first of elder places, fourteen places, the first of fourteen steps. For Bhauma, this and the other steps, jina and so forth, make "in total" fourteen places of lunar mansions, "an arrangement of elder places." "It should be understood that all the planets are reckoned in this same manner; leader of men."

> From "Saumya," the longitude of Saumya, and "Śukra, the Sun is subtracted," "Saumya," yields the planet Mercury, and "Śukra," yields accurate Śukra; these come from the longitudes of Saumya and Śukra. Thus is accurate Maṅgala.

As with the other planets, the full list of the step values for the fast motion of Mars is not given here, but in another part of the Tantra. The reason for this is presumably to concentrate here on the method and not detract from this with long lists of numbers—fourteen for each of the five planets.

The longitude of Mercury

Multiply by zero sky (0) Moon (1) the whole count of days, and subtract fire (3) Sun (12) mountain (7). Divide by mountain (7) orifice (9) mountain (7) and nāga (8), and separate the remainder into mansions, and so forth. The stated divisor yields the mansions and then nāḍī of the longitude of Saumya; The subtraction for Saumya, from the mean Sun remove, excellent lord of men, lord of men mansions and also a half. [45]

> Now the planet Mercury is explained, with "Multiply by zero sky Moon the whole count of days." "Multiply by zero sky Moon," by one hundred, the whole previous true count of days. And, "subtract fire Sun mountain," means that seven thousand one hundred and twenty-three is subtracted from this count of days multiplied by one hundred.
>
> "Divide by mountain orifice mountain and nāga," means "by mountain," by seven, and "orifice mountain and nāga," by eight thousand seven hundred and ninety-seven, its period in solar days; with this "mountain orifice mountain and nāga," "divide," to separate.
>
> "And separate the remainder into mansions, and so forth," means that the count of days that remains from the division by the period in days, this is separated into "mansions, and so forth," "multiplied" by twenty-seven.

> By "and so forth" is meant that the remainder from again dividing by the period is multiplied by sixty, and then multiplied again by pala and by six breaths.
>
> From "the stated" days of the period, "divisor," the quotient yields "mansions," "and then nāḍī," in the nāḍī place, and similarly in the pala and breaths there are quotients. These yield the components of the longitude, "the longitude of Saumya."
>
> "The subtraction for Saumya, from the mean Sun remove, excellent lord of men, lord of men mansions and also a half," means that whatever is the result of having divided by the period of mountain, and so forth, the longitude of "Saumya," in order to determine the true fast motion, there is a "subtraction." This is "from the mean Sun," O, "excellent lord of men, lord of men," sixteen, "mansions and also a half," from the nāḍī place of the Sun, thirty nāḍī.

This verse starts the description of the calculation of the longitude of Mercury. First of all, the general day count is multiplied by 100, and then the epoch value, of 7,123, is subtracted. This is then divided by the period in terms of hundredths of a solar day, 8,797, to yield the slow, or heliocentric, longitude.

When calculating the fast, or geocentric, longitude for the inner planets, the correction for the variable speed of the planet is not applied to the slow motion, as with the outer planets, but it is applied to the mean longitude of the Sun. This is because the geocentric mean position of the inner planets is identical to that of the Sun.

> *The method with the remainder, the slow and fast motion with additions and subtractions, is done as with Mars. The slow motion steps of Saumya are ten mountain (7) fire (3); the fast motion, lord of men (16), and so forth. Having reduced the count of days by sky (0) sky (0) taste (6) and eye (2), divide by tooth (32) fire (3) ocean (4). The remainder multiplied by mansions is mansions, continue with nāḍī, and this is the slow motion of Guru. [46]*

As with the previous definition, if the subtraction does not go, add a circle of lunar mansions and then perform the subtraction. "The method with the remainder," meaning, "the slow and fast motion with additions and subtractions, is done as with Mars," this is easy to understand.

Regarding "The slow motion steps of Saumya are ten mountain fire," "Saumya" is Mercury. Of the "slow motion," the sign-motion has the first and latter of six places, and in the first sign-place is "ten." The second sign-place is "mountain," seven, and the third sign-place "fire," three. These are for the first half. For the latter half, in the fourth sign-place is three, the fifth sign-place seven, and the sixth sign-place ten. "Ten mountain fire" are the slow motion steps.

For "the fast motion," the mansion-motion, there are fourteen steps in fourteen places, "lord of men, and so forth," meaning sixteen, and so forth. There will be further explanation (of the fast steps) taught later. This completes the planet Mercury.

The longitude of Jupiter

Now Jupiter is explained, with "Having reduced the count of days by sky sky taste and eye." "The count of days" is the previous count of days, and this is reduced by twenty-six hundred: "sky sky taste and eye," which is from the point of view of karaṇa and not siddhānta. "Divide by tooth fire ocean" means that this is then divided by four thousand three hundred and thirty-two.

"The remainder," the remainder from the division, is "multiplied by mansions," meaning that it is multiplied by twenty-seven, divided by the period divisor, to produce "mansions." "Continue" as the previously explained method, for the "nāḍī" and so forth of Guru (Jupiter).

From the mansions subtract Sun (12), and the slow motion steps are Remover (11) nine and summit (3). Then for the fast, the steps in an arrangement of elder (14) places are direction (10), and so forth. Multiply the days by sky (0) and Moon (1), subtract ocean (4) Vasu (8), and divide by mountain (7) jina (24) eye (2). Multiply by mansions for the mansions of longitude, and then nāḍī, for the fast motion of Venus. [47]

"From the mansions subtract Sun," means that from this longitude of Jupiter twelve mansions are subtracted, and the rest of the method is as with Mars. "The slow motion steps are Remover nine and summit," means that, similarly to before, in the six sign-places are Remover, eleven, then nine and then summit, three. In the latter half they are the reverse of these.

"Then for the fast" motion, "the steps in an arrangement of elder places" means that in fourteen places there are "direction, and so forth," meaning direction, ten, and so on. The explanation of the steps moving through the mansions will be taught later. This completes Jupiter.

The longitude of Venus

Now Venus is explained. "Multiply the days by sky and Moon" means that having multiplied the count of days by ten, "subtract ocean Vasu," subtract eighty-four. "Divide by mountain jina eye" means that for the fast steps, divide by the step period in days, of two thousand two hundred and forty-seven.

To the remainder "multiply by mansions for the mansions of longitude, and then nāḍī" of the longitude, continuing with pala, and so forth, as with Mars, this being for the "fast motion" of "Venus."

The terminology here might seem the wrong way around, but it is not. This last calculation is described as being for the fast motion of Venus, because the slow motion is the same as the mean motion of the Sun, and it is to that that the correction for the variable speed of the planet is applied. This is the subject of the next couple of lines.

The calculation given here in verse 47 is for what in the West would be called the heliocentric motion of Venus, and, as with the other inner planet, Mercury, only the mean of this is calculated, and this is used to determine the fast motion.

> *Season (6) mansions subtract to the Sun, arrow (5) age (4) 'having a hare' (1) are the slow motion steps. For fast, the list of reality (25), and so forth, in an arrangement of elder (14) places, addition and subtraction being as with Mars. Subtract sky (0) eye (2) nāga (8) and knowledge (4) from the correct day count, and with six taste (6) mountain (7) sky (0) Moon (1), Divide, multiply by mansions for mansions, and to be subtracted for Saturn is eighteen. [48]*

For the slow motion of Venus, "season mansions" means that six mansions "subtract to the Sun," meaning to the longitude of the Sun, but it should be understood that here the locative case is used instead of the ablative. "Arrow age 'having a hare' are the slow motion steps," means that, as before, in the six sign-places there are in the first half arrow, meaning five, age, four, and 'having a hare,' one. In the latter half they are the reverse of these.

"For fast," for the fast motion, "the list of reality and so forth" means the list of twenty-five and so forth, this "the list of reality and so forth" being "in an arrangement of elder places," the fourteen places of the lunar mansion steps. "Addition and subtraction being as with Mars" means that the addition and subtraction of the motion steps are done just as with Maṅgala. This completes Venus.

The slow motion of Saturn

Now Saturn is explained. "Subtract sky eye nāga and knowledge" from the correct count of days. The previous "correct day count" is reduced by four thousand eight hundred and twenty, and this reduction is from the point of view of the karaṇa and not the siddhānta.

"With six taste mountain sky Moon, divide," divide by the period of ten thousand seven hundred and sixty-six days. "Multiply by mansions" the remainder, divide by the divisor of the period in days "for mansions" as the quotient. Continuing similarly yields the pala, and so forth, of the longitude.

"To be subtracted for Saturn is eighteen," means that from the longitude of Saturn eighteen mansions are to be subtracted. If this would leave a deficit then add a circle and then subtract. This is similar to the previous definition to determine the movement from the birth-mansion (*skye ba'i skar ma, janma nakṣatra*).

The steps are twenty-two, lunar day (15) and season (6), arranged in taste (6) places; for fast motion taste (6) and so forth. Fast and slow motions are progressive traversing of the steps; reversing is regressive. In the first half, and in the latter half, due to the motion of the Sun, the planets are advancing. Through thirty-seven times hand (2) months Ketu performs both fast and reverse motions. [49]

For the slow motion "the steps are twenty-two, lunar day and season," meaning that of the steps of the six sign-places, in the first sign is twenty-two, in the second "lunar day," fifteen, and then "season," six. And it is stated "arranged in taste places," because the latter half can in that way also be understood.

"For fast motion taste and so forth," means that for the fourteen places of the fast mansion-motion, there are steps of "taste and so forth," six and so on, which are to be added and subtracted. Further explanation will be taught later, and with Saturn this completes the description of the steps of the planets.

The four motions of the planets

> Now is explained the nature of the motions, with "fast and slow motions are progressive traversing of the steps." This indicates fast motion, when the planet is traversing the first half of the nāḍī of the fourteen planetary steps, and is appearing from the disk of the Sun, this is called fast motion. Because this is progressive traversal of the steps it is "progressive traversing of the steps," and when it is traversing the latter half this is called slow motion.
>
> Then, "reversing is regress" refers to the regress of the planet when half a circle is subtracted. "The first half," (of) the regress is called reversing motion. And, "in the latter half, due to the motion of the Sun," the planets are "advancing." This is called advancing motion, returning from the reversal.
>
> Here, from its appearance, through the progress, in the first half there is an increasing increment, and in the second half a decreasing increment.
>
> Then, when a half circle has been subtracted, for the first half of regress there is an increasing decrement, and in the second half, until it enters the Sun's lunar mansion, a decreasing decrement. Then it disappears, and again appears, and this is understood as due to the progress.

This description makes the meaning of these terms 'progress' and 'regress' perfectly clear. For one of the outer planets such as Mars, after conjunction with the Sun the geocentric planet is moving ahead of its heliocentric position for half a circle, and therefore this is called progress. The second half it is moving behind the heliocentric, and so this is regress. It starts travelling fast, moves ahead of the heliocentric, slows down, and eventually reverses and becomes retrograde, putting it behind the heliocentric. The planet speeds up again, returning from the reversal but still travelling behind the heliocentric until the next conjunction.

"Through thirty-seven times hand months Ketu performs both fast and reverse motions." This single line is a brief description of Ketu (comet), and this is explained extensively later, together with the planets.

The visibility of the planets

One that exists in the longitude of the Sun, this planet is for certain invisible. Having escaped the Sun it becomes visible, and its path is divided between the movement of the passages. Those that are on the left path, move from the left due to the motion of the Sun. Those on the right, from the right, and it is true that these conflict with each other as they are enemies. [50]

Now the timing of the visibility of the planets is explained, with "one that exists in the longitude of the Sun, this planet is for certain invisible." This means that the planets are said to be invisible when they cannot be seen due to the light from the disk of the Sun, but it is not the case that they are not there.

"Having escaped the Sun it becomes visible," means that a planet that had been invisible, due to its motion escapes the Sun and becomes visible again, because of escaping from the light of the Sun. "Its path is divided between the movement of the passages" means that the path of this visible planet is divided between the movement of the passages.

Regarding being divided between the passages, this division of the passages means division of the movement of the Sun into passages of one hundred and eighty-two and a half days, from the disk of fire to Himavat, north of Kailash, and from Himavat to the disk of fire in the south.

"Those that are on the left path, move from the left due to the motion of the Sun." Here, those that are on the left path are the peaceful planets of Saumya (Mercury)

> and the others. This is because the planets Mercury, Venus, and Ketu arise from the left side.
>
> When they disappear into the disk of the Sun they enter from the left side, and when they appear, they also come from the left side. For this reason, a planet that is on the left path is moving left of the wrathful planets, just as is the Sun.
>
> "Those on the right, from the right," means that those that are on the right, that from the right path disappear into the Sun, are Maṅgala, Jupiter, and Saturn. These are wrathful, and move to the right of the peaceful planets because they arise from the right side.
>
> Here, because Ketu arises from the left side it is peaceful in its body aspect, and because it arises from the right side Jupiter is peaceful in its body aspect.
>
> In this way, "it is true that these conflict with each other as they are enemies"; meaning that these peaceful and wrathful planets, Mercury and Maṅgala, Jupiter and Venus, Saturn and Ketu, these will conflict with each other because they are enemies.

The best way to understand the usage here of the terms "left path" and "right path" is to imagine an observer in the northern hemisphere looking south towards the ecliptic, passing from the east on the left horizon, up into the sky, and down to the west on the right horizon. Just after their superior conjunction, the inner planets Mercury and Venus appear as evening stars, just to the left of the Sun—along that line of the ecliptic—after the Sun has just set. They therefore appear "from the left."

The text does not make this particularly clear, seeming to make out that the inner planets can only disappear into, and appear again from the Sun on the left side. They are of course also seen as morning stars, after their inferior conjunction. In his commentary on this point (Tskhaga, p. 254) Buton makes this point: "It should be understood that because of their stepping, the three planets Mercury, Venus, and Ketu sometimes appear east of the Sun and sometimes west of the Sun."

However, the outer planets such as Mars, just after their conjunction with the Sun are first seen rising just before the Sun in the east, therefore to the right of the Sun along the line of the ecliptic. They therefore appear "from the right," and set just before the Sun. Buton states that the outer planets appear from the west (the right) of the Sun because they travel more slowly than the Sun.

When a comet, Ketu (*mjug rings*), is visible, it will most likely be inside the orbit of the Earth and will therefore behave just like one of the inner planets, appearing as they do after superior conjunction.

> *Those that are in their own realm, if an enemy appears, they will certainly conflict. In their mansion there is, but in others no conflict, and for certain they are neutral to each other. If the Moon is to the left of the Sun, having arisen on the left, The northern cusp is raised, but some say its motion can come from the south, the right. [51]*

> "Those that are in their own realm, if an enemy appears, they will certainly conflict." This means that when Mars is in its own realm, the sign Aries or the sign Scorpio, if at that time the planet Mercury is moving through that realm, they will certainly conflict.
>
> Similarly, the realm of Mercury is Gemini or Virgo, and if the movement of Mars takes it there they will conflict. Similarly, the realm of Jupiter is Sagittarius and Pisces, and if Venus moves there, then Jupiter and Venus will be in conflict. Similarly, the realm of Venus is Taurus and Libra. Similarly, the realm of Saturn is Capricorn and Aquarius, and if Ketu moves there, at the time they will conflict. Similarly, the realm of 'having a hare' (the Moon) is Cancer, and if Saturn moves there, at that time will conflict with Ketu. This is because Ketu is born on the left side.

There is some confusion in this last point, as there are differences between the Tibetan and Sanskrit texts.

Mipham (MiKal 1, p. 175) explains this comment by saying: "Furthermore, if Saturn is in the Moon's realm of Cancer, if at that time Ketu is also there, those two will conflict. When Saturn is in the Sun's realm of Leo, if Ketu comes there, it will be in conflict with Saturn."

This seems to be given for completeness' sake. Each pair of planets conflict with each other when together in each other's own signs. Ketu is included here as effectively an inner planet (born on the left side), as the enemy of Saturn, but Ketu does not have its own signs within the zodiac. From what Mipham says, Ketu seems to have joint rulership over the signs of the Moon and the Sun, Cancer and Leo.

He also adds that the rulerships of the Head and Tail of Rāhu are respectively Virgo and Aquarius, but that they do not conflict with the Sun and Moon.

> "In their mansion, but in others there is no conflict." Here, "in their mansion" refers to the planets' birth-mansions. They do not only conflict in the signs of their own realms, but will also be in conflict with enemies in their birth mansions. That of Venus is the mansion Punarvasu, of Maṅgala the mansion Maghā, of Jupiter the mansion Hastā, of the planet Mercury the mansion Anurādhā, of Saturn the mansion Mūla, and of Ketu, the mansion Uttarāṣāḍhā.
>
> Saumya (Mercury) and Maṅgala conflict in each others' mansions. Similarly do Venus and Jupiter, and Saturn and Ketu. Apart from each others' mansions, in other mansions or realms they are not in conflict, and this is "for certain," without doubt. In other mansions "they are neutral to each other."
>
> Regarding the elevation of the cusps of the Moon, "if the Moon is to the left of the Sun, having arisen on the left," at that time "the northern cusp is raised, but some say its motion can come from the south," moving to the south. This is not in the nature of the causes of famine and drought.

This very short comment about the cusps of the Moon is disputing bad omens such as those found in Bṛhat Saṃhitā, chapter IV, v. 16 (Bṛhat 1, p. 37): "…northern cusp of the Moon be raised…timely rains in the country. On the other hand, with the southern cusp raised she portends the threat of famine."

The logic here seems to be that the southern cusp can rarely be seen elevated, and this is referring to the period shortly after new Moon.

The new Moon always appears from the left of Sun, and is visible following new Moon, after the Sun has set and just before the Moon follows it. In the northern hemisphere the northern cusp is usually higher than the southern one, although at certain times, near the equator, the southern cusp can be elevated. This can occur if the Moon passed the Sun to the north.

The elevation of the cusp depends on the angle the path of the setting Moon makes with the western horizon, and the southern cusp can only be raised (above the northern one) when the position of the Moon's nodes causes the Moon to be to the north of the ecliptic just after new Moon, having passed north of the zenith shortly after noon.

The point that some "some say its motion can come from the south" is probably a reference to the fact that south of the equator, the southern cusp can be elevated when the Moon passes the Sun on the southern side.

Such indications were of importance in Indian astronomy and astrology, and for a discussion of the calculation methods for the attitude of the Moon's cusps, see Varāhamihira in *Pañcasiddhāntikā* (Pañca, p. 137ff.).

Rāhu's eclipses of the Sun and Moon

At the juncture and again, when Rāhu's Head moves together, only then can the capture be direct. When moving on the left, not from the right, but due to the motion of the Sun, on the right, the right part. In that way Rāhu captures from cardinal and intermediate directions, captures the hare; when emerging, this is behind. The line of the orbit is from Aśvinī and so forth, through half of Citrā, the middle points where day and night are equal. [52]

Now is explained the entry into Rāhu. "At the juncture" refers to the juncture of full Moon, the word "again" refers to the juncture of new Moon.

> "When Rāhu's Head moves together" with the Moon, "only then can the capture be direct." Here direct means capture on the east. This should be understood as due to the passing of Rāhu, and as this is well known in other karaṇas, the Tathāgata Mañjuśrī did not make effort (to explain further).
>
> "When moving on the left, not from the right" means that when Rāhu passes on the left (east) the Moon will be captured from the left (north) and not the right. "Due to the motion of the Sun, on the right, the right part"; due to the motion of the Sun means that due to the motion of the Moon arising from the position of the Sun. On the right, when passing on the right, the Moon will be captured on the right (south).
>
> "In that way Rāhu captures from cardinal and intermediate directions, captures the hare," means that because of passing in these ways as described and capturing the hare (the Moon), Rāhu captures from different cardinal and intermediate directions.
>
> "When emerging, this is behind." Passing from the east, and so forth, when it emerges this is from behind, passing from the west. More on the passing of Rāhu, and so forth, should be understood from the Mūlatantra and the karaṇas of others.

This brief description of lunar eclipses needs some explanation. The main point is that the manner in which the Moon is eclipsed—the direction from which the shadow starts to cross it and the depth of the eclipse—depends on the relative positions of three things—the Earth's shadow which is exactly opposite the Sun, the Moon's node, Rāhu, and the path taken by the Moon as it passes the point of conjunction. If the Moon passes almost exactly over Rāhu at the point of conjunction, then the east limb of the Moon will enter the shadow first, the eclipse will be total, and when the Moon emerges from the shadow, the last limb to be exposed will be the western one.

There are two other extremes. The first described here is when Rāhu (Rāhu's Head, the ascending node) is to the left (east) of both the shadow and the Moon when conjunction occurs (the Moon passes Rāhu shortly after the conjunction). In that instance the Moon will be on the south side of the shadow, and so its northern limb will be touched by the shadow. When Rāhu is on the right of the conjunction, and the Moon passes it shortly before the conjunction, the opposite will be the case.

The eclipse will occur from intermediate directions at the points between these extremes.

The opposite case for Rāhu's Tail, the descending node, is not given here, and is easily understood.

This ends the section of the Vimalaprabhā that describes the calendar. Further details are given elsewhere in the text on the general topics of astronomy and astrology. These cover such topics as the length of day and night at different places, the Kālacakra view on cosmology, full details of the step functions for the fast motions of the planets, considerable detail on the astrological significance of the vowels and consonants, and so forth.

Chapter VI

Different Calculation Systems

Tantra Karaṇa system

For the descriptions of the calculations for the Tibetan calendar in the first three chapters of this book I relied mainly on one system—the siddhānta calculations of the Phugpa tradition. In this chapter I shall give the details of other important traditions of calculation, and compare all of these with a modern understanding of the motion of the Sun, Moon, and planets.

In chapter five I gave the translation of the original description of the karaṇa calendrical calculations from the Vimalaprabhā, and the best place to start is with a recap of the figures in those calculations.

There are two key differences between the various systems of siddhānta calculation and the karaṇa: the values for the mean change of weekday and solar longitude during a month are different between the two systems. Other than these figures, the principles of the calculations are the same, the same values are used in all the step functions, and the same values are used for the periods of the planets (at least, when measured in solar days).

Using the same notation as for the epoch data from Chenrab Norbu given at the end of chapter three, the data for the Tantra epoch is as follows:

Epoch: Monday 23rd March 806. Julian day: 2015531

True month:	m × 1;2	+ 0;0 (1,65)
Mean weekday:	M × 1;31,50	+ 2;30,0
Anomaly:	M × 2;1	+ 5;112 (28,126)
Mean Sun:	M × 2;10,58,2,10	+ 26;58,0,0,0 (13)
General day:	No general day figures are given.	
Mars:	167	
Jupiter:	-2600 (or, +1732)	
Saturn:	-4820 (or, +5946)	
Mercury:	-7123 (or, +1674)	
Venus:	-84 (or, +2163)	
Rāhu:	122	

The calculations yield for the epoch the true weekday as: 3;4,45,4,8, with a true solar longitude of: 0;8,59,0,8. This means that the true new Moon occurred early on Tuesday 24th March, and that the Kālacakra new year started on the following day.

One thing that just about all Tibetan writers agree on, with the notable exception of Zhonnu Pal (Khrulsel), is that the Tantra epoch refers to the year 806 CE. (They of course express this as the Fire-Dog year, 221 years before the start of the first prabhava cycle used in Tibet, 1027 CE.) However, there are many interpretations of these epoch figures in the Tibetan literature.

Some consider them to be actual mean positions of the Sun, Moon, and planets at the epoch, while others (e.g., Khrulsel) consider that the true epoch positions were hidden amongst these data and other factors given in the Vimalaprabhā. Another point of view expressed (Padzhal, Nangser) is that the values given in the Tantra have been adjusted so that using the inaccurate calculations of the Karaṇa method (i.e., the mean values for the monthly weekday and solar longitude change) the results obtained for the epoch in the year 1027—considered to be the "real" epoch of the Tantra—are in fact correct.

These variations in the interpretations of this original material are clearly a major cause of the multiplicity of calculation methods that evolved in Tibet, but in trying to settle the particular issue of the meaning of these figures, I should first consider the mean figures for the weekday and solar longitude.

Starting with the mean weekday, the monthly change given in the karaṇa is 1;31,50, meaning that the length of the synodic month is 29;31,50 solar days. This is equivalent to 29.5305556 days.

In chapter one the siddhānta synodic month was determined to be 29.5305870 solar days, and this compared well to the true value a thousand years ago of 29.5305867. All these numbers certainly seem very close, but the error (compared to modern figures) in the karaṇa system is about 100 times greater than that in the siddhānta.

Crucially for those trying to interpret the Tantra information, with the siddhānta weekday advancing each month by 1;31,50,0,480 (707), and the karaṇa weekday by 1;31,50, then the calculated time of any lunar phase is getting progressively later in the siddhānta system compared to the karaṇa. This difference amounts to nearly one and a half nāḍī in each 60 year cycle.

Another way of expressing the karaṇa relationship between the synodic month and solar days that can readily be calculated is that:

10,800 lunar days = 360 lunar months = 10,631 solar days.

This figure indicates the origin of at least part of the karaṇa calendar, as it is exactly equal to the standard cycle in the Islamic calendar of 30 lunar years, consisting of 19 normal years of 354 days each, and 11 leap years each of 355 days.

This relationship is needed in order to calculate the length of the solar year in terms of solar days. The change each month in the karaṇa Sun is 2;10,58,2,10 (13), and multiplying this out to the lowest fractional part gives a result of 612,960. The total number of those lowest fractional parts in an entire circle of the zodiac is:

$$27 \times 60 \times 60 \times 6 \times 13 = 7581600$$

The mean motion of the karaṇa Sun in one lunar month can now be represented as a fraction of the whole zodiac:

$$\frac{612960}{7581600} = \frac{1277}{15795}$$

Divide this into a full circle, convert to lunar days by multiplying by 30, and then use the relationship that 10,800 lunar days is equal to 10,631 solar days, and the length of the solar year is determined as:

$$\frac{15795 \times 30 \times 10631}{1277 \times 10800} = 365.258516 \text{ solar days.}$$

This is a surprising figure as it is in fact closer to the modern figure for the length of the year (either sidereal or tropical) than the siddhānta figure (365.270645), which is supposedly more accurate. In fact, it is in very close agreement with the length of the sidereal year, which around the time of the Tantra epoch was 365.256364 days. Presumably these figures were derived from a system of sidereal measurement, even though it was made clear in the last chapter that the Kālacakra expects corrections to be made that would result in a tropical zodiac. Perhaps this is precisely why such corrections are needed, and that accurate mean figures for the tropical Sun were not available.

I should point out that the length of the solar day is itself changing over time, and I have not taken this into account. There are increasing uncertainties regarding this variability the further one looks back in time, and so any adjustment would be uncertain. However, the range of errors due to this and any other errors in the modern calculations are well understood, and are very much smaller than the differences that are being compared here.

When comparing the karaṇa Sun to the siddhānta, the monthly difference between the two is 2;10,58,2,10 (13) - 2;10,58,1,17 (67). This amounts to 1.5155 breaths each month, or 3 nāḍī 23 pala each 60 year cycle. So, the calculated time of lunar events is creeping behind in the karaṇa compared to the siddhānta, and the solar longitude is creeping ahead. These figures were much discussed and considered by the Tibetans, as they considered the siddhānta figures to be precisely accurate.

Having compared the solar year length with modern values, now would be a good point at which to recap the three values for the solar year length that occur in the Kālacakra literature, and compare them with other Indian systems. The three are from the siddhānta and karaṇa calculations, and the karaṇa year change given in the Vimalaprabhā. Their values, together with a modern value (for 1000 CE) in similar units, are:

Siddhānta:	365;16,14,1,12,121 (13,707)
Karaṇa:	365;15,30,3,1209 (1277)
Year change:	365;15,31,1,121 (317)
Modern:	365;14,32,0,8,31 (13,707)

Converting all their fractional parts to sexagesimal, they become, correct to their fourth fractional places:

Siddhānta:	365;16,14,19,22
Karaṇa:	365;15,30,39,28
Year change:	365;15,31,13,49
Modern:	365;14,32,6,11

The siddhānta figure does not come close to any of the old Indian systems, but the other two Tantra figures bear close comparison with:

Ārya Siddhānta (499 CE):	365;15,31,15,0
Original Sūrya Siddhānta:	365;15,31,30,0
Pauliśa Siddhānta:	365;15,30,0,

The fractional parts of these figures are all sexagesimal. Lists of the lengths of the solar year from these and other Indian astronomical systems are given by Sewell (Sewell, p. 6) and Pant (KBhaga, p. 103). They give values derived from as early as the 5th century CE, and in these and similar sources I have not found any figure that comes close to this siddhānta year length. This suggests that it is an anomaly produced from the overall structure of the calendar—essentially the cycles of intercalary months—and was never intended by the authors of the Kālacakra system to be used as the Tibetans have used it, as an accurate description of the motion of the Sun.

Regarding the epoch values given in the Tantra, the first one to check is the weekday of the epoch new Moon. The mean weekday is given as 2;30,0 and the true weekday works out to 3;4,45,4,8, these days being on the 23rd and 24th March respectively.

In order to compare with modern calculations, it is necessary to choose a meridian for the calculation, as the time will be needed in terms of the solar day. The obvious one to choose is the main meridian that has for long been in use in India, that of Ujjain, at longitude 75°78.

By modern calculations, the time for mean new Moon, measured from mean daybreak, and converted into the familiar units of nāḍī, pala, and breaths is: 23rd March 806 at 26,27,5 (nāḍī, pala, and breaths), and for true new Moon: 24 March at 1,26,5. These are so close to the Karaṇa figures of 30,0,0 and 4,45,4 that they must surely be considered as real epoch data. There is nothing being hidden here.

Notice that the modern figure for mean new Moon is 3,32,1 less than the karaṇa figure, and for true new Moon 3,18,5 less. That they are both less than the karaṇa figures by very similar amounts is due to the fact that they are related by calculation, and that calculation is based on the anomaly, which itself will soon be shown to be fairly accurate.

The discrepancy between the modern and karaṇa figures is most likely due to three possibilities. The first is that observational error is the cause. Similarly, it is possible that they are calculated figures based on earlier observations, and that calculation errors cause the difference.

The other main possibility is that the figures are based on a meridian further east of Ujjain. If these figures are considered to be highly accurate, then the longitude this suggests for the meridian is about 96° east. This is about as far east in India as is possible—the eastern end of Assam—and seems very unlikely. Perhaps more than one of these factors play a part in creating the error.

One further issue worth considering here is the definition of the start of the solar day. It was common in India to define the solar day as starting at mean sunrise, 6 AM L.M.S.T. in western terms. This is an hour later than the start of the day in the Tibetan calendar. If this start of the day is used in calculating the mean and true new Moon times by modern methods, it would nearly double the discrepancy between the karaṇa and western figures. This is not conclusive, but is evidence that the Kālacakra system used mean daybreak rather than mean sunrise as the start of the solar day. Unfortunately there is no unambiguous definition in the Kālacakra Tantra or Vimalaprabhā.

The next epoch figure to consider is the longitude of the Moon's perigee. The anomaly represents the distance of the mean Moon from its apogee, and to find the distance from the perigee, one simply adds or subtracts half a circle. At the time of the epoch, the modern figure for the longitude of the Moon's perigee is 108°4057. (This, and all other longitudes that will be used later, is in a tropical zodiac, relative to the mean equinox of date.)

To convert the epoch anomaly figure of 5;112 to degrees of longitude, it can simply be treated as a complex fraction of a full circle. It represents the distance of the Moon from its apogee, as the following fraction of a full circle:

$$\frac{5\times126+112}{28\times126} = 0.210317. \text{ This is equivalent to } 75.^{\circ}7143.$$

It is now necessary to convert the measure of the longitude of the Moon at the epoch, which of course is equal to that of the Sun. The easiest way to do this, as the epoch value is 26;58,0, is simply to subtract two nāḍī from 360°. This gives 359.°5556.

If the Moon is 75.°7143 ahead of its apogee, then the apogee is at:

$$359.^{\circ}5556 - 75.^{\circ}7143 = 283.^{\circ}8413.$$

Subtracting 180° to determine the perigee yields 103.°8413. As this is not something that can be observed particularly easily, this compares well with the modern figure of 108.°4057 (the difference is -4.°5644).

The next epoch figure that should be considered is that of the mean solar longitude. We have seen that the karaṇa mean Sun at epoch is 359.°5556. Modern calculations give a figure of 4.°4348, a difference of just less than five (-4.°8792) degrees, almost exactly the same difference for the perigee.

One thing that should be considered here is that the data given in the Tantra might be based on an Indian sidereal zodiac. The first point of Aries in the tropical zodiac is slowly moving backwards (the process of precession) through the stellar constellations of the zodiac. The sidereal zodiac remains fixed relative to the stars, although there are many views regarding precisely where it begins.

There is therefore some uncertainty over the time that the two zodiacs matched, but it was approximately the first half of the sixth century. At that time the tropical first point of Aries was near the junction between the stellar constellations of Pisces and Aries.

If the longitude of the Sun is converted into a sidereal zodiac, assuming a date of equivalence between sidereal and tropical zodiacs as 500 CE, the amount of precession by 806 CE, i.e., the difference between longitude measurements in the two zodiacs, is just over 4°. In this case the error in the karaṇa figures almost disappears. This is what should be expected, as the mean motion of the Sun is clearly also a sidereal figure.

This is very strong evidence that the Kālacakra calendar is based on an earlier Indian calendar, and did not come from a land far to the north, as the Vimalaprabhā suggests. Around the sixth century Indian astronomers paid surprisingly little attention to the issue of precession, and the methods of the Kālacakra calendar are clearly intended to take this into account and adjust to a tropical zodiac.

We should next consider the five planets. Their mean longitudes at epoch are given in terms of a count of days (or tenths and hundredths of days with Venus and Mercury) since they last passed the first point of Aries. To convert to degrees we simply multiply by 360 and then divide by the respective period of the planet.

These figures are for the end of the solar day of the epoch, and so to compare with modern figures we should calculate the mean planetary positions for that time, and it is best to continue to use the Ujjain meridian. The results are as follows:

	Karaṇa data	**Karaṇa degrees**	**Modern degrees**	**Difference**
Mercury	1674/8797	68°.505	80°.778	-12°.273
Venus	2163/2247	346°.542	14°.878	-28°.336
Mars	167/687	87°.511	93°.425	-5°.914
Jupiter	1732/4332	143°.934	148°.828	-4°.894
Saturn	5946/10766	198°.826	204°.613	-5°.787

Again, considering a sidereal zodiac makes the errors for Mars, Jupiter, and Saturn almost disappear. The larger errors for Mercury, and particularly Venus, suggest that these data derive from earlier calculations and that accumulated errors are to blame. Such errors should be expected to be much greater with these two planets than with the others.

One possible source suggests itself, the Saura Siddhānta, one of the four mentioned in the Vimalaprabhā. Based on an epoch of midnight at the beginning of Monday 21st March 505 CE, calculations for the mean planetary positions from this siddhānta survive in the *Pañcasiddhānta* of Varāhamihira (Pañca. p. 294ff.). This is worth considering in some detail.

The periods of the planets are the first quantities to consider. As with the karaṇa system, the periods of Venus and Mercury are given in the *Pañcasiddhānta* in terms of tenths and hundredths of a day. Unlike the karaṇa system however, the periods of Jupiter and Saturn are given in terms of hundredths and thousandths of a day:

In the two systems, the periods of the planets in solar days are:

	Pañca	**Karaṇa**
Mercury	87.97	87.97
Venus	224.7	224.7
Mars	687	687
Jupiter	4332.32	4332
Saturn	10766.066	10766

The greater accuracy obtained by using fractions of a day makes a lot of sense with the fast moving inner planets Mercury and Venus, but not so much sense with the very much slower outer planets, Jupiter and Saturn. It may well be the case that the Kālacakra values for the periods of these two are slightly simplified versions of those in the Saura Siddhānta.

Another quantity that should be compared is the position of the aphelion of the planets. After converting the Kālacakra values to degrees, the two systems have:

	Pañca	**Karaṇa**
Mercury	220° (234.°26)	220° (238.°92)
Venus	80° (290.°38)	80° (294.°68)
Mars	110° (128.°57)	126.°67 (134.°10)
Jupiter	160° (170.°47)	160° (175.°24)
Saturn	240° (243.°87)	240° (249.°73)

The figures in brackets are modern values calculated for the respective epochs of these systems, 505 and 806 CE. These figures are identical with the one exception of Mars, and notice again the large error they both have for Venus. Whatever the origin of the error in the Venus figure in the Pañcasiddhānta, it appears to have simply been copied into the Kālacakra Tantra.

The best way of comparing the epoch values for the mean positions for the planets between these two systems is to calculate the mean positions for the 806 epoch based on the data in the *Pañcasiddhānta.* The 505 epoch is midnight at the end of Sunday 20th March 505, Julian day number 1,905,588. The 806 epoch is the end of the solar day of Monday 23rd March 806, Julian day: 2,015,531. The end of that solar day is actually five hours after midnight at the end of the day in western terms, and I shall ignore those five hours. The count of days between the epochs is:

2015531 - 1905588 = 109943 solar days.

The Tantra karaṇa data has already been converted into degrees. Using the calculations given on p. 295 of Sarma's translation of the *Pañcasiddhāntikā* to derive mean positions from the Saura Siddhānta yields the following comparison:

	Pañca	**Karaṇa**	**Difference**
Mercury	68°.509	68°.505	-0°.004
Venus	12°.612	346°.542	-26°.070
Mars	87°.646	87°.511	-0°.135
Jupiter	143°.967	143°.934	-0°.033
Saturn	198°.798	198°.826	+0°.028

Another way of looking at this comparison is to convert the results from the *Pañcasiddhānta* calculation into days or fractions of days of revolution, correct to the nearest whole number. These are the terms in which the Kālacakra Tantra expresses these quantities, and if those figures were derived from the *Pañcasiddhānta*, just such a calculation would have been done. The result of doing this is:

	Pañca	**Karaṇa**
Mercury	1674	1674 (hundredths of a day)
Venus	79	2163 (tenths of a day)
Mars	167	167
Jupiter	1732	1732
Saturn	5945	5946

The match is very close, with the exception of the strange figures for Venus. It is my opinion that there is an error in the Kālacakra Tantra, perhaps an old scribal error, and that the epoch value, instead of being described as to subtract 84 should in fact be to add 84. If this is accepted, then the mean longitude of Venus that this represents is 13°.458. This is much closer to the figure calculated from the *Pañcasiddhānta* of 12°.612, and also much closer to the modern figure of 14°.878.

Incidentally, the epoch value of the mean position of Mercury in the *Pañcasiddhānta* is 148°.283, and this compares favourably with a modern figure of 151°.866. As the match between the two systems for the longitude of Mercury is so close, this shows that the large discrepancy between the karaṇa and modern figures for Mercury is mainly due to accumulated calculation error.

None of this proves that the Tantra figures were derived from precisely the calculations of the Saura Siddhānta as preserved by Varāhamihira. His text just happens to be the one that survives today, and no doubt in the eight and ninth centuries there were many texts in existence describing Saura Siddhānta calculations, and others closely related to them. However, this comparison certainly suggests very strongly the origin of these Kālacakra planetary calculations in an earlier Indian system, most probably the Saura Siddhānta.

There is one other component in the karaṇa epoch data that should be considered before looking at the Tibetan systems of calculation. This is the longitude of Rāhu, important in predicting eclipses. The epoch value of 122 months translates into a longitude of Rāhu's Head of 169°.043. A modern figure is 173°.921, and again, with the Tantra figure 4°.878 less than the modern result, this suggests that the calculation is based on a sidereal system.

In fact, this difference is very close indeed to that between the karaṇa mean Sun and a modern figure, which was 4°.879. This means that the karaṇa figure for the difference between the position of Rāhu and the Sun—so important for eclipse prediction—was correct at the epoch to an accuracy of one thousandth of a degree. This could be due to luck or coincidence, but probably not. Given the poor granularity (1°.65) in the measurement of the longitude of Rāhu, this is actually an exact fit, and may well have been set as such.

Eclipses are good data points for anybody trying to set up astronomical and calendrical calculations and, as it happens, as was pointed out in the previous chapter, the Sun rose partially eclipsed by the Moon on the morning of the new Moon day of the Tantra epoch. This event, and the preceding lunar eclipse at sunset on 8th March may well have been used to adjust the longitude of the Sun and/or Rāhu.

As for comparisons between the Tantra figures for the calculation of the position of Rāhu and earlier Indian systems, checking several calculations in the *Pañcasiddhānta* reveals no obvious match. All the figures derived in that way are between about 2° and 3° greater than the Tantra figure.

It is said that the Kālacakra Tantra and its commentary the Vimalaprabhā were translated into Tibetan around 1027 CE, the beginning of the first prabhava cycle adopted by the Tibetans. In the following decades two other main works describing the calendar were also translated. With an epoch date of 1087, the Kālacakrāvatāra of Abhayākaragupta (Ktsjug) reproduces the Tantra calculations, working back from its epoch to the epoch of the Tantra, reproducing the same epoch figures as the Tantra.

Later, three texts by Śākya Śrībhadra, who is said to have visited Tibet in 1208 CE, were translated. These are clearly to be used together, and the first of these, the Kālacakragaṇopadeśa (Ktsman) has as its epoch 1206 CE, and gives epoch data for that time, rather than working back to the Tantra epoch.

Interestingly, the third text in the group, which deals with the planets for the same epoch, the Pañcagrahapṛthaggaṇanopadeśa (Ktsgza), gives data for Venus which differs from results calculated on the basis of the Tantra. Presumably some attempt was made to correct the increasing error in the position of Venus, but unfortunately the effort failed and Śrībhadra's Venus is actually less accurate than the Tantra's.

This and other errors became increasingly obvious to the Tibetans. It was clear from the Kālacakra literature that the karaṇa calculations were not to be considered accurate, and eventually attempts were made to create a new set of calculations altogether, based on the scant information given in the Vimalaprabhā concerning the Kālacakra siddhānta methods.

In a short space of time towards the middle of the 15th century CE, these efforts gave rise to three distinct calculation systems, all based on the concept that the siddhānta system in the lost Kālacakra Mūlatantra would, or could, have included a set of accurate calculations for the production of the calendar.

This view does not explain why the Vimalaprabhā gives a method using the solsticial shadow for correcting the karaṇa calendar, but the assumption seems to have been that all that was needed was accurate epoch data for the position of the Sun, Moon, and planets, and that if these data are combined with the siddhānta mean data for the weekday and solar calculations, the result would be a calendar accurate over very long periods of time.

My translation of the relevant section of the Vimalaprabhā in the previous chapter interprets the intentions of the Kālacakra somewhat differently. Rather than the siddhānta providing highly accurate calculations for the calendar, it instead provides a methodology for regular observation and correction of the calendar, based on the solsticial adjustment to the longitude of the Sun. That interpretation is compatible with the fact that the Vimalaprabhā is critical of Hindu systems of calendrical calculation that rely on complex calculations alone, which then become inaccurate over long periods of time.

The "Error Correction" system

With a date of publication said to be 1443 CE, the text by Zhonnu Pal (1392–1481) entitled "The Correction of Errors in Astronomy" (*rtsis la 'khrul pa sel ba*, Khrulsel) appears to be the oldest surviving attempt to create a system of siddhānta calculation (*grub rtsis*) for the calendar.

It has to be said that Zhonnu Pal's views on chronology are highly unorthodox, and received much valid criticism. For a start, he confuses the beginning of the prabhava cycle of years with that of the Chinese cycle, and instead of identifying Prabhava with Fire-Rabbit as is normal, he identifies it with Wood-Mouse, three years earlier, the start of the Chinese sixty-year cycle.

It is not clear why he does this, but one possible explanation is confusion with the sixty-year cycle in northern India in which years are expunged. In that system the year Prabhava did coincide with Wood-Mouse on two occasions, in 1084 and 1144 CE.

Zhonnu Pal also places the Buddha very early, giving his birth as 1387 BCE, and the epoch of the Kālacakra Tantra as 340 CE. These controversial views on chronology and the criticism they attracted may well have played a part in preventing his calendar becoming widely accepted.

However, his method for calculating the calendar is based upon some basic assumptions and the application of the method given in the Vimalaprabhā for fixing the solar longitude at the solstice. The main assumption that he makes, in common with other Tibetans, is that the fundamental cycle of 65 solar years being equivalent to 804 lunar months is highly accurate and repeats itself indefinitely.

He also assumes that there must be a point within this cycle that is a starting point, where a month of Caitra begins with the entry of the Sun into Aries at the exact time of mean new Moon—an image that is almost exactly depicted in the Tantra epoch data. The final main assumption is that this starting point must equate on some occasions to the beginning of the prabhava cycle of sixty years. This means that the two cycles of 65 and 60 years combine to make up a larger cycle of 780 years in total.

These assumptions lead to a structure of the calendar that will repeat itself exactly. That structure will be independent of the weekdays, but will be fixed as far as the solar longitude and intercalary months are concerned. In other words, given that in a certain year the month of Caitra starts with the mean new Moon at the first point of Aries, 65 years later exactly the same will occur, although on a different weekday, with the intercalary months of each 65 year cycle being the same. Some of these cycles will also start in Wood-Mouse years, which Zhonnu Pal equates with Prabhava.

If such a 65 year cycle starts with Wood-Mouse, the last year of the cycle would be Earth-Dragon. The next cycle would start with Earth-Snake and end with Water-Bird. In full, the possible combinations with the Chinese sexagenary cycle are:

1. Wood-Mouse to Earth-Dragon
2. Earth-Snake to Water-Bird
3. Wood-Dog to Earth-Tiger
4. Earth-Rabbit to Water-Sheep
5. Wood-Monkey to Earth-Mouse
6. Earth-Ox to Water-Snake
7. Wood-Horse to Earth-Dog
8. Earth Pig to Water-Rabbit
9. Wood-Dragon to Earth-Monkey

10. Earth-Bird to Water-Ox
11. Wood-Tiger to Earth-Horse
12. Earth-Sheep to Water-Pig

This gives the full cycle of 780 years. Having described this structure, Zhonnu Pal makes the comment that: "The succession of intercalary months and changes of zodiacal sign (occupied by the Sun) within these 780 years, cycle repeatedly through the aeon, without even the slightest variation."

Zhonnu Pal fills out the details of the structure of the calendar by calculating from the start of the cycle for Sun-sign changes and intercalary months. He makes use of a couple of interesting mathematical innovations for the calculation. These simplify the calculation without any loss of accuracy, and also provide an elegant way of interpreting the meaning of the intercalation index.

For the determination of the structure of the calendar, the defining points are the entry of the Sun into the various signs of the zodiac. The mean motion of the Sun in one lunar day in the siddhānta calculations is given by: 0;4,21,5,43 (67). This can be simplified to 134th fractions of a nāḍī as: 0;4,49 (134).

The size of a zodiacal sign is 2;15,0 (134) and a simple division shows that the time taken for the mean Sun to move through a single sign of the zodiac is: 30 12/13th lunar days.

In this way the structure of the calendar can be constructed by describing the mean motion of the Sun in terms of 134th parts of a nāḍī, and measuring time in terms of 13th parts of a lunar day.

Zhonnu Pal describes the start of the cycle as being "the first white lunar day of the month of Caitra in the first Prabhava year, as the Sun first entered the sign of Aries." In other words, at the beginning of the very first cycle, at the time of the mean new Moon at the beginning of the month of Caitra, the solar longitude was exactly zero. Also, the intercalation index was zero. It is important to point out that Zhonnu Pal uses the month count itself as the intercalation index, and so his index is half of that in the normal Phugpa calculations.

So, simple division can determine when during this first year of Prabhava the mean Sun enters Capricorn—winter solstice, the defining point according to the Kālacakra Tantra. The first point of Capricorn has a longitude of 20;15,0, and division by the mean motion of the Sun gives the time elapsed from the very beginning of the cycle at the new Moon of Caitra as 9 months 8 4/13th lunar days.

The next significant point is the beginning of the next year of Vibhava. At that point the intercalation index is 12, and multiplying this by 4 gives a result of 48, suggesting that the first month of the new year is not intercalary (it has not reached 130). Now, given that the lunar months are a little less than one-twelfth of a solar year, the Sun will enter Aries during this first month of Caitra in the new year.

Again, simple division will yield the time that this occurs. Dividing a full circle of 27;0,0 by the mean solar motion of 0;4,49 (134) yields that the Sun enters Aries for the second time after 12 months 11 1/13th lunar days.

So, in the month Caitra of this second year of the cycle Vibhava, the Sun enters Aries 11 1/13th lunar days after new Moon. Another way of looking at this is to say that at that new Moon at the beginning of Caitra, the Sun still had a certain distance to travel before it would next enter Aries. That distance is easily calculated by multiplying the time between new Moon and the entry to Aries by the mean daily motion of the Sun:

11;1 (13) × 0;4,49 (134) = 0;48,48 (134)

This is an important result. The intercalation index of 12, multiplied by 4, gives a result of 48, and if this number is placed in the nāḍī and 134th fractional places, it gives an exact measure of the distance the Sun has to travel before it next enters Aries.

In fact, this works for all months and all zodiacal signs, and the intercalation index is therefore a simple measure at the time of a new Moon of the distance the Sun has to travel before it next changes zodiacal sign.

So, why does this work? The point here is that the distance the mean Sun travels in a lunar month is a bit less than a whole zodiac sign. Therefore, each lunar month, the position of the end of the current Sun sign moves forward by:

2;15 - 2;10,58,1,17. Converting this to 134th fractional parts, yields:
2;15 - 2;10,130 (134) = 0;4,4 (134)

Therefore, the distance to be travelled by the Sun from each new Moon to the next change in sign increases by 0;4,4 (134) each month. As the intercalation index increases by one each month, and as the distance to be travelled when that index is zero is an entire Sun sign, then by multiplying that index by 4 will produce the result as described by Zhonnu Pal. Of course, using the intercalation index as was done in chapter one and multiplying it by two would produce exactly the same result. (It is interesting to note that Zhonnu Pal is keeping close to the Kālacakra Tantra here, where the month count was multiplied by 4 rather than 2.)

Continuing, the next winter solstice is again easily determined, by further division. It occurs nine months and 19 5/13th lunar days after the new Moon at the beginning of the year Vibhava, 21 months and 19 5/13th lunar days after the beginning of the whole cycle. For this month the intercalation index is 22, which when multiplied by four yields 88, suggesting (as it has not reached 130) that this is also not an intercalary month.

During the next year, the third in the cycle, Śuklata, the intercalation index does reach over 130.

One point that must be mentioned here is that although he does not explicitly state this, Zhonnu Pal uses a somewhat different way of naming intercalary months. For example, if an intercalary month falls between the months of Caitra and Vaiśākha, in the normal way of naming the months the intercalary month would be called an extra Vaiśākha, and the month following it the delayed Vaiśākha.

An alternative method is to name the intercalary month after the month that precedes it. The mathematics of Zhonnu Pal's calendar suggests that he used this latter method, and he was not alone in this. This view was also put forward in the *Pad dkar zhal lung* by Lachen Thinle Gewai Wangpo (*bla mkhyen 'phrin las dge ba'i dbang po*, Padzhal, p. 604). This is also the same method as used in China.

There is a strong logic to this method, as if a month is defined by entry into a particular sign, if the next month is intercalary, then the Sun does not change sign and remains in the same sign for the whole of that month.

Given that a 65 year cycle is equivalent to 804 lunar months, an intercalary month should occur after every 32 1/2 months. In the third year of the cycle, the beginning of the month of Mārgaśīrṣa is exactly 32 months after the start of the cycle. The 32 1/2 month point is effectively reached in the middle of this month. It is therefore duplicated, and the next month (which would otherwise be called Pauṣa) should be intercalary.

The beginning of that next month is 33 months after the start of the cycle. The intercalation index is therefore 33, and this multiplied by four yields 132—going over 130 for the first time. The solar longitude at the beginning and end of that month is easily calculated by multiplication as before:

Beginning:	18;2,2 (134)
End:	20;12,132 (134)

The first of these longitudes is eight zodiacal signs (18;0) + 0;2,2, and the second is eight signs + 2;12,132. It is therefore clear that during this month the Sun does not change sign and that this is an intercalary month, the duplicated Mārgaśīrṣa.

Similarly, the month following Śrāvaṇa in the sixth year of the cycle is exactly 66 lunar months after the beginning of the cycle. This is 32 1/2 months, plus one intercalary that has been added, plus another 32 1/2 months.

At the beginning of that month the solar longitude is 9;4,4 (134), or four signs (9;0) + 0;4,4, and at the end it is 11;15,0 (134), or exactly five signs. During that month the Sun does not change sign, and therefore it is intercalary. The month Śrāvaṇa is therefore duplicated.

For the first of these two intercalary months, Mārgaśīrṣa in the third year of the cycle, the 32 1/2 month intercalary indication occurs in the very middle of the month that is to be duplicated. In the second of these intercalations, the month of Śrāvaṇa in the sixth year of the cycle, the 32 1/2 month point is at the very end of the month that will be duplicated. This pattern repeats through the 24 intercalations of the 65 year cycle.

In this way, working through the entire cycle, a structure can be built up identifying the changes of sign of the Sun, particularly the entries into Aries and Capricorn, and the intercalary months.

Zhonnu Pal gives a list of the intercalary months, and then builds a table indicating in which years of the Chinese sexagenary cycle they fall. The list of intercalary months (notice that each occurs twice) is as follows:

1. Mārgaśīrṣa	13. Jyeṣṭha
2. Śrāvaṇa	14. Māgha
3. Vaiśākha	15. Kārtikka
4. Pauṣa	16. Āṣāḍha
5. Āśvina	17. Caitra
6. Jyeṣṭha	18. Mārgaśīrṣa
7. Phālguna	19. Bhādrapada
8. Kārtikka	20. Vaiśākha
9. Śrāvaṇa	21. Māgha
10. Caitra	22. Āśvina
11. Pauṣa	23. Āṣāḍha
12. Bhādrapada	24. Phālguna

Zhonnu Pal then goes into some detail describing a set of five tables for the winter solstice points—he in fact describes these as wheels, with one set of values in the middle, each surrounded by another 12. However, for the purposes of describing these it is easiest to place the values in tables, with his central figures in the leftmost columns.

The entry of the Sun into Capricorn in the first year of the cycle was calculated above as occurring 9 months 8 4/13th lunar days after the beginning of the year. By definition the solstice must occur in the tenth Kālacakra month, Pauṣa, and all we need to identify the time is the elapsed number of lunar days, 8, and the number of 13th fractional parts of a lunar day, 4. Notice that in terms of the calendar, it would be normal to express this by saying that the solstice occurs during the ninth lunar day of Pauṣa. These two values, 8 and 4, are the first values in the first of the five tables.

The next solstice calculated occurred at nine months and 19 5/13th lunar days after the next new year, and so the figures 19 and 5 become the first values in the second of the five tables. This procedure continues, until the sixth solstice, the figures for which, 3 and 9, are placed in the second column of the first table. The full set of five tables is as follows:

Table one

8	3	29	24	19	15	10	6	1	26	22	17	12
4	9	1	6	11	3	8	0	5	10	2	7	12
Mouse, Tiger, Dragon, Horse, Monkey, Dog–Male–Wood												
Ox, Rabbit, Snake, Sheep, Bird, Pig–Female–Earth												
Intercalary: 2, 4, 13, 15												

Table two

19	14	10	5	30	26	21	17	12	7	3	28	24
5	10	2	7	12	4	9	1	6	11	3	8	0
Mouse, Tiger, Dragon, Horse, Monkey, Dog–Male–Iron												
Ox, Rabbit, Snake, Sheep, Bird, Pig–Female–Wood												
Intercalary: 6, 8, 17, 19, 21												

Table three

30	25	21	16	12	7	2	28	23	18	14	9	5
6	11	3	8	0	5	10	2	7	12	4	9	1
Mouse, Tiger, Dragon, Horse, Monkey, Dog–Male–Fire												
Ox, Rabbit, Snake, Sheep, Bird, Pig–Female–Iron												
Intercalary: 1, 10, 12, 14, 23												

Table four

11	6	2	27	23	18	13	9	4	30	25	20	16
7	12	4	9	1	6	11	3	8	0	5	10	2
Mouse, Tiger, Dragon, Horse, Monkey, Dog–Male–Water												
Ox, Rabbit, Snake, Sheep, Bird, Pig–Female–Fire												
Intercalary: 3, 5, 7, 16, 18												

Table five

22	18	13	8	4	29	24	20	15	11	6	1	27
8	0	5	10	2	7	12	4	9	1	6	11	3
Mouse, Tiger, Dragon, Horse, Monkey, Dog–Male–Earth												
Ox, Rabbit, Snake, Sheep, Bird, Pig–Female–Water												
Intercalary: 9, 11, 20, 22, 24												

In these tables are included not only the winter solstice times but also the alignment with the Chinese sexagenary cycle and the 24 intercalary months.

Taking the first year of the cycle, Wood-Mouse, the combination of wood and Mouse occurs only in the first table, and it is in that table that the first figures were placed. The next year, Wood-Ox, can only refer to the second table, and it is in the first row of that table that the second set of solstice figures were placed.

The third year of the cycle Fire-Tiger, is the one calculated as containing the first intercalary month, and this is indicated in the third table. The first intercalary month in the list is Mārgaśīrṣa, as calculated earlier. The second intercalary month in a cycle occurs in the first of these five tables. This is therefore during the sixth year of the cycle, Earth-Snake, and the intercalary month that is second in the list is Śrāvaṇa.

If the first cycle of 65 years starts with Wood-Mouse, as described earlier, the second cycle must start with Earth-Snake. Clearly, this lies also in the first of these tables, with the winter solstice values again being 8 and 4. This pattern repeats itself through the entire 780 year cycle, and then starts again.

Zhonnu Pal states that tables like these can be established for other phenomena, such as summer solstice, or the entry of the Sun into Aries. Having described how to construct these tables, he then goes on to describe how to use them in establishing a calendar.

Zhonnu Pal applies the method of correction as described in the Vimalaprabhā, of observing the winter solstice by means of determining when the length of the midday shadow of a gnomon starts again to shorten. The Vimalaprabhā does not describe how to set up these tables and use them in the way that Zhonnu Pal does, and so what follows is his adaptation of the correction.

No doubt many observations will have been performed over a number of years, but he describes just one, and fixes his calendar on the basis of that. Presumably the text by Zhonnu Pal that I am using is very early, as Norzang Gyatso (Padzhal, p. 443) mentions solstice determinations in Zhonnu Pal's tradition, taking place in 1466, 1467 and 1468. These all fit perfectly with the one described by Zhonnu Pal himself.

In the Water-Dog year, 1442 CE, he observed on the 13th lunar day (of the month of Pauṣa) that the shadow had reversed (i.e., started to shorten). Referring to the tables, the Water-Dog year can only be found in the fourth table, and only the first set of values, 11 and 7, can fit the observation. For example the seventh values of 13 and 11 mean that the solstice occurs 13 11/13th lunar days after new Moon, i.e., during the 14th lunar day. Zhonnu Pal observed the shadow having turned during the 13th lunar day, and so this is not possible.

Similarly, the eighth values in the table, 9 and 3, are too early, and the turn of the shadow would have been observed a couple of days earlier than he reports.

Of course, the main weakness of this method is that it assumes that he can already determine the timing of lunar days reasonably accurately, rather than just estimating from the appearance of new and full Moons. Unfortunately, Zhonnu Pal gives no indication how this is done, although he later fits the weekday calculation of his calendar to his interpretation of the data given in the Kālacakra Tantra—maybe an iterative process was involved here, and he is just describing his final results.

That result is that the mean longitude of the Sun was defined as 20;15 at 11 7/13ths lunar days after the new Moon at the start of the month of Pauṣa in the Water-Dog year, 1442 CE.

From his calendar as he later constructed it, the mean weekday for the beginning of the 12th lunar day was 4;33,45,0,0; this is on Wednesday 12th December 1442. Adding 7/13ths of a lunar day takes this figure to 5;5,33,0,552, early morning on the Thursday, about 7.13 AM L.M.S.T. My calculations using modern methods make the time of the solstice at 8.09 AM L.M.S.T. (Central Tibet) on that same Thursday. This seems very accurate, but the accuracy is misleading.

Certainly, Zhonnu Pal got the day right. Presumably his detection of the reversal of the midday shadow took place on the Friday, but looking at the actual solstice, the distance between the mean Moon and Sun at that time was 124°.89, and so the solstice occurred during the 11th lunar day, not the 12th, and about 5/13th through that lunar day, not 7/13ths. It seems to be mainly coincidence that the figures in Zhonnu Pal's tables place the time of the solstice very close to the real time at which it occurred.

There is clearly quite an error in his weekday calculation. Using modern methods, I place both the mean and true new Moon at the start of the month of Pauṣa during which this solstice occurred as happening about 27 1/2 hours later than as given by Zhonnu Pal's calendar. The relationship between mean and true lunar days (dependent upon the accuracy of the anomaly) is quite good: his new Moon is earlier than the true by 4 hrs 10 mins, and using modern calculations I make it 4 hrs 17 mins earlier.

But this error in the actual timing of the lunar days—i.e., the weekday calculation—is extraordinary. Just one eclipse, occurring a day later than the predicted new or full Moon, should have been enough to demonstrate this error, and no doubt it did, contributing to the lack of acceptance of this calendar. Unfortunately, the materials I have available to me on Zhonnu Pal's methods make no mention of eclipse prediction or analysis. The epoch data that I have used in reconstructing his calendar is not dependent on his text alone, but exactly the same data is reproduced by both Lhundrup Gyatso (Padzhal, p. 31) and Norzang Gyatso (Padzhal, p. 461).

As it happens, Norzang Gyatso (Padzhal p. 446) does discuss an eclipse of the Moon predicted by Zhonnu Pal's calculations as occurring in 1469, but does not use this to criticize the weekday figure, rather the apparent position of the Moon in the lunar mansions. The eclipse did take place, and Zhonnu Pal's calendar predicts that it would occur shortly before 10.00 PM L.M.S.T. on Thursday 26th January 1469. It in fact occurred about 27 hours later, just after midnight local time on the Friday. Given clear skies, it would have been clearly visible from Tibet.

The main epoch data is described by Zhonnu Pal after the description of the solstice determination and how this fits into the five tables that hold the structure of the calendar.

His solstice determination took place in the Water-Dog year, 1442, and this refers to the first entry in the fourth table. This means that the beginning of the 65 year cycle current at that time must have been the Earth-Sheep year, 1439. Therefore, at the very beginning of the first lunar day (mean new Moon) of the month of Caitra in that year, the mean Sun has to be fixed as entering Aries, and the intercalation index as zero. This was Saturday 14th March 1439.

Thanks to his solstice determination this solar longitude is very accurate. At the solar time (mean weekday) given for the new Moon at which the mean Sun was set to zero degrees Aries, modern calculations give the position of the mean Sun as just 0°.03 before the first point of Aries. However, that time was a little over a day before the real new Moon.

Zhonnu Pal then calculates back to the year he takes as the base-epoch, the year for which the calculations are given in the Kālacakra Tantra. As mentioned earlier, he considers this to have been the Iron-Mouse year, 340 CE. This is 1099 years before 1439, and dividing by 65 leaves a result of 59. This is 6 less than 65, and so the base-epoch year is 6 years after the start of a cycle. The intercalation index is then easily calculated, being zero at Caitra at the beginning of a cycle. Multiply the years by 12 and then divide by 65:

$$6 \times 12 = 72 \div 65 = 1 \text{ rem. } 7$$

This remainder of 7 is therefore the base-epoch value for the intercalation index (this is simply measured in months, and is half the value that would normally be used). The next step is to derive the epoch position of the Sun as this is linked with the intercalation index. Using the method described earlier, if the intercalation index for base-epoch Caitra is 7, multiplying this by four gives the distance the mean Sun has to travel before entering Aries as: 0;28,28. The longitude of the Sun at epoch is then easily calculated by subtraction:

27;0,0 - 0;28,28 = 26;31,106 (134) = 26;31,47,2,52 (67)

These results are derived from observation, but from here on the epoch values used by Zhonnu Pal depend solely upon his interpretation of the data in the Kālacakra Tantra, and his views on this are highly controversial.

The next value that he discusses in his text is that of the mean weekday at epoch. There are three comments in the literature that Zhonnu Pal interprets together. These are the addition of 8 to the year count in the karaṇa new year calculation, the addition of an apparent epoch value of 2;30, and the curious comments that occur twice in the Vimalaprabhā about "reduction of Mars and development of Sun."

Zhonnu Pal considers that the true epoch value is the addition of 8 to the year count. This means that at Caitra, eight years before the base-epoch, the mean weekday was exactly zero. This is a completely different definition of new year from that understood by other writers, and as explained in the Vimalaprabhā itself. There the definition is of the entry of the Sun into Aries, not the timing of the new Moon at the beginning of

Caitra. To Zhonnu Pal this is not contradictory, as he considers the true epoch data to be hidden within the Tantra information, which therefore needs special interpretation.

In those eight years, it is easily calculated that there were a total of 99 months, including intercalaries. (The intercalaries occurred in 334, 336 and 339 CE.)

Using the karaṇa mean weekday calculation for this month count gives the weekday at base-epoch as:

99 × 1;31,50 = 4;31,30

This is intended to be the epoch value for the Tantra calculations. Zhonnu Pal states that the curious comments about Mars and the Sun refer to values such as that for Mars (3) being replaced by those for the Sun (1), in other words, reduced by 2. His point is that the epoch value given in the Tantra, 2;30, is 2 less than the true epoch value of 4;31, ignoring the small difference in the nāḍī value.

In actual usage, he performs the calculation according to the siddhānta figures and takes as his weekday epoch value: 4;31,41,1,151.

This is the single source of his error in the weekday calculations. His determination of the mean new Moon occurring on Wednesday 13th February 340, is just less than 26 hours before the mean new Moon actually occurred, on the Thursday.

He goes on to point out that the epoch value given in the Tantra and that intended by the Tantra (2;30 and 4;30) are equivalent to each other if the first is subtracted. In other words, subtracting 2;30 is the same as adding 4;30 (the two added together total 7;0). For Zhonnu Pal this is another way in which the true epoch values are hidden in the writings of the Tantra, and he extrapolates from this to other epoch values.

He states that just as the weekday value should be subtracted, so should the epoch value for the anomaly. That epoch value is 5;112 and subtracting this is equivalent to adding 22;14, and it is this that he takes as his base-epoch value.

As before, combining this with the epoch value for the Sun gives the value for the Moon's perigee as 249°.45. This is fortuitously accurate, as the modern figure for the perigee at the time is 221°.31.

Zhonnu Pal continues with this thinking for the position of Rāhu and states that the Tantra figure of 122 also needs to be subtracted. This means an actual epoch figure of (adding) 108. This gives a value for the Head of Rāhu at the epoch as 190°.96. This is also surprisingly accurate as modern calculation gives a result of 189°.24.

However, this is where fortunate accuracy runs out. The copy I have of Zhonnu Pal's text is incomplete, and does not give his derivation of the planetary positions. However, according to the otherwise accurate information given by Norzang Gyatso (Padzhal, p. 461), Zhonnu Pal used the epoch values given in the Tantra directly. If so, his planetary positions are completely wrong, being effectively random:

	Zhonnu Pal	**Modern**
Mercury	68°.505	336°.600
Venus	346°.542	134°.687
Mars	87°.511	153°.306
Jupiter	143°.934	36°.537
Saturn	198°.826	261°.851

Because of his direct application of the methods given for the adjustment of the solar longitude, Zhonnu Pal's calendar is in some ways the most accurate that was produced in Tibet. There was no problem with the months as mentioned in chapter four, and his Caitra, etc., agreed with the Indian systems. His month definitions also appear to have been properly compatible with the Chinese system, and so his calendar is the only Tibetan system for which details survive that would have been compatible with both the Indian and Chinese systems. (However, see the contemporary Sherab Ling calendar described below.)

I am not aware of any later attempts to correct for errors in the weekday calculation, but that was certainly the weakest link in his calendar. In summary, the epoch values that he describes for the Tantra base-epoch are as follows:

Epoch: Wednesday 13th February 340. Julian day: 1845286

True month:	m × 1;2	+ 0;14 (1,65)
Mean weekday:	M × 1;31,50,0,480	+ 4;31,41,1,151 (707)
Anomaly:	M × 2;1	+ 22;14 (28,126)
Mean Sun:	M × 2;10,58,1,17	+ 26;31,47,2,52 (67)
Rāhu:		+ 108

I have mentioned before that perhaps an iterative process was used in the development of these figures. As with other writers Zhonnu Pal goes on to describe how his calculations fit with the historical data for events concerning the Buddha. Looking at this in detail is beyond the scope of the current work, but it includes such things as the entry of the Buddha into the womb of his mother, the timing of his birth, in particular the lunar mansion at that time, the eclipse at the time of the Buddha's enlightenment, and so on.

Such astronomical details as are given in the Indian texts quoted by Zhonnu Pal and others, such as the Sūryagarbha Sūtra, are rather scant, and are often in need of interpretation. However, most Tibetan calendar makers considered it very important to make the results produced by their calendars agree with the historical data. Unfortunately, Zhonnu Pal's methods are not described in full in texts currently available, and it is not clear whether his calendrical calculations influenced the timing as he saw it of the Buddha's life, or whether such chronology influenced the calculations.

However, his description of the structure of the calendar, and the tables used for the 780 year cycle are the fullest description of the methods used to create these siddhānta calendars that I have been able to find, and it is clear that others used similar techniques. I also suspect that his definition of intercalary months more properly fits the intentions of the original Kālacakra authors.

The Phugpa system

The main text describing the theory underlying the development of the Phugpa calendar system, the "Oral Instructions of Puṇḍarīka" (Padzhal) consists of a primary work by Phugpa Lhundrup Gyatso together with several explanatory works, all of which are by Norzang Gyatso (1423–1513) with the exception of one by Lachen Thinle Gewai Wangpo.

Unfortunately, the practical derivation of the calendar is not explained as fully as in the work by Zhonnu Pal, and some of the arguments presented seem rather circular, but the main assumptions underlying the derivation of the calendar are clearly presented. Certainly much attention is paid to fitting the calendar with the Phugpa understanding of chronology, and this is combined with observation and theoretical assumptions.

The key assumption is that the winter solstice, and therefore other seasonal points, are observed to occur at different times from Tibet and India, and that the calculations given in the Kālacakra Tantra are designed for the central meridian passing through India. For this reason, the method of correction of the solar longitude given in the Vimalaprabhā cannot apply directly to Tibet. The position of the Sun, Moon, and planets within the zodiac and lunar mansions will be the same at any one time when viewed from different places such as Tibet and India, but the timing of the seasonal points will be different. The longitude of the Sun will therefore be different at the moment of solstice when viewed from Tibet.

There is some justification for this view based on an extrapolation of ideas presented in the Kālacakra Tantra, starting in verse 55 of the first chapter. The cosmology described envisages a great mountain, Meru, around which are arranged 12 great continents. We are said to be located on the southernmost of these. The lunar mansions and the Sun, Moon, and planets that move across them circle around Mt. Meru, above these continents.

The key point made is that the seasons occur at different times in these continents. For example, winter solstice is the time of the Sun's most southerly passage in the southern continent, and at that same time, although the Sun is still seen as being in the same position within the zodiac, from the point of view of the opposite northern continent, the Sun is at its most northern position, and therefore that continent experiences summer solstice. Similarly, spring and autumn equinoxes are experienced on the continents to the east and west of Meru.

In this way, the seasons rotate around the 12 continents, and the Phugpa tradition interprets the definitions of the seasons in each continent to apply strictly to the central meridian passing through that continent. To the east or west of that meridian, the seasonal points will be experienced at different times. Tibet is considered to be far to the east of India, and an exact figure is given for the difference this makes to the timing of the seasons. The solstice is said to occur in Tibet a little over 23 lunar days before it is experienced on the central meridian passing through India. (For those not familiar with astronomy, this is quite wrong, and a solstice is actually observed to occur at the same time from any point on the Earth.)

A single wheel or table, very much like the five constructed by Zhonnu Pal, is used in the Phugpa tradition, but it is not clear that is was used in exactly the same way to fix the solar longitude. The way the figures are discussed it seems more to have confirmed the results of visual observations. Again, this is only mentioned very briefly, but in my opinion much use was made of observations against the fixed stars in order to determine longitude.

The key problem for the Phugpa calendar makers was to determine the difference in the timing of the solstices as observed from Tibet and India, and it seems that this was done by measuring longitude by direct observation and then calculating the difference in time. I have not been able to find mention of any way by which that time difference could be determined more directly, and Norzang Gyatso states (Padzhal, p. 449) that the siddhānta calculations agree with visual observation. The method he describes, unfortunately only briefly, is that the longitude of the Moon that is derived from that of the Sun is checked by observation as it passes against the stars that are assumed to comprise the lunar mansions.

The one particular solstice the detection of which is discussed the most frequently in the Phugpa literature took place very late on Friday 12th December 1466, about an hour before daybreak of the Saturday. This solstice is described twice in the "Oral Instructions of Puṇḍarīka" (Padzhal, p. 458 and 530) and also by Norzang Gyatso in his general commentary to the Kālacakra system (Kdgyan, p. 118, and in English translation: Kilty, p. 127).

There are mistakes in both the data presented and the calculations described in these texts (at least in currently available editions), but with three descriptions the correct figures are easily pieced together. This shows the values used for the difference between seasonal timings thought to have existed between India and Tibet, and the impact these had on the Phugpa calendar.

According to Norzang Gyatso, starting on the 26th of the 11th month, the method described by Abhayākaragupta in his Kālacakrāvatāra (Ktsjug) for using a gnomon to determine a solstice was used. Abhaya expands on the very brief details given in the Vimalaprabhā, and in particular explains how to construct on the base on which the gnomon is set up the north-south line. This ensures that the midday examination of the shadow is performed correctly.

Norzang Gyatso states that the midday shadow was observed to have turned during the fifth lunar day of the 12th month, and that the solstice actually occurred during the 4th lunar day, at 3;6,4 (13,5). In this notation, 3 is a full count of completed lunar days, 6 is a number of 13th parts of a lunar day, and 4 is a further subdivision into 5ths. This is therefore just over halfway through the fourth lunar day of the month.

In the Phugpa calendar, this 4th lunar day started at mean weekday 4;17,10,0,690. Adding 0;6,4 (13,5) to this takes the time to 4;48,3,4,459. This is late on the Wednesday 10th December, and is just over two days (nearly 52 hours) before the actual solstice occurred—a very inaccurate observation.

At that time, the mean Sun is given a value of 18;31,30, and this is taken as the equivalent to the figure of 20;15 given in the Vimalaprabhā for the position of the mean Sun at the winter solstice.

The difference between these two figures is 1;43,30. Interestingly, this is an exact number (23) of degrees, and this offers a possible clue regarding the derivation of these values.

The whole number of degrees seems strong evidence that the theory of variable solstices around the twelve continents considered there to be 360 discrete solstices observed from 360 subdivisions of the 12 major continents. These are associated with the 360 zodiacal days, or degrees of the zodiac, and therefore the solar longitude at different locations at the time of solstice must be whole numbers of zodiacal days.

This speculation is not fully supported by the texts. Norzang Gyatso actually writes (Padzhal, p. 529) in terms of 365 discrete solstices, but this does not fit the mathematics easily. Also, he later (Padzhal, p. 529) aligns the solstices with the zodiacal days, and describes how to take the difference of 23 zodiacal days, convert this into solar longitude, and then subtract this from 20;15 in order to derive the mean Sun at solstice in Tibet. There are other inconsistencies like this in his descriptions and his mathematics.

Assuming my hypothesis is correct, the necessarily approximate estimations of the longitudes of the Sun and Moon derived from observations would have produced an estimate of the longitude of the Sun at solstice, and this would have been adjusted to fit the nearest whole number of zodiacal days.

Given the mean motion of the Sun per lunar day, by means of division the supposed time difference between the seasonal points in Tibet and India can be calculated. Given the mean motion of the Sun in a lunar day as 0;4,21,5,43, this yields:

1;43,30 ÷ 0;4,21,5,43 = 23;42,27,4,108,10 (707,13)

Converting this to 13ths and 5ths, as above, this becomes 23;9,1 (13,5).

This is an important figure, and we now have the supposed seasonal difference between Tibet and India expressed in three different units, two of solar longitude and one of time:

longitude:	23°
	1;43,30
time:	23;9,1

The table that is used in the Phugpa tradition is a little different from those used by Zhonnu Pal. Where he had 5 tables each of 13 entries, the Phugpa combines all the information into one with 65 entries. Just as with his table, the first entry is placed in the centre of a circle, with the other entries arranged around. Also as with Zhonnu Pal, the Phugpa tradition makes the assumption that the 65 year cycle aligns with the 60 year prabhava cycle.

As with Zhonnu Pal's wheels it is easiest to represent these here in tabular form rather than circles. The Phugpa table contains data for the timings of both summer and winter solstices, the upper values being for the summer.

1	2	3	4	5	6	7	8	9	10	11	12	13	14	15	16	17
9	20	1	12	23	4	15	26	7	18	29	10	21	3	14	25	6
0	1	2	3	4	5	6	7	8	9	10	11	12	0	1	2	3
4	4	4	4	4	4	4	4	4	4	4	4	4	4	4	4	4
14	25	6	17	28	9	21	2	13	24	5	16	27	8	19	30	11
7	8	9	10	11	12	0	1	2	3	4	5	6	7	8	9	10
4	4	4	4	4	4	4	4	4	4	4	4	4	4	4	4	4

18	19	20	21	22	23	24	25	26	27	28	29	30	31	32	33	34
17	28	9	20	1	12	23	4	15	27	8	19	30	11	22	3	14
4	5	6	7	8	9	10	11	12	0	1	2	3	4	5	6	7
4	4	4	4	4	4	4	4	4	4	4	4	4	4	4	4	4
22	3	15	26	7	18	29	10	21	2	13	24	5	16	27	9	20
11	12	0	1	2	3	4	5	6	7	8	9	10	11	12	0	1
4	4	4	4	4	4	4	4	4	4	4	4	4	4	4	4	4

35	36	37	38	39	40	41	42	43	44	45	46	47	48	49	50	51
25	6	17	28	9	21	2	13	24	5	16	27	8	19	30	11	22
8	9	10	11	12	0	1	2	3	4	5	6	7	8	9	10	11
4	4	4	4	4	4	4	4	4	4	4	4	4	4	4	4	4
1	12	23	4	15	26	7	18	29	10	21	3	14	25	6	17	28
2	3	4	5	6	7	8	9	10	11	12	0	1	2	3	4	5
4	4	4	4	4	4	4	4	4	4	4	4	4	4	4	4	4

52	53	54	55	56	57	58	59	60	61	62	63	64	65
3	15	26	7	18	29	10	21	2	13	24	5	16	27
12	0	1	2	3	4	5	6	7	8	9	10	11	12
4	4	4	4	4	4	4	4	4	4	4	4	4	4
9	20	1	12	23	4	15	27	8	19	30	11	22	3
6	7	8	9	10	11	12	0	1	2	3	4	5	6
4	4	4	4	4	4	4	4	4	4	4	4	4	4

It is clear that the figures in this table have been calculated in exactly the same way as described by Zhonnu Pal. The first figure in his table for the occurrence of a winter solstice was 8;4, and the first winter figure in this Phugpa table is 14;7,4 (13,5). The relationship is easily derived. The value found above for the time difference between Tibet and India was 23;9,1 lunar days. Subtracting this amount from each of the figures in Zhonnu Pal's table yields the equivalent figures in the Phugpa table. For example:

8;4,0 - 23;9,1 = 14;7,4 (30 is added as there are 30 lunar days in each month.)

The meaning of this difference is that the Sun reaches the point in the zodiac where a solstice is observed in Tibet 23;9,1 lunar days before it reaches the equivalent point where the solstice is observed in India. In other words, the mean Sun reaches longitude 18;31,30 that same number of lunar days before it reaches longitude 20;15.

We can now understand some of the other characteristics of the Phugpa calendar, particularly those associated with the definitions of the months, which depend upon the position of the Sun.

The intercalation index is tied to the longitude of the Sun in exactly the same way as with the "Error Correction" calendar. When the Sun is at the very beginning of a zodiacal sign, such as 0° Aries, at the exact moment of mean new Moon, the intercalation index is zero.

However, such a value does not indicate an intercalary month in the Phugpa system. Instead, values of either 48 or 49 indicate intercalation. Given the rule established earlier, multiply these numbers by 2 (not by 4, as with Zhonnu Pal, as the Phugpa index is already twice his), and then place them as nāḍī and 134th fractional parts. These then give the distance the Sun has to travel before entering the next sign:

0;96,96 = 1;36,96 = 21°.49
0;98,98 = 1;38,98 = 21°.94

The points defining the months have been offset by a distance of nearly 22°. Looking at the behaviour of the solar longitude more closely, there is a range of values within a zodiacal sign that represent the definition point for a month. These are 0;34,34 to 0;36,36, equivalent to 7°.612 to 8°.060—the difference of approximately 22°. This is not exactly the

23° offset described above, but it is very close, and clearly these are equivalent.

The important point is that the seasonal points still define the months. Whereas in the Kālacakra and Zhonnu Pal's system the vernal equinox, the Sun's entry into Aries, defines the month of Caitra, in the Phugpa system the vernal equinox, which is considered to occur at approximately 8° Pisces, defines the previous month, Phālguna.

This was set as the definition of Phālguna presumably because the authors of this system believed that the equinox occurred in Tibet about 23 days before it did in India, nearly a month earlier. In fact, it occurs at the same time, and it is this that causes the Phugpa months to be one month behind the Indian systems, as was the subject of the complaints by Paṇḍita Vimalaśrī and others.

The key point that was not realized when this system was developed was that instead of being very precise, the siddhānta mean motion of the Sun is actually less accurate than that of the karaṇa, and there is no real proof that it was ever intended to be used in this way. This greater error resulted in the divergence of the calculated position of the Sun from the true position, and the postulated seasonal time difference between Tibet and India is an attempt to explain this.

The creators of this system could not accept the inaccuracies in the siddhānta mean Sun, and of course the error has been accumulating all the time this system has been in use. At the time of writing (2003) the Phugpa position of the Sun is just over 36° behind the tropical Sun.

Just as with the creators of other siddhānta systems such as Zhonnu Pal, the authors of the Phugpa system also made efforts to match their calculations with the chronology of the Buddha and particularly with the data given in the Kālacakra Tantra.

Lochen Dharmaśrī points out that the Phugpa system considers the data given in the Tantra to be correct, except for the weekday and solar longitude calculations. However, small changes have been made in the Phugpa calendar to such things as the calculated positions of the planets, and the justification for these is not made clear. I presume these adjustments were made on the basis of observations.

As far as the weekday and Sun are concerned, the Phugpa tradition interprets the data in the light of the fact that the Tantra in one sense gives two epochs. Calculations start from the first Tibetan-adopted Prabhava, 1027, and then work back to the main epoch of 806. The Phugpa explanation is that there are errors in the karaṇa calculations, compared to the accurate siddhānta methods, and in the Tantra the true figures were hidden, being adjusted so that they would produce accurate results at the epoch of 1027.

The easiest way of comparing the figures is to work backwards with the Phugpa calculations to the beginning of Caitra in 806, thereby determining these hidden epoch values. The figures this gives for the mean weekday and Sun are:

Weekday: 2;22,34,2,518
Sun: 0;8,3,3,33

The difference between the mean monthly changes in both systems for the weekday and solar longitude are easily calculated. Each month the karaṇa mean weekday falls behind the siddhānta by 480 of the smallest 707-units. In the 221 years between the 806 and 1027 epochs, a total of 2,733 synodic months, this amounts to 0;5,9,1,355.

In order to be correct by karaṇa calculation in 1027, the siddhānta figure for the mean weekday at the Tantra epoch therefore has to be increased. It becomes:

2;22,34,2,518 + 0;5,9,1,355 = 2;27,43,4,166

The figure given in the Tantra is 2;30. As I mentioned during the discussion of eclipse predictions in chapter three, at the time that the Phugpa tradition was developed, the figure for the mean weekday was giving mean new Moon as 8.3 nāḍī earlier than modern calculations suggest.

For the Sun, the karaṇa longitude is increasing faster than the siddhānta by a figure of (44×30)/(13×67) parts of a breath each month. In 221 years this amounts to 0;11,30,1,57,8 (67,13).

Similarly, the siddhānta figure for the mean Sun at the Tantra epoch has to be decreased. It therefore becomes:

0;8,3,3,33 - 0;11,30,1,57,8 (67,13) = 26;56,33,2,22 (13)

The epoch figure in the Tantra is 26;58. These small differences are effectively ignored by the Phugpa tradition and are put down to compositional needs of the Tantra—presumably such as poetics, style, and so forth.

The following is a list of all the components of the Phugpa calendar calculated backwards for the epoch of the Tantra, together with the equivalent data from the Tantra for the original karaṇa system.

Epoch: Monday 23rd March 806. Julian day: 2015531

	Siddhānta	**Karaṇa**
True month:	0;63	0;0
Mean weekday:	2;22,34,2,518	2;30,0
Anomaly:	5;98	5;112
Mean Sun:	0;8,3,3,33	26;58,0,0,0
Mars:	168	167
Jupiter:	1731	1732
Saturn:	5953	5946
Mercury:	1777	1674
Venus:	2172	2163
Rāhu:	122	122

Perhaps the most famous of all works on astronomy and astrology written in Tibet was from the Phugpa tradition, the "White Beryl" (Baidkar), attributed to Sangye Gyatso. This text properly established the Phugpa system of calculation. It is a compendium of astrology and divination, covering much more than the computation of the calendar, and is one of the most authoritative sources on such subjects as Indian and Chinese astrology, Tibetan geomancy, and much more. Large portions of the sections of this work that deal with Chinese elemental divination have been translated by Gyurme Dorje in "Tibetan Elemental Divination Paintings" (Gyurme).

The epoch for the "White Beryl" is 1687, 10,897 synodic months after the Tantra epoch, and 2,968 months before the 1927 epoch of the "Essence of the Kalkī." The epoch data for the "White Beryl" is as follows:

Epoch: Saturday 12th April 1687. Julian day: 2337326

True month:	m × 1;2	+ 0;15 (1,65)
Mean weekday:	M × 1;31,50,0,480	+ 0;10,57,2,692 (707)
Anomaly:	M × 2;1	+ 18;33 (28,126)
Mean Sun:	M × 2;10,58,1,17	+ 26;29,46,3,27 (67)
General day:	+52,+220	
Mars:	447	
Jupiter:	2958	
Saturn:	4768	
Mercury:	1851	
Venus:	171	
Rāhu:	209	

The "White Beryl" and other texts in the Phugpa tradition make use of a theoretical calculation that has strong echoes of Hindu systems of astronomical calculation—the very systems criticized by the Kālacakra. The theory behind this calculation is that there was a point in time when all the planets, and the Sun and Moon, were at zero degrees Aries, and at the same time other key cycles were also at their beginnings. From that moment in time, they have all maintained constant mean motions, and their positions at any moment in time could be calculated given this initial starting point and the mean motions.

In Hindu systems such calculations were often performed, with a point in time in 3102 BCE being taken as the start of the current Kali age. Calculations were often made using this as a base-epoch with all, or most, longitudes equal to zero.

A Great Age of 4,320,000 years is mentioned in Hindu literature, and just the same period of time is also found in the Kālacakra system, but it is not tied in literally to the calculations of the calendar.

However, the theory that there was a point in time when everything was at zero longitude is taken literally in the Phugpa tradition, and this moment has been calculated. The derivation of this is given much prominence in the "Oral Instructions of Puṇḍarīka," and Norzang Gyatso spends many pages examining this. It is certainly impressive that the Tibetans were able to perform these calculations by hand. In order to reproduce their work I resorted to a modern and highly specialized mathematical programming language (muMATH).

The "Essence of the Kalkī" gives for its epoch of 1927 the years that have elapsed since zero longitude, and the remaining years until this will occur again. Adding these together gives the total length of one of these postulated great ages:

Years elapsed at 1927:	82,776,132,766,945,179,840 years
Total length of age:	2,796,235,115,048,502,090,600 years

The best way of calculating such a number as this total would be to take the lowest common multiple (L.C.M.) of the periods of the planets and other cycles concerned. Norzang Gyatso goes through these one at a time, but using the modern method of the L.C.M. is best for the current purposes.

Taking the various periods in their prime factors, all figures in days, the first step is to find the L.C.M. of the following (with stops indicating multiplication):

2.7.769	(Saturn)
2.2.3.19.19	(Jupiter)
3.229	(Mars)
3.7.107	(Venus)
19.463	(Mercury)
3.3.5.17.67.131	(Solar days)
3.5.5.5.17.23.131	(Rāhu cycles)
3.3.3.5.5.7.17.131	(Anomalistic cycles)

This gives a result (L.C.M.) of:

2.2.3.3.3.5.5.5.7.17.19.19.23.67.107.131.229.463.769

This is a number of solar days, and now has to be converted to years by multiplying by 18,382 (2.7.13.101) and dividing by 7,614,405 (3.3.5.17.67.131):

$$2.2.3.3.3.5.5.5.7.17.19.19.23.67.107.131.229.463.769 \times \frac{2.7.13.101}{3.3.5.17.67.131} \Rightarrow$$

2.2.2.3.5.5.7.7.13.19.19.23.101.107.229.463.769

When multiplied out in full this does indeed yield:

2,796,235,115,048,502,090,600 years.

The next step is to see if the count of years given from the time of zero longitude will produce the epoch data of the "Essence of the Kalkī." Naturally, in these calculations all epoch values are zero and all that is needed is to multiply the true month at 1927 by the relevant factors.

For the true month:

82776132766945179840 × 12 = 993313593203342158080

993313593203342158080 × 1;2 = 1023877088378829609097;55

For the mean weekday:

1023877088378829609097 × 1;31,50,0,480 = 6;57,53,2,20

For the mean longitude of the Sun:

1023877088378829609097 × 2;10,58,1,17 = 25;9,10,4,32

For the anomaly:

1023877088378829609097 × 2;1 = 13;103

To convert the month count to lunar days:

1023877088378829609097 × 30 = 30716312651364888272910

For the general day (calculating from the bottom, as usual):

30716312651364888272910 - 480621228720967576406 =
30235691422643920696504
30716312651364888272910 + 43445986777036617076 =
30759758638141924889986 ÷ 64 = 480621228720967576406 rem. 2
30716312651364888272910 ÷ 707 = 43445986777036617076 rem. 178

Weekday check:

30235691422643920696504 ÷ 7 = 4319384488949131528072 rem. 0

Having determined the general day:

For Mars, 30235691422643920696504 modulo 687 = 157

For Jupiter, 30235691422643920696504 modulo 4332 = 3964

For Saturn, 30235691422643920696504 modulo 10766 = 6286

For Mercury, 100 × 30235691422643920696504 modulo 8797 = 4639

For Venus, 10 × 30235691422643920696504 modulo 2247 = 301

For Rāhu: 102387708837882960909 7 ÷ 230 = 445163951469056351 7 rem. 187

All of these figures agree exactly with the 1927 epoch data given by Chenrab Norbu.

A more practical example of longer calculations in this tradition is recorded by the Jonang writer Banda Gelek (Bgrinnye, p. 571). He takes as an epoch the new Moon at the beginning of the third Mongolian month in the Earth-Tiger year of 1638 CE (Wednesday 14th April). As this is about 50 years before the epoch given in the "White Beryl" by Sangje Gyatso, Banda Gelek may well be referring to one of the earliest practical systems of calendrical calculation to be derived from the Phugpa tradition. He gives the author of this system as Drakpa Palzang (*grags pa dpal bzang*).

According to Lodro Drakpa (*blo gros grags pa*, Rigsgye, p. 522), Drakpa Palzang was a student of Tāranātha, and his text, which appears now to be lost, formed the basis of the calendrical calculations used by the Jonang tradition. Quite how this fits in with the Phugpa tradition is not clear, but certainly Drakpa's work was based on that of earlier Phugpa writers such as Lhundrup Gyatso. However, the latter's "Oral Instructions of Puṇḍarīka" (Padzhal) gives no similar set of calculations but rather sets out the theory on which they would later be based.

This system is clearly of historical interest, and Banda Gelek gives two forms of the calculation. The second of these is the usual method as described in chapter one, but the first method is no longer used, and is probably the system as described originally by Drakpa Palzang. I presume that Banda Gelek includes this system (three times in three different texts) out of historical respect.

The basic calculation derives the mean weekday, anomaly, and mean solar longitude, and I shall describe these calculations for the example date that was used in chapter one. That was 1st March 1995, and the results determined in chapter one were:

Mean weekday:	4;39,28,2,230
Anomaly:	20;61
Mean Sun:	22;44,6,1,41

The calculation starts with the derivation of the true month count in the usual way, with an intercalation index of 9. From the 1638 epoch to 1st March 1995 the true month count is 4,414. I shall start the calculations here.

For the mean weekday, add 6,707 to the true month, and then multiply by 8,657. Divide by 39,592 and discard the quotient. Multiply the remainder by 7, and divide again by 39,592. The quotient that results is the weekday value, and the calculation continues using the remainder.

Multiply that remainder by 60, again divide by 39,592, and the quotient is the number of nāḍī. Continue with the remainder, multiplying again by 60, then 6 and 707, and the final division by 39,592 will have no remainder.

Working downwards, the calculation is as follows:

4414 + 6707 = 11121
11121 × 8657 = 96274497 ÷ 39592 = 2431 rem. 26345
26345 × 7 = 184415 ÷ 39592 = 4 rem. 26047
26047 × 60 = 1562820 ÷ 39592 = 39 rem. 18732
18732 × 60 = 1123920 ÷ 39592 = 28 rem. 15344
15344 × 6 = 92064 ÷ 39592 = 2 rem. 12880
12880 × 707 = 9106160 ÷ 39592 = 230 rem. 0

The quotients 4, 39, etc., are the expected values for the weekday. Of the three calculations, this one is the least easy to understand. It is using the relationship that 39,592 lunar months is exactly equal to 175,682 weeks.

The length of a lunar month in terms of solar days is given in the Phugpa siddhānta system as 29;31,50,0,480. As 28 days is exactly 4 weeks, the 28 can be discarded as in the usual monthly calculation of the mean weekday, and just the change in weekday each month can be considered. This is 1;31,50,0,480. In 39,592 lunar months, this amounts to a change in weekday of:

$$39592 \times 1;31,50,0,480 = 60599;0,0,0,0 = 7 \times 8657;0,0,0,0$$

This means that in 39,592 lunar months, the monthly advance in the weekday is exactly equal to 8,657 weekday cycles, or weeks. Hence the use of the number 8,657 in the calculation. The value of 6,707 on the line before is an epoch value.

For the anomaly, add 435 (epoch value) to the true month and then multiply by 253. Divide by 3,528 and discard the quotient (completed whole cycles). Multiply the remainder by 28, dividing again by 3,528. The quotient is the anomaly. Multiply the remainder by 126, again divide by 3,528. The quotient is the anomaly fractional part, and there will be no remainder. For the example month:

4414 + 435 = 4849
4849 × 253 = 1226797 ÷ 3528 = 347 rem. 2581
2581 × 28 = 72268 ÷ 3528 = 20 rem. 1708
1708 × 126 = 215208 ÷ 3528 = 61 rem. 0

The values of 20 and 61 are those expected. This is using the relationship that 3,528 lunar months is equal to 3,781 anomalistic cycles. As with the weekday, only the advance of the cycle each month is used, i.e.:

3781 - 3528 = 253

Finally, for the mean longitude of the Sun, add 507 (epoch value) to the true month, multiply by 65 and then divide by 804, discarding the quotient (completed cycles).

Multiply the remainders successively by 27, 60, 60, 6 and 67, each time dividing by 804, with the last division leaving no remainder. The quotients give the mean longitude of the Sun. For the example day:

4414 + 507 = 4921
4921 × 65 = 319865 ÷ 804 = 397 rem. 677
677 × 27 = 18279 ÷ 804 = 22 rem. 591
591 × 60 = 35460 ÷ 804 = 44 rem. 84
84 × 60 = 5040 ÷ 804 = 6 rem. 216
216 × 6 = 1296 ÷ 804 = 1 rem. 492
492 × 67 = 32964 ÷ 804 = 41 rem. 0

The quotients again yield the expected solar longitude of 22;44,6,1,41. This calculation uses the well known relationship that 65 solar cycles are equivalent to 804 lunar months.

The Tsurphu system

The derivation of the "Error Correction" calendrical system is well described by Zhonnu Pal, but there are many gaps in the surviving record of the development of the Phugpa tradition; particularly the observations that were made and the reasoning employed in developing the calendar. Unfortunately, there is even less information available to us about the development of the Tsurphu tradition.

This goes back to the third Karmapa Rangjung Dorje (1284–1339), author of the "Compendium of Astronomy." His text is commented upon in the "Treasury of Jewels" (Tlkuntu) by Pawo Tsuklag (1504–1566). This commentary is an excellent work on the subject, and in my opinion should stand alongside the famous "White Beryl" as the two greatest works on astronomy and astrology produced in Tibet.

The "Treasury of Jewels" offers unique insights into many of the relevant sections of the Kālacakra Tantra, but unfortunately does not give any description of the construction of the siddhānta calculation of the Tsurphu calendar.

The original development of that calendar, based also on the work of Rangjung Dorje, was by Jamyang Dondrup Wozer. He is said to have used the same epoch as the authors of the Phugpa tradition, 1447 CE. His text presumably contained the descriptive information regarding the creation of the calendar that I would like to comment upon here. This is usually referred to simply as the "Great Text on Astronomy" (*rtsis gzhung chen mo*), and appears also to be lost.

Some clues regarding the development of the Tsurphu calendar do survive. Pawo Tsuklag describes how the circular world system that surrounds Mt. Meru is divided into 360 minor continents, and that these are associated with the 360 zodiacal days. In other words, the division is regular, with the minor-continents all the same size, divided into 360 sections just as the zodiac is divided into 360°, or zodiacal days.

He goes on to say that there are 360 solstices, meaning that the solstices and other seasonal points are observed at different times in the different minor continents. He explains that when one minor continent experiences summer solstice, the one opposite to it experiences winter solstice, and the ones at east and west, 90 around in each direction, experience the equinoxes.

He is therefore describing a theory very similar to that put forward in the Phugpa tradition, and gives a time difference between the experience of solstice in Tibet and India of 14 days (he states that some claim 13 days). He also describes a longitude difference of about one nāḍī, and if by 14 days he means 14 zodiacal days, this would mean that the longitude of the Sun at winter solstice should be 1;3,0 less than the figure given in the Vimalaprabhā, i.e.: 19;12,0.

Certainly, at the time of the development of this system, the calculated mean solar longitude at the times of winter solstice was very close to that figure.

This longitude difference is much less than the 23° of the Phugpa system. In the Tsurphu tradition it is 14°, so we would expect the solar longitude in the Tsurphu to be 9° greater than that in the Phugpa. However, the difference between the solar longitudes in the two systems is less than this expected gap of 9°.

Ignoring the small difference between the two systems in their values for the mean weekday, in the Tsurphu tradition the mean longitude of the Sun is greater than that in the Phugpa by 0;21,31,2,4. This is equivalent to 4°.8.

The reason for this lies in observational error. I showed earlier that the Phugpa determination of solstices was actually a couple of days before the true occurrence of the solstice. This would make their solar longitude greater than if an accurate observation had been made. The reverse is the case with the Tsurphu tradition whose observations placed the solstice about a day after it actually happened, making the solar longitude less than would have been derived from accurate observation. (This last comment comes from an examination of the calculations, in the absence of any written description of eclipse observations.)

These differences just about account for the longitude difference of the Sun between the two systems.

I am assuming that the developers of the Tsurphu tradition used solstice determination of some kind to derive their calendar, but they seem not to have followed the method used by Zhonnu Pal and the Phugpa of developing a set of tables defining the structure of the calendar and then applying the results of observations to that structure.

I have not come across any such set of tables in texts on the Tsurphu tradition, and the calculations that are described do not fit any such theoretical table. For example, in both the Phugpa and "Error Correction" systems, every 65 years the solar longitude is exactly 0;0,0,0,0 at mean new Moon at the start of the month Caitra. In each case the tabular structure of the theoretical calendar is calculated from that point.

In the Tsurphu tradition the calculations simply never produce such a value of zero in the mean longitude of the Sun (nor for that matter in the true longitude). Also, in the other two traditions, because of the use of the table as a means of defining the possible times of solstice, those timings are expressed in relatively simple values, such as the first figure in the Phugpa table of 14;7,4 (13,5). The Tsurphu solstices do not occur at similarly simple values.

I have used two main texts for analysing the calculations of the Tsurphu tradition, and the epoch data given in these agree completely (one can be derived from the other). The first such text is the "Excellent Flask of Essentials" (Bumzang) by Karma Ngelek Tendzin. The epoch data given in that text is as follows:

Epoch: Wednesday 26th March 1732. Julian day: 2353745

True month:	m × 1;2	+ 1;-6 (1,65)
Mean weekday:	M × 1;31,50,0,8,584	+ 4;14,6,2,2,666 (13,707)
Anomaly:	M × 2;1	+ 14;99 (28,126)
Mean Sun:	M × 2;10,58,1,3,20	- 1;29,17,5,6,1 (13,67)
General day:	+12,-12	
Mars:	377	
Jupiter:	2050	
Saturn:	10414	
Mercury:	7406	
Venus:	321	
Rāhu:	75	

The other text is the "Compendium of Practical Astronomy" (Kongleg) by Jamgon Kongtrul. Its epoch data is:

Epoch: Monday 19th April 1852. Julian day: 2397598

True month:	m × 1;2	+ 0;14 (1,65)
Mean weekday:	M × 1;31,50,0,8,584	+ 2;9,24,2,5,417 (13,707)
Anomaly:	M × 2;1	+ 0;72 (28,126)
Mean Sun:	M × 2;10,58,1,3,20	+ 0;1,22,2,4,18 (13,67)
General day:	+16,-3	
Mars:	262	
Jupiter:	2583	
Saturn:	437	
Mercury:	3003	
Venus:	686	
Rāhu:	180	

Notice that both these writers use an extra fractional unit for the figures for both weekday and solar longitude. This makes conversion unnecessary whenever such figures have to be used together, and the lowest significant figure can simply be ignored. The mean motions are the same as in other siddhānta systems.

One point worth noting is that most of the data is derived directly from the Kālacakra Tantra, and if these Tsurphu calculations are worked backwards to the Tantra epoch in 806 CE, the same data is derived for the intercalation index, the anomaly, the five planets, and Rāhu. The only major differences are with the weekday and solar longitude.

One small difference that should be mentioned is that this tradition gives no calculation for the mean Sun at the end of the solar day for use in the planetary calculations. Both Jamgon Kongtrul and Karma Ngelek Tendzin describe using the mean Sun derived during the main calendrical calculations, and Pawo Tsuglak describes using the true Sun from those same calculations.

The values used for the mean weekday—which maintains accuracy over very long periods of time—are somewhat more accurate than the Phugpa weekday, which is behind by 8.3 nāḍī. The Tsurphu weekday is similarly behind, in 1447 CE giving mean new Moon 5.5 nāḍī earlier than modern calculations suggest.

Kongtrul also gives a set of data for what he terms the fusion of karaṇa and siddhānta (*byed grub zung 'brel*). The data he gives is as follows:

Epoch: Monday 19th April 1852. Julian day: 2397598

True month:	m × 1;2 - 0;51 (1,65)
Mean weekday:	M × 1;31,50,0,30 + 2;9,46,1,10 (44)
Anomaly:	M × 2;1 - 27;54 (28,126)
Mean Sun:	M × 2;10,58,2,20 + 0;16,51,3,18 (38)

In these calculations the mean change in weekday has a different lowest fractional part and is almost exactly the average of the two mean motions from the karaṇa and the siddhānta. However, this is not the case with the mean motion of the Sun. The "fusion" mean motion is much closer to the more accurate karaṇa mean Sun than to the siddhānta Sun. This suggests the very interesting possibility of an awareness of the error in the siddhānta Sun.

No indication is given how these figures were derived, or how they should be used, but there would be problems in using them unless they were combined with observation and correction. The main problem would be that the new figure for the mean motion of the Sun is out of step with the structure that is clearly implied by the intercalation index.

As it happens, the use of the intercalation index and its relationship to the months is the most problematic aspect of the Tsurphu calendar. For a start, the intercalation index is no longer tied to the longitude of the Sun in the same way as with the "Error Correction" and Phugpa systems.

In those systems, when the intercalation index is zero at the exact moment of mean new Moon, the Sun is at the very beginning of a zodiacal sign, such as 0° Aries. When the intercalation index is zero in the Tsurphu tradition, the mean Sun is instead at a position of 6.°57 at mean new Moon. For example, when the index is zero at the new Moon at the beginning of the third month of Caitra, the mean Sun has a longitude of 0;29,34,5,37, equivalent to 6.°57 Aries.

The intercalation index defines the intercalary months, and an inspection of the solar longitude shows a range of values within the zodiacal signs that are equivalent to the monthly definition points. That range is 0;29,78 (134) to 0;31,80 (134), or, 6.°574 to 7.°022.

Because the main siddhānta calculation used keeps step with the intercalation index, this range remains stable through time. But it is not what would be expected given the supposed time difference between Tibet and India for the seasonal points.

That difference is equivalent to 14° motion of the mean Sun, and one would therefore expect the definition points to be close to 16° in each sign.

A contemporary attempt at reform

Just before this book went to press, I was contacted on behalf of Sherab Ling monastery in Bir, Himachal Pradesh, India, the Indian seat of H.E. Tai Situ Rinpoche. The astrologer there, Kojo Tsewang Namgyal (*go 'jo tshe dbang rnam rgyal*, Tsenam) has for many years been investigating the origins of the Tibetan calendar and the cause of the errors it contains, with a view to developing his own reformed calendar. His wish to have the system he has developed computerized led one of his students to get in touch. Tsenam refers to his calendar as the Tantra method (*rgyud lugs*), but as we shall see, this is something of a misnomer, although his calendar is a significant improvement on the Phugpa and Tsurphu systems as they exist today.

I shall refer to this calendar as the Sherab Ling system. It has not yet been documented, and to some extent is still under development, but sufficient information has been passed to me to describe it reasonably completely. Its main data are as follows:

Epoch: Sunday 29th March 1987. Julian day: 2446884

True month:	m x 1;2 + 0;38 (1,65)
Mean weekday:	M x 1;31,50,0,480 + 1;42,47,3,465 (707)
Anomaly:	M x 2;1 + 19;111 (28,126)
Mean Sun:	M x 2;10,58,2,564,5546 + 25;41,58,2,25,6655 (707,6811)
General day:	18,250
Mars:	94
Jupiter:	4105
Saturn:	6867
Mercury:	6104
Venus:	1561
Rāhu:	8

The most noticeable feature of this calendar is the unusual calculation for the solar longitude. The mean monthly motion of the Sun is here much closer to that in the karaṇa system than in the siddhānta system as used by the Phugpa and Tsurphu systems. The figure is in fact easily derived, and is taken directly from the Tantra, by converting the karaṇa year change solar year length of 365;15,31,1,121 (317). If this value is divided into the length of the lunar month, and multiplied by 27 (for the number of lunar mansions in a solar cycle) the result is the mean monthly solar motion given here:

$$\frac{29;31,50,0,480 \times 27}{365;15,31,1,121} = 2;10,58,2,564,5546(707,6811)$$

Quite why this rather odd value of the length of the solar year has been taken is not clear. This certainly makes the calculations more accurate, but also more complex, and it also means that the structure used by all three siddhānta systems described above breaks down. There is no longer any simple integer relationship between a number of solar cycles and a number of lunar months. In fact, the calculation for the true month was given to me in the form:

m x 1;287179 + 0;5566410 (1,9343575)

Apart from the epoch value of 5,566,410, this calculation is easily derived from the mean monthly motion. In one month, the Sun moves, as a fraction of a full circle:

$$2;10,58,2,564,5546\ (707,6811) = \frac{227048872500}{2808327866400}$$

To move a full circle of 27 mansions it takes the Sun:

$$\frac{28083278664}{2270488725} \text{ lunar months.}$$

Therefore, 2,270,488,725 solar years are equivalent to 28,083,278,664 lunar months:

ie., 3114525 solar years = 38523016 months

Or, 9343575 years = 115569048 months = 9630754 x 12 months

These are the two key numbers, that 9,343,575 solar years is equivalent to 9,630,754 sets of 12 lunar months. The difference between these two figures is the number of intercalary months in 9,343,575 solar years: 287,179. The relationship between solar (zodiacal) and lunar months can therefore be expressed as:

m x 1;287179 (1,9343575)

In practice, instead of this complex calculation, one can instead use (including now the addition of an epoch value):

m x 1;2 + 0;38 (1,65)

This would only need rare adjustment, with intercalary months indicated by the intercalation index equalling 16 or 17.

Unfortunately, the Sherab Ling calendar does not correct the error introduced into the Phugpa system by subtraction of a correction at the time of solstice. Tsenam has performed his own solstice determinations through a period of 30 years, and sets the longitude of the Sun at solstice as 18;31,30. This is the same figure as originally used in the Phugpa system, 1;43,30 less than the figure of 20;15 specified in the Vimalaprabhā.

This correction of 1;43,30 is used twice in the calculation of the basic Sherab Ling calendar. Once the mean solar longitude has been calculated, this is written down twice, and the two instances are treated rather differently. With the first, the correction of 1;43,30 is added to the figure for the mean Sun, and from this is derived the stepping correction to be applied to the mean Sun to yield the true Sun.

Instead of then applying this correction again to the semi-true weekday to derive the true weekday, the second value of the mean Sun is used to calculate the solar stepping again, but this time without the adjustment of 1;43,30. These two methods produce different values.

In the epoch data above I gave the values used in the calculation to find the general day as 18 and 250. Given the availability of modern calculators, Tsenam has introduced a variation on this that is more straightforward, but generates much larger numeric values. In his method, to convert lunar days to solar days, first multiply by 11,135, add an epoch value of 8,068 to the result, and take the quotient after dividing by 11,312. This is exactly equivalent to the traditional method given in chapter one, but requires fewer steps. Also, in the traditional method the values used are effectively subtracted, and represent the remainder from mean new Moon to the end of the epoch solar day. In the modern method, the epoch value of 8,068 represents the fraction of the epoch solar day between the start of that day and mean new Moon.

Another interesting feature of this calendar is the fact that the Tibetan months are aligned properly with the Indian months, the first month of the year being Phālguna, rather than Māgha. However, the controversial Phugpa definition of the Tiger month as the 11th Tibetan month is also used.

Apart from that last point, if only the Kālacakra value for the solar longitude at solstice had been used, this calendar would be a significant improvement on the "Error Correction" system of Zhonnu Pal, and so although this calendar fulfils some of the criteria for a properly reformed calendar, it falls short in this one key respect.

In addition, a variant on the Sherab Ling calendar is currently being published by the Jyotish Department of the Central Institute for Higher Tibetan Studies in Sarnath, India. This uses the same calculations derived by Tsewang Namgyal, but structures the months with the waning fortnight coming before the waxing fortnight. Such a system was described in chapter four as being attributed to the Kālacakra Mūlatantra. This means, for example, that the third month Vaiśākha, that fell in 2006, lasted from 14th April until 13th May in the Sarnath calendar. In the Sherab Ling calendar, Vaiśākha ran from 28th April until 27th May. The printed Sarnath almanac is also styled rather differently from other Tibetan almanacs, particularly with daily information being printed in concise tables rather than boxes, more in line with Indian almanacs.

Conclusions

Looking at the description of the calculations for the calendar in the Kālacakra Tantra commentary, the Vimalaprabhā, translated in chapter five, it strikes me that the Kālacakra system expresses a reforming spirit, criticizing the loss of accuracy in general Indian systems and encouraging the proper use of a tropical zodiac based upon the observation of solstices.

It is certainly true that around the sixth and seventh centuries CE Indian astronomers paid little—perhaps too little—attention to the effects of precession. In his translation of the Sūrya Siddhānta (Sūrya, p. 117), Burgess writes that "the earliest Hindu astronomers were ignorant of, or ignored, the periodical motion of the equinoxes." He also considers the possibility that the Hindu adoption of the sidereal system was the result of "a failure to recognise the fact that the equinox was variable."

He goes on to describe how difficult it would have been for them to fit corrections for precession into their theories and calculations once they had finally realized the important effect it was having. This is a cogent point, and the Vimalaprabhā similarly criticizes the Indian heterodox astronomers for creating complex systems that they eventually themselves failed to understand, and that subsequently became inaccurate with the passage of time.

These views expressed by Burgess are very similar to my interpretation of the Kālacakra criticism of Hindu astronomers—that they had drifted by neglect into using a sidereal zodiac. It is this error that the

Kālacakra authors want to see corrected in a reform of the calendar. A Kālacakra point of view would accept the basic structure of the Indian calendar and its symbolism, but adjust it to the tropical zodiac. Not by some tortuous manipulation of theories and complex calculations as in the Hindu siddhāntas, but by the simple application of observation.

In the Vimalaprabhā this could hardly be expressed more clearly, and the order in which these topics are presented in both the Kālacakra Tantra and its commentary make sense when viewed in this way.

To recap, at the very beginning of the section describing the calculations the Vimalaprabhā explains that there are inaccuracies in the calculation systems in use at that time in India—it calls them corrupt—and explains that this is due to an inaccurate knowledge of the solar longitude.

It then explains that this inaccuracy comes from not using the shadow determination of the solstice to correct the solar longitude, and that if as a result the solar longitude is wrong, then all the planetary positions will also be wrong. It then states that if the positions of the Sun and the planets are wrong, then any astrology performed using these positions will be meaningless.

The language used is quite strong, and this is clearly considered an important and fundamental point. It is worth noting that this is in the introduction to the whole set of calculations. What more natural place to stress a point that is considered an axiom of the system?

Furthermore, the longitude of the Sun that is applied after the solstice determination is later called the primary definition (*rtsa ba'i nges pa, mūladhruvaka*). The use of this term certainly suggests that this point is axiomatic for the whole calendar.

After the introduction, the Vimalaprabhā goes on to give the definitions and calculations for the basic calendar—the cycles of months, intercalary months, the lunar days, and so forth. The basic quantity on which all this depends, the mean relative motion of the Sun and Moon, is very accurate, and so, given an accurate value for the solar longitude, the calendar derived would have a strong basis.

Only then comes the description of how to detect the winter solstice and go back and correct the results of the previous calculations for the solar longitude. The logic is simple: set up the basic structure or skeleton of the calendar, and then fine-tune it on the basis of observation. As described above, the Vimalaprabhā gives at this point the basic relationships and some calculations that aid in adjusting the longitude of the Sun.

The next natural topic should be the calculations for the planetary positions, as these are dependent on an accurate solar longitude. After just a couple of pages discussing the change in the length of day through the months and the position of the Moon's node, that is exactly the subject next discussed in the Vimalaprabhā.

In 10th or 11th century India, a calendrical system such as that described by the Kālacakra Tantra would have been seen as quite radical when compared to those in general use at that time. By then the use of a sidereal zodiac had become standard, and it is interesting to speculate that the Kālacakra authors felt it necessary to claim authority from outside of the traditional Indian systems, and perhaps this is one reason behind the claim that the Kālacakra came from a long line of righteous kings in Sambhala, who had not been subject to Islamic invasion and whose calendrical methods had not been corrupted.

In the introduction to the calendar the Vimalaprabhā states that the definitions for the calendar need to be re-established every sixty years. This seems an excessively long time, and in practice this would certainly have been done more regularly. Perhaps the sixty-year figure represents how often all the basic data should be reset in textbooks; observational adjustments would need to continue regularly.

For a start, given the original epoch in 806 CE for the karaṇa calendar, the first year in which the intercalation index wrongly identifies an intercalary month—as judged by the karaṇa solar longitude—is 849 CE, after 43 years. A few years later and they are all wrong. The structure implied by the intercalation index is clearly very useful, just so long as it is not left uncorrected for too long.

The siddhānta figure for the length of the solar year, 365;16,14,1,12,121 (13,707), that is so clearly out of line with other, and much older Indian values, is not given in the Kālacakra literature, or used. In the section on the siddhānta corrections, the Vimalaprabhā does describe how to derive it from the basic structure of the calendar, the fundamental relationship between lunar months and solar cycles.

This section describes how to manipulate the various values, and reads to a certain extent like an arithmetic lesson on the methods to be used when applying the solar longitude correction, rather than a statement of values to be used in a set of precise, but otherwise secret, siddhānta calculations.

The way the corrections are described strongly suggests that the solar longitude is to be corrected by solstice observation every year. This is a more natural way to proceed, and such repeated observations would enable a finer determination of the timing of the solstice. It is easy to imagine the use of a set of tables such as those described by Zhonnu Pal, but with the tables undergoing regular adjustment and revision.

This tabular structure is an approximation, but the Tibetans took it literally as an exact representation of the calendar. Unfortunately, the relationship that is the basis of that structure, that 65 years equals 804 lunar months, is the source for the siddhānta mean motion of the Sun, which is the common weak link in all the Tibetan derived siddhānta calendars.

This structure must have seemed very compelling to the Tibetan calendar makers, and they seem to have become tied into this. As they considered these siddhānta relationships to be exact, then regularly adjusting the solar longitude, with the implied change to the mean motion of the Sun, would have broken that structure.

I have never found any comment in the Tibetan material to explain why they did not accept the Vimalaprabhā instruction to re-establish the calendar definitions regularly. Presumably it was because that instruction refers to the karaṇa calendar, and the Tibetans devised the concept of a siddhānta calendar that entailed precisely accurate calculations and therefore only needed a single set of observations to establish the solar longitude. There is in fact much discussion in the literature about how to correct the karaṇa calculations on the basis of siddhānta quantities.

This hypothetical siddhānta calculation system was assumed to have been included in the lost Kālacakra Mūlatantra, but there is no real evidence in the original Indian material to suggest that such a system of calculation ever existed. Quite the contrary, and it seems to be a purely Tibetan construction.

Mipham basically supports this view that the early Tibetan astronomers did not accept the need for repeated observation and correction. He discusses this in his commentary (MiKal 1, p.206) to the Kālacakra Tantra, and, referring to the solstice detection described in the Vimalaprabhā, writes that "the earlier writers investigating this had difficulty in making new observations and did not accept the method."

They were left with the problem of how to interpret the calculations given in the Tantra and the increasing deviation from observations of the results of those calculations. It is easy now to consider it quite extraordinary that the view could have developed that the solstice is observed from Tibet three weeks before it is from India. But Tibet was a very isolated country, and actual travel to India took many weeks, if not months, and so proper comparisons were not readily available. We have also seen how the Tibetans would sometimes ignore the criticisms of visiting Indian masters.

Norzang Gyatso makes it quite clear that if it were not the case that the solstice occurred at different times, then the longitude of the Sun at winter solstice would be set at 20;15—just as was done by Zhonnu Pal, in accordance with the Vimalaprabhā. Of course, Norzang Gyatso wrongly assumes that this would only happen if Tibet lay on the same central Indian meridian, and he considered it to be far to the east.

There are two basic areas where most Tibetan astronomers reinterpreted the intentions of the Kālacakra system. They took the siddhānta discussion regarding the corrections to the calendar to imply that there did at one time exist a set of precise calculations for the derivation of the calendar, and they considered that the solstice adjustment given in the Vimalaprabhā referred to the karaṇa calculations alone. It would therefore not be needed again once the supposed siddhānta calculations had been (re-)established.

With this interpretation, and their subsequent reliance on sets of complex calculations, it is ironic indeed that with the exception of a few, the Tibetans, who have otherwise preserved the Kālacakra system so well, when deriving their calendars have fallen victim to precisely those same errors that the Kālacakra system so strongly criticizes.

APPENDIX I

The Sixty-Year Cycles

The following table lists the names of the sexagenary cycles, from both Indian and Chinese systems. The first column gives the name from the Chinese system. The next two columns contain the names from the Indian system, first in Tibetan and then Sanskrit. Depending on the source used there are many small variations in the spelling of these names. The last two columns identify the western years for the current and previous prabhava cycles.

Fire-Rabbit	rab byung	prabhava	1927	1987
Earth-Dragon	rnam byung	vibhava	1928	1988
Earth-Snake	dkar po	śuklata	1929	1989
Iron-Horse	rab myos	pramadī	1930	1990
Iron-Sheep	skyes bdag	prajapati	1931	1991
Water-Monkey	anggi ra	aṅkira	1932	1992
Water-Bird	dpal gdong	śrīmukha	1933	1993
Wood-Dog	dngos po	bhava	1934	1994
Wood-Pig	na tshod ldan	yuvika	1935	1995
Fire-Mouse	'dzin byed	dhṛitu	1936	1996
Fire-Ox	dbang phyug	īśvara	1937	1997
Earth-Tiger	'bru mang po	vahūdhvanya	1938	1998
Earth-Rabbit	myos ldan	pramādī	1939	1999
Iron-Dragon	rnam gnon	vikrama	1940	2000
Iron-Snake	khyu mchog	bṛiṣabha	1941	2001
Water-Horse	sna tshogs	citra	1942	2002
Water-Sheep	nyi ma	bhānu	1943	2003
Wood-Monkey	nyi sgrol byed	bhānutāra	1944	2004
Wood-Bird	sa skyong	virthapa	1945	2005
Fire-Dog	mi zad	akṣaya	1946	2006
Fire-Pig	thams cad 'dul	sarvajit	1947	2007
Earth-Mouse	kun 'dzin	sarvadhāri	1948	2008
Earth-Ox	'gal ba	virodhi	1949	2009
Iron-Tiger	rnam 'gyur	vikrita	1950	2010
Iron-Rabbit	bong bu	khara	1951	2011
Water-Dragon	dga' ba	nanda	1952	2012
Water-Snake	rnam rgyal	vijaya	1953	2013

Wood-Horse	rgyal ba	jaya	1954	2014
Wood-Sheep	myos byed	mada	1955	2015
Fire-Monkey	gdong ngan	durmukha	1956	2016
Fire-Bird	gser 'phyang	hemalaṃbha	1957	2017
Earth-Dog	rnam 'phyang	vilaṃbhi	1958	2018
Earth-Pig	sgyur byed	vikāri	1959	2019
Iron-Mouse	kun ldan	sarvavati	1960	2020
Iron-Ox	'phar ba	slava	1961	2021
Water-Tiger	dge byed	śubhakrita	1962	2022
Water-Rabbit	mdzes byed	śobhana	1963	2023
Wood-Dragon	khro mo	krodhi	1964	2024
Wood-Snake	sna tshogs dbyig	viśvabandhu	1965	2025
Fire-Horse	zil gnon	parabhava	1966	2026
Fire-Sheep	spre'u	pravaṃga	1967	2027
Earth-Monkey	phur bu	kīlaka	1968	2028
Earth-Bird	zhi ba	saumya	1969	2029
Iron-Dog	thun mong	sādharaṇa	1970	2030
Iron-Pig	'gal byed	virobhakrita	1971	2031
Water-Mouse	yongs 'dzin	paradhari	1972	2032
Water-Ox	bag med	pramādi	1973	2033
Wood-Tiger	kun dga'	ānanda	1974	2034
Wood-Rabbit	srin bu	rākṣasa	1975	2035
Fire-Dragon	me	anala	1976	2036
Fire-Snake	dmar ser can	viṅgala	1977	2037
Earth-Horse	dus kyi pho nya	kāladūti	1978	2038
Earth-Sheep	don grub	siddhārtha	1979	2039
Iron-Monkey	drag po	rudra	1980	2040
Iron-Bird	blo ngan	durmati	1981	2041
Water-Dog	rnga chen	dundubhi	1982	2042
Water-Pig	khrag skyug	rudhirura	1983	2043
Wood-Mouse	mig dmar	rāktākṣi	1984	2044
Wood-Ox	khro bo	krodhana	1985	2045
Fire-Tiger	zad pa	kṣayaka	1986	2046

The Chinese sexagenary cycle

The following table contains the various elements associated with the Chinese sexagenary cycle. Because 60 is not a multiple of 9, three different numbers can be associated with each year of the cycle. For the three columns of numbers given, 1 White in the first position of the central column was the number for Fire-Rabbit, 1927 CE. At the end of that cycle the numbers continue into the third column, for 4 Green in Fire-Rabbit, 1987 CE. The next cycle then continues in the first column, with 7 Red for 2047 CE, finally coming back to the top of the middle column for the next prabhava cycle.

	Life	**Body**	**Power**	**Fortune**	**Nine numbers**
Fire-Rabbit	Wood	Fire	Fire	Fire	7 1 4
Earth-Dragon	Earth	Wood	Earth	Wood	6 9 3
Earth-Snake	Fire	Wood	Earth	Water	5 8 2
Iron-Horse	Fire	Earth	Iron	Iron	4 7 1
Iron-Sheep	Earth	Earth	Iron	Fire	3 6 9
Water-Monkey	Iron	Iron	Water	Wood	2 5 8
Water-Bird	Iron	Iron	Water	Water	1 4 7
Wood-Dog	Earth	Fire	Wood	Iron	9 3 6
Wood-Pig	Water	Fire	Wood	Fire	8 2 5
Fire-Mouse	Water	Water	Fire	Wood	7 1 4
Fire-Ox	Earth	Water	Fire	Water	6 9 3
Earth-Tiger	Wood	Earth	Earth	Iron	5 8 2
Earth-Rabbit	Wood	Earth	Earth	Fire	4 7 1
Iron-Dragon	Earth	Iron	Iron	Wood	3 6 9
Iron-Snake	Fire	Iron	Iron	Water	2 5 8
Water-Horse	Fire	Wood	Water	Iron	1 4 7
Water-Sheep	Earth	Wood	Water	Fire	9 3 6
Wood-Monkey	Iron	Water	Wood	Wood	8 2 5
Wood-Bird	Iron	Water	Wood	Water	7 1 4
Fire-Dog	Earth	Earth	Fire	Iron	6 9 3
Fire-Pig	Water	Earth	Fire	Fire	5 8 2
Earth-Mouse	Water	Fire	Earth	Wood	4 7 1
Earth-Ox	Earth	Fire	Earth	Water	3 6 9
Iron-Tiger	Wood	Wood	Iron	Iron	2 5 8
Iron-Rabbit	Wood	Wood	Iron	Fire	1 4 7
Water-Dragon	Earth	Water	Water	Wood	9 3 6
Water-Snake	Fire	Water	Water	Water	8 2 5
Wood-Horse	Fire	Iron	Wood	Iron	7 1 4
Wood-Sheep	Earth	Iron	Wood	Fire	6 9 3
Fire-Monkey	Iron	Fire	Fire	Wood	5 8 2
Fire-Bird	Iron	Fire	Fire	Water	4 7 1

	Life	Body	Power	Fortune	Nine numbers
Earth-Dog	Earth	Wood	Earth	Iron	3 6 9
Earth-Pig	Water	Wood	Earth	Fire	2 5 8
Iron-Mouse	Water	Earth	Iron	Wood	1 4 7
Iron-Ox	Earth	Earth	Iron	Water	9 3 6
Water-Tiger	Wood	Iron	Water	Iron	8 2 5
Water-Rabbit	Wood	Iron	Water	Fire	7 1 4
Wood-Dragon	Earth	Fire	Wood	Wood	6 9 3
Wood-Snake	Fire	Fire	Wood	Water	5 8 2
Fire-Horse	Fire	Water	Fire	Iron	4 7 1
Fire-Sheep	Earth	Water	Fire	Fire	3 6 9
Earth-Monkey	Iron	Earth	Earth	Wood	2 5 8
Earth-Bird	Iron	Earth	Earth	Water	1 4 7
Iron-Dog	Earth	Iron	Iron	Iron	9 3 6
Iron-Pig	Water	Iron	Iron	Fire	8 2 5
Water-Mouse	Water	Wood	Water	Wood	7 1 4
Water-Ox	Earth	Wood	Water	Water	6 9 3
Wood-Tiger	Wood	Water	Wood	Iron	5 8 2
Wood-Rabbit	Wood	Water	Wood	Fire	4 7 1
Fire-Dragon	Earth	Earth	Fire	Wood	3 6 9
Fire-Snake	Fire	Earth	Fire	Water	2 5 8
Earth-Horse	Fire	Fire	Earth	Iron	1 4 7
Earth-Sheep	Earth	Fire	Earth	Fire	9 3 6
Iron-Monkey	Iron	Wood	Iron	Wood	8 2 5
Iron-Bird	Iron	Wood	Iron	Water	7 1 4
Water-Dog	Earth	Water	Water	Iron	6 9 3
Water-Pig	Water	Water	Water	Fire	5 8 2
Wood-Mouse	Water	Iron	Wood	Wood	4 7 1
Wood-Ox	Earth	Iron	Wood	Water	3 6 9
Fire-Tiger	Wood	Fire	Fire	Iron	2 5 8

The 24 solar terms

The following is a list of the 24 solar terms (*dus gzer nyer bzhi, jì jié de biāo* 季节的标志). The Tibetan terms are in the left column, taken from the "Cloud of Offerings pleasing Mañjuśrī" (Citsjam, p. 172/3). The numbers in the second column refer to the positions (in degrees) of these terms in a tropical zodiac. Those that are multiples of 15 are the minor terms (*dbugs thob, jié qì* 节氣), and those that are multiples of 30 are the major terms (*dbugs sgang, zhōng qì* 中氣). The final column contains English translations of the names of the terms, together with some additional comments, mainly taken from the "White Beryl" (Baidkar 1, pp. 154, etc.).

dpyid tshigs	315	Beginning of Spring; geese come out from the swamps.
kha ba char	330	Rain Water; snow starts to turn to rain.
srin bu 'gul	345	Stirring of Insects; the stirring of life, the arising of the great wind of spring.
dpyid mnyam	0	Spring Equinox.
dwangs gsal	15	Clear Brightness; clear, bright skies; time to plant seedlings, the rising of sap.
'bru char	30	Grain Rain; rain for crops, time to sow all fields.
dbyar tshugs	45	Beginning of Summer; the arrival of cuckoos.
bri ba gang	60	Grain Full; blooming of rhododendrons, and 'sewa' flowers; time to renew old scarecrows.
myur 'debs	75	Quick Planting; time quickly to plant all major seeds; first crops mature.
dbyar nyi ldog	90	Summer Solstice.
tsha ba chung	105	Slight Heat; return of the heat.
tsha ba che	120	Great Heat; monsoon rains, the swelling of rivers.
ston tshugs	135	Beginning of Autumn; the crowing of roosters, first reduction in the heat, cuckoos return (south) to Mon.
bsil 'gug	150	Cooling; rivers recede.
bad dkar	165	White Dew; it starts to get cold.
ston mnyam	180	Autumn Equinox; beginning of frosts; leaves changes colour.
bad nag	195	Black Dew, the dew turns cold.
ba mo 'bab	210	Start of Frost; frosts take hold, geese head south.
dgun tshugs	225	Beginning of Winter, cold increases, ice forms.
kha ba chung	240	Slight Snow, the cold gathers strength.
kha ba che	255	Great Snow.

dgun nyi ldog	270	Winter Solstice.
grang ngar chung	285	Slight Cold; the cold increases.
grang ngar che	300	Great Cold; very cold, extreme cold.

The lunar mansions

The following is a list of the lunar mansions, together with their Tibetan and Sanskrit names. There are some small variations in the spelling of the Sanskrit names, and I have taken the list from the translation by Ramakrishna Bhat of Varāhamihira's Bṛhat Saṃhitā (Bṛhat, p. 879), mainly because these spellings are close to those used in the Vimalaprabhā, the Kālacakra Tantra commentary. The final column gives the element associated with each mansion in the Indian symbolic system. The Chinese system is different.

Index	**Tibetan**	**Sanskrit**	**Element**
0	tha skar	Aśvinī	wind
1	bra nye	Bharaṇī	fire
2	smin drug	Kṛittikā	fire
3	snar ma	Rohiṇī	earth
4	mgo	Mṛigaśiras	wind
5	lag	Ārdrā	water
6	nabs so	Punarvasu	wind
7	rgyal	Puṣya	fire
8	skag	Āśleṣā	water
9	mchu	Maghā	fire
10	gre	Pūrvaphalgunī	fire
11	dbo	Uttaraphalgunī	wind
12	me bzhi	Hastā	wind
13	nag pa	Citrā	wind
14	sa ri	Svātī	wind
15	sa ga	Viśākhā	wind
16	lha mtshams	Anurādhā	earth
17	snron	Jyeṣṭha	earth
18	snrubs	Mūla	water
19	chu stod	Pūrvāṣāḍhā	water
20	chu smad	Uttarāṣāḍhā	earth
21	gro bzhin	Śravaṇa	earth

Index	Tibetan	Sanskrit	Element
21	byi bzhin	Abhijit	earth
22	mon gre	Dhaniṣṭhā	water
23	mon gru	Śatabhiṣaj	earth
24	khrums stod	Pūrvabhādrapāda	fire
25	khrums smad	Uttarabhādrapāda	water
26	nam gru	Revatī	water

Notice that there are two mansions with number 21. If they are both included this gives a list of 28 mansions, the same as is in use in China. For most purposes in India and Tibet a list of 27 is used, and one of these two that are numbered 21 is left out.

There is some confusion over the correct Tibetan equivalents to the Sanksrit names here. Some give *gro bzhin* as the Tibetan for Abhijit, and others give it as the Tibetan for Śravaṇa. As it happens, for the list of 27 mansions, the Indians leave out the first of these two, and the Tibetans the second. In this list I have therefore given the Tibetan equivalents as they are found in the Vimalaprabhā, which makes the two lists of 27 match up.

The weekdays

The following list gives the index number for each of the weekdays, the name in Tibetan and Sanskrit, the weekday in English, the planet associated, and then the relevant element. The latter is principally used with the conjunction of weekday and lunar mansion elements in an almanac's daily information. The Sanskrit names are those given in the standard list in the Vimalaprabhā. There are many variations in other Sanskrit listings.

0	spen pa	śanina	Saturday	Saturn	Earth
1	nyi ma	aditya	Sunday	Sun	Fire
2	zla ba	soma	Monday	Moon	Water
3	mig dmar	maṅgala	Tuesday	Mars	Fire
4	lhag pa	budha	Wednesday	Mercury	Water
5	phur bu	bṛihaspati	Thursday	Jupiter	Wind
6	pa sangs	śukra	Friday	Venus	Earth

The double-hours

The following is a list of the Tibetan names of the double-hours, their English equivalents, the 12 animals associated with them from the Chinese system, and the period of time they represent in a 24 hour L.M.S.T. clock. There is one term that is repeated twice, the Tibetan *phyed yol*, which indicates that a halfway point, noon or midnight, has been passed. Usefully, we have a very close equivalent to this in the now archaic English midnoon, which indicates either afternoon or the period following midnight.

nam langs	Daybreak	Rabbit	5–7
nyi shar	Sunrise	Dragon	7–9
nyi dros	Mid-morning	Snake	9–11
nyi phyed	Noon	Horse	11–13
phyed yol	Midnoon	Sheep	13–15
nyi myur	Late afternoon	Monkey	15–17
nyi nub	Sunset	Bird	17–19
sa srod	Twilight	Dog	19–21
srod 'khor	Evening	Pig	21–23
nam phyed	Midnight	Mouse	23–1
phyed yol	Midnoon	Ox	1–3
tho rangs	Pre-dawn	Tiger	3–5

The Indian months

The months in the Indian calendar are named after the approximate lunar mansion in which full Moon occurs during the month in question. The names of the months and their respective lunar mansions are exactly the same in Tibetan, but there are differences in Sanskrit, as the names have evolved over the centuries. The following listing is in the order of the months in the Kālacakra year, with the seasons according to the Kālacakra system.

——Month——			
Tibetan	**Sanskrit**	**Lunar Mansion**	**Seasonal name**
nag pa	Caitra	Citrā (13)	Early-spring
sa ga	Vaiśākha	Viśākhā (15)	Late-spring
snron	Jyeṣṭha	Jyeṣṭha (17)	Early-summer

——Month——			
Tibetan	**Sanskrit**	**Lunar Mansion**	**Seasonal name**
chu stod	Āṣāḍha	Pūrvāṣāḍhā (19)	Late-summer
gro bzhin	Śrāvaṇa	Śravaṇa (21)	Early-rains
khrums	Bhādrapada	Pūrvabhādrapāda (24)	Late-rains
tha skar	Āśvina	Aśvinī (0)	Early-autumn
smin drug	Kārtikka	Kṛittikā (2)	Late-autumn
mgo	Mārgaśīrṣa	Mṛigaśiras (4)	Early-pre-winter
rgyal	Pauṣa	Puṣya (7)	Late-pre-winter
mchu	Māgha	Maghā (9)	Early-winter
dbo	Phālguna	Uttaraphalgunī (11)	Late-winter

There are variations in the spellings of the names of the months. The Vimalaprabhā usually has Kārtika instead of Kārtikka, and also uses both Puṣya and Pauṣa.

The Yogas

The following is a list of the names of the yogas, in Tibetan followed by Sanskrit, from the five components of the calendar, together with their index numbers, taken from Chenrap Norbu.

	Tibetan	Sanskrit
0	sel ba	Viṣkambha
1	mdza' ba	Prīti
2	tshe dang ldan pa	Āyuśmat
3	skal bzang	Saubhāgya
4	bzang po	Śobhana
5	shin tu skrang	Atigaṇḍa
6	las bzang	Sukarman
7	'dzin pa	Dhṛiti
8	zug rngu	Śūla
9	skrang	Gaṇḍa
10	'phel ba	Vṛiddhi
11	nges pa	Dhruva
12	kun 'joms	Vyāghāta
13	dga' ba	Harṣaṇa
14	rdo rje	Vajra

	Tibetan	Sanskrit
15	grub pa	Siddhi
16	shin tu lhung	Vyatipāta
17	mchog can	Varīyas
18	yongs 'joms	Parigha
19	zhi ba	Śiva
20	grub pa	Siddha
21	bsgrub bya	Sādhya
22	dge ba	Śubha
23	dkar po	Śukla
24	tshangs pa	Brahman
25	dbang po	Indra
26	khon 'dzin	Vaidhṛiti

There is a problem with the Sanskrit of the Vimalaprabhā, in that between numbers 11 and 12, the Vimalaprabhā list adds Śaṅku, and leaves out Siddha (20). This is not reflected in the Tibetan translation. Also, in the Tsurphu tradition the list is shifted along by one, and Vaidhṛiti is given the index number zero. It appears this is not a mistake in one of the texts, but a difference between the traditions. Banda Gelek, the only writer who treats both traditions in detail, gives Vaidhṛiti as index zero for the Tsurphu tradition (Bgbumrin, p. 34) and Viṣkambha as index zero for the Phugpa tradition (Bgrinnye, p. 600).

The Karaṇas

As was made clear in chapter one, the karaṇas are divided into two groups. Four are called fixed (*rtag pa'i byed pa, dhruvakaraṇa*), and seven changing (*'pho ba'i byed pa, carakaraṇa*), making a total of eleven:

Fixed karaṇas:

Tibetan	Sanskrit
bkra shis	Śakuni
rkang bzhi	Catuṣpada
klu	Nāga
mi sdug pa	Kintughna

Changing karaṇas:

Tibetan	**Sanskrit**
gdab pa	Vava
byis pa	Vālava
rigs can	Kaulava
til rdung	Taitila
khyim skyes	Gara
tshong ba	Vaṇija
viṣṭi	Viṣṭi

Each of the karaṇas occupies one-half of one of the 30 lunar days in a month. Each of the fixed karaṇas occur just once each month around the time of new Moon.

Śakuni is the second half of the 29th lunar day; Catuṣpada is the first half of the 30th lunar day, and Nāga the second half; Kintughna is the first half of the first lunar day.

This leaves a total of 56 half lunar days, from the second half of the first to the first half of the 29th lunar day, inclusive. The changing karaṇas, in the order given above, rotate through these 56 half lunar days. The following table lists the assignment of all the karaṇas with the half lunar days.

Lunar day	**First half**	**Second half**
1	Kintughna	Vava
2	Vālava	Kaulava
3	Taitila	Gara
4	Vaṇija	Viṣṭi
5	Vava	Vālava
6	Kaulava	Taitila
7	Gara	Vaṇija
8	Viṣṭi	Vava
9	Vālava	Kaulava
10	Taitila	Gara
11	Vaṇija	Viṣṭi
12	Vava	Vālava
13	Kaulava	Taitila
14	Gara	Vaṇija

Lunar day	First half	Second half
15	Viṣṭi	Vava
16	Vālava	Kaulava
17	Taitila	Gara
18	Vaṇija	Viṣṭi
19	Vava	Vālava
20	Kaulava	Taitila
21	Gara	Vaṇija
22	Viṣṭi	Vava
23	Vālava	Kaulava
24	Taitila	Gara
25	Vaṇija	Viṣṭi
26	Vava	Vālava
27	Kaulava	Taitila
28	Gara	Vaṇija
29	Viṣṭi	Śakuni
30	Catuṣpada	Nāga

The Chinese lunar mansions

In the list of the names of the lunar mansions given from the Indian tradition, the first mansion, given an index number of zero, was Aśvinī. It is normal in lists of the Chinese mansions, at least when cited in Tibetan sources, to give instead the index number of zero to Citrā, number 13 in the Indian lists. In the following, the Chinese name is given twice, first in the transliteration system as used by Jamgon Kongtrul and followed in Tsurphu almanacs, and then in modern Pinyin Chinese together with the Chinese character.

0	Citrā	gyo	jiǎo (角)
1	Svātī	khang	kàng (亢)
2	Viśākhā	tis	dī (氐)
3	Anurādhā	spu	fáng (房)
4	Jyeṣṭha	gsin	xīn (心)
5	Mūla	dbis	wěi (尾)
6	Pūrvāṣāḍhā	kyī	jī (箕)
7	Uttarāṣāḍhā	rū	dǒu (斗)
8	Śravaṇa	nyi'u	niú (牛)

9	Abhijit	gnyos	nǔ (女)
10	Dhaniṣṭhā	shu'i	xū (虚)
11	Śatabhiṣaj	wu	wēi (危)
12	Pūrvabhādrapāda	zhi	shì (室)
13	Uttarabhādrapāda	dbi'i	bì (壁)
14	Revatī	kho'i	kuí (奎)
15	Aśvinī	lū	lóu (娄)
16	Bharaṇī	dbu'i	wèi (胃)
17	Kṛittikā	ma'u	mǎo (昴)
18	Rohiṇī	bi'i	bì (毕)
19	Mṛigaśiras	tsu'i	zuǐ (嘴)
20	Ārdrā	kīn	cān (参)
21	Punarvasu	tsing	jǐng (井)
22	Puṣya	ku'i	guǐ (鬼)
23	Āśleṣā	li'u	liǔ (柳)
24	Maghā	gsing	xīng (星)
25	Pūrvaphalgunī	tswang	zhāng (张)
26	Uttaraphalgunī	gzhi'i	yì (翼)
27	Hastā	cing	zhěn (轸)

APPENDIX II

Chronology of the Sambhala Kings

The following is a list of the names, in Sanskrit and Tibetan, of the Dharma- and Kalkī-kings of Sambhala, together with their most commonly given dates. Most writers agree on these dates because the dating of King Aja, 806 CE, is largely unavoidable as being 221 years before 1027 CE, the first prabhava cycle adopted in Tibet. However, one writer, Zhonnu Pal, gives the date of Aja and the epoch of the Kālacakra calculations, instead as 340 CE. (See chapter six.)

The dharma-kings

Sucandra	zla ba bzang po	977 BCE
Sureśvara	lha'i dbang po	877
Tejī	gzi brjid can	777
Somadatta	zla bas byin	677
Sureśvara	lha'i dbang phyug	577
Viśvamūrti	sna tshogs gzugs	477
Sureśāna	lha'i dbang ldan	377

The kalkī-kings

Yaśas	grags pa	277
Puṇḍarīka	padma dkar po	177
Bhadra	bzang po	77
Vijaya	rnam rgyal	24 CE
Sumitra	bshes gnyen bzang po	124
Raktapāṇi	phyag dmar	224
Viṣṇugupta	khyab 'jug sbas pa	324
Arkakīrti	nyi ma grags	424
Subhadra	shin tu bzang po	524
Samudravijaya	rgya mtsho rnam rgyal	624
Aja	rgyal dka'	806
Sūrya	nyi ma	1027
Viśvarūpa	sna tshogs gzugs	1127

Śaśiprabha	zla 'od	1227
Ananta	mtha' yas	1327
Mahīpāla	sa skyong	1427
Śrīpāla	dpal skyong	1527
Hari	seng ge	1627
Vikrama	rnam par gnon pa	1727
Mahābala	stobs po che	1827
Aniruddha	ma 'gags pa	1927
Narasiṃha	mi'i seng ge	2027
Maheśvara	dbang phyug chen po	2127
Anantavijaya	mtha' yas rnam rgyal	2227
(Yaśas)	(grags pa)	
Cakrī	'khor lo can	2327

There are some problems with the number of kalkī-kings. The list above contains 25 names, but the great Indian Kālacakra teacher Vibhūticandra pointed out to Tibetan colleagues that the names of the 18th and 19th in this list, Hari and Vikrama, belonged together as one name, Harivikrama. He also pointed out to them that some Tibetan lists similarly split up the name of number 24 in the list above into two names, Ananta and Vijaya. This persists to this day. (See for example Bgbumrim, p. 15.)

The advice of this great Kālacakra teacher was duly noted by the Tibetans but in practice ignored, and their misreading of the Sanskrit when translating into Tibetan was not corrected. Accepting his advice would reduce the list to 24 kings, although the predecessor to Cakrī is in fact another by the name of Yaśas, and his inclusion returns the list to the correct count of 25. The additional error of splitting the name of Anantavijaya would produce a list of 26, unless of course the second Yaśas is omitted, which was generally the case in Tibetan lists.

Not all writers accept that Samudravijaya reigned for 182 years and Aja for 221 years. Banda Gelek, for example (Bgbumrim, p. 5) describes a chronology which has them both reigning for 100 years. This means that in this listing the reign of Kalkī Sūrya would start in 824 CE, bring the reign of Cakrī (26th in this list) forwards to 2224 CE.

General chronology

The following is a list of most of the general events that are mentioned in the chronology section of Tibetan almanacs. These have been taken from a variety of sources, including the "White Beryl," the "Excellent Flask of Essentials," the "Compendium of Tibetan Astronomy," and several almanac examples. It should be born in mind that the western year given is the year in which the Tibetan year (element and animal combination) starts. Although they mostly overlap, an event occurring late in the Tibetan year may occur very early in the next western year.

1027 BCE, Wood-Tiger: Birth of the Buddha according to the tradition of the story of the sandalwood image of the Buddha made in his lifetime.

962 BCE, Earth-Sheep: On 15th of the month of Pūrvāṣāḍhā, the Buddha entered the womb of his mother, according to the Phugpa tradition.

961 BCE, Iron-Monkey: On 7th of the month of Viśākhā, having completed 10 months in the womb, the birth of the Buddha. (Phugpa tradition)

933 BCE, Earth-Mouse: The Buddha observes suffering and leaves the palace. (Phugpa tradition)

927 BCE, Wood-Horse: At the time of the lunar eclipse on the 15th of the month of Viśākhā, the enlightenment of the Buddha. On 4th of month of Pūrvāṣāḍhā, the first turning of the Wheel of the Dharma, the teaching of the four truths. (Phugpa tradition)

915 BCE, Fire-Horse: Birth of the Buddha according to the tradition of Buton.

881 BCE, Iron-Dragon: On 15th of the month of Citrā, the Buddha revealed the Kālacakra Mūlatantra. On the 15th of the month of Viśākhā, Nirvāṇa of the Buddha. (Phugpa tradition)

880 BCE, Iron-Snake: Sucandra writes down the Kālacakra Mūlatantra. (Phugpa tradition)

837 BCE, Wood-Mouse: On the 15th of the month of Mārgaśīrṣa, the birth of Mañjughoṣa in the form of a youth, at Mt. Wutai (*ri bo rtse lnga*) in China.

624 BCE, Fire-Bird: Birth of the Buddha according to the Theravada tradition.

481 BCE, Iron-Monkey: Birth of Nāgarjuna.

277 BCE, Wood-Monkey: The first kalkī-king, Mañjuśrī Yaśas, enthroned in Sambhala, brought the four castes into one, and taught the Kālacakra Laghutantra.

127 BCE, Wood-Tiger: enthronement of King Nyatri Tsenpo (*gnya' khri btsan po*) at Yarlung Thangri (yar klungs thang ri).

77 BCE, Wood-Dragon: Birth of Asaṅga.

254 CE, Wood-Dog: Birth in Tibet of king Thothori Nyentsen.

298 CE, Earth-Horse: Birth of Candrakīrti.

624 CE, Wood-Monkey: Samudravijaya ascends the throne in Sambhala. Time of the barbarians in Mecca. Start of the count of years known as "fire sky ocean."

617 CE, Fire-Ox: Birth of Songtsen Gampo.

629 CE, Earth-Ox: Start of the reign of Songtsen Gampo.

641 CE, Iron-Ox: Arrival in Lhasa of the Chinese wife of Songtsen Gampo, Kongjo, together with the first translations into Tibetan of Chinese astrological methods.

730 CE, Iron-Horse: Birth of king Trisong Detsen.

749 CE, Earth-Ox: Guru Rinpoche (Padmasambhava) first visits Tibet.

751 CE, Iron-Rabbit: Establishment of Samye (*bsam yas*) monastery.

806 CE, Fire-Dog: Establishment of the corrected Kālacakra calendar by Kalkī Aja.

863 CE, Water-Sheep: Birth of Lang Darma, the Tibetan persecutor of Buddhism.

901 CE, Iron-Bird: Lang Darma becomes king of Tibet. Six months later is the suppression of the Buddhist teachings.

902 CE, Water-Dog: Assassination of Lang Darma.

956 CE, Fire-Dragon: Birth of Nāropa.

967 CE, Fire-Rabbit: Cilupa brought the Kālacakra teachings from Sambhala to India.

973 CE, Water-Bird: Start of the later spread of the teachings according to Buton.

978 CE, Earth-Tiger: Start of the later spread of the teachings according to Dromton (*'brom ston*).

982 CE, Water-Horse: Birth of Atiśa.

1004 CE, Wood-Dragon: Birth of Dromton Gyalwai Jungne (*'brom ston rgyal ba'i 'byung gnas*). Birth of Abhayākaragupta.

1012 CE, Water-Mouse: Birth of the translator Marpa.

1027 CE, Fire-Rabbit: Start of the Tibetan counting of sixty-year prabhava cycles. Kālacakra teachings brought to Tibet.

1031 CE, Iron-Sheep: Birth of Machig Labdron (*ma gcig lab sgron*). (Some sources say 1055 or 1103.)

1034 CE, Wood-Dog: Birth of Khon Konchog Gyalpo (*'khon dkon mchog rgyal po*).

1040 CE, Iron-Dragon: Birth of Milarepa and the translator Bari (*ba ri lo tsā ba*).

1042 CE, Water-Horse: Atiśa arrives in Tibet. (Some sources give 1039.)

1059 CE, Earth-Pig: Birth of translator Ngog Lodan Sherab (*rngog blo ldan shes rab*).

1079 CE, Earth-Sheep: Birth of Gampopa (*sgam po pa*).

1084 CE, Wood-Mouse: Birth of Rechung Dorje Drakpa (*ras chung rdo rje grags pa*).

1092 CE, Water-Monkey: Birth of Sachen Kunga Nyingpo (*sa chen kun dga' snying po*).

1110 CE, Iron-Tiger: Birth of Phagmo Drubpa Dorje Gyalpo (*phag mo grub pa rdo rje rgyal po*), and the 1st Karmapa, Dusum Chenpa (*dus gsum mkhyen pa*).

1123 CE, Water-Rabbit: Birth of Drogon Yudrag (*'gro mgon g.yu brag*).

1127 CE, Fire-Sheep: Birth of Pandita Shakyashri (*paṇḍi ta śakya śrī*) in Kashmir.

1147 CE, Fire-Rabbit: Birth of Sachen Jetsun Drakpa Gyaltsen (*sa chen rje btsun grags pa rgyal mtshan*).

1161 CE, Iron-Snake: Birth of Tsangpa Gyare (*gtsang pa rgya ras*).

1179 CE, Earth-Pig: Establishment of Drigung (*'bri gung*) monastery.

1180 CE, Iron-Mouse: Establishment of Staklung (*stag lung*) monastery.

1182 CE, Water-Tiger: Birth of Sakya Panchen Kunga Gyaltsen (*sa skya paṇ chen kun dga' rgyal mtshan*).

1189 CE, Earth-Bird: Establishment of Tsurphu (*mtshur phu*) monastery by the 1st Karmapa.

1204 CE, Wood-Mouse: Birth of 2nd Karmapa, Karma Pakṣi.

1230 CE, Wood-Mouse: Birth of Siddha Orgyanpa (*grub thob o rgyan pa*).

1235 CE, Wood-Sheep: Birth of Drogon Phagpa (*'gro mgon 'phags pa*).

1243 CE, Water-Rabbit: Birth of Kunpang Thugje Tsondru (*kun spangs thugs rje brtson 'grus*).

1253 CE, Water-Ox: Chogyal Phagpa (*chos rgyal 'phags pa*) assumes control of the whole of Tibet.

1284 CE, Wood-Monkey: Birth of 3rd Karmapa, Rangjung Dorje (*rang byung rdo rje*).

1290 CE, Iron-Tiger: Birth of Buton Rinchen Drup (*bu ston rin chen grub*).

1292 CE, Water-Dragon: Birth of Dolpopa Sherab Gyaltsen (*dol po pa shes rab rgyal mtshan*).

1295 CE, Wood-Sheep: Birth of Longchen Rabjampa (*klong chen rab 'byams pa*). (Some sources give 1308.)

1318 CE, Earth-Horse: 3rd Karmapa writes the "Compendium of Astronomy" (*rtsis kun las btus pa*), the first native Tibetan text on astronomy and astrology.

1335 CE, Iron-Horse: Opening of the pilgrimage site of Kongpo Bonri (*kong po bon ri*).

1340 CE, Iron-Dragon: Birth of 4th Karmapa, Rolpai Dorje (*rol pa'i rdo rje*).

1349 CE, Earth-Ox: Birth of Thegchen Chogyal (*theg chen chos rgyal*), and Rendawa Zhonnu Lodro (*red mda' ba gzhon nu blo gros*).

1357 CE, Fire-Bird: Birth of Tshongkhapa.

1364 CE, Wood-Dragon: Birth of Gyaltsab Darma Rinchen (*rgyal tshab dar ma rin chen*).

1368 CE, Earth-Monkey: Start of the Ming dynasty in China.

1375 CE, Wood-Rabbit: Birth of Zhalu Legpa Gyaltsen (*zhwa lu legs pa rgyal mtshan*) and Bodong Chogle Namgyal (*bo dong phyogs las rnam rgyal*).

1384 CE, Wood-Mouse: Birth of 5th Karmapa, Deshin Shegpa (*de bzhin gshegs pa*).

1385 CE, Wood-Ox: Birth of Thangtong Gyalpo (*thang stong rgyal po*) and Khedrub Geleg Palzang (*mkhas grub dge legs dpal bzang*).

1391 CE, Iron-Sheep: Birth of 1st Dalai Lama, Gendun Drubpa (*dge 'dun grub pa*).

1405 CE, Wood-Bird: Birth of Tagtsang Lotsawa Sherab Rinchen (*lo chen shes rab rin chen*).

1409 CE, Earth-Ox: Establishment of Ganden (*dga' ldan*) monastery.

1416 CE, Fire-Monkey: Establishment of Drepung (*'bras spung*) monastery. Birth of 6th Karmapa, Thongwa Donden (*mthong ba don ldan*).

1419 CE, Earth-Pig: Establishment of Sera (*se ra*) monastery.

1423 CE, Water-Rabbit: Birth of Khedrub Norzang Gyatso (*mkhas grub nor bzang rgya mtsho*).

1428 CE, Earth-Monkey: Birth of Sakya Panchen Shakya Chogden (*sa skya paṇ chen śākya mchog ldan*).

1429 CE, Earth-Bird: Start of the Tsurphu tradition of siddhānta calculations by Tsurbu Jamyang (*mtshur bu 'jam dbyangs*).

1435 CE, Wood-Rabbit: Establishment of Nalendra monastery. (*nālendra yi chos sde*).

1441 CE, Iron-Bird: Birth of the translator Chochong Zangpo (*lo tsā ba chos skyong bzang po*).

1447 CE, Fire-Rabbit: Establishment of Tashilhunpo (*bkra shis lhun po*) monastery.

1453 CE, Water-Bird: Birth of Shamar Chochi Drakpa (*zhwa dmar chos kyi grags pa*) and Drubthob Tsangnyon (*grub thob gtsang smyon*).

1454 CE, Wood-Dog: Birth of 7th Karmapa, Chodrag Gyatso (*chos grags rgya mtsho*).

1459 CE, Earth-Rabbit: Establishment of Chone (*co ne*) monastery.

1476 CE, Fire-Monkey: Birth of 2nd Dalai Lama, Gendun Gyatso (*dge 'dun rgya mtsho*). Composition of the Blue Annals (*deb ther sngon po*) by Geulo Zhonnu Pal (*'gos lo gzhon nu dpal*).

1504 CE, Wood-Mouse: Birth of Pawo Tsuklag Threngwa (*dpa' bo gtsug lag phreng ba*).

1507 CE, Fire-Rabbit: Birth of 8th Karmapa, Micheu Dorje (*mi bskyod rdo rje*).

1523 CE, Water-Sheep: Birth of Mangtho Ludrub Gyatso (*mang thos klu sgrub rgya mtsho*).

1527 CE, Fire-Pig: Birth of Drukpa Pema Karpo (*'brug pa padma dkar po*).

1537 CE, Fire-Bird: Birth of Khedrub Palgyi Sengge (*mkhas grub dpal gyi seng ge*).

1543 CE, Water-Rabbit: Birth of 3rd Dalai Lama, Sonam Gyatso (*bsod nams rgya mtsho*).

1556 CE, Fire-Dragon: Birth of 9th Karmapa, Wangchuk Dorje (*karma pa dbang phyug rdo rje*).

1574 CE, Wood-Dog: Birth of Situ Chochi Gyaltsen (*si tu chos kyi rgyal mtshan*).

1575 CE, Wood-Pig: Birth of Tāranātha.

1589 CE, Earth-Ox: Birth of 4th Dalai Lama, Yontan Gyatso (*yon tan rgya mtsho*).

1595 CE, Wood-Sheep: Birth of Drigung Chochi Drakpa (*'bri gung chos kyi grags pa*).

1604 CE, Wood-Dragon: Birth of 10th Karmapa, Choying Dorje (*chos dbyings rdo rje*).

1617 CE, Fire-Snake: Birth of 5th Dalai Lama, Ngawang Lozang Gyatso (*ngag dbang blo bzang rgya mtsho*).

1645 CE, Wood-Bird: Start of construction of the Potala palace in Lhasa.

1653 CE, Water-Snake: Birth of Sangje Gyatso (*sangs rgyas rgya mtsho*).

1654 CE, Wood-Horse: Birth of Lochen Dharmaśrī (*lo chen dharma śrī*).

1676 CE, Fire-Dragon: Birth of 11th Karmapa, Yeshe Dorje (*ye shes rdo rje*).

1683 CE, Water-Pig: Birth of 6th Dalai Lama, Tshangyang Gyatso (*tshangs dbyangs rgya mtsho*).

1700 CE, Iron-Dragon: Birth of Situ Chochi Jungne (*si tu chos kyi 'byung gnas*).

1703 CE, Water-Sheep: Birth of 12th Karmapa, Jangchup Dorje (*byang chub rdo rje*).

1704 CE, Wood-Monkey: Birth of Sumpa Yeshe Paljor (*sum pa ye shes dpal 'byor*).

1708 CE, Earth-Mouse: Birth of 7th Dalai Lama, Kalzang Gyatso (*skal bzang rgya mtsho*).

1728 CE, Earth-Monkey: Birth of Kunchen Jigme Wangpo (*kun mkhyen 'jigs med dbang po*).

1729 CE, Earth-Bird: Birth of Kunchen Jigme Lingpa (*kun mkhyen 'jigs med gling pa*).

1733 CE, Water-Ox: Birth of 13th Karmapa, Dudul Dorje (*bdud 'dul rdo rje*).

1737 CE, Fire-Snake: Birth of Thukwen Chochi Nyima (*thu'u bkwan chos kyi nyi ma*).

1758 CE, Earth-Tiger: Birth of 8th Dalai Lama, Jampal Gyatso (*'jam dpal rgya mtsho*).

1772 CE, Water-Dragon: Birth of Ngulchu Dharma Bhadra (*dngul chu dharma bhadra*).

1798 CE, Earth-Horse: Birth of 14th Karmapa, Thegchok Dorje (*theg mchog rdo rje*).

1805 CE, Wood-Ox: Birth of 9th Dalai Lama, Lungtog Gyatso (*lung rtogs rgya mtsho*).

1813 CE, Water-Bird: Birth of Kongtrul Yonten Gyatso (*kong sprul yon tan rgya mtsho*).

1816 CE, Fire-Mouse: Birth of 10th Dalai Lama, Tsultrim Gyatso (*tshul khrims rgya mtsho*).

1820 CE, Iron-Dragon: Birth of Jamyang Chentse Wangpo (*'jam dbyangs mkhyen brtse'i dbang po*).

1838 CE, Earth-Dog: Birth of 11th Dalai Lama Khedrub Gyatso (*mkhas grub rgya mtsho*).

1846 CE, Fire-Horse: Birth of Mipham Namgyal Gyatso (*mi pham rnam rgyal rgya mtsho*).

1852 CE, Water-Mouse: Birth of 4th Shamarpa Gendun Tendzin Gyatso (*dge 'dun bstan 'dzin rgya mtsho*).

1856 CE, Fire-Dragon: Birth of 12th Dalai Lama Thrinle Gyatso (*'phrin las rgya mtsho*).

1871 CE, Iron-Sheep: Birth of 15th Karmapa, Khachap Dorje (*mkha' khyab rdo rje*).

1876 CE, Fire-Mouse: Birth of 13th Dalai Lama, Thubten Gyatso (*thub bstan rgya mtsho*).

1883 CE, Water-Sheep: Birth of Chenrab Norbu (*mkhyen rab nor bu*).

1908 CE, Earth-Monkey: Composition of the great commentary on the Kālacakra Tantra, "Illuminations of the Vajra Sun" (MiKal), by Mipham. (*mi pham rnam rgyal rgya mtsho*).

1924 CE, Wood-Mouse: Birth of 16th Karmapa, Rangjung Rigpai Dorje (*rang byung rig pa'i rdo rje*).

1935 CE, Wood-Pig: Birth of 14th Dalai Lama, Tendzin Gyatso (*bstan 'dzin rgya mtsho*).

Commemorative and other special days

The following is a list of special days highlighted in Tibetan almanacs. This list is taken from several sources, and I only point out the tradition from which they are taken where there are differences between those traditions. The numbering is in terms of Mongolian month-lunar date, and so 1-14 refers to the 14th of the first Mongolian month.

1-1 to 1-4. The great prayer festival in Lhasa.

1-10. The Samye 10th day, commemorating the time that Guru Rinpoche, Padmasambhava, left the country to perform disciplined conduct in the Sitavana charnel ground.

1-14. Commemoration of Milarepa.

1-15. Commemoration of the translator Marpa.

1-15. Offerings made on the completion of the fortnight commemorating the performance of miracles by the Buddha.

2-28. Commemoration of Tāranātha.

3-15. Revelation by the Buddha of the Kālacakra Tantra.

4-7. Birth of the Buddha (Phugpa).

4-8. Birth of the Buddha (Tsurphu).

4-15. Enlightenment and Nirvāṇa of the Buddha. (Some also consider this to be the day of his birth.)

6-4. First turning of the Wheel of the Dharma, the first teaching by the Buddha, of the four Noble Truths, in the deer park near Varanasi.

6-15. Entry of the future Buddha into the womb of his mother.

6-22. Commemoration of Buton Rinchen Drub.

9-6. Commemoration of Dolpopa Sherab Gyaltsen.

9-22. Descent of the Buddha back to Earth from the 33 realms of the gods.

10-25. Commemoration of Tsongkhapa.

11-3. Commemoration of the Karmapa Dusum Chenpa.

12-17. Commemoration of the great translator Rinchen Zangpo.

12-29. "Nine-torma." Day of the completion of protector practices to prevent obstacles and evil influences in the coming new year.

Glossary

As explained in the introduction, not all the Tibetan terms used in the discussion of the calendar have a traceable Sanskrit equivalent. Where these are known from the Kālacakra literature, the Sanskrit term follows the Tibetan in the following list. Where the term is Chinese in origin, the Chinese is given if known.

keg skar	Obstacle mansion.
dkar po, śukra	Venus.
rkang sdom	Total.
rkang 'dzin	Step index.
rkyang pa'i dgu mig	Solitary sign calculation.
skyes khyim, janmarāśi	Birth-sign (apogee).
skye ba'i skar ma, janma nakṣatra	Birth mansion (apogee).
skra can, romaka	One of the four siddhāntas.
khams kyi sbyor ba	Elemental yogas.
khams lnga, pañcadhātu	Five elements.
khug pa'i dgu mig	Combined sign calculation.
khyim, rāśi	Sign of the zodiac.
khyim gyi 'khor lo, rāśicakra	Zodiac of (12) signs.
khyim zhag	Zodiacal day, degree.
khyim zla	Zodiacal month.
'khyogs po, vakra	Reversing.
gab pa'i sa bdag	Hidden earth-lord.
go log	Contrary (regarding solar eclipses).
grub rtsis	Siddhānta calculation.
dgu mig	Nine-sign calculations.
bgrod pa, ayana	Passage (of the Sun).
'gros bzhi	The four motions of the planets, fast, slow, reversing, and advancing.
rgyu skar, nakṣatra	Lunar mansion.
rgyu zhing yod pa, saccāra	Interpolation variable.
sgang, dbugs sgang	Definition point, major solar term.
sgos zhag	Particular day.
sgra gcan, rāhu	The nodes of the Moon's orbit.

lnga bsdus (yan lag lnga), pañcāṅga	The five components.
gcer bu pa, yamanaka	One of the four siddhāntas.
cha shas, bhāga	Fractional part.
chags pa'i rus sbal	Material turtle.
chad pa, ūna	Omitted lunar day.
chu tshod, nāḍī, ghaṭikā	Unit of time or angle.
chu srang, pāṇīpala	Unit of time or angle.
mjug ma, puccha	Tail of Rāhu.
mjug rings, ketu	A comet.
nyi ma pa, sūrya, saura	One of the four siddhāntas.
nyi ma phyed dag	Semi-true solar longitude.
nyi ma bar pa	Mean solar longitude.
nyi ma'i dhru ba, sūryadhruvaka	Monthly mean solar longitude.
nyi ma'i bu, ravija	Saturn.
nyin zhag, dina	Solar day.
bstan rtsis	Account/calculation of the teachings. Chronology.
rtag pa'i byed pa, dhruvakaraṇa	Fixed karaṇa.
rtag longs	Mean longitude, mean motion.
stong pa chen po yi ge lnga, pañcākṣaramahāśūnya	The five "letters of great emptiness."
thig le stong pa yi ge drug, binduśūnyaṣaḍakṣara	The six "letters of empty potential."
the se rgyal po, tài suì 太岁	The earth-lord, King The-se.
thong gshol 'khor lo	Plough cycle.
dar gud bcu gnyis, shí èr shèng shuāi 十二盛衰	The twelve phases.
dal ba, manda	Slow, slow component of a planet's motion, heliocentric longitude.
dal ba dag pa, dal dag	True slow component.
dal ba bar pa, dal bar	Mean slow motion longitude.
dur mig	Tomb-sign calculations.
dus sbyor, lagna	Ascendant, rising sign.
dus me, kālāgni	Tail of Rāhu.
dus gzer nyer bzhi, jì jié de biāo zhì 季节的标志	24 solar terms.

drag gsum rkang 'dzin	Step index for the three wrathful planets.
gdong, vaktra	Head of Rāhu.
bdud skar	Demon mansion.
nam langs, pratyūṣa	Daybreak.
gnam gyi rtsa ba, tiān gān 天干	Celestial stems (10).
gnas pa'i rus sbal	Natural turtle.
gnas mal	House (as in 12 houses in a horoscope).
spar kha brgyad	bā guà 八卦. Eight trigrams.
spyi zhag	General day.
sprul pa'i rus sbal	Turtle of emanation.
phug lugs	Phugpa calendrical tradition.
'pho ba'i byed pa, carakaraṇa	Changing karaṇa.
byed pa, karaṇa	Practical calendrical system; one of the five components.
byed rtsis	Karaṇa calculation.
bla skar	Spirit mansion.
bla ma, guru	Jupiter.
bla gza'	Spirit weekday.
dbang skar	Power mansion.
dbugs, śvāsa	Breath (unit of time or angle).
dbugs sgang, zhōng qì 中氣	Major solar term. Definition point.
dbugs thob, jié qì 节氣	Minor solar term.
dbyug gu, daṇḍa	Unit of time, equal to one nāḍī.
'byung 'phrod	Elemental yogas.
'byung ba, nirgama	Advancing.
'byung ba lnga, wǔ xíng 五行	Five elements.
'byung rtsis	Elemental calculation or divination.
'bras rtsis	Interpretative calculation, astrology.
sbyor ba, yoga	Conjunction, union; one of the five components.
mar ngo	Waning fortnight.
mun can, tamin	Dark One, Rāhu.
myur ba, śīghra	Fast component of a planet's motion.

sman rtsis khang	Institute of Medicine and Astrology (Lhasa).
sme ba dgu, jiǔ gōng 九宫	Nine numbers.
rtsa ba	Source of Rāhu.
rtsa ba'i nges pa, mūladhruvaka	Primary definition.
rtsis, gaṇanā	Calculation, astronomy.
rtsis 'phro	Values of astronomical variables at an epoch; epoch values.
tshes zhag, tithi	Lunar day.
tshes 'khyud	Exact lunar day; the moment the lunar day changes.
tshangs pa, brahma	One of the four siddhāntas.
tshes zhag, tithi	Lunar day; one of the five components.
mtshur lugs	Tsurphu tradition of calendrical calculation.
zhi gnyis rkang 'dzin	Step index for the two peaceful (inner) planets.
zla skyes, saumya	Mercury.
zla ba rnam par dag pa, zla dag, māsa viśuddha	True lunar month.
zla bshol, adhikamāsa	Intercalary month.
zla ba lhag pa ba, adhikamāsa	Intercalary, or extra, month.
gza', graha	Planet.
gza', vāra	Weekday, short for *res gza'*.
gza' phyed dag pa	Semi-true weekday.
gza' bar pa	Mean weekday.
gza' yi dhru ba, vāradhruvaka	Monthly mean weekday.
yan lag lnga (lnga bsdus), pañcāṅga	The five components.
yar ngo	Waxing fortnight.
rab byung, prabhava	First year in the Indian sexagenary cycle.
ri bo rtse lnga, wǔ tái shān 五台山	Mount Wu Tai.
rim pa, krama	Progessive.
rim min, utkrama	Regressive.
ril po, piṇḍa	Anomaly of the Moon.

ril po'i cha shas, piṇḍāvayava	Fractional part of the Moon's anomaly.
res gza', vāra	Weekday; one of the five components.
lo 'go 'khrul med	Correct (Chinese) new year.
log men	Reverse-year.
longs spyod, bhoga	Longitude.
gshed skar	Adversary mansion.
gshed gza'	Adversary weekday.
sa skyes, bhauma	Mars.
sa glang, niú chūn 牛春	Earth Ox, Spring Ox.
sa bdag, bhūmipati	Earth-lord.
sa'i yan lag, dì zhī 地支	Earthly branches (12).
so nam 'khor lo	Farming cycle.
srid pa'i rus sbal	Existent turtle.
srog skar	Life mansion.
srog gza'	Life weekday.
bslu ba med pa'i gzer	Unerring determinant.
hor zla	Mongolian month.
lhag pa, adhika	Duplicated, extra lunar day.

Bibliography

Tibetan sources

Tibetan sources are cited throughout the text by these abbreviations:

Baidkar: *Phug lugs rtsis kyi legs bshad mkhas pa'i mgul rgyan bai ḍūr dkar po'i do shal dpyod ldan snying nor.* sDe srid sangs rgyas rgya mtsho. Beijing, 1997.

Bgbumrin: *rTsis gzhung 'dod 'jo'i bum bzang gi 'das mo nyung ngur bsdus pa legs bshad rin po che'i 'phreng ba.* 'Ba' mda' dge legs, collected works, vol. 20, pp. 1–207. Dzamthang.

Bgglang: *Sa glang brtsi tshul.* 'Ba' mda' dge legs, collected works, vol. 20, pp. 211–218. Dzamthang.

Bggsert: *Sa gsum kun gyi rna bar snyan pa'i rgyud mang sgra las 'khrungs pa'i snying po gcig tu bsdus pa'i rgya nag gser rtsis.* 'Ba' mda' dge legs, collected works, vol. 20, pp. 397–404. Dzamthang.

Bgrinnye: *Grags pa dpal gyi rtsis gzhung 'bru mang gi lhan thabs rtsis rigs 'dod 'jo'i snye ma'i lhan thabs rin chen snye ma las bstan rtsis kyis lhan thab.* 'Ba' mda' dge legs, collected works, vol. 20, pp. 541–727. Dzamthang.

Brasrat: *dPyad gsum 'bras rtsis ratṇa'i bang mdzod snang ba'i dga' ston.* 'Jigs med nam mkha'i rdo rje. Delhi.

Bujigle: *'Jig rten khams kyi le'u'i 'grel bshad dri med 'od mchan bcas.* Bu ston rin chen grub. *The Collected Works of Bu-ston.* Vol 1. Śata-pitaka series. Indo-Asian Literatures.

Bumzang: *gTsug lag rtsis rigs tshang ma'i lag len 'khrul med mun sel nyi ma nyer mkho'i 'dod pa 'jo ba'i bum bzang.* Si tu dbon karma nges legs bstan 'dzin. Delhi, 1977.

Citsjam: *Ma hā tsi na'i rtsis gzhung 'jam dpal dgyes pa'i mchod sprin.* Ed. by Shes rab chos 'phel. Kan su'u mi rigs dpe skrun khang, 1994.

Citsmel: *rGya rtsis myur sgrub kyi ri mo'i lag len gnad kun gsal por ston pa dri bral man shel dkar po'i me long*. Padma bdud 'dul. mTsho sngon mi rigs dpe skrun khang, 1996.

Kal: *mChog gi dang po'i sangs rgyas las phyung ba rgyud kyi rgyal po dpal dus kyi 'khor lo*. Kālacakra Tantra, Kangyur, Tengyur.

Kdgyan: *Phyi nang gzhan gsum gsal bar byed pa dri med 'od kyi rgyan. mkhas grub nor bzang rgya mtsho*. Topden Tshering, 1975.

KDkhas1: *dPal dus kyi 'khor lo'i 'grel chen dri ma med pa'i 'od kyi rgya cher bshad pa de kho na nyid snang bar byed pa*. mKhas grub rje. rJe yab sras gsungs 'bum, vol. 28, pp. 3–696. Dharamsala, 1998.

Khrulsel: *rTsis la 'khrul pa sel ba*. 'Gos lo tsā ba gzhon nu dpal. Incomplete copy. 1443.

Kongleg: *rTsis kyi bstan bcos nyer mkho bum bzang las skar rtsis kyi lag len 'jug bder bsdebs pa legs bshad kun 'dus*. 'Jam mgon kong sprul. Kong sprul gsungs 'bum, vol. 14, 199–547.

Ktsgza: *gZa' lnga so so'i rtsis kyi man ngag (Pañcagrahapṛthaggaṇanopadeśa)*. Śākya Śrībhadra. Tengyur.

Ktsjug: *Dus kyi 'khor lo la 'jug pa zhes bya ba (Kālacakrāvatāra)*. 'Jigs med 'byung gnas sbas pa (Abhayākaragupta). Tengyur.

Ktsman: *dPal dus kyi 'khor lo'i rtsis kyi man ngag ces bya ba (Śrī-Kālacakragaṇopadeśa)*. Śākya Śrībhadra. Tengyur.

Ktszin: *Nyi zla 'dzin pa'i rtsis*. Śākya Śrībhadra. Tengyur.

Kunnor: *sKar rtsis kun 'dus nor bu*. Ed. by bSam 'grub rgya mtsho. 2 volumes. Krung go'i bod kyi shes rig dpe skrun khang, 1988.

Lithsh: *Li tho'i shes bya rab gsal*. Tshe dbang lha mo. Si khron mi rigs dpe skrun khang, 1997.

MiKal: *dPal dus kyi 'khor lo'i rgyud kyi tshig don rab tu gsal byed rdo rje nyi ma'i snang ba*. Mi pham rgya mtsho. 2 volumes. Gangtok: Sonam T. Kazi, 1969.

Miptsug: *gTsug lag rtsis kyi sngon 'gro rab gsal me long*. Mi pham rgya mtsho. Collected works of Jamgon Kongtrul, vol. 14, pp. 561–577.

Nangrtsa: *rTsis kyi man ngag nyin mor byed pa'i snang ba*. sMin gling lo chen dharma śrī, 1714.

Nangser: *rTsis kyi man ngag nyin byed snang ba'i rnam 'grel gser gyi shing rta*. sMin gling lo chen dharma śrī. Bod ljangs mi dmangs dpe skrun khang, 1983.

Nyernag: *Nyer mkho'i bum bzang nag rtsis kyi sngon 'gro*. Karma nges legs bstan 'dzin. Delhi, 1977.

Padzhal: *Legs par bshad pa padma dkar po'i zhal gyi lung*. Phug pa lhun grub rgya mtsho, mkhas grub nor bzang rgya mtsho. Beijing: Mi rigs dpe skrun khang, 2002.

Pktant: *mChog gi dang po'i sangs rgyas rnam par phye ba gsang ba thams cad bshad pa'i mdzod*. Padma dkar po, collected works, vol. 13. Darjeeling: Kagyu Sungrab Nyamso Khang, 1973.

Rigsgye: *dKar rtsis byed grub zung gi khungs las brtsam pa'i nyer mkho'i don nyung bsdus su brjod pa rigs ldan bla ma dgyes byed*. bLo gros grags pa, collected works, vol. 10, pp. 513–533. Dzamthang.

Rigthig: *bsTan bcos bai ḍūra dkar po dang nyin byed snang ba'i dgongs don gsal bar ston pa rtsis gzhi'i man ngag rigs ldan snying gi thig le*. mKhyen rab nor bu. Bod gzhung dga' ldan pho brang phyogs las rnam rgyal, 1968.

Rdelgre: *Nag rstis rdel 'grem 'bras bshad. lha mo tshul khrims*. Kan su'u mi rigs dpe skrun khang, 1995.

Takhist: *dPal dus kyi 'khor lo'i chos bskor gyi byung khungs nyer mkho*. Tāranātha. The Collected Works of Tāranātha, vol. 2, pp. 1–43. Smanrtsis Shesrig Dpemzod.

Tansal: *bsTan rtsis gsal ba'i nyin byed*. Mang thos klu sgrub rgya mtsho. Bod ljongs mi dmangs dpe skrun khang, 1988.

Tlkuntu: *dPal dus kyi 'khor lo'i man ngag rtsis kyi bstan bcos kun nas btus pa chen po'i rgyas 'grel rin po che'i gter mdzod.* dPa' bo gtsug lag phreng ba.

Tsgodon: *Bod kyi rtsis rig gi go don dang lag len.* Phyad mdzod gsung rab & mā yang bzod pa rgyal mtshan. Mi rigs dpe skrun khang, 1988.

Tsinamz: *Bod kyi skar rtsis rig pa'i rnam gzhag.* Sha bo tshe ring & blo yangs rgyal. Kan su'u mi rigs dpe skrun khang, 1997.

Tskhaga: *dPal dus kyi 'khor lo'i rtsis kyi bstan bcos mkhas pa rnams dga' bar byed pa.* Bu ston rin chen grub. Bod ljangs mi dmangs dpe skrun khang, 1987.

Tsrikun: *Bod kyi rtsis rig kun 'dus chen mo.* byams pa 'phrin las. 5 volumes. Si khron mi rigs dpe skrun khang, 1998.

Zlazer: *'Byung rtsis man ngag zla ba'i 'od zer.* sMin gling lo chen dharma śrī. Dharmsala, 1968.

Non-Tibetan Sources

The following non-Tibetan sources are cited throughout the text by these abbreviations:

Bṛhat: Varāhamihira. 1981. *Bṛhat Saṃhitā.* Trans. by M. Ramakrishna Bhat. Two volumes. Delhi: Motilal Banarsidass.

Chinrec: *Chinese Recorder and Missionary Journal.* Foochow.

ESAA: Seidelmann. P.K., ed. 1992. *Explanatory Supplement to the Astronomical Almanac.* Mill Valley, California: University Science Books.

KBhaga: Nayarāj Pant. 1987. *Kālacakrako Jyautiṣabhāga* (includes the Sanskrit text of the *Kālacakra Anusāri Gaṇita*). Kathmandu: Mahendrasaṃskṛtaviśvavidyālaya.

Mawangdui: Shaughnessy, Edward L., trans. 1997. *I Ching: The Classic of Changes.* New York: Ballantine Books.

Pañca: Varāhamihira. 1993. *Pañcasiddhāntikā*. Trans. by T.S. Kuppanna Sastry. Adyar, Madras: P.P.S.T. Foundation.

Sūrya: Burgess, Rev. Ebenezer, trans. 2000. *The Sūrya Siddhānta*. Delhi: Motilal Banarsidass.

Vimala: Kalkī Puṇḍarīka. 1986. *Śrī Laghu-kālacakratantrarāja ṭīkā vimalaprabhā*. Sarnath: Central Institute of Higher Tibetan Studies.

The following non-Tibetan sources are cited throughout the text by author-date:

Daniélou, Alain. 1991. *The Myths and Gods of India*. Rochester, Vt.: Inner Traditions International.

Grönbold, Günther. 1995. *The Date of the Buddha according to Tantric Texts*. Bibliotheca Indo-Buddhica Series No. 165. Delhi: Sri Satguru Publications.

Gyurme Dorje. 2001. *Tibetan Elemental Divination Paintings*. London: John Eskenazi.

Kilty, Gavin, trans. 2004. *Ornament of Stainless Light: An Exposition of the Kālacakra Tantra*. Boston: Wisdom Publications.

Meeus, Jean. 1998. *Astronomical Algorithms*. Richmond, Va.: Willmann-Bell.

Nebesky-Wojkowitz, René de. 1993. *Oracles and Demons of Tibet*. Tiwari's Pilgrims Book House reprint.

Neugebauer, O. 1969. *The Exact Sciences in Antiquity*. New York: Dover.

Newman, John. 1987. The Outer Wheel of Time: Vajrayāna Buddhist Cosmology in the Kālacakra Tantra. Ph.D. dissertation. Madison: University of Wisconsin.

———. 1998a. Islam in the Kālacakra Tantra. *Journal of the International Association of Buddhist Studies* 21, no. 2: 311–371.

———. 1998b. The Epoch of the Kālacakra Tantra. *Indo-Iranian Journal* 41: 319–349.

Needham, Joseph. 1962. *Science and Civilisation in China.* Cambridge, England: Cambridge University Press.

Pingree, David. 2001. Ravikās in Indian Astronomy and the Kālacakra. In *Le Parole E I Marmi*, Serie Orientale Roma XCII, 2, pp. 655–664. Roma: Istituto Italiano per l'Africa e l'Oriente.

Sewell, Robert, and Sankara Balkrishna Dikshit. 1995. *The Indian Calendar*. Delhi: Motilal Barnarsidass.

Smith, E. Gene. 2001. *Among Tibetan Texts*. Boston: Wisdom Publications.

Index

A

advancing motion, 71, 82, 110
Aja, 152, 212
almanac, 9, 141
angular measure, 10, 13
animals, twelve, 168
anomalistic month, 28
anomaly, 21, 27, 38, 228, 300, 319
apogee, 27, 38
ascendant, 201
astrology, 1, 141, 173, 249
astrology, Kālacakra, 213
awarenesses, five, 158

B

Babylonian methods, 8, 12
Banda Gelek, 3, 44, 334
birth-mansion, 286, 291
birth-sign, 31, 58, 89, 239
body factor, 172
breath, unit of measurement, 12
Buddha, historical information, 150, 367

C

Caitra, 16, 146
calendar, 141
celestial stems, ten, 144, 196
Chenrab Norbu, 2
chi, Chinese term for wind, breath, 50
Chinese calendar, 195, 209
Chinese symbolism, 163
civil day, 11
coefficient, interpolation, 25, 26, 27, 34, 235
colour, of an eclipse, 124, 137
combined sign calculation, 187
comet, 290
commemorative days, 200, 374
components of the calendar, five, 40, 246
conjunction, 67, 287
contrary position, 126

D

Dark One, Rāhu, 273
daybreak, 10, 300
deferent, 63
degree, unit of angular measure, 14
dependent origination, twelve links, 199, 205
Desi Sangje Gyatso, 3, 101, 104
Dhānyakaṭaka, great stūpa, 144, 211
dharmadhātu, 165
direction, of an eclipse, 121, 135, 293
double-hours, 145, 204, 358
Drogon Chogyal Phagpa, 145
duplicated lunar date, 41, 203
duration, of an eclipse, 116, 119, 134

E

Earth Ox, 142, 176
earth-lord, 142, 190, 199
earthly branches, twelve, 145
eclipse, 95, 98, 180, 269, 272, 293
  lunar, 100
  solar, 125

ecliptic, 13, 289
elemental yogas, 203
elements, five, six, 157, 163
emotional defilements, 157
empowerment, 213
empty flask, 199
enemy-tomb, 189
epicycle, 56, 63
epoch, 1, 48, 139, 329, 339
epoch of Kālacakra Tantra, 212, 221, 295, 304, 348
Error Correction, 307
expunged years, 143, 224
extra lunar date, 41

F

fast longitude, 56, 278
fast motion, 69, 81, 110
five components of the calendar, 40, 246
fortune factor, 172
Fú Xī, 164

G

general day, 46, 57
generation process, 213
geocentric longitude, 56, 62, 77
Geu Lotsawa Zhonnu Pal, 3, 307
gnomon, 258, 259, 315

H

Head, of Rāhu, 95, 201
heliocentric longitude, 56
Hindu siddhāntas, 233, 347
houses, twelve, 201

I

I Ching, 164
index, into a table, 25
inferior conjunction, 79, 289
initiation, 213
inner planets, 76
intercalary month, 15, 51, 53, 311
intercalation index, 16, 51, 225, 309, 327, 348
interpolation, 24, 26, 59, 234, 278
interpolation correction, 25
interpolation variable, 33, 237, 269
Islamic calendar, 223, 297

J

Jamgon Kongtrul, 3, 104, 340
Jamyang Dondrup Wozer, 3, 337
Jonang tradition of Buddhism, 3
Jovian year, 143
Julian day, 39, 49
Jupiter, 61, 74, 279, 283

K

Kālacakra maṇḍala, 159, 213
Kālacakra Mūlatantra, 98, 144, 146, 151, 306
Kālacakra siddhānta, 259
Kālacakra symbolism, 155, 215
Kālacakra Tantra, 1, 211
Kālāgni, the Tail of Rāhu, 95
Kali, age of, 331
Kalkī kings, 211, 365
karaṇa, 9
karaṇa calculation, 9, 202, 295
karaṇa year, 249
karaṇa, one of five components, 40, 44, 245, 247, 360

Karma Ngelek Tendzin, 3
Karmapa, 2, 260
King The-se, earth-lord, 191
Kongjo, 147

L

Lalitavistāra Sūtra, 153
letters of empty potential, six, 159
letters of great emptiness, five, 159
Lhundrup Gyatso, 3
life factor, 172
Local Mean Solar Time (L.M.S.T.), 11, 300, 358
longitude, 14, 236
lunar day, 7, 21, 23, 40
lunar mansions, 14, 40, 244, 246, 356, 362
lunar month, 7
luni-solar calendar, 7

M

Madhumatī, 223
magnitude, of an eclipse, 108, 131
maṇḍala, 159, 213
Mañjughoṣa, 166
maõóala, 154, 157
Mars, 56, 274
mean daybreak, 10
mean motions, 264
mean slow longitude, 58
mean solar longitude, 21, 230, 256, 301
mean weekday, 18, 226, 297, 318
Mercury, 85, 279, 281
meridian, 11, 299
Minling Lochen Dharmaśrī, 3, 97
Mipham, 2, 99, 150, 349
Mongolian month, 145, 194
months, names of, 195, 358
Moon, 14
motions, four, 69, 287

N

nāḍī, 12
natal-central number, 185
natal-trigram, 186
new year, 10, 145
nine-sign, 186
Nirvāṇa of the Buddha, 151
node of Moon's orbit, 1, 95
node-distance, 100
Norzang Gyatso, 3, 138, 315
number, progressed, 184
numbers, nine, 164, 167, 175

O

obscuration, of an eclipse, 108
observations of eclipses, 137
omitted lunar date, 42, 203
own-tomb, 189

P

pala, 12
particular day, 57
passage, 220, 241, 270
Pawo Tsuklag, 2, 260, 337
peaceful planets, 55
penumbra, 106, 118, 126
perfection process, 213
perigee, 27, 241
period, of the Sun, 260
period, planetary, 57, 89
phases, twelve, 170
Phugpa tradition of calculation, 2, 321
planet, 11, 55, 273, 302

planets, visibility of, 288
power factor, 172
Prabhava, 8, 144, 222, 307
precession, 219, 301
primary definition, of the siddhānta, 258, 347
progressed attributes, 183
progressive, 24, 32, 68, 276, 287
Ptolemaic theory, 57, 63

Q

quadrant, 67

R

Rāhu, ascending node, 1, 95, 180, 201, 268, 271, 292, 305, 319
Rangjung Dorje, 2, 260, 337
regressive, 25, 33, 276
reverse-year, 183
reversing motion, 70, 82, 110, 287

S

Sambhala, 150, 211, 217, 348, 365
Sangje Gyatso, Desi, 3, 101
Saturn, 61, 75, 279, 285
seasons, 195, 322
 six, 195
semiduration, of an eclipse, 119
semi-true solar longitude, 239
semi-true weekday, 26, 36, 234
sexagenary table, 182
sexagesimal notation, 12
siddhānta, 9, 258
siddhānta calculation, 9, 307, 349
sidereal year, 37, 298
sidereal zodiac, 15, 219, 346
signs of the zodiac, twelve, 13, 162, 199
sixty-year cycle, 8, 142, 351
skandhas, five, six, 157
slow longitude, 56, 77, 79
slow motion, 70, 82, 110, 287
solar day, 10, 19
solar longitude, 21, 238
solar longitude, true, 30, 258
solar term, 51, 177, 200, 354
solitary sign calculation, 187
solstice, 138, 210, 220, 259, 313, 322
Songtsen Gampo, king of Tibet, 147
Source, of Rāhu, 96
spirit factor, 175
Spring Ox, 176
step function, 24
step index, 63, 77
Sucandra, 153, 211
superior conjunction, 79, 289
superstition, 7, 42
Sūryagarbha Sūtra, 153
symbolic information, 154
synodic month, 7, 19, 297

T

Tail, of Rāhu, 95
Tāranātha, 211, 334
Teliṅga system, 143
The-se, King, earth-lord, 191
time, 7, 10, 215
timing, of an eclipse, 119, 134
tomb-sign, 186
trigram, progressed, 184
trigrams, eight, 164, 168
tropical zodiac, 15, 148, 219, 346
true heliocentric longitude, 60

true lunar month, 15, 225
true solar longitude, 30, 258, 266
true weekday, 30, 233
Tsurphu, tradition of calculation, 2, 337
turtle, mythical, 164

U

Ujjain, 299
umbra, 106, 118
unerring determinant, 101

V

vajra-time, 215
Varāhamihira, 99, 124, 175, 220, 292, 302, 356
Venus, 76, 279, 284
Vibhūticandra, 366
Vimalaprabhā, 1, 109, 211, 216
vowels and consonants, 154

W

waning fortnight, 146
waxing fortnight, 146
weekday, 11, 18, 40, 246, 357
  true, 30
western dates, 45
Wheel of Life, 199
wrathful planets, 55
Wu Tai, Mount, 166

Y

yang, 144, 158
Yaśas, 152, 211, 217
year, Jovian, 143
yin, 144, 158
yoga, one of five components, 40, 43, 204, 245, 246, 359
Yungton Dorjepal, 145

Z

Zhonnu Pal, Geu Lotsawa, 3, 307, 349
zodiac, 13, 259, 346
  sidereal, 15
  tropical, 15
zodiacal day, 14, 202, 263
zodiacal month, 16